Human Rights and the Protection of Domestic Workers in Labour and Migration Law

OXFORD LABOUR LAW

***General Editors*:** Alan Bogg, Professor of Labour Law at University of Bristol Law School; A. C. L. Davies, Dean of the Oxford Law Faculty; Keith Ewing, Professor of Public Law at King's College London; and Mark Freedland, Emeritus Research Fellow in Law at St John's College and Emeritus Professor of Employment Law in the University of Oxford.

The *Oxford Labour Law* series (formerly known as the *Oxford Monographs on Labour Law* series) has come to represent a significant contribution to the literature of British, European, and international labour law. The series recognizes the arrival not only of a renewed interest in labour law generally, but also the need for fresh approaches to the study of labour law following a period of momentous change in the UK and Europe. The series is concerned with all aspects of labour law, including traditional subjects of study such as collective labour law and individual employment law. It also includes works that concentrate on the growing role of human rights and the combating of discrimination in employment, and others that examine the law and economics of the labour market and the impact of social security law and of national and supranational employment policies upon patterns of employment and the employment contract. Two of the contributing authors to the series, Lucy Vickers and Diamond Ashiagbor, have received awards from the Society of Legal Scholars in respect of their books.

Also Available in the Series

Freedom of Association
From Labour Law to the Constitution
ALAN BOGG

Workplace Investigations
Justice and the Legal Regulation of Employer Conduct
ADRIANA ORIFICI

Underpaid and Unrecognized
State-Induced Unfree Labour
KATIE BALES AND AMIR PAZ-FUCHS

Shaping Contracts for Work
The Normative Influence of Terms Implied by Law
GABRIELLE. GOLDING

Human Rights Due Diligence and Labour Governance
INGRID LANDAU

Catholic Social Teaching and Labour Law
An Ethical Perspective on Work
MARK BELL

Structural Injustice and Workers' Rights
VIRGINIA MANTOUVALOU

Reforming Age Discrimination Law
Beyond Individual Enforcement
ALYSIA BLACKHAM

Putting Human Rights to Work
Labour Law, the ECHR, and the Employment Relation
PHILIPPA COLLINS

Strike Ballots, Democracy, and Law
BREEN CREIGHTON, CATRINA DENVIR, RICHARD JOHNSTONE, SHAE MCCRYSTAL, ALICE ORCHISTON

Living Wage
Regulatory Solutions to Informal and Precarious Work in Global Supply Chains
SHELLEY MARSHALL

A Purposive Approach to Labour Law
GUY DAVIDOV

Human Rights and the Protection of Domestic Workers in Labour and Migration Law

NATALIE SEDACCA
Associate Professor in Employment Law, Durham Law School, Durham University, UK

OXFORD
UNIVERSITY PRESS

OXFORD
UNIVERSITY PRESS

Great Clarendon Street, Oxford, OX2 6DP,
United Kingdom

Oxford University Press is a department of the University of Oxford.
It furthers the University's objective of excellence in research, scholarship,
and education by publishing worldwide. Oxford is a registered trade mark of
Oxford University Press in the UK and in certain other countries.

Published in the United States of America by Oxford University Press
546 Fifth Avenue, New York, NY 10036, United States of America.

British Library Cataloguing in Publication Data
Data available

Library of Congress Control Number: 2026946796

ISBN 9780198985235

DOI: 10.1093/9780198985266.001.0001

Printed and bound by
CPI Group (UK) Ltd., Croydon, CR0 4YY

The manufacturer's authorized representative in the EU for product safety is
Oxford University Press España S.A. of Parque Empresarial San Fernando de Henares,
Avenida de Castilla, 2 – 28830 Madrid (www.oup.es/en or product.safety@oup.com).
OUP España S.A. also acts as importer into Spain of products made by the manufacturer.

FSC www.fsc.org MIX Paper | Supporting responsible forestry FSC® C013604

Preface

In many countries, there is a pattern of exclusion of domestic workers from the protection of employment law, through legislative exceptions, disadvantageous visa conditions and a lack of visibility to labour inspectorates. This pattern of exclusion is clearly discriminatory: most domestic workers are women, and they are often also either international migrants or members of an ethnic minority in the country in which they work. It also leaves some of the most vulnerable members of society exposed to exploitation and abuse.

In this important addition to Oxford Monographs in Labour Law, Natalie Sedacca offers a critical account of the law's treatment of domestic workers and uses human rights law to develop a case for reform. Her detailed doctrinal analysis is backed up by empirical evidence of domestic workers' lived experiences across four continents: in Chile, the UK, India, and South Africa. The voices of domestic workers and their advocates are heard throughout the book, explaining in detail the problems they face and making a powerful case for change. The author outlines and advocates for a rich understanding of human rights law which emphasizes the protection of socio-economic rights, the imposition of positive obligations on the state, a feminist critique of notions of privacy, and a strong universalism to include marginalized groups in the scope of protection. She uses this to produce a range of reform proposals: for example, the right to respect for private and family life is used to challenge the absence of any proper limits on domestic workers' working time or right to family reunification, and the right not to be subjected to forced labour is used as an important counterweight to employers' arguments that labour inspection should not take place in private homes on privacy grounds.

The book as a whole makes a compelling case for much stronger protection of the human rights of domestic workers and should be required reading for scholars, lawyers, campaigners, and policymakers. It shines a light on injustices which have been allowed to go unchallenged for far too long.

Acknowledgements

The work for this book began during my PhD at University College London (UCL) in 2017–21, with later research undertaken including the addition of further case studies from 2022–25. My PhD fees and stipend were generously funded by the London Arts and Humanities Partnership and the UCL Faculty of Laws, each of which also provided additional funding for research and conference trips. The latter stages of research and writing benefited greatly from two terms of research leave granted by Durham University and Durham Law School from October 2024 to March 2025.

I am immensely grateful to all the interviewees in Chile, the UK, South Africa, and India, who are listed by name or pseudonym in the Appendix, for generously taking the time to speak to me and share such rich insights and experiences.

Virginia Mantouvalou was a fantastic and inspirational PhD supervisor, sharing immense knowledge and insight and pushing me to sharpen my ideas. Her support extended beyond academic guidance to other practical areas, including introducing me to the charity Kalayaan, which gave me the links to develop my empirical research as well as facilitating my broader understanding of, and participation in, domestic workers' rights campaigns. She has continued to provide invaluable guidance and mentorship since I completed my PhD, including during the book-writing process, from giving feedback on the proposal to reading four of its chapters.

I am also grateful to my secondary PhD supervisor, Par Engstrom, who was a great source of expertise on the Latin American region and practicalities of research, including the framing of questions and the development of an overall methodology. My PhD examiners Tonia Novitz and Colm O'Cinneide gave very insightful feedback that assisted me in framing the subsequent book project and identifying changes to be made within it.

During my later work on the manuscript, I am particularly thankful to Elizabeth (Lizzy) O'Loughlin, who has been my mentor at Durham Law School since October 2023. Lizzy has read drafts of almost all the book's chapters, often within short time periods, providing very helpful feedback and encouragement. As my mentor in the previous academic year 2022–23, Hannah Bows assisted me with the development of the proposal and responses to initial comments; I also discussed the plans with Deirdre McCann and, in my previous position at Exeter, with Catherine Dupre.

My work for the PhD and the book has been improved by comments and questions at the London Labour Law Discussion Group and the UCL PhD Work in

Progress Forum, and internal discussions at UCL, Exeter, and Durham. I have also received helpful feedback while presenting at various external conferences, such as the Society of Legal Scholars, Labour Law Research Network, and Socio-Legal Studies Association, and at various specialist seminars and events. I am grateful to the National Law School of India, Bengalaru, particularly Saurabh Bhattacharjee and the Centre for Labour Studies, who hosted me for a two-week visit in January 2025 and gave insightful feedback during a faculty seminar and in other discussions. My work has also benefited from feedback from OUP, the series editors, and the anonymous peer reviewers. All errors remain my own.

Many thanks are also due to those who assisted me in facilitating the empirical research by suggesting or introducing me to contacts. For Chile, this included Jorge Contesse, Jorge Leyton-García, Ernesto Vargas Weil, Guillermo Jimenez, Victoria Martínez Placencia, and Par Engstrom. Ruth Olate and the interviewee with pseudonym 'Catalina' both kindly introduced me to domestic worker interviewees at their organizations. I am also grateful to Verónica García De Cortázar Galleguillos and Javier Alonso Belaunde for correcting my draft Spanish translations of my questions for participants in Chile, and of a summary of the research to send them afterwards, respectively. In the UK, many thanks go to the migrant domestic worker NGO Kalayaan, particularly Avril Sharp, who worked jointly with me on the research project for which we undertook worker interviews. I became a trustee for Kalayaan in 2020 and have continued to learn a great deal from all the staff and fellow trustees. In addition, Jamila Duncan-Bosu of the Anti-Trafficking and Labour Exploitation Unit facilitated my observation of employment tribunal hearings for the *Puthenveettil* case and shared relevant documents with me. In South Africa, introductions to or suggestions of interviewees were assisted by Marlese von Broembsen, Jane Barrett, Abigail Osiki, and Anashri Pillay, while in India I am grateful for the same to Neha Wadhawan, Prabha Kotiswaran, Samita Sen, Parvati Raghuram, Nalini Nayak, and Supurna Banerjee.

My former UCL PhD colleagues, including Aleisha Ebrahimi, Hitesh Dhorajiwala, Inga Thiemann, Eleni Frantziou, Conor Crummey, Daniella Lock, Joe Atkinson, and Luminita Olteanu, have been a great source of camaraderie and inspiration. I am similarly grateful to many other academic friends such as Dafni Lima, Clara Martins-Pereira, Demet Asli Caltekin, Kim Bouwer, and Maayan Niezna. Last but not least, I am very grateful to my family, particularly my mother Ann, who has given me so much support over the years, and my friends outside academia. A special thanks goes to my wonderful partner, Luke Cooper, who first encouraged me to make the switch from legal practice to academia and has fiercely supported me and kept me positive throughout.

Contents

Table of cases

INTERNATIONAL AND REGIONAL BODIES

Human Rights Committee

Committee on the Elimination of Discrimination against Women

Committee on the Rights of the Child

Inter-American Commission on Human Rights

Inter-American Court of Human Rights

African Commission on Human and People's Rights

African Court of Human and People's Rights

European Court of Human Rights

European Committee of Social Rights

Court of Justice of the European Union

Domestic courts

United Kingdom / England and Wales

South Africa

India

Table of instruments and legislation

INTERNATIONAL AND REGIONAL MATERIALS

International

Americas (Organization of American States)

Africa (African Union)

Europe (Council of Europe)

European Union

UNITED KINGDOM

Statutes

Statutory instruments

Other

Bill (at time of writing)

CHILE

Constitution

Codes and statutes

Other

SOUTH AFRICA

Constitution

Statutes

Other

INDIA

Constitution

Codes and Statutes

Other

Abbreviations

ACHPR	African Charter on Human and People's Rights
ACHR	American Convention on Human Rights
AComHPR	African Commission on Human and People's Rights
ACtHPR	African Court on Human and People's Rights
C-189	ILO Convention 189 Concerning Decent Work for Domestic Workers
C-190	ILO Convention 190 Concerning the Elimination of Violence and Harassment in the world of work
CCMA	Commission on Conciliation, Mediation and Arbitration (South Africa)
CEDAW	Convention on the Elimination of All Forms of Discrimination against Women
CGD	Conclusive Grounds Decision (UK)
COIDA	Compensation for Occupational Injuries and Diseases Act (South Africa)
CRC	UN Convention on the Rights of the Child
ECHR	European Convention on Human Rights
ECSR	European Committee of Social Rights
ECtHR	European Court of Human Rights
ESC	European Social Charter (original 1961 version)
GC23	UNCESCR General Comment No 23 on the Right to Just and Favourable Conditions of Work
GLAA	Gangmasters and Labour Abuse Authority (UK)
IAComHR	Inter-American Commission on Human Rights
IACtHR	Inter-American Court of Human Rights
ICCPR	International Covenant on Civil and Political Rights
ICESCR	International Covenant on Economic, Social and Cultural Rights
ILO	International Labour Organisation
IMF	International Monetary Fund
MERCOSUR	Mercado Común del Sur—The Common Market of the South (South America)
NRM	National Referral Mechanism (UK)
NRTPF	No Recourse to Public Funds (UK)
ODWV	Overseas Domestic Worker Visa (UK)
RGD	Reasonable Grounds Decision (UK)
SADSAWU	South African Domestic Service and Allied Workers Union
SERI	Socio-Economic Rights Institute of South Africa
SEWA	Self-Employed Women's Association (India)
UDHR	Universal Declaration of Human Rights
UNCESCR	UN Committee on Economic, Social and Cultural Rights
WTR	Working Time Regulations (UK)

PART 1

DOMESTIC WORKERS, EXCLUSION, AND HUMAN RIGHTS

1
Introduction

Domestic workers carry out essential but undervalued labour like cooking, cleaning and laundry, and caring for children and elderly, sick, and disabled people, in private households.[1] They are overwhelmingly women and disproportionately migrants and ethnic minorities.[2] Despite the vital role domestic workers play, their work is routinely undervalued and unrecognized, with working lives frequently marked by low pay, long and undefined hours, conditions that are unsafe and do not respect workers' privacy, a lack of freedom to move between employers, and separation from family members. These indignities stem in some respects from a lack of legal protection, with domestic workers specifically excluded from provisions applicable in other sectors and subjected to distinct, less favourable labour standards. But even where the same standards apply in principle to domestic workers as other workers, there are often practical difficulties in realising these entitlements. Protections that are supposed to apply to domestic workers are not properly enforced because of the isolated nature of the work, which takes place in private homes that are outside the purview of labour inspection. Domestic workers are also frequently prevented or deterred from enforcing their rights or leaving exploitative situations because of vulnerabilities arising from their immigration status.

This book conceptualizes these various deficits of protection collectively as the 'exclusion' of domestic workers. It examines the role of human rights law in challenging this exclusion and extending protection to domestic workers in labour and migration law. Its analysis proceeds by examining a series of issues that commonly affect domestic workers: limitations to enforcement of rights, including workplace inspection in private households; the application of minimum wage legislation and working time limits; and visa regimes as they affect migrant domestic workers' position, ability to enforce rights, and family lives. The book examines these phenomena in four case study countries—Chile, the UK, South Africa, and India—combining first-hand empirical research with doctrinal materials.[3] It analyses

[1] ILO, 'Formalizing Domestic Work' (ILO 2016) 3.

[2] Sabrina Marchetti, 'The Global Governance of Paid Domestic Work: Comparing the Impact of ILO Convention No. 189 in Ecuador and India' (2018) 44 Critical Sociology 1191, 1194; ILO, 'Making Decent Work a Reality for Domestic Workers: Progress and Prospects Ten Years after the Adoption of the Domestic Workers Convention, 2011 (No 189)' (ILO 2021) 10–17.

[3] For an explanation, see the subsections 'Case study selection' and 'Researching domestic workers' exclusion' in this chapter.

Human Rights and the Protection of Domestic Workers in Labour and Migration Law. Natalie Sedacca, Oxford University Press. © Oxford University Press 2026. DOI: 10.1093/9780198985266.003.0002

these areas of exclusion using two main organising themes. The first, 'lack of accountability', refers to a lack of visibility, scrutiny, and regulation via objective rules and standards of actions within the home and family, and is manifested in matters such as non-applicability of labour inspection procedures to domestic work and a lack of regulation of hours. The second theme, 'devaluation', denotes the denial of the value of work in the private sphere to the economy and society, which combines with the concentration of women who are structurally disadvantaged on the basis of characteristics such as migration status and/or ethnicity, as well as gender. This manifests in phenomena like persistent low pay in the domestic work sector, the presentation of paid domestic workers as being 'like a member of the family', their depiction as 'low-skilled workers', and their consequent subjection to restrictive visa schemes that lead to a lack of rights and labour mobility.

The book provides new insights into the exclusion of domestic workers from protection, how this exclusion falls short of human rights standards, and the ways in which human rights law can support the case for improved and better enforced rights. The relationship between labour law and human rights is controversial, with some arguing that human rights are unsuitable for protecting workers' rights because they are too individualistic and based on state restraint, are legalistic and remove agency from workers, fail to prioritize economic and social rights, and are not genuinely universalistic, while others counter these claims and view human rights as more fruitful for the protection of workers.[4] My argument intervenes in this debate by making a distinct and positive case for the role of human rights law in extending protection to domestic workers. It is not dismissive of critiques of dominant approaches to human rights but instead examines how responding to these criticisms can spur reform to better reflect the movement's core principles.[5]

I posit a specific approach to human rights that I argue is most promising for challenging domestic workers' exclusion. This has four main features. First, bearing in mind that labour law frequently concerns relationships with private employers, the approach centres a move beyond a view of human rights based solely on state restraint to encompass positive duties on the state to prevent and punish violations that are perpetrated by private actors.[6] Secondly, it views the shift in

[4] For detailed citations on this topic, see Chapter 3. Significant works include: Philip Alston (ed), *Labour Rights as Human Rights* (OUP 2005); Jay Youngdahl, 'Solidarity First: Labor Rights Are Not the Same as Human Rights' (2009) 18 New Labor Forum 30; Kevin Kolben, 'Labor Rights as Human Rights?' (2009) 50 Virginia Journal of International Law 449; Colin F Fenwick and Tonia Novitz (eds), *Human Rights at Work: Perspectives on Law and Regulation* (Hart 2010); Virginia Mantouvalou, 'Are Labour Rights Human Rights?' (2012) 3 European Labour Law Journal 151; Janice R Bellace, 'Human Rights at Work: The Need for Definitional Coherence in the Global Governance System' (2014) 30 International Journal of Comparative Labour Law and Industrial Relations 175; Judy Fudge, 'Labour Rights as Human Rights: Turning Slogans into Legal Claims' (2014) 37 Dalhousie Law Journal 601.

[5] Gráinne De Búrca, *Reframing Human Rights in a Turbulent Era* (OUP 2021) 4.

[6] See eg Sandra Fredman, 'Poverty and Human Rights: A Peril and a Promise' in Dapo Akande and others (eds), *Human Rights and 21st Century Challenges: Poverty, Conflict, and the Environment* (OUP 2020) 224–32.

human rights towards greater scrutiny of the private sphere (for example, in relation to domestic violence)[7] as promising for the protection of domestic workers, because of the parallels with the family home as a workplace. Thirdly, the approach requires significant weight to be given to social and economic rights and distributional issues as well as (but not instead of) civil and political entitlements.[8] Finally, it argues that the practical realization of claims to universalism in human rights is hindered when too great a weight is placed on state sovereignty, especially in the context of migration.[9] It therefore argues for a rebalancing in favour of migrants' rights that recognizes factors like the context for large-scale migration and the vital role that domestic workers play in destination countries. Throughout the book, I use this framework to criticize the lack of protection offered to domestic workers, focusing primarily on the right to private and family life, the right to work, the prohibition of forced labour, and relevant anti-discrimination provisions.

Defining domestic work

The International Labour Organisation (ILO) defines domestic work as 'work performed in or for a household or households' and a domestic worker as any person engaged in such work within an employment relationship, except where this is sporadic or occasional and not on an occupational basis.[10] While casual work is excluded,[11] this definition otherwise encompasses a broad variety of work patterns, from cleaners and carers working across several different households to domestic workers performing a range of tasks in a single home. This book focuses on the latter category, primarily those working full-time for a single employer and engaged directly rather than through an intermediary.[12] This focus was chosen

[7] Paulina García-Del Moral and Megan Alexandra Dersnah, 'A Feminist Challenge to the Gendered Politics of the Public/Private Divide: On Due Diligence, Domestic Violence, and Citizenship' (2014) 18 Citizenship Studies 661.

[8] This draws on an 'integrated approach' where social and economic rights are used to interpret civil and political rights—Virginia Mantouvalou, 'Labour Rights in the European Convention on Human Rights: An Intellectual Justification for an Integrated Approach to Interpretation' (2013) 13 Human Rights Law Review 529.

[9] Judy Fudge, 'Making Claims for Migrant Workers: Human Rights and Citizenship' (2014) 18 Citizenship Studies 29.

[10] ILO, 'C-189—Convention Concerning Decent Work for Domestic Workers, 2011' (100th ILC Session 2011) Article 1.

[11] For criticism of this exclusion, see Tonia Novitz and Phil Syrpis, 'The Place of Domestic Work in Europe: An Analysis of Current Policy in the Light of the Council Decision Authorising Member States to Ratify ILO Convention No. 189' (2015) 6 European Labour Law Journal 104, 117.

[12] There is a growing literature on domestic work performed via intermediaries, including digital platforms—see eg Abigail Hunt and Emma Samman, 'Domestic Work and the Gig Economy in South Africa: Old Wine in New Bottles?' (2020) 15 Anti-Trafficking Review 102; Ambika Tandon and Aayush Rathi, 'Sustaining Urban Labour Markets: Situating Migration and Domestic Work in India's "Gig" Economy' (2024) 56 Environment and Planning A: Economy and Space 1245; Paula Rodríguez-Modroño, Astrid Agenjo-Calderón, and Purificación López-Igual, 'Platform Work in the Domestic and Home Care Sector: New Mechanisms of Invisibility and Exploitation of Women Migrant Workers' (2022) 30 Gender and Development 619. I have also written on this elsewhere, eg James Muldoon,

because relations of this nature give rise to a distinctive set of concerns. The dynamic in which one individual—usually a woman—performs a range of tasks is heavily associated with devaluation and lack of recognition. In contrast to the expectation in most jobs of specified responsibilities and hours,[13] domestic workers' tasks are often poorly defined and can appear limitless.[14] The labour of the domestic worker performing these tasks, even if paid, is therefore often conflated with work that would otherwise be provided for free, usually by women, within the family.[15] The intensity and abilities required for each individual task, which include 'corporeal' and emotional qualities, are often unrecognized, with work assumed to be 'simple labour' that does not require specific skills or specialization.[16] This characterization relates not only to the work's reproductive nature but also to the 'cultural codification' drawn from the legacy of the work having been traditionally performed by workers from marginalized ethnic minorities, and the depiction of their work as inferior because of its association with the body and emotions rather than rationality.[17]

Domestic work comprising a spectrum of tasks often takes place on a 'live-in' basis, meaning the worker lives in the home they work in, in contrast to 'live-out' domestic work where the worker visits (a) household(s) to work and then returns to a separate home. Live-in work brings pronounced challenges, including isolation, an expectation of constant availability, the potential for tasks to be increased, and difficulty contesting unreasonable employer instructions.[18] The provision of accommodation increases dependency on employers, creating an extra obstacle to leaving a job,[19] and can pose serious privacy issues such as lacking an individual bedroom, monitoring of communications, and intrusive surveillance.[20] Despite these disadvantages, live-in work can be appealing, particularly for migrant domestic workers,

Natalie Sedacca, and Paul Apostolidis, 'Matchmakers: Placement Agencies and Digital Platforms in the UK Childcare Market' (2025) 5 Work in the Global Economy 6.

[13] Sophie Henderson, *Protecting the Rights of Women Migrant Domestic Workers: Structural Violence and Competing Interests in the Philippines and Sri Lanka* (Routledge 2022) 2.

[14] ILO, 'Report IV(1)—Decent Work for Domestic Workers—99th Session of the International Labour Conference' (2010) 7.

[15] Rosie Cox, 'Gendered Work and Migration Regimes' in Liam Leonard (ed), *Transnational Migration, Gender and Rights* (Emerald 2012) 45–46.

[16] Encarnación Gutiérrez Rodríguez, *Migration, Domestic Work and Affect: A Decolonial Approach on Value and the Feminization of Labor* (Routledge 2010) 89–92, 110.

[17] ibid 92.

[18] Bridget Anderson, *Doing the Dirty Work? The Global Politics of Domestic Labour* (Zed 2000) 41–43; Einat Albin, 'From "Domestic Servant" to "Domestic Worker"' in Judy Fudge, Shae McCrystal, and Kamala Sankaran (eds), *Challenging the Legal Boundaries of Work Regulation* (Hart 2012) 248; Novitz and Syrpis (n 11) 109.

[19] European Union Agency for Fundamental Rights, 'Out of Sight: Migrant Women Exploited in Domestic Work' (2018) 8 <http://fra.europa.eu/en/publication/2018/exploited-domestic-workers> accessed 25 August 2025.

[20] Anderson (n 18) 43; Gutiérrez Rodríguez (n 16) 117; European Union Agency for Fundamental Rights (n 19) 5.

to avoid separate challenges associated with live-out work like the need to travel between jobs and to find and pay for accommodation, which may be shared and/or in poor condition.[21] Migrant domestic workers often begin on a live-in basis and then move to live-out work after several years in the host country, once they have settled and paid off debts,[22] as a way to establish a degree of autonomy.[23] However, where visa regimes are strict and allow only short-term residence without renewal options, there is little to no scope for such a transition to take place.

The term 'domestic worker' both contrasts and overlaps with other roles such as nanny, au pair, and care worker. A nanny is ostensibly a distinct occupation with specialism in childcare reflected in higher salaries and lower expectation to complete household work such as cleaning, except where directly related to the children being cared for.[24] However, the term is increasingly also used to refer to low-paid domestic workers who perform domestic work alongside childcare.[25] The descriptor 'au pair' traditionally referred to an individual on a linguistic and cultural exchange performing limited amounts of household labour or childcare, but again, the increasing work expected from many labelled in this category has made it difficult to divide their role sharply from that of domestic workers.[26] The relationship between domestic and care work is more complex. In certain cases, there are clear distinctions between the roles, particularly where care work takes place in an institutional setting or entails a series of short, often high-pressure visits to different households, or the receipt of direct payments allowing professionalized workers to provide care packages.[27] But for care workers based in a private home, there are important areas of overlap with domestic workers, including the lack of appreciation of work in private homes as being a public good, the invisibility of the labour, the wrongful depiction of the work as 'unskilled' and its conflation with work provided for free by women in the family, which may then be used to justify low pay.[28] This book therefore also considers these other categories of

[21] Anderson (n 18) 46; Marta Kindler, 'Risk and Risk Strategies in Migration: Ukrainian Domestic Workers in Poland' in Helma Lutz (ed), *Migration and Domestic Work: A European Perspective on a Global Theme* (Ashgate 2008) 154; Gutiérrez Rodríguez (n 16) 69.

[22] Anderson (n 18) 47.

[23] Adelle Blackett, *Everyday Transgressions: Domestic Workers' Transnational Challenge to International Labor Law* (Cornell University Press 2019) 6.

[24] Rosie Cox, *The Servant Problem: Domestic Employment in a Global Economy* (Bloomsbury 2006) 72; Sara R Farris, 'The Business of Care: Private Placement Agencies and Female Migrant Workers in London' (2020) 27 Gender, Work, and Organization 1450, 1456.

[25] Irma Arriagada and Rosalba Todaro, *Cadenas Globales de Cuidados: El Papel de La Migrantes Peruanas En La Provisión de Cuidados En Chile* (ONU Mujeres 2012) 18; Nicky Busch, 'The Employment of Migrant Nannies in the UK: Negotiating Social Class in an Open Market for Commoditised in-Home Care' (2013) 14 Social & Cultural Geography: Gendered Spaces of Commoditised Care 541, 546.

[26] Busch (n 25) 546–48; See also Rosie Cox and Nicky Busch, *As an Equal? Au Pairing in the 21st Century* (Zed 2018).

[27] LJB Hayes, *Stories of Care: A Labour of Law: Gender and Class at Work* (Palgrave, Macmillan Education 2017) 72–76, 162–72.

[28] ibid 36–37, 48–52, 118–43.

worker where there is an overlap with domestic work as defined in this section, but not where there is a clear distinction.

Domestic work, gender, race, and migration

Paid domestic work has been a 'typically female occupation' since the nineteenth century,[29] and remains so to date. Women account for 76.2 per cent of domestic workers worldwide, with regional variation—the highest proportion is 89 per cent in the Americas.[30] Men working as domestic workers are more likely to be concentrated in niche areas such as driving, security, and gardening,[31] where the erasure of skill or conflation with 'non-work' is less likely. The women performing domestic work are disproportionately from ethnic minorities and/or international migrants, such that the sector 'perpetuates hierarchies based on race, ethnicity, indigenous status, caste and nationality'.[32] The groups dominating the sector range from indigenous and rural populations in South America, persons of lower 'caste' in India, Black people in previously colonized countries like South Africa, and international migrants from the Global South in Europe and North America.[33] Hierarchies also exist between ethnic groups, with some employers expressing preference for Filipina migrant workers over those from African countries and other Asian countries like India and Sri Lanka.[34]

The concentration of minority women in domestic work can be helpfully understood through the concept of 'racialization', which refers to racial meanings being 'constructed by powerful institutions and groups and used to justify discrimination, stereotyping, violence and othering of ethnic and religious groups'.[35] The roots of this connection can be traced back to slavery, which had long been associated with ethnic or national difference, as well as with reproductive and household labour.[36] The formal end of slavery as an institution did not put an end to

[29] Raffaella Sarti, 'The Globalisation of Domestic Service: An Historical Perspective' in Helma Lutz (ed), *Migration and Domestic Work: A European Perspective on a Global Theme* (Ashgate 2008) 91.

[30] ILO, 'Making Decent Work a Reality' (n 2) 13.

[31] ILO, 'Report IV(1) 99th Session' (n 14) 7.

[32] ibid 5.

[33] Marchetti (n 2) 1194. The 'Global South' refers to the regions of Latin America, Asia, Africa, and Oceania, which are 'mostly (though not all) low-income and often politically or culturally marginalized', although they are far from homogenous—Nour Dados and Raewyn Connell, 'The Global South' (2012) 11 Contexts 12, 12; Meron Zeleke and Lahra Smith, 'Introduction: Intra-Continental Migration Dynamics in Africa and the Importance of South-South Migration (SSM)' in Meron Zeleke and Lahra Smith (eds), *African Perspectives on South–South Migration* (Routledge 2024) 5–6.

[34] Fiona Williams and Anna Gavanas, 'The Intersection of Childcare Regimes and Migration Regimes: A Three-Country Study' in Helma Lutz (ed), *Migration and Domestic Work: A European Perspective on a Global Theme* (Ashgate 2008) 22; Henderson (n 13) 97.

[35] Amnesty International, 'Policing the Pandemic: Human Rights Violations in the Enforcement of Covid-19 Measures in Europe' (2020) EUR 01/2511/2020 4 FN 3.

[36] Anderson (n 18) 128.

racist conceptions of Black or other racialized people as particularly suited to certain types of physical labour, including domestic work, or the expectation to serve more privileged groups.[37] This is a self-perpetuating process: racialized women are pushed towards domestic work by a combination of factors, including economic necessity and a lack of other opportunities, and once in the sector their association with 'degraded' labour reinforces notions of 'their supposed natural inferiority' projected by more privileged groups.[38]

Understanding the socio-economic context for domestic work also requires an examination of the factors driving widespread demand, including for international migration. Migrant domestic workers make up around 17.2 per cent of all domestic workers worldwide, and a large majority (almost 80 per cent) work in high-income countries.[39] A key factor in the demand for domestic work in industrialized countries is women's increased participation in labour outside the home, combined with an intensification of work and a lack of reconciliation with family life.[40] Standardized hours of work were created in many high-income countries in the post-World War II era based on a 'male-breadwinner' model that was reliant on support from a woman undertaking reproductive labour in the home.[41] This conception of women's non-participation in waged work was never universally true, particularly for Black and working-class women,[42] but it is clearly unrealistic today, with wide acceptance that families need two incomes in many countries.[43] The hours designed around a male worker supported by a female 'reproductive' worker at home are now, in many families, being worked by two people. Rather than adjusting work demands around family and other responsibilities, there is often an increased expectation on employees to be flexible.[44]

Despite this shift, there has not been a significant corresponding increase in the share of household labour performed by men or a decline in the expectation of

[37] ibid 148–49; Iris Marion Young, *Justice and the Politics of Difference* (Paperback reissue, Princeton University Press 2011) 52.

[38] Evelyn Nakano Glenn, 'From Servitude to Service Work: Historical Continuities in the Racial Division of Paid Reproductive Labor' (1992) 18 Signs 1, 32.

[39] Maria Gallotti, 'Migrant Domestic Workers Across the World: Global and Regional Estimates' (ILO 2015) 1–2. Although this document is not that recent, it still appears on the relevant ILO resources page: ILO, 'Data on Domestic Workers' (*ILO*, undated) <https://www.ilo.org/topics-and-sectors/domestic-workers/data-domestic-workers> accessed 29 August 2025.

[40] ILO, 'Report IV(1) 99th Session' (n 14) 5.

[41] Carole Pateman, *The Sexual Contract* (Polity 1988) 131; Judy Fudge and Rosemary J Owens, 'Introduction' in Judy Fudge and Rosemary J Owens (eds), *Precarious Work, Women and the New Economy: The Challenge to Legal Norms* (Hart 2006) 21.

[42] Diamond Ashiagbor, 'The Intersection between Gender and "Race" in the Labour Market: Lessons for Anti-Discrimination Law' in Anne E Morris and Thérèse O'Donnell (eds), *Feminist Perspectives on Employment Law* (Cavendish 1999) 145; Joanne Conaghan, 'Gender and the Labour of Law' in Hugh Collins, Virginia Mantouvalou, and Gillian Lester (eds), *Philosophical Foundations of Labour Law* (OUP 2018) 275–83.

[43] Novitz and Syrpis (n 11) 106.

[44] Fudge and Owens (n 41) 21; Conaghan (n 42) 283.

women's contribution,[45] nor a comprehensive questioning of the 'sexual, class and racial division of domestic labour'.[46] This leads to a demand for domestic workers to make up for these hours of work by being available for longer periods, although the option of employing a domestic worker is often unaffordable to working-class families, particularly in industrialized countries.[47] Onerous working hours patterns cause particular difficulties for women wanting to take up professionalized occupations; where they cannot afford the support required to work long hours, they are increasingly concentrated in zero hours contracts and other 'flexible'/precarious forms of work.[48] Domestic workers are in an even more precarious position, since they continue to carry out labour that is viewed as outside of the main workforce.[49]

In addition, many industrialized states (with certain exceptions like Denmark and Sweden) have failed to make adequate provision of care services to make up for women's increasing work outside the home, at the same time as care and other social reproductive needs are steadily increasing, driven by factors such as a growing elderly population.[50] These shortcomings in state support stem in large part from the tendency to cut welfare under 'financialized capitalism',[51] and were exacerbated by the financial crisis of 2008 and the ensuing recession.[52] For example, in European countries, nurseries and creches are often expensive and there is a tendency to transfer these responsibilities to the private sector rather than to increase public provision.[53]

A lack of high-quality care provision also has negative implications for the human rights of those relying on these services, including children, disabled persons, and people who work outside the home—particularly working women, to whom the remaining caring burden mainly falls.[54] While recognising these manifold human rights considerations, the book maintains that domestic workers

[45] Fudge and Owens (n 41) 21, 15; Barbara Ehrenreich and Arlie Russell Hochschild, 'Introduction' in Barbara Ehrenreich and Arlie Russell Hochschild (eds), *Global Woman: Nannies, Maids and Sex Workers in the New Economy* (Granta Books 2003) 9.

[46] Rosario Fernández, 'Commodification of Domestic Labour, the Culture of Servitude and the Making of the Chilean Nation' (2018) 43 Österreichische Zeitschrift für Soziologie 49, 51.

[47] ILO, 'Report IV(1) 99th Session' (n 14) 9.

[48] Novitz and Syrpis (n 11) 107–8.

[49] ibid 109; Inga K Thiemann, 'Beyond Victimhood and Beyond Employment? Exploring Avenues for Labour Law to Empower Women Trafficked into the Sex Industry' (2019) 48 Industrial Law Journal 199, 215.

[50] Ehrenreich and Hochschild (n 45) 8–9; Novitz and Syrpis (n 11) 107; Irma Arriagada, 'La Injusta Organización Social de Los Cuidados En Chile' in Nadya Araujo Guimarães and Helena Hirata (eds), *El cuidado en América Latina* (Fundación Medifé Edita 2020) 133.

[51] Nancy Fraser, 'Crisis of Care? On the Social-Reproductive Contradictions of Contemporary Capitalism' in Tithi Bhattacharya (ed), *Social Reproduction Theory: Remapping Class, Recentering Oppression* (Pluto Press 2017) 32.

[52] Novitz and Syrpis (n 11) 108.

[53] Gutiérrez Rodríguez (n 16) 74, 87.

[54] Human Rights Council, 'Resolution Adopted on 11 October 2023 on Centrality of Care and Support from a Human Rights Perspective—A/HRC/RES/54/6'.

cannot be expected to bear the burden of failings in broader care work provision by working for unlimited hours, with low pay, and in conditions that deny basic rights. Apart from being unjustifiable from the workers' rights perspective, this does not necessarily lead to better outcomes for 'recipients' of care or other domestic work. For example, the UN's Independent Expert on the Enjoyment of All Human Rights by Older Persons has noted 'evidence that the satisfaction of persons receiving care correlates with the well-being of their care workers'.[55] Likewise, a recent Advisory Opinion of the Inter-American Court of Human Rights (IACtHR) identified a 'right to care' as an autonomous right that comprises both the right to *receive* care and the right to *provide* care in dignified conditions, whether paid or unpaid,[56] thus viewing the rights of providers and recipients holistically rather than being in conflict. It should also be noted that the understanding of a 'care crisis' is not universally the key factor behind demand for domestic work. India, for example, has relatively low women's participation in paid work outside the home, yet there is a significant demand for domestic workers to allow their employers to maintain middle-class status and avoid tasks that are viewed as unattractive.[57]

Apart from demand, it is equally important to understand the factors driving outward migration for domestic work. Many migrant domestic workers are from countries that were impoverished by colonialism or related processes,[58] who may migrate to countries of the Global North, more prosperous nations within their region, or internally to richer cities or areas. Countries of the Global South have been significantly impacted by the move that took place across the world from the late 1970s to a favoured system of 'neoliberalism': an economic programme requiring market deregulation, privatization of public services, and a shrinking of the welfare state's role.[59] This took place alongside globalization, comprising enhanced economic and political integration worldwide, with an increase in trade, investment and capital flows.[60] Loans were made conditional on 'structural adjustment programmes' entailing cuts, currency devaluation, and reduction of certain industries, making an adequate standard of living much more difficult to achieve.[61]

[55] Rosa Kornfeld-Matte, 'Report of the Independent Expert on the Enjoyment of All Human Rights by Older Persons—A/HRC/30/43' (UN Human Rights Council 2015) [80].

[56] *The Content and Scope of the Right to Care and Its Interrelationship with Other Rights—Advisory Opinion OC-31/25* IACtHR 12 June 2025, Ser A No 31.

[57] Raka Ray and Seemin Qayum, *Cultures of Servitude: Modernity, Domesticity, and Class in India* (Stanford University Press 2009) 9.

[58] Gul Ozyegin and Pierette Hondagneu-Sotelo, 'Conclusion: Domestic Work, Migration and the New Gender Order in Contemporary Europe' in Helma Lutz (ed), *Migration and Domestic Work: A European Perspective on a Global Theme* (Ashgate 2008) 196.

[59] Joseph R Slaughter, 'Hijacking Human Rights: Neoliberalism, the New Historiography, and the End of the Third World' (2018) 40 Human Rights Quarterly 735, 767.

[60] Fudge and Owens (n 41) 4–5.

[61] Ehrenreich and Hochschild (n 45) 8; Silvia Federici, *Revolution at Point Zero: Housework, Reproduction, and Feminist Struggle* (PM Press 2012) 69, 102–4.

This compelled many in the Global South to migrate to escape a lack of opportunity, low wages, and poor conditions, and for a chance to send back remittances that constitute a major international monetary flow and may be essential to meet basic needs.[62] Outward migration is often encouraged by governments keen to benefit from remittances, upon which many Global South states depend to service debts and allow families and communities to survive in the face of high unemployment.[63] These phenomena are exemplified by the Philippines, a key country of origin for migrant domestic workers worldwide, where governments have actively promoted this migration path since the early 1970s.[64] As public services have been minimized and working conditions declined, remittances have been used to strengthen foreign exchange reserves in order to repay heavy debts to organizations like the World Bank and International Monetary Fund (IMF).[65]

Apart from these economic incentives, there are also important gender-based factors driving migration. Women may decide to become domestic workers to escape feminized poverty: a distinct impact of poverty resulting from factors like discrimination, lower participation in the labour market and segregation to informal and low-paid roles, domestic violence, and an unequal division of labour.[66] Taken together with demand, this gives rise to the 'feminization of migration': the large-scale migration of mainly female workers to carry out roles that were traditionally performed for free by women in the family, and which are integral to their host societies' functioning.[67] Migration to support family members can have a distinct meaning for women in allowing them to escape traditional gender roles by becoming the family's income provider.[68] Large-scale feminized migration can therefore be understood as a survival strategy in response to gendered discrimination alongside poverty and lack of opportunity. Yet, even as domestic workers perform work that is indispensable to the countries or regions they migrate to, harsh migration laws and a lack of labour protection often mean that this survival strategy is curtailed or takes place in hostile conditions.

[62] Federici (n 61) 66–70.

[63] Ehrenreich and Hochschild (n 45) 7; Fudge (n 9) 29; Henderson (n 13) 4.

[64] Rhacel Salazar Parreñas, *Servants of Globalization: Migration and Domestic Work* (2nd edn, Stanford University Press 2015) 3–4.

[65] Robyn Magalit Rodriguez, *Migrants for Export: How the Philippine State Brokers Labor to the World* (University of Minnesota Press 2010) xvi–xix.

[66] Parreñas (n 64), ch 2; Urmila Bhoola, 'Report of the Special Rapporteur on Contemporary Forms of Slavery, Including Its Causes and Consequences—UN Doc A/HRC/39/52' (2018) 7; Henderson (n 13) 45.

[67] Ehrenreich and Hochschild (n 45) 4–5. The importance of domestic workers to the global economy is also acknowledged in the preamble to C-189.

[68] Parreñas (n 64) 32.

Contesting domestic workers' exclusion: ILO Convention 189 and beyond

As a result of their labour being conceptualized as distinctive and less valuable, domestic workers are often excluded from protections applicable to others, or subject to special forms of regulation that are inadequate to protect them.[69] Worldwide, 36.1 per cent of domestic workers are entirely outside labour law coverage, with the remainder varying between coverage in general labour laws in full (11.4 per cent), in part (30.2 per cent), coverage by specific laws or subordinate legislation (11.8 per cent) and varied coverage depending on state in federal systems (10.5 per cent).[70] Beyond this, there is frequently a gap between legal entitlements and the treatment of domestic workers in practice, since the work takes place behind closed doors, is isolated, and is usually not subject to labour inspection.

Domestic workers and their organizations were central to the movement that pressed against this widespread, systemic exclusion from labour law standards, towards the development of a specific ILO Convention on domestic work.[71] A coalition of Latin American domestic workers and European advocates carried out intensive campaigning, leading to the 2008 meeting of the ILO Governing Body commissioning academic expert Adelle Blackett to draft an urgent report on decent work for domestic workers.[72] The resulting report recognized the factors driving increased demand for domestic work, its undervaluation, and its frequent informal nature and invisibility,[73] with developments culminating in the agreement of ILO Convention 189 on domestic work (C-189) and the accompanying Recommendation 201[74] at the ILO's 100th session in 2011.

An approach to labour rights based on human rights protections and standards played a crucial role in the adoption of C-189. Understanding domestic workers' claims as a human rights concern helped to make the case for their inclusion in a framework that had long excluded them, as well as contributing to specific entitlements that became part of the Convention, such as respect for privacy and a prohibition on employers retaining travel documents.[75] A human rights-based approach therefore counteracted exclusion while recognising the distinctive position of domestic workers. By adopting C-189, a hard law instrument—as opposed to previous soft law approaches—the ILO demonstrated the importance now placed on the

[69] Virginia Mantouvalou, 'Human Rights for Precarious Workers: The Legislative Precariousness of Domestic Labor' (2012) 34 Comparative Labor Law & Policy Journal 133, 136–37.

[70] ILO, 'Making Decent Work a Reality' (n 2) 60.

[71] Blackett, *Everyday Transgressions* (n 23) 6.

[72] Merike Blofield and Merita Jokela, 'Paid Domestic Work and the Struggles of Care Workers in Latin America' (2018) 66 Current Sociology 531, 538; Blackett, *Everyday Transgressions* (n 23) 9–10.

[73] ILO, 'Report IV(1) 99th Session' (n 14) 1–5.

[74] ILO, 'ILO Convention 189' (n 10); ILO, 'R-201—Recommendation concerning Decent Work for Domestic Workers, 2011 (No. 201)' (100th ILC Session 2011).

[75] ILO, 'Report IV(2)—Decent Work for Domestic Workers—99th Session of the International Labour Conference' (2010) 12, 151, 192; Blackett, *Everyday Transgressions* (n 23) 13–34.

regulation of domestic work, comprehensively acknowledging the role and poor conditions workers had been subjected to for the first time.[76] C-189 sets out entitlements that range from civil rights like protection against abuse, harassment and violence, respect for privacy, and access to justice, to social and labour rights like minimum wage coverage, and a safe and healthy working environment, as well as rights specific to domestic workers' position such as providing that they cannot be forced to live in their employer's home or to remain there during rest or annual leave if they do.[77]

C-189 represents a major advance for domestic workers' rights and is testament to the determined and successful campaigning of domestic workers and their allies. However, there are certain limitations to its impact, including the relatively low level of ratification, which stands at forty countries worldwide.[78] For the remaining countries, campaigns for ratification are vital, but it is also valuable to examine alternative justifications for improved entitlements based on states' existing human rights obligations. Secondly, despite its generally very progressive nature, C-189 leaves some areas of ambiguity, which could be interpreted as allowing lesser forms of protection. In relation to these, I argue that a human rights analysis allows for greater precision in determining the entitlement to ensure domestic workers do not remain excluded because of the priority given to employers' privacy and other interests. For example, C-189 Article 17 requires each member state to develop and implement measures for labour inspection, enforcement, and penalties 'with due regard for the special characteristics of domestic work', and states that measures specifying the conditions should have 'due respect for privacy'. This can be interpreted as meaning that the employer's privacy is a bar on *any* power of entry to the home for inspection, which, I argue, would be too deferential to the employer's interests and fail to adequately protect domestic workers. I therefore set out principles for inspections in a private home that are based on, and compliant with, human rights. This clarifies that a power of entry should be included, and that random rather than only complaint-led inspections should be carried out. I also explore and clarify what 'due respect for privacy' should be understood to entail, arguing that this means powers of entry being limited to measures needed to check workers' rights and well-being as opposed to granting sweeping powers, e.g. to search through correspondence.

Another example is C-189 Article 10, which requires consideration of the 'special characteristics of domestic work' in ensuring equal treatment regarding hours of work, overtime, rest, and leave. This is a weaker wording than was originally proposed,[79] and is open to interpretation, being potentially available to justify hours that are significantly longer than in other sectors. My argument therefore

[76] Einat Albin and Virginia Mantouvalou, 'The ILO Convention on Domestic Workers: From the Shadows to the Light' (2012) 41 Industrial Law Journal 67, 71.

[77] Articles 5, 6, 16, 11, 13, and 9 respectively.

[78] Ratification figures are from 4 August 2025.

[79] ILO, 'Report IV(1) 99th Session' (n 14) 419.

moves beyond the stipulations of C-189 by addressing reasonable limitations on working time as part of the right to a private and family life. Building on previous related arguments,[80] I draw on empirical materials to examine and critique justifications given for extended hours in domestic work, which include the necessity of supporting working families but also encompass cultural expectations of constant availability for live-in domestic workers.

Thirdly, while C-189 Article 8 includes stipulations to assist migrant domestic workers relating to contracts, cooperation between member states, and entitlement to repatriation, its provisions do not directly address the limitations of visa regimes nor the question of family reunification. I examine the former through the prism of the right to work, arguing that undue restrictions on access to the labour market infringe on the right to gain a living by freely chosen work as part of the 'negative' right to work, and examining how this links to civil and political rights. I also consider family reunification based on the right to private and family life, drawing on empirical materials to highlight relevant factors such as the structural disadvantage forming the background to migration for domestic work and the pain caused by long-term family separation, which, I argue, are relevant in assessing justifications for limiting this right.

Case study selection

This book takes a global focus by examining the protection of domestic workers' human rights in one country from each of four continents in which domestic work is highly feminized:[81] the Americas (Chile), Europe (the United Kingdom),[82] Africa (South Africa) and Asia (India).

Within the Americas, the vast majority of domestic workers are in the Latin American and Caribbean sub-regions.[83] Apart from the regional prevalence of domestic work,[84] Latin America is of great interest to domestic workers' rights because of its strong movements and initiatives towards their protection.[85] Of the forty countries that have ratified C-189, almost half (nineteen) are in Latin

[80] Deirdre McCann, 'Decent Working Hours as a Human Right: Intersections in the Regulation of Working Time' in Colin F Fenwick and Tonia Novitz (eds), *Human Rights at Work: Perspectives on Law and Regulation* (Hart 2010).

[81] ILO, 'Making Decent Work a Reality' (n 2) 13. The Arab states are distinctive as a region where only 36.6 per cent of domestic workers are women (ibid).

[82] The United Kingdom comprises four nations, with some powers in certain legal areas devolved to the Northern Ireland Assembly, Scottish Parliament, and Welsh Parliament. Immigration and nationality are not devolved in any nation, and employment law in Northern Ireland only—David Torrance, 'Reserved Matters in the United Kingdom' (2019) House of Commons Library Briefing Paper CBP 8544 33–39.

[83] ILO, 'Making Decent Work a Reality' (n 2) 29.

[84] ILO Regional Office for Latin America and the Caribbean, '2015 Overview Latin America and the Caribbean' (2015) 13.

[85] Blofield and Jokela (n 72) 538.

America and the Caribbean. Chile is an example of a country that ratified C-189 quite promptly (in 2015) and made significant legislative reforms alongside this, adding to earlier incremental steps to improve domestic workers' rights. The 2015 reforms included provisions for limits on the working day, conditions on payments in kind, and preventing the employer from unilaterally reducing remuneration following reduced working days or an increase in rest days. They also introduced a notable system of inspection without entry to the home, whereby the employer can choose to accept an inspector's entry or attend the office of the labour inspectorate.

In Europe, the domestic work sector is proportionately smaller,[86] but concerns about exploitation within it are central in discussions of severe labour abuses.[87] Ratifications of C-189 are lower than in Latin America at eleven countries. While details vary, a number of countries in the region have 'outdated and even regressive' laws on domestic workers' rights,[88] or had until recently. This includes the UK, which has declined to ratify C-189 and abstained from the vote on it in the ILO proceedings. Domestic workers are excluded from some key provisions on working time, including the maximum hourly working week of 48 hours,[89] and private households are exempted from health and safety provisions on inspections.[90] Until April 2024, live-in domestic workers deemed to be treated as akin to family members were even excluded from minimum wage entitlement.[91]

In Africa, domestic work employs around 9.6 million people, amounting to 2.1 per cent of overall work, and making the continent the third largest regional employer of domestic workers after Asia and Pacific and the Americas.[92] South Africa is the continent's largest employer of domestic workers, with around 1,335,343 workers in this role,[93] an estimated 6 per cent of the country's workforce.[94] Since the end of apartheid, South Africa has seen incremental reforms to improve the legal position of domestic workers following campaigns by unions and allies, including a Sectoral Determination mandating a minimum wage and basic working conditions in 2002, and ratification of C-189 in 2013.[95] It has arguably been at the 'vanguard of domestic workers' rights', having long recognized domestic workers' labour as work,[96] yet serious inequalities and compliance failings persist in practice.[97]

[86] ILO, 'Making Decent Work a Reality' (n 2) xviii.
[87] See eg European Union Agency for Fundamental Rights (n 19).
[88] Adelle Blackett, 'The Decent Work for Domestic Workers Convention and Recommendation, 2011' (2012) 106 American Journal of International Law 778, 793–94 fn 3.
[89] See Chapter 6.
[90] See Chapter 4.
[91] See Chapter 5.
[92] ILO, 'Making Decent Work a Reality' (n 2) 41.
[93] ibid.
[94] Hunt and Samman (n 12) 103.
[95] ibid 107.
[96] Blackett, *Everyday Transgressions* (n 23) 138.
[97] See eg Q Dawood and M Seedat-Khan, 'The Unforgiving Work Environment of Black African Women Domestic Workers in a Post-Apartheid South Africa' (2023) 33 Development in Practice 168.

The Asia-Pacific region has the highest concentration of domestic workers globally, encompassing over 50 per cent of the sector worldwide.[98] The only state in this region to have ratified C-189 is the Philippines, which is a major country of origin for migrant domestic workers. India is an example of a country with a very sizeable domestic work sector, estimated at 4.8 million, alongside an inconsistent framework for rights.[99] While domestic work is the largest single employer for women in urban areas, domestic workers are not covered under most national labour laws.[100] There is substantial variation between different states as to the level of protection provided, including domestic workers' eligibility for the minimum wage.[101] Important advocacy for more comprehensive protection has taken place in recent years, including during the Covid-19 pandemic, with domestic workers protesting to call for improvements and assert their status as workers entitled to legal protection.[102]

There are several comparable features between the case studies. All are large economies within their regions, formally democratic systems—albeit with some degree of regression[103]—and all have ratified the main generalist international human rights treaties.[104] Chile and the UK are subject to the jurisdiction of the relevant regional human rights courts, the IACtHR and European Court of Human Rights (ECtHR) respectively, and South Africa also accepted the overall jurisdiction of the African Court on Human and People's Rights (ACtHPR).[105] No direct equivalent of these courts exists for the Asian continent,[106] but the Indian Supreme Court

[98] ILO, 'Making Decent Work a Reality' (n 2) 26.

[99] ibid 31.

[100] Srijani Datta and others, 'Domestic Workers from Margin to Center: Protest, Opportunity and Threat in Pandemic Politics' (2022) 26 Journal for Cultural Research 39, 42.

[101] N Neetha, 'Minimum Wages for Domestic Work: Mirroring Devalued Housework' (2013) 48 Economic and Political Weekly 77, 77–83.

[102] Datta and others (n 100) 40–41.

[103] There is no uncontroversial way of measuring the extent of democratic deficit, and various indices exist for this comparison. For example, Freedom House categorizes Chile, the UK, and South Africa as free and India as partly free, while the Economist Democracy Index categorizes the UK as a full democracy and Chile, South Africa, and India as 'flawed democracies'—Freedom House, 'Countries and Territories' (*Freedom House*) <https://freedomhouse.org/countries/freedom-world/scores> accessed 25 August 2025; Lucia Garcia, 'Democracy Index: Conflict and Polarisation Drive a New Low for Global Democracy' (*Economist Intelligence Unit*, 15 February 2024) <https://www.eiu.com/n/democracy-index-conflict-and-polarisation-drive-a-new-low-for-global-democracy/> accessed 25 August 2025.

[104] United Nations, 'International Covenant on Economic, Social and Cultural Rights (Adopted 16 December 1966, Entered into Force 23 March 1976) 993 UNTS 3'; United Nations, 'International Covenant on Civil and Political Rights (Adopted 16 December 1966, Entered into Force 23 March 1976) 999 UNTS 171'.

[105] Although it has not made the specific declaration required to allow direct petitions to it by individuals and NGOs—Organization of African Unity, 'Protocol to the African Charter on Human and Peoples' Rights on the Establishment of an African Court on Human and Peoples' Rights—10 June 1998', Art 34(6). On the regional systems, see further Chapter 3 and Table 3.1.

[106] The closest equivalent is the ASEAN Human Rights Declaration in Southeast Asia, which is a binding treaty but has no judicial enforcement mechanism and is for a separate part of Asia.

engages significantly with international legal norms.[107] All case study countries have seen significant concern about the conditions of domestic workers, although progress in addressing their marginalization is more advanced in Chile and South Africa, which have ratified C-189 and made legislative changes to improve rights, than in the UK and (at national level) India. It is instructive to examine a combination of countries that have and have not ratified C-189, since an analysis based on human rights is relevant to both in varying ways: where not ratified, other human rights obligations may develop the case for improving the position of domestic workers regardless, and where ratified, human rights standards can help to identify gaps in protection that provide normative support for further development.

In all case study countries, domestic workers are predominantly women, many coming from groups that are marginalized on other axes, including migration status and ethnicity.[108] In Chile, domestic work was traditionally performed by rural and indigenous Chilean women.[109] Although international migration is increasingly superseding this internal migration,[110] similar patterns are replicated in this context. Peruvian migrants are often perceived by employers as 'more indigenous' and therefore more loving and subservient, in contrast to Chilean women who are viewed as being too conscious of their rights.[111] Domestic workers in the UK are often migrants from the Philippines and other countries in the Global South, including South/South East Asia and Africa.[112] In South Africa, the apartheid system 'framed black labour as cheap, informal and irregular' and, despite crucial legal reforms, there is an enduring legacy of discriminatory attitudes towards the Black women who overwhelmingly perform this work.[113] South Africa is also a significant destination country for workers from other Southern African countries, particularly Zimbabwe, but there are few relevant labour migration routes, leaving many in a situation of irregularity.[114] In India, persons categorized

[107] Neha Jain, 'The Democratizing Force of International Law: Human Rights Adjudication by the Indian Supreme Court' in Anthea Roberts and others (eds), *Comparative International Law* (OUP 2018) 320.

[108] Marchetti (n 2) 1194; International Lawyers Assisting Workers Network, 'Mapping Domestic Work and Discrimination in Africa' (ILAW 2023) 60; Datta and others (n 100) 42.

[109] Karolina Stefoni and Rosario Fernández, 'Mujeres Inmigrantes En El Trabajo Doméstico. Entre El Servilismo y Los Derechos' in Karolina Stefoni (ed), *Mujeres inmigrantes en Chile: ¿Mano de obra o trabajadoras con derechos?* (Ediciones Universidad Alberto Hurtado 2011), ebook LOC 543–73.

[110] ILO, 'Making Decent Work a Reality' (n 2) 30.

[111] Stefoni and Fernández (n 109), ebook LOC 573–659; Claudia Mora and Eduardo A Undurraga, 'Racialisation of Immigrants at Work: Labour Mobility and Segmentation of Peruvian Migrants in Chile' (2013) 32 Bulletin of Latin American Research 294, 294–99; Fernández (n 46) 54–57.

[112] Selim Yilmaz and Caroline Emberson, 'Exploring the Nature of Labour Exploitation among Domestic Workers in the UK' (University of Nottingham Rights Lab 2023) 6.

[113] Abigail Hunt and Fortunate Machingura, 'Working Paper 07: A Good Gig? The Rise of on-Demand Domestic Work' (ODI 2016) 18; Wandile Sibiya and David du Toit, 'Sweeping up Decent Work: Paid Domestic Work and Digital Platforms in South Africa' (2022) 30 Gender and Development 637, 638. Quotation from Hunt and Machingura.

[114] Zaheera Jinnah, 'Negotiated Precarity in the Global South: A Case Study of Migration and Domestic Work in South Africa' (2020) 2020 Studies in Social Justice 210, 212–18.

as belonging to a lower 'caste', particularly Dalits, alongside Adivasi tribal people, suffer disadvantage and entrenched discrimination,[115] and women carrying out domestic work, especially cleaning, are primarily poor and from disadvantaged caste groups.[116] The most significant migration in the sector is internal, from rural and poorer areas to cities, which has similar causes to international migration elsewhere, such as escaping abuse, poverty, and lack of opportunity.[117] It can also raise similar challenges, particularly where it crosses state lines, such as barriers to social security access and family separation.[118]

Taking these four case studies together allows for a multi-focal examination of the phenomenon of migration for domestic work. While the UK is an example of international migration from the Global South to an industrialized country of the Global North, Chile and South Africa mainly exemplify the growing phenomenon of 'South-South' migration, an understanding of which is crucial to explaining 'the international division of reproductive labour'.[119] India is important for examining internal migration, which has received less attention in recent literature than international migration.[120]

Researching domestic workers' exclusion

The key objective of the research has been to address the contribution of human rights to challenging domestic workers' exclusion, understood through the themes of 'lack of accountability' and 'devaluation'. This question has been addressed partly through an analysis of relevant primary legal materials (spanning the period up to August 2025), policy documents, and existing empirical and other academic studies. I have also supplemented this with first-hand qualitative research, comprising interviews with domestic workers and with others whose work or expertise is relevant to domestic workers' rights, which illuminated practical experiences

[115] Alpa Shah and Jens Lerche, 'Tribe, Caste, Class: New Mechanisms of Exploitation and Oppression' in Alpa Shah and others, *Ground Down by Growth: Tribe, Caste, Class and Inequality in 21st Century India* (Pluto Press 2017). On the complexity of caste and the need to avoid essentialized understandings, see Surinder S Jodhka and Jules Naudet, 'Introduction—Studying Caste: Conceptual Currents and Emergent Perspectives' in Surinder S Jodhka and Jules Naudet (eds), *The Oxford Handbook of Caste* (OUP 2023).

[116] Samita Sen and Nilanjana Sengupta, *Domestic Days: Women, Work, and Politics in Contemporary Kolkata* (OUP 2016) 99–100; Datta and others (n 100) 43.

[117] Sen and Sengupta (n 116) 73.

[118] Shraddha Chigateri, Mubashira Zaidi, and Anweshaa Ghosh, 'Locating the Processes of Policy Change in the Context of Anti-Rape and Domestic Worker Mobilisations in India' (United Nations Research Institute for Social Development 2016) 102–33.

[119] Parreñas (n 64) 40; Alan Desmond, 'From Complementarity to Convergence: The UN Global Compact for Migration and the UN Migrant Workers Convention' (2022) 55 World Comparative Law 83, 91–92.

[120] Ray and Qayum (n 57) 10.

and views on the legal frameworks. The hybrid approach of combining empirical research with 'black letter' analysis draws on methods pioneered by labour law scholars such as Barmes, who utilized interviews alongside analysis of case law and other materials.[121] Similarly, it is influenced by Hayes' use of doctrinal analysis and social theory alongside ethnographic work in her study of care workers in the UK, which intentionally foregrounds the impact of the law on those who are the object of its regulation as opposed to voices of already powerful actors such as employers.[122] The empirical research provides a deepened and enriched understanding of the ways domestic workers are excluded from or incorporated within labour law protection, by examining how the law and its impacts are experienced and thought about by workers and others with practical, professional, and academic knowledge of the field.

The first set of empirical research took place during 2018–20 as part of my doctoral project, which examined the two primary case studies, the UK and Chile. I undertook research in Chile in April to June 2019, interviewing sixteen academic and professional respondents, including the General Secretary of the main domestic workers' union and the General Coordinator of a migrant rights organization, and eleven domestic workers that these two organizations introduced me to. The interviews focused on the position following the 2015 reforms implemented alongside C-189 ratification, a subject on which few other empirical studies existed.[123] They were semi-structured and covered five key areas: working hours and their impact on private and family life; the procedure for inspection without entry to the home; the undervaluation of domestic work and conflation of domestic workers with family members; the impact of migration laws on migrant domestic workers; and strategies for improving rights. They were conducted in Spanish with the exception of one participant, Granados Zambrano, who chose to be interviewed in English.

The situation in the UK was distinctive in some respects. There had not been substantial recent reform to the labour rights of domestic workers, and pre-existing empirical studies covered the position of domestic workers under the restrictive visa and limited regulatory situation.[124] This meant that a central outstanding area for examination was the impact of changes that had been made to the immigration

[121] Lizzie Barmes, *Bullying and Behavioural Conflict at Work: The Duality of Individual Rights* (OUP 2016) 4–8.

[122] Hayes (n 27) 11–12, 27–28.

[123] A key exception was Férnandez's work—Rosario Fernández, 'Mujeres de elite y trabajo doméstico remunerado en Chile: ¿crisis de cuidados o de la familia?' (2017) 12 La Manzana de la Discordia 33; Fernández (n 46). As this drew on interviews with employers, my research with workers complements it well.

[124] See eg Virginia Mantouvalou, '"Am I Free Now?" Overseas Domestic Workers in Slavery' (2015) 42 Journal of Law and Society 329; Zhe Jiang and Marek Korczynski, 'When the "Unorganizable" Organize: The Collective Mobilization of Migrant Domestic Workers in London' (2016) 69 Human Relations 813.

rules in 2016 relating to the right to work for domestic workers identified as potential victims of trafficking or 'modern slavery'.[125] I undertook research on this matter as a volunteer for the migrant domestic worker NGO Kalayaan from May to September 2018. This entailed interviewing 21 workers identified as potential victims of trafficking or modern slavery, of whom eleven had permission to work while waiting for a final decision and ten did not, leading to a co-authored policy report.[126] Some of these interviews were in English, where the worker felt confident enough, while others were in Tagalog (spoken in the Philippines) with a telephone interpreter.

The variance in the work within this first phase reflects differing situations with regard to legislative changes and the availability of pre-existing research. In Chile, the comprehensive scope of the 2015 reforms and the relatively limited empirical studies subsequent to these changes called for a wide-ranging enquiry to ascertain experiences and views of these changes. In the UK, with some key areas having already been covered by existing studies, the research focused on an area that the main NGO for domestic workers identified as a gap in their current knowledge, which also allowed me to 'give back' to participants through policy work.[127] I supplemented that work by carrying out online interviews in 2020 with two professionals in the domestic work field, to address broader questions of relevance to the full range of research themes.

In addition, I undertook a secondary phase of research in 2022–25, examining the two additional case study countries, South Africa and India, which had not been part of my doctoral project, to increase the breadth of the investigation. As well as analysing doctrinal materials and the rich existing empirical literature on domestic workers in both these countries, I carried out online interviews in autumn 2024 with eight experts on India[128] and eight in South Africa, including trade union and NGO workers, and researchers in academic and other institutions. These interviews were in English since all interviewees were fluent English speakers. Again, this covered each major area of the book's analysis.

I obtained ethics approval from the respective institutions (University College London for my doctoral research and Durham for the interviews in 2024) and obtained informed consent from all interviewees. Domestic worker interviewees were given a shop voucher to thank them for their time. When citing the interviews, I use pseudonyms for all domestic workers, and for non-domestic workers

[125] I define this term in chapter Chapter 2 and explain the changes in Chapter 7.

[126] Natalie Sedacca and Avril Sharp, 'Dignity, Not Destitution: The Impact of Differential Rights of Work for Migrant Domestic Workers Referred to the National Referral Mechanism' (Kalayaan 2019). After completing this research project I became a trustee for Kalayaan in 2020.

[127] Jiang and Korczynski (n 124) 821.

[128] One of the India interviewees, Samita Sen, was based in the UK but with extensive expertise on India.

who chose to be referred to by a pseudonym, while others in the latter group opted to be cited using their full name. A list of interviewees is found in the Appendix. I draw on direct quotes and citations from the interviews in chapters four to eight; all references in those chapters that contain only a name or pseudonym are references to interview material.

Structure and outline of the book

The book has three parts. The first, comprising Chapters 2 and 3 as well as this introductory chapter, sets out the conceptual framework, including my understanding of domestic workers' exclusion based on the organizing themes of 'lack of accountability' and 'devaluation', and the value of human rights in addressing this exclusion. Chapter 2 provides an overview of the failings in labour law's protection for the sector, outlining the position in the case study countries. It then elaborates on the book's understanding of domestic workers' *exclusion*—the lack of formal coverage of labour standards alongside the non-enforcement of those standards that formally apply—via two central organizing themes, 'lack of accountability' and 'devaluation'. I explain the linkage between these themes and their manifestation in the regulation of paid domestic work.

Chapter 3 develops the argument that human rights law can play a positive role in progressing domestic workers' inclusion: the goal that domestic workers are covered by labour law standards, that those standards are properly enforced, and that workers are not prevented from enforcing rights because of vulnerabilities arising from immigration status. After arguing that the values of labour law and human rights are primarily shared rather than in opposition and tracing their convergence, I examine critiques of human rights from a labour law perspective: the relative neglect of socio-economic rights, the charge that human rights are too individualistic to be of value to workers' rights, and the suggestion that a human rights framework relies too heavily on legalistic means, de-prioritizing workers' agency. I then present universality as a normative feature of human rights that has significant value for addressing the position of domestic workers, who frequently fall outside the protection of labour law because of their work's location in the private sphere and migration-related vulnerabilities. Finally, the chapter sets out the scope and relevance of a human rights approach for domestic workers' inclusion, highlighting the concept of the 'positive obligation' that has made human rights law increasingly relevant in regulating private relationships, feminist developments regarding domestic violence progressing accountability for abuses that take place within the 'private sphere', and the salience of an 'integrated approach' to human rights in allowing for an extension of protection for social and economic rights.

Part 2 addresses manifestations of exclusion in the labour law field: a lack of enforcement of labour standards (Chapter 4), a failure to recognize domestic work as 'real work' and consequential low pay (Chapter 5) and excessive working hours (Chapter 6). Each of these chapters explains the phenomenon as it arises in the case study countries with reference to empirical studies, links it to the analysis based on 'lack of accountability' and/or 'devaluation', and sets out how human rights law and principles can challenge the exclusion.

Chapter 4 examines regimes for labour inspection and enforcement, which is generally precluded for domestic work in the UK and India, whereas in Chile and South Africa, some provision exists, but it is subject to limits, including on powers of entry to private homes. I explore how the human right to decent work creates a requirement for enforcement mechanisms, while the prohibition on forced labour requires preventative elements and reform to legal systems. I also critique limitations on inspections in domestic work that arise from an understanding of the employer's privacy as paramount. While accepting that employers' privacy is a salient factor, I argue that it should not be viewed as automatically 'trumping' workers' rights. By analogy with the increasingly proactive role of human rights law in justifying intrusion into the 'private sphere' and the family in relation to domestic abuse, I propose that it cannot be acceptable to preclude any intervention in a non-family working relationship simply because it takes place in the home. Drawing on the proportionality test, as developed in human rights jurisprudence, I develop a justification for inspections of homes employing domestic workers alongside safeguards to avoid giving inspectors excessive powers. The proposals expand on the existing specifications of C-189, using a human rights-based interpretation to argue against a reading that is unduly oriented to the employer's privacy at the expense of other factors.

In Chapter 5, I examine the devaluation of domestic work as manifested in the conflation of domestic workers with members of the family employing them ('the familial discourse'), the failure to recognize their work as real or 'skilled' work, and its manifestation in systemic low pay. While acknowledging complexities in the ways that workers and others think about the familial discourse, I argue that its overall impact is to perpetuate devaluation—for example, through stifling workers' demands for improvements and extracting additional work from them. The chapter then examines exclusion from minimum wage entitlements, discussing the relatively strong regulatory frameworks that exist in Chile and South Africa alongside countervailing factors maintaining devaluation. It then considers the state-based variation in India, and the exemption from minimum wage that existed for some live-in domestic workers until recently in the UK. In addition to challenges through anti-discrimination frameworks, I explore how human rights law can address devaluation through the right to a living wage and to fair pay, alongside the prohibition on forced labour.

Chapter 6 addresses the persistent difficulty in regulating working time for domestic workers, particularly those who live with their employers. Apart from South Africa, all the case study countries contain some differential treatment of at least live-in domestic workers in their regulatory framework, while in all cases, compliance issues and expectations of constant availability mean that workers often work well beyond formal limits. After noting the relevant social and economic rights provisions, I explore how limitation of working time forms part of the right to a private and family life, with excessive hours leaving domestic workers little or no time to engage in other activities or develop relationships with others beyond their employers. Drawing on my empirical findings, I explore purported justifications for longer hours, including cultural expectations of constant availability and the notion of supporting working families. While the latter is potentially a legitimate aim vis-à-vis interference with the right, I argue that measures to pursue it are unlikely to be proportionate where they have a significant negative effect on the family life of domestic workers.

The book's third part addresses particular exclusions of migrant domestic workers, based on restrictive visa regimes and limited opportunities for family reunification, again drawing on empirical research to ground its human rights analysis. Chapter 7 examines how visa conditions shape migrant domestic workers' labour market access and rights at work, exploring the specific, restrictive visa scheme for the sector in the UK, the restrictions and potentials for domestic workers in the general visa regimes in Chile and South Africa, and the regulation of internal migration in India. Measures arising in these contexts that restrict or prevent access to the labour market are discussed as an infringement on the negative aspect of the right to work, which entails protection against state interference in being able to seek employment, or being coerced into labour. I argue that justifications for restricting the right to work based on migration control should be treated with great caution, particularly when the differential treatment is based on notions of 'skill-level', which facilitates gender-based discrimination given the low statuses available to women migrants. The chapter also explores how the restrictiveness of migration regimes pushes workers towards irregular or precarious immigration statuses, and analyses the right to decent work and the prohibition on forced labour as supporting a series of core standards that apply to all, regardless of migration status.

Chapter 8 considers the restrictions migrant domestic workers face in relation to family reunification (having their family members join them at their destination), both directly through restrictions in immigration law, and indirectly through practical barriers. Drawing on empirical material, it explores the impact of these restrictions on workers and their families. The chapter outlines relevant social rights provisions before analysing the extent of protection for the right to family reunification under international and regional human rights obligations on family life. It highlights the recognition of the state's obligation to promote the development and enhancement of the family unit in the Inter-American system. While the European context has often seen greater deference to the concept of state sovereignty, the chapter discusses notable exceptions, including in cases that involve potential discrimination in access to rights. The chapter argues for a 'contextualised proportionality analysis' that brings to the forefront structural questions, including the socio-economic context for large-scale migration, when considering justifications for limiting rights. I contend that the proportionality exercise should give proper weight to the serious harm caused by denying family reunification, which creates prolonged separation and can put severe strains on relationships.

Chapter 9's Conclusion reiterates the core argument that current labour and migration law regimes are driving systemic exclusion of domestic workers and draws together cross-cutting issues in human rights violations that have arisen across the thematic chapters. It reiterates how the negative aspect of the right to work is denied through restrictive visa regimes, while the right to decent work is breached by unsafe working and living conditions, the exclusion of domestic work from labour enforcement, low pay, and excessive hours. Other violations include fuelling forced labour through a lack of proper inspection regimes, and undermining the right to private and family life through excessive working hours and a lack of family reunification. Noting that a demand for greater inclusivity and universality supported by human rights provides a basis for recognising domestic workers' exclusion as unacceptable, I restate key reforms that my reading of human rights law supports from across the chapter themes. These comprise equalization of the minimum wage with other sectors or its improvement beyond this where existing levels are inadequate to meet standards of fairness and a decent standard of living, ensuring the enforceability of labour rights even for irregular migrants, proper restrictions on working hours that leave adequate time for a family life, and an effective, proactive system of inspection that includes a proportionate power of entry to homes and is clearly separated from immigration enforcement. In addition, inclusion requires secure visa systems with simple mechanisms for extension and change of employer and viable access to family reunification. The Conclusion also contains some reflections on the implications of the material for the relationship between human rights and domestic workers' rights, and the book's relevance to other countries and sectors.

2
Understanding domestic workers' exclusion
'Lack of accountability' and 'devaluation'

Introduction

This chapter introduces the book's framing of domestic workers' 'exclusion'—the lack of formal coverage of labour standards alongside the non-enforcement of applicable standards—which underly its arguments on the role of human rights law. It first provides an overview of the legal position of domestic workers in each case study country to set the scene, with later chapters to elaborate on each aspect (including by referring to details from the empirical research). Against this background, I explain the two central organizing themes the book uses to explain and critique domestic workers' exclusion. The first is 'lack of accountability', which denotes a deficiency of visibility, scrutiny and regulation via objective rules and standards within the 'private sphere' of the home and family. In explaining this, I draw a parallel between the law's traditional failures in accountability for violence and abuse occurring within the private sphere and the ongoing limits on inspection in domestic work. I argue that exclusions from labour inspection are centred on protecting the rights of the employing family, being typically justified through conceptions of the employer's privacy and the 'sacrosanct' nature of the family home.

The second central organizing theme is 'devaluation', which refers to the denial of the value of domestic and caring labour to the wider economy and society. This can be traced in part to its association with the 'private sphere', with domestic labour viewed as 'unproductive' and less valuable than work in the public sphere. Yet it is also crucial to examine the impact of other factors such as ethnicity, migration status, and class, as well as the legacy of slavery and servitude, in constructing the work as unskilled and the worker as 'like a family member'. I trace how these forms of devaluation are manifested in the exclusion of domestic workers from minimum wage and social security coverage, the expectation of constant availability and longer working hours, and the applicability of unfavourable visa regimes. Finally, I introduce the argument for a human rights-based approach to challenging both lack of accountability and devaluation, which will be further elaborated in Chapter 3.

Human Rights and the Protection of Domestic Workers in Labour and Migration Law. Natalie Sedacca, Oxford University Press. DOI: 10.1093/9780198985266.003.0003

Gaps and progression in protecting domestic workers—An overview of the case studies

This section provides a contextual overview of domestic workers' rights in each case study country, including its development in recent decades and comparison to the broader labour law framework. It begins with Chile and South Africa, the two countries that have ratified C-189, which both demonstrate concerted attempts to regulate domestic work with progressive changes alongside the continued existence of implementation challenges.

In Chile, there have been cumulative progressive changes to the regulation of domestic work since the fall of Augusto Pinochet's military dictatorship in 1990. Pinochet's rule was characterized by extreme repression of workers, unions, and left-wing organizations, and the imposition of an early and extreme form of the neoliberal model, including a reduction in collective bargaining and job security, and the abolition of special labour courts.[1] The period since the end of the dictatorship has seen some progressive labour law reforms in areas such as dismissal and unemployment protection, but constraints remain, including a lack of sectoral-level collective bargaining and restrictions on strike action.[2] Against a starting point where domestic workers were paid 75 per cent of the national minimum wage, had twelve-hour working days and only a half-day off for public holidays for live-in workers, and were excluded from severance pay and maternity leave,[3] there have been significant improvements to rights. Early reforms before the advent of C-189 included domestic workers' right to severance pay in 1990, to maternity leave in 1998, equalization of the minimum wage between 2008 and 2011, and stipulations on rest and days off in 2009.[4]

When Chile ratified C-189 in 2015, it made further substantial reforms via Law 20.786.[5] On working time, this provides for live-out workers to be subject to a usual

[1] Peter Winn, 'The Pinochet Era' in Peter Winn (ed), *Victims of the Chilean Miracle: Workers and Neoliberalism in the Pinochet Era, 1973–2002* (Duke University Press 2004) 19–35; Irma Arriagada and Rosalba Todaro, *Cadenas Globales de Cuidados: El Papel de La Migrantes Peruanas En La Provisión de Cuidados En Chile* (ONU Mujeres 2012) 24; Cesar F Rosado Marzán, 'The Labor Judge Unleashed: Rule of Law and Labor Rights in "Neoliberal" Chile' (2018) 43 Law and Social Inquiry 1574, 1583.

[2] Volker Frank, 'The Elusive Goal in Democratic Chile: Reforming the Pinochet Labor Legislation' (2002) 44 Latin American Politics and Society 35, 39–42; Rosado Marzán (n 1) 1581–83. See also Chapter 6 on more recent reforms to cut the working week.

[3] Merike Blofield, *Care Work and Class: Domestic Workers' Struggle for Equal Rights in Latin America* (Penn State University Press 2012) 118–19.

[4] Ley No 19.010—establece Normas sobre Terminación del contrato de trabajo y estabilidad en el empleo 1990; Ley No 19.591—Modifica el Código del Trabajo en Materia de Protección a la Maternidad 1998; Ley No 20.279—Reajusta Monto del Ingreso Mínimo Mensual 2008; Ley No 20.336—Modifica el Artículo de Código del Trabajo, relativo al Descanso Semanal de los Trabajadores de Casa Particular 2009; see Lidia Casas and Helena Olea, 'Trabajadoras de Casa Particular—Invizibiladas y Discriminadas' in Centro de Derechos Humanos (ed), *Informe Anual sobre Derechos Humanos in Chile 2014* (Ediciones Universidad Diego Portales 2014) 150.

[5] Ley No 20.786—Modifica la Jornada, Descanso y Composición de la Remuneración de los Trabajadores de Casa Particular, y Prohíbe La Exigencia de Uniforme en Lugares Públicos 2014. This was implemented in 2015 alongside ratification.

maximum of forty-five hours weekly, completed over a maximum of six days, with weekly rest governed by the same norms as other workers and the possibility of agreeing up to fifteen further hours payable at an enhanced rate.[6] By contrast, live-in domestic workers still do not have a fixed timetable; instead, they are normally expected to have a total of twelve hours' daily rest, including nine continuous hours between days.[7] The law also prohibits employers from unilaterally reducing remuneration as a consequence of changes to the working week and rest days,[8] deductions from the wage to account for the provision of food and accommodation ('payment in kind'), and requirements to wear a uniform.[9] It introduces a notable provision for 'inspection without entry to the home', which gives an employer the option of accepting an inspector's entry or attending the office of the labour inspectorate.[10] The changes are thus significant and broadly positive, yet distinctions from other sectors remain in relation to working hours and inspections.

The situation of domestic workers in South Africa takes place against the background of significant reform to labour rights following the end of apartheid. South Africa's post-apartheid constitution has been described as 'transformative' because, as well as limiting the state's power, it directs state intervention and social change to meet its aims.[11] The 1996 constitution encompasses a comprehensive labour clause, which can be directly relied on in court and is given further effect through three key labour statutes.[12] While labour law standards are favourable to workers, they are far from universally implemented, with two separate economies arguably co-existing: a 'third world informal sector' where labour rights are generally absent, alongside the modern rights-compliant one.[13] The post-apartheid era has seen a noteworthy shift in the rights of domestic workers. Having been marked by domineering, racist, and sexist relations with barely any legal protections during apartheid, within a decade of Mandela's release from prison the sector had undergone wide-ranging and pioneering reform aimed at treating domestic work as employment, with related rights, contracts, and formalization.[14] Beyond

[6] ibid, unitary article para 3(a)–(d).

[7] Código del Trabajo—Edición actualizada al 8 de agosto de 2025 ('Labour Code—Chile 2025'), Art 149(e).

[8] Ley 20.786, third transitory article.

[9] Labour Code—Chile 2025, Art 151, 151bis.

[10] ibid, Art 146 ter.

[11] Darcy Du Toit, 'Situating Domestic Work in a Changing Global Labour Market' in Darcy Du Toit (ed), *Exploited, Undervalued and Essential: Domestic Workers and the Realisation of Their Rights* (Pretoria University Law Press 2013) 3.

[12] The Constitution of the Republic of South Africa 1996, s23; Labour Relations Act—Act No 66 of 1995 (South Africa); Basic Conditions of Employment Act—Act 75 of 1997 (South Africa) ('BCEA'); Employment Equity Act—Act No 55 of 1998 (South Africa); see Stefan van Eck, 'Constitutionalisation of South African Labour Law: An Experiment in the Making' in Colin F Fenwick and Tonia Novitz (eds), *Human Rights at Work: Perspectives on Law and Regulation* (Hart 2010) 268–71.

[13] van Eck (n 12) 259–65.

[14] Shireen A Ally, *From Servants to Workers: South African Domestic Workers and the Democratic State* (Cornell University Press 2009) 2–3; Adelle Blackett, *Everyday Transgressions: Domestic Workers' Transnational Challenge to International Labor Law* (Cornell University Press 2019) 137–38.

including domestic workers in the general labour law statutes, a 2002 regulation, Sectoral Determination 7, contains sector-specific provisions on matters including wage calculation and deduction, accommodation standards, working hours, and termination of employment.[15] This provision was highlighted in the ILO report that preceded the agreement of C-189, with South Africa going on to ratify the convention in 2013.[16]

Despite South Africa's progressive and pioneering role, major power inequalities and paternalist relationships between domestic workers and employers remain.[17] There are limited enforcement mechanisms for applicable labour rights, with inspectors only allowed to enter private homes with written authorization from a labour court or the consent of the owner/occupier.[18] Until 2020, domestic workers were excluded from a key provision on compensation for occupational injuries and disease;[19] since then, efforts have been made to rectify the position through accelerating pre-existing legislative reform projects and awareness-raising campaigns, although levels of compliance and registration remain a challenge.[20] As with Chile, then, progressive developments have represented substantial advances, but certain important distinctions between domestic work and other sectors either remain or did so until quite recently.

The discussion now moves to the case studies that have seen less significant national progress. The UK (like Chile) was an early adopter of a neoliberal approach under Conservative governments of the 1980s and 1990s, which significantly reduced union power and workers' rights.[21] After partial reverses during the 1997 to 2010 Labour government,[22] the deregulatory trend was further consolidated by governments of and led by the Conservative party from 2010 to 2024.[23] The

[15] Basic Conditions of Employment Act—Act 75 of 1997—Sectoral Determination 7: Domestic Worker Sector [updated to 26 November 2014] 2002.

[16] Blackett, *Everyday Transgressions* (n 14) 142. The report referenced is ILO, 'Report IV(1)—Decent Work for Domestic Workers—99th Session of the International Labour Conference' (2010).

[17] Abigail Hunt and Emma Samman, 'Domestic Work and the Gig Economy in South Africa: Old Wine in New Bottles?' (2020) 15 Anti-Trafficking Review 102, 105; Q Dawood and M Seedat-Khan, 'The Unforgiving Work Environment of Black African Women Domestic Workers in a Post-Apartheid South Africa' (2023) 33 Development in Practice 168, 173–74; Candice James, Fairuz Mullagee, and Abigail Osiki, 'Domestic Workers in South Africa: Inclusion Under the Compensation for Occupational Injuries and Diseases Act' (2023) 96 The Thinker 13, 15–16.

[18] Basic Conditions of Employment Act 1997, s65; Zaheera Jinnah, 'Negotiated Precarity in the Global South: A Case Study of Migration and Domestic Work in South Africa' (2020) 2020 Studies in Social Justice 210, 215.

[19] Compensation for Occupational Injuries and Diseases—Act 130 of 1993 (South Africa). The case that led to the repeal is discussed in Chapters 3 and 5.

[20] James, Mullagee, and Osiki (n 17) 19–22.

[21] Sandra Fredman, 'Precarious Norms for Precarious Workers' in Judy Fudge and Rosemary J Owens (eds), *Precarious Work, Women and the New Economy: The Challenge to Legal Norms* (Hart 2006) 183; Lord Wedderburn, 'Labour Law 2008: 40 Years On' (2007) 36 Industrial Law Journal 397, 405; ACL Davies, 'Workers' Human Rights in English Law' in Colin F Fenwick and Tonia Novitz (eds), *Human Rights at Work: Perspectives on Law and Regulation* (Hart 2010) 176–77.

[22] Davies (n 21) 177.

[23] Michael Ford and Tonia Novitz, 'Legislating for Control: The Trade Union Act 2016' (2016) 45 Industrial Law Journal 277; KD Ewing and John Hendy QC, 'The Trade Union Act 2016 and the

Employment Rights Bill, which is awaiting its third reading in the House of Lords at the time of writing, stands to improve overall labour market regulation in some respects.[24] Beyond the overall regulatory context, domestic workers face a set of specific exclusions from labour rights applicable in other sectors. The UK has not only declined to ratify C-189 but was also one of eight countries to abstain from the relevant vote in the ILO proceedings that agreed the Convention. The representative argued that this was because the UK already provided 'comprehensive employment and social protection to domestic workers', but that the overall strength of its labour provisions made it 'occasionally inappropriate to treat domestic workers identically'.[25] In reality, C-189 does not require fully identical protection, but the level of divergence in the UK is indeed likely to fall foul of the Convention's requirements. Domestic workers are outside key working time protections, including the maximum working week of forty-eight hours,[26] while the private households where they work are excluded from ordinary labour inspection.[27]

While recent years have seen an increasing recognition of domestic workers' vulnerability to exploitation, this has not been met by an extension of labour rights to the sector as a whole—for example, by repealing these legislative exemptions. Instead, regulation has primarily targeted the most severe forms of exploitation. The Modern Slavery Act 2015 contains a series of legal measures directed at the phenomenon of 'modern slavery', an 'umbrella term',[28] encompassing human trafficking, slavery, servitude, and forced or compulsory labour.[29] It introduced some support provisions and immigration safeguards for domestic workers subjected to the most severe forms of abuse and exploitation, explored further in Chapter 7.

Failure of Human Rights' (2016) 45 Industrial Law Journal 391; Ioannis Katsaroumpas, 'Crossing the Rubicon: The Strikes (Minimum Service Levels) Act 2023 as an Authoritarian Crucible' (2023) 52 Industrial Law Journal 513.

[24] Alan Bogg and Michael Ford KC, 'From "Fairness at Work" to "Making Work Pay": A Preliminary Assessment of the Employment Rights Bill' (*UK Labour Law*, 14 October 2024) <https://uklabourlawblog.com/2024/10/14/from-fairness-at-work-to-making-work-pay-a-preliminary-assessment-of-the-employment-rights-bill-by-professor-alan-bogg-and-professor-michael-ford-kc/> accessed 31 August 2025.

[25] Fiona Mactaggart MP, HC Deb 29 June 2011, vol 530, col 269.

[26] Working Time Regulations 1998—SI 1998/1833, reg 19 for England, Wales and Scotland; Working Time Regulations (Northern Ireland) 2016—SI 2016/49 reg 23 for Northern Ireland.

[27] Health and Safety at Work Act 1974, s51, applicable in England, Wales and Scotland.

[28] Nicole Siller, '"Modern Slavery" Does International Law Distinguish between Slavery, Enslavement and Trafficking?' [2016] Journal of International Criminal Justice 405, 405–7.

[29] Trafficking involves (1) an action such as 'recruitment' or 'transportation', (2) the involvement of means such as 'coercion', 'deception', or 'abuse of power', and (3) the 'purpose of exploitation'—United Nations, 'Protocol to Prevent, Suppress and Punish Trafficking in Persons, Especially Women and Children, (Adopted 15 November 2000, Entered into Force 25 December 2003) 2237 UNTS 319—"The Palermo Protocol"' (2000). There is extensive literature problematising the categories of 'modern slavery' and 'trafficking', eg JC Hathaway, 'The Human Rights Quagmire of "Human Trafficking"' (2009) 49 Virginia Journal of International Law 1; Janie Chuang, 'Exploitation Creep and the Unmaking of Human Trafficking Law' (2014) 108 American Journal of International Law 609. However, this book's key concerns are the shortcomings of the regime for survivors of modern slavery and the failure to extend similar protections to workers who have suffered other abuses.

However, it has serious shortcomings, including its predominantly criminal law focus and the inadequate protection for those identified or in the process of being identified as victims.[30] In relation to migrants, its protective intentions are undermined by the government's anti-immigration policies,[31] and do not go far enough to protect domestic workers.

The final case study, India, also lacks comprehensive regulation of domestic work at national level. In general, India's labour laws offer a high level of protection but apply to a fairly small proportion of the workforce, which is mainly comprised of informal workers who are low paid, usually non-unionized, and lacking job security.[32] While this has some parallels to other case studies, including South Africa, it is not solely an issue of under-enforcement. Rather, certain groups of workers are expressly excluded from protection—for example, because of the size or sector of the enterprise they work for.[33] In 2020, four new Labour Codes were passed by parliament, which are yet to be implemented nationally at the time of writing.[34] There are concerns that the Codes will weaken the power of trade unions and their scope to take industrial action, make employment more flexible, and diminish the applicability of health and safety laws via threshold requirements and exemptions.[35]

Domestic workers are generally classified as providing a personal service in the home rather than as workers, and are consequently excluded from many key labour law provisions, including on wages and maternity benefits.[36] Provisions for domestic workers at national level are mainly confined to welfare benefits entitlement under legislation on unorganized workers,[37] alongside protection from sexual harassment and child labour.[38] The 2025 Supreme Court judgment *Malik v Uttarkhand*—although arising from a specific criminal law matter—was highly

[30] Virginia Mantouvalou, 'The UK Modern Slavery Act 2015 Three Years On' (2018) 81 Modern Law Review 1017.

[31] Judy Fudge, 'Why Labour Lawyers Should Care About the Modern Slavery Act 2015' (2018) 29 King's Law Journal 377.

[32] Ramapriya Gopalakrishnan, 'Enforcing Labour Rights through Human Rights Norms: The Approach of the Supreme Court of India' in Colin F Fenwick and Tonia Novitz (eds), *Human Rights at Work: Perspectives on Law and Regulation* (Hart 2010) 195; Anil Verma and Shyam Sundar, 'Employment Relations in India' in Greg Bamber and others (eds), *International and Comparative Employment Relations: National Regulation, Global Changes* (6th edn, Routledge 2020) 317–19; Adwitiya Mishra and Aasheerwad Dwivedi, 'Labour Laws in India: History, Evolution and Critical Analysis' [2023] Labor History 1, 5–6.

[33] Kamala Sankaran, 'Labour Law in South Asia: The Need for an Inclusive Approach' in Teklè Tzehainesh (ed), *Labour Law and Worker Protection in Developing Countries* (International Labour Office 2010) 229; Gopalakrishran (n 32) 203.

[34] Puneet Gupta, 'How New Labour Codes Will Impact Your Salary, Gratuity and Provident Fund Payments Once Implemented' (*Economic Times*, 8 July 2025) <https://economictimes.indiatimes.com/wealth/earn/how-new-labour-codes-will-impact-your-salary-gratuity-and-provident-fund-payments-once-implemented/articleshow/122201449.cms?from = mdr> accessed 30 August 2025.

[35] Mishra and Dwivedi (n 32) 12–14.

[36] Srijani Datta and others, 'Domestic Workers from Margin to Center: Protest, Opportunity and Threat in Pandemic Politics' (2022) 26 Journal for Cultural Research 39, 42.

[37] The Unorganised Workers' Social Security Act—Act No 33 of 2008, s2(k–n).

[38] Rina Agarwala and Shiny Saha, 'The Employment Relationship and Movement Strategies among Domestic Workers in India' (2018) 44 Critical Sociology 1207, 1220.

critical of the gaps in the national legislative framework and the lack of progress in addressing them, most recently through a 2017 initiative to formulate a national policy for domestic workers that appears to have stalled.[39] It consequently directed relevant government departments, including the Ministry of Labour, to constitute an expert committee 'to consider the desirability of recommending a legal framework for the benefit, protection and regulation of the rights of domestic workers'.[40] This stands to increase the prospects of national-level reform, but its outcome is not known at the time of writing.

For the meantime, as a federal country, the position in India varies between states. For example, domestic workers in the southern states of Kerala, Tamil Nadu, and Karnataka are entitled to labour contracts akin to those of other workers, while nine states (out of twenty-eight) have included domestic workers in their schedules of occupations entitled to minimum wages.[41] That said, even in states with minimum wage coverage, difficulties with enforcement may remain where the household is still viewed as a private space that is not generally amenable to inspection, and domestic work continues to be understood as a mainly voluntary agreement.[42] Domestic workers are frequently engaged based on individual verbal agreements and generally excluded from provisions on working hours, leave, overtime, and night shifts, meaning low wages and poor conditions are prevalent.[43] Therefore, there is currently a lack of systematic, national regulation to promote the rights of domestic workers.

Migration status and domestic workers' exclusion

Discrepancies in the realization of rights also arise from migration, since it is more difficult for workers who lack a secure, long-term status to enforce their rights.[44] In India, while there are some international migrants from Bangladesh and Nepal in domestic work,[45] internal migration is a more prominent concern for the sector. Where migrants cross state lines within India, they can experience barriers to

[39] *Ajay Malik v State of Uttarakhand and Anr* [2025] INSC 118 [48–50]. On the 2017 initiative, see Datta and others (n 36) 49.

[40] *Malik v Uttarakhand* (n 39) [48–55].

[41] Sabrina Marchetti, 'The Global Governance of Paid Domestic Work: Comparing the Impact of ILO Convention No 189 in Ecuador and India' (2018) 44 Critical Sociology 1191, 1186; Samita Sen, 'Regulating Wage, Realizing Rights: Domestic Workers in India' in Pedro Ramos Pinto and Massimo Asta (eds), *The Value of Work since the 18th Century: Custom, Conflict, Measurement and Theory* (Bloomsbury Publishing 2023) 128.

[42] Amrita Ghatak and Kingshuk Sarkar, 'Status of Domestic Workers in India: A Tale of Two Cities' (2022) 65 Indian Journal of Labour Economics 863, 864–74.

[43] N Neetha, 'Misconstrued Notions and Misplaced Interventions: An Assessment of State Policy on Domestic Work in India' (2021) 64 Indian Journal of Labour Economics 543, 545–52.

[44] See Chapter 7.

[45] Marchetti (n 41) 1196.

obtaining identification documents needed to access security, while language barriers and limited social networks compound problems.[46] The legislation in place to protect internal migrants between states only applies to establishments and contractors employing at least five inter-state workers,[47] therefore excluding most private employers of domestic workers.

In the remainder of the countries, international migration is a central issue, with restrictions to migration regimes posing a challenge to domestic workers' rights. Chile has seen a rapid increase in international migration since the early 2000s, including to the domestic work sector.[48] Until 2022, it was possible for migrants to enter the country as a tourist and later change to a work visa or temporary residence permit, usually a 'visa subject to contract' where their permission to stay was conditioned on a contract with an employer.[49] The possibility of changing status from tourist to worker has been removed with a new migration law in force from 2022;[50] the requirement to apply from outside the country is likely to be difficult for domestic workers to comply with, potentially fuelling more irregular work.[51] In South Africa, a sizeable minority of domestic workers are migrants from surrounding countries, particularly Zimbabwe, yet the migration regime makes it very difficult for workers classed as 'low-skilled' to obtain work permits, leaving many in an irregular situation.[52] The UK's approach is distinct in that it has a sector-specific visa, the Overseas Domestic Worker Visa, which is highly restrictive: it is only available to those who have already been working for the employer outside the UK for at least twelve months just before applying, is limited to a six-month non-renewable period, and (like most visas in the UK) bars access to most publicly funded benefits.[53]

Therefore, whether through the denial of any accessible visa system or the imposition of harsh restrictions, domestic workers are frequently subjected to

[46] Shraddha Chigateri, Mubashira Zaidi, and Anweshaa Ghosh, 'Locating the Processes of Policy Change in the Context of Anti-Rape and Domestic Worker Mobilisations in India' (United Nations Research Institute for Social Development 2016) 132.

[47] The Inter-State Migrant Workmen Act—Act No 30 of 1979 (India) s1(4). See Chapter 7.

[48] Paulina Granados Zambrano, María Fernanda Toledo Badilla and Nicolás Rivera González, 'Documento de Trabajo N° 63: Caracterización de La Población Inmigrante En El Sistema de Pensiones y Seguro de Cesantía' (Superintendencia de Pensiones, Chile 2019) 6–7, 45; Victoria Finn and Sebastián Umpierrez de Reguero, 'Inclusive Language for Exclusive Policies: Restrictive Migration Governance in Chile, 2018' (2020) 11 Latin American Policy 42, 45.

[49] Rodrigo Sandoval Ducoing, 'Una nueva Política Migratoria para los trabajadores migrantes en Chile' (2016) 4 Relaciones Laborales y Derecho del Empleo 1; Carol Chan, 'Patchwork Infrastructures: Indonesian and Filipino Multinational Migratory Trajectories to Chile' (2023) 0 Applied Mobilities 1, 6.

[50] Ley No 21.325—Ley de Migración y Extranjería 2021.

[51] Research participants cited in Chapter 7.

[52] Jinnah (n 18) 212–18.

[53] Home Office, 'Immigration Rules (UK)—Updated 13 August 2025' <https://www.gov.uk/guidance/immigration-rules> accessed 22 August 2025, Appendix Overseas Domestic Worker, ODW 5.1–5.7, 8.1–8.2.

unfavourable migration regimes. This amounts to a further gap in protection, which leaves workers at risk of becoming irregular if they leave an abusive employer or if their visa becomes invalid, including where their employer fails to renew documents.[54] Both workers on a valid but restrictive visa, and those with irregular status, have their labour mobility severely hindered, making it more difficult to change employers or challenge abuse.[55] Alongside features like the cost of migration, resulting debt, and lack of information, this increases susceptibility to forced labour and exploitation.[56] In addition, many migrant domestic workers are denied a route to family reunification—that is, to bring members of their family to live with them in the country where they are working—meaning their own care needs are erased.[57] This leads to separation that can be long-term and causes serious suffering for both the migrant workers and their children.[58]

The protection offered to domestic workers is therefore fragmented and often far from complete, comprising limitations to inspection that impede effective enforcement, less strict regulation of working time, low pay, and unfavourable migration regimes. There is variation in each of these respects between the case studies, with Chile and South Africa having generally gone further to equalize applicable labour laws than the UK and India. Yet all countries show at least some differential treatment and shortcomings in implementing those rights that are formally applicable to domestic workers. These lacunae in protection are perpetuated in ways that can be understood through two key themes: 'lack of accountability', denoting a deficiency of visibility, scrutiny, and regulation via objective rules and standards within the 'private sphere' of the home and family, and 'devaluation', which refers to denial of the value of domestic and caring labour to the wider economy and society. The next section explores these themes conceptually and examines their parallels in other social phenomena, before analysing their application to the protection of domestic workers.

[54] UN High Commissioner for Human Rights, 'Behind Closed Doors: Protecting and Promoting the Human Rights of Migrant Domestic Workers in an Irregular Situation—Report No HR/PUB/15/4' (2015) 4.

[55] Virginia Mantouvalou, '"Am I Free Now?" Overseas Domestic Workers in Slavery' (2015) 42 Journal of Law and Society 329.

[56] Cathryn Costello, 'Migrants and Forced Labour: A Labour Law Response' in Alan Bogg and others (eds), *The Autonomy of Labour Law* (Hart 2015) 207–9. See further Virginia Mantouvalou, 'Legal Construction of Structures of Exploitation' in Hugh Collins, Gillian Lester, and Virginia Mantouvalou (eds), *Philosophical Foundations of Labour Law* (OUP 2018).

[57] Rhacel Salazar Parreñas, *Servants of Globalization: Migration and Domestic Work* (2nd edn, Stanford University Press 2015) 18–20; Blackett, *Everyday Transgressions* (n 14) 3.

[58] Arlie Russell Hochschild, 'Love and Gold' in Barbara Ehrenreich and Arlie Russell Hochschild (eds), *Global Woman: Nannies, Maids and Sex Workers in the New Economy* (Granta Books 2003) 22; ILO, 'Report IV(1) 99th Session' (n 16) 9–10; Parreñas (n 57), ch 4.

Conceptualizing the exclusion of domestic workers

To elucidate the themes of lack of accountability and devaluation, a helpful starting point is the classic feminist critique of the 'public/private' sphere divide.[59] The divide is a liberal concept in which the public sphere associated with men, law, work, and politics is seen as superior to and distinct from the private sphere of women, the home, and the family.[60] Since the private sphere tends to be associated with women, its denigrated position acts to marginalize women and their work, such that it is not seen as 'real work' with economic value or or as being subject to the same standards as other sectors.[61] The public/private sphere divide is therefore important to understanding both lack of accountability and (alongside other factors) devaluation.

Lack of accountability in the private sphere

The public/private sphere divide frequently works to conceal the power relationships that exist within the family, based on an assumption that 'altruism and the harmony of interests' prevail.[62] Drawing on enlightenment theorists such as Kant, Rousseau, and Hegel, the family is constructed as a uniquely altruistic 'haven in a heartless world' which needs protection from legal and state-based scrutiny, in contrast to the state as a site of rationality.[63] This presentation conceals the existence of systematic injustices within the family and leads to an understanding that the requirements for free consent and justifications of the exercise of power in the private sphere do not apply in the same way as they would in public.[64] The private sphere is therefore understood as closed to scrutiny, permitting abuses to go unchecked.

The aim of countering the lack of visibility, accountability, and scrutiny of activities in the private sphere and extending the 'protection of the public sphere' to areas categorized as private has been a central theme of feminist thought and

[59] This section draws on the analysis in Natalie Sedacca, 'Domestic Workers, the "Family Worker" Exemption from Minimum Wage, and Gendered Devaluation of Women's Work' (2022) 51 Industrial Law Journal 771.

[60] Hilary Charlesworth, Christine Chinkin, and Shelley Wright, 'Feminist Approaches to International Law' (1991) 85 American Journal of International Law 613, 626; Susan Moller Okin, 'Gender, the Public, and the Private' in Anne Phillips (ed), *Feminism and Politics* (OUP 1998) 116.

[61] Charlesworth, Chinkin, and Wright (n 60) 640.

[62] Susan Moller Okin, *Justice, Gender and the Family* (Basic Books 1989) 128.

[63] Carole Pateman, *The Sexual Contract* (Polity 1988) 168–88; Susan B Boyd, 'Challenging the Public/Private Divide: An Overview' in Susan B Boyd (ed), *Challenging the Public/Private Divide: Feminism, Law, and Public Policy* (University of Toronto Press 1997) 9; Okin, 'Gender, the Public, and the Private' (n 60) 119.

[64] Carole Pateman, 'Feminist Critiques of the Public / Private Dichotomy' in SI Benn and Gerald F Gaus (eds), *Public and Private in Social Life* (Croom Helm 1983) 283–84; Okin, *Justice, Gender and the Family* (n 62) 31.

action, particularly in the 1980s and 1990s.[65] As part of this critique, the mantra 'the personal is political' challenges the view of the domestic sphere and family as sharply divided from other social and political life and therefore as being immune from ordinary scrutiny, or as not requiring attention from the state and political theories.[66] This concept can bring to light the power relations which underlie the state's implementation of decisions on privacy, which make its practical application inconsistent with its own standards, thus reproducing an established model of the family.[67] The regulation of domestic work requires a similar 'opening up' of the private sphere, into which the domestic worker may otherwise be subsumed, to scrutiny.

To understand this, it is helpful to consider another manifestation of the idea of the private sphere as immune from scrutiny: the way many legal systems have traditionally treated violence and sexual abuse in the context of intimate relationships as a private matter and distinct from other forms of violence.[68] Whereas the starting point in the public sphere is that violence must either be justified on a particular basis, such as self-defence, or will be viewed as unlawful, this expectation has often been waived in the private sphere. English law condoned domestic violence until the late nineteenth century as a way to restrain and chastise wives,[69] with similar principles reflected in India under colonial rule.[70] When legislation has been introduced to address domestic violence, this has often started with the focus of preserving and reconciling the family unit rather than holding perpetrators accountable. This was seen in legislation passed in Chile in 1994, with a revised law more focused on accountability and protective measures subsequently introduced in 2005, following criticism from women's organizations.[71] A 2002 legislative project in India that similarly focused on preservation of the household lapsed in 2004 and was superseded by a more protective act the following year.[72]

[65] Boyd, 'Challenging the Public/Private Divide' (n 63) 11.

[66] Okin, *Justice, Gender and the Family* (n 62) 124–27; Iris Marion Young, *Justice and the Politics of Difference* (Paperback reissue, Princeton University Press 2011) 120.

[67] Catherine Moore, 'Women and Domestic Violence: The Public/Private Dichotomy in International Law' (2003) 7 International Journal of Human Rights 93, 103–4.

[68] ibid 95.

[69] Jennifer Koshan, 'Sounds of Silence: The Public/Private Dichotomy, Violence, and Aboriginal Women' in Susan B Boyd (ed), *Challenging the Public/Private Divide: Feminism, Law, and Public Policy* (University of Toronto Press 1997) 89.

[70] Uma Chakravarti, 'Some Thoughts on Domestic Violence: Using Violence to Regulate a Patriarchal Family' in Indira Jaising and Pinki Mathur Anurag (eds), *Conflict in The Shared Household: Domestic Violence and the Law in India* (OUP 2019) 34–35.

[71] Ley No 19.325—establece normas sobre procedimiento a los actos de violencia intrafamiliares 1994; Ley No 20.066—Establece Ley de Violencia Intrafamiliar 2005; Susan Franceschet, 'Explaining Domestic Violence Policy Outcomes in Chile and Argentina' (2010) 52 Latin American Politics and Society 1, 2–9.

[72] The Protection from Domestic Violence Bill 2002; Protection of Women from Domestic Violence Act—Act No 3 of 2005; see Asmita Basu, 'Building Strong Alliances: The Politics of the Protection of Domestic Violence Act in India (2006)' in Sohela Nazneen, Samuel Hickey, and Eleni Sifaki (eds), *Negotiating Gender Equity in the Global South: The Politics of Domestic Violence Policy* (Taylor & Francis 2019) 177–81.

In South Africa, the apartheid era saw a lack of willingness to address abuse in the private sphere, which was not fully addressed by 1993 legislation, although a more progressive law came into force in 1998.[73]

Rape and sexual violence in the context of marriage and intimate relationships remain 'drastically under-recognized' even compared to domestic violence.[74] In India, the definition of rape in the penal code contains an explicit exclusion for 'sexual intercourse or sexual acts by a man with his own wife' unless she is under fifteen years old,[75] although more recent civil legislation defines the phenomenon as domestic violence.[76] In the other case study countries, exemptions for marital rape were only removed in the 1990s, through a judgment in England,[77] and legislation in South Africa and Chile.[78] For a long time, then, exclusions have perpetuated a situation where marriage 'establishes legitimate access to sexual property in the person' for men.[79] Even after legislation is formally changed, significant obstacles to protection of victims and accountability for perpetrators can remain, with police and judicial systems often focusing on promoting family reconciliation and failing to recognize abuse within a family setting.[80]

Attempts to justify limited intervention on these forms of abuse based on the privacy of the family relationship within which it takes place are problematic. If anything, more rather than less scrutiny is needed in this situation, because the abuse is less obviously visible and therefore greater efforts must be made to detect and prevent it.[81] Purported justifications based on the idea of a general principle against state intervention in the family also do not stand up to scrutiny. In practice, the state routinely makes judgements that amount to intervention, from reinforcing parental authority to determining which groups are counted as families and therefore entitled to protection.[82] The question is therefore not whether the state intervenes, but which decisions it makes in its interventions. Choices not to take action over matters such as domestic violence do not create a position of 'neutrality'. Rather, they reflect a particular orientation: one that protects the existing

[73] Prevention of Family Violence Act—Act No 133 of 1993; Domestic Violence Act—Act No 116 of 1998; see Lillian Artz and Valérie Grand'Maison, 'Achieving a Broad-Based Coalition: The Politics of South Africa's Domestic Violence Act (1998)' in Sohela Nazneen, Samuel Hickey, and Eleni Sifaki (eds), *Negotiating Gender Equity in the Global South: The Politics of Domestic Violence Policy* (Taylor & Francis 2019) 113–17.

[74] Melanie Randall and Vasanthi Venkatesh, 'The Right to No: The Crime of Marital Rape, Women's Human Rights, and International Law' (2015) 41 Brooklyn Journal of International Law 153, 155.

[75] Indian Penal Code—Act No 45 of 1860 (as amended), s375.

[76] Protection of Women from Domestic Violence Act—Act No 3 of 2005, s3.

[77] *R v R* [1992] AC 599; Stephanie Palmer, 'Rape in Marriage and the European Convention on Human Rights: C.R. v. U.K. and S.W. v. U.K.' (1997) 5 Feminist Legal Studies 91.

[78] Prevention of Family Violence Act (Act No 133 of 1993), s5; Ley No 19.617—modifica el código penal en materias relativas al delito de violación 1999, s15.

[79] Pateman, *The Sexual Contract* (n 63) 168.

[80] Koshan (n 69) 89–90; Randall and Venkatesh (n 74) 160; Chakravarti (n 70).

[81] Ruth Gavison, 'Feminism and the Public/Private Distinction' (1992) 45 Stanford Law Review 1, 12.

[82] Frances E Olsen, 'The Myth of State Intervention in the Family' (1985) 18 University of Michigan Journal of Law Reform 835, 836–51.

power relations within the family, particularly as regards men's right of access to women's bodies and power over children.[83] In this context, feminists and advocates for children's rights have pointed to the rights of individuals within families to protection against more powerful members of the family or the family unit itself.[84]

A parallel can be drawn to the critique of the state's non-intervention into domestic work, which takes place through the application of less stringent rules on the enforcement of standards based on the work's association with the private sphere. Domestic work tends to be associated with the private sphere because of its location within the family household and the fact that it is work that might otherwise be performed for free by women in the family.[85] Accepting the feminist argument that privacy rights are needed even for individuals within the family unit, there is, by analogy, a compelling case for strong rights for domestic workers in a household of which they are not actually family members. If the state can intervene even within an actual family relationship, the same must certainly be true of a relationship that is just *represented* as family-like, while in reality being marked by paternalism and dependency.[86] By declining to intervene, the state is not remaining neutral but making a political decision in favour of the dominant party in the relationship, the employer. Just as feminist theory has increasingly called into question exceptionalism for violence within the family unit, the same critique should be harnessed to examine the ongoing gaps in the regulation of paid domestic work.

Manifestations of lack of accountability in domestic work regulation

A key example of the state's hesitancy to intervene is reflected in the limited enforcement of labour standards, including the tendency to exclude homes that employ domestic workers from labour inspections. Labour inspections are generally a central way of enforcing workers' rights and labour law,[87] and have been a priority for the ILO since its inception.[88] They are especially helpful in the context of low unionization,[89] as is found in domestic work, where collective organization is limited by practical difficulties even where a legal right to unionize exists.[90] The

[83] Boyd, 'Challenging the Public/Private Divide' (n 63) 13. Also Veronica Garcia de Cortazar Galleguillos, discussant comments, October 2018.
[84] Okin, 'Gender, the Public, and the Private' (n 60) 132.
[85] Rosie Cox, 'Gendered Work and Migration Regimes' in Liam Leonard (ed), *Transnational Migration, Gender and Rights* (Emerald 2012) 45–46.
[86] ibid 46; Einat Albin and Virginia Mantouvalou, 'The ILO Convention on Domestic Workers: From the Shadows to the Light' (2012) 41 Industrial Law Journal 67, 68.
[87] ILO, 'Report IV(1) 99th Session' (n 16) 72.
[88] ILO, 'Labour Inspection—Report III (Part 1B), International Labour Conference 95th Session' (2006) [3].
[89] Michael J Piore and Andrew Schrank, 'Toward Managed Flexibility: The Revival of Labour Inspection in the Latin World' (2008) 147 International Labour Review 1, 17–18.
[90] ILO, 'Domestic Workers across the World: Global and Regional Statistics and the Extent of Legal Protection' (ILO 2013) 70. See Chapters 4 and 6.

exclusion of domestic workers' places of work from inspection is therefore a significant disadvantage. Its justification generally rests on the idea of the home and family being part of the private sphere in which the usual standards of regulation are not applicable, and is part of a broader exclusion of domestic workers from protections granted to others because their work is not deemed to be taking part in public and is therefore not subject(able) to scrutiny.

Despite its positive attributes, C-189 is somewhat deferential in relation to inspections. Its Article 17 refers to developing and implementing measures for labour inspection, enforcement, and penalties, 'with due regard for the special characteristics of domestic work'. It further stipulates that measures should specify the conditions under which access to household premises may be granted, 'having due respect for privacy'. The reference to 'special characteristics' can be taken to imply that domestic work does not merit the same level of scrutiny as other work because of its location in the private household and family. The requirement to give 'due respect for privacy' might seem neutral in relation to the different parties' privacy rights, but when understood in context, it can be seen to prioritize the employer's privacy at the worker's expense. The debates leading up to C-189's agreement show that the overwhelming reason for resisting more prescriptive requirements stemmed from the needs of the employer.[91] States had been asked about arrangements to ensure compliance, including labour inspection, with the question already containing the proviso 'with due regard to privacy'. Despite the presence of this proviso, several responses made reference to the need for privacy, including the employer group stating that 'the family home is sacrosanct and the police need with good cause a warrant from a judge before entering a home'.[92] This demonstrates that privacy, rather than being a neutral value, has tended in this context to reflect the interest of the employer as the more powerful party in the relationship.

While it is reasonable for privacy to be a consideration, it is problematic to allow it to preclude inspections involving entry to the home in any form. In allowing it to form an absolute bar, the state does not remain neutral but rather allows employers to adopt and continue abusive practices without much likelihood of consequences. The lack of clear direction on this point in turn affords a degree of flexibility to states to allow the continuation of legal frameworks that prevent the working conditions of domestic workers from being subject to the same scrutiny as other sectors. As discussed in the summary of case studies above, there are full or partial exclusions for domestic work from inspection across all case study countries. Even in Chile and South Africa, where the position is more progressive, entry to the home is only possible with the permission of the occupier, or with labour court

[91] ILO, 'Report IV(2)—Decent Work for Domestic Workers—99th Session of the International Labour Conference' (2010) 204–6.

[92] ibid.

authorization in the latter. In Chapter 4, I will argue that human rights principles call into question the bar on inspection in private households, while also setting limits in law to the contents and intrusiveness of such inspections based on the criteria of justification and proportionality.

Devaluation in the private sphere

Other than 'lack of accountability', the other organizing theme I use for understanding domestic workers' exclusion is 'devaluation'. The public/private sphere divide means that work performed in the private sphere, typically by women, is systematically constructed as inferior to and less important than work in the 'public' sphere. The separation obscures the work and requirements of women through the assumption that only paid work in the public sphere makes a contribution to the economy, or indeed is properly counted as work.[93] The performance of domestic labour is conflated with work that women would often otherwise carry out for free in the family home and that is perceived to be 'innate' to them.[94] This leads to such tasks being constructed as inherent to women, at best viewed as 'unskilled' work and at worst not acknowledged as work at all.[95]

Central to this process is the presentation of work in the private sphere as being detached from the arena where value is generated, and the idea that it does not contribute to the economy in the same way as 'productive' work in the public sphere. Feminist theorists have traced the intensification of this strict separation to industrialization, which removed much of production from the family remit and separated it from economic exchanges.[96] Whereas the pre-industrial economy was 'centred in the home and its surrounding farmland', meaning women's work completed there was no less respected than the labour of men,[97] the process of land privatization brought an end to the subsistence economy and led to monetary relations dominating economic life.[98] It therefore came to be understood that only production for market exchange created value, while 'the reproduction of the worker began to be considered as valueless from an economic viewpoint and even ceased to be considered as work'.[99] Therefore, the creation of the 'private sphere'

[93] Charlesworth, Chinkin, and Wright (n 60) 640.

[94] ILO, 'Report IV(1) 99th Session' (n 16) 5.

[95] Silvia Federici, *Revolution at Point Zero: Housework, Reproduction, and Feminist Struggle* (PM Press 2012) 16; LJB Hayes, *Stories of Care: A Labour of Law: Gender and Class at Work* (Palgrave, Macmillan Education 2017) 52, 81; Lourdes Peroni, 'The Borders That Disadvantage Migrant Women in Enjoying Human Rights' (2018) 36 Netherlands Quarterly of Human Rights 93, 97.

[96] Boyd, 'Challenging the Public/Private Divide' (n 63) 8; Sandra Fredman and Judy Fudge, 'The Contract of Employment and Gendered Work' in Mark Freedland (ed), *The Contract of Employment* (OUP 2016) 232.

[97] Angela Y Davis, *Women, Race & Class* (Penguin Classics 2019) 28.

[98] Silvia Federici, *Caliban and the Witch: Women, the Body and Primitive Accumulation* (2nd edn, Autonomedia 2014) 63–74.

[99] ibid 74–75.

as separate took place simultaneously with the devaluation of work in and related to that sphere. This is mirrored in today's understanding of childcare and other domestic work as a private responsibility and a gendered, nurturing activity that should not be performed for economic reward,[100] and the labelling of those who do not work outside the home as 'inactive'.[101]

Tracing the development of devaluation and paid domestic work

While much feminist analysis of the devaluation of reproductive labour has centred around unpaid work, there is increasing recognition of the need for a broader analysis encompassing 'the parallel devaluation of paid reproductive labor'.[102] The devaluation of paid domestic work reflects the lack of social value conferred on unpaid work within the household.[103] The concept of a 'continuum' between market-based domestic labour and work carried out in the context of marriage[104] is helpful in allowing both overlaps and distinctions to be accounted for. Rather than impacting all women uniformly, the gendered public/private sphere divide has differential effects based on factors including race, class, and sexual identity.[105] Even at the height of expectations for women to remain in the home in the nineteenth century, working-class women and those from racialized groups were much more likely to engage in outside paid work while also being expected to complete unpaid tasks in their own home.[106] The analysis relating to public and private spheres is still relevant because the lower wages for work categorized as 'women's work'—even when completed on a paid basis—stem partly from its gendered association with the private sphere. However, it is also vital to consider other factors. The devaluation of paid domestic work is strongly shaped by the concentration within it of women who are disadvantaged through other characteristics, such as ethnicity, migration status, and class. The designation of domestic tasks as unskilled and non-productive, which provides the state with a justification for failing

[100] Katherine Teghtsoonian, 'Who Pays for Caring for Children? Public Policy and the Devaluation of Women's Work' in Susan B Boyd (ed), *Challenging the Public/Private Divide: Feminism, Law, and Public Policy* (University of Toronto Press 1997) 117; Hayes (n 95) 26.

[101] Encarnación Gutiérrez Rodríguez, 'The Precarity of Feminisation' (2014) 27 International Journal of Politics, Culture, and Society 191, 196.

[102] Mignon Duffy, 'Doing the Dirty Work: Gender, Race, and Reproductive Labor in Historical Perspective' (2007) 21 Gender & Society 313, 315–16.

[103] Kamala Sankaran, 'Domestic Work, Unpaid Work and Wage Rates' (2013) 48 Economic and Political Weekly 85.

[104] Prabha Kotiswaran, 'Abject Labors, Informal Markets: Revisiting the Law's (Re)Production Boundary' (2014) 18 Employee Rights and Employment Journal 111, 117–20.

[105] Boyd (n 63) 12; Shreya Atrey, 'Women's Human Rights: From Progress to Transformation: An Intersectional Response to Martha Nussbaum' (2018) 40 Human Rights Quarterly 859, 903.

[106] Nancy Fraser, 'Crisis of Care? On the Social-Reproductive Contradictions of Contemporary Capitalism' in Tithi Bhattacharya (ed), *Social Reproduction Theory: Remapping Class, Recentering Oppression* (Pluto Press 2017) 27; Davis (n 97) 2, 208.

to invest in them, draws not only from their gendered nature but also from their relationship to colonial power structures, with the labour of outsider figures like the 'undocumented migrant' particularly devalued.[107] The situation can be further complicated by distinct levels of valuation between different domestic tasks. In India, for example, many accounts of domestic work note that persons of lower caste are more likely to be hired for cleaning, while cooking is viewed as more suitable for those of higher caste.[108]

This combined impact of gender with other factors demonstrates the need for an 'intersectional' approach to the question of women in domestic work, which recognizes how the interaction between attributes leads to 'compounded' forms of exclusion that go beyond forms of discrimination experienced by someone disadvantaged on only one axis.[109] This compounded disadvantage causes practical difficulties for domestic workers, who have often been neglected both by unions focusing on their existing, more privileged members, and by feminist groups that may not prioritize domestic worker rights.[110] An intersectional approach also allows for a structural understanding of disadvantage, which recognizes the interrelation between multiple characteristics and moves beyond viewing forms of exclusion as isolated incidents.[111]

In the domestic work context, a structural understanding of disadvantage requires recognition of how negative connotations associated with household and reproductive labour can be traced to an association with slavery and servitude rather than ordinary paid labour.[112] In many countries, including South Africa and Chile, domestic work began as a form of colonial servitude, which subsequently transformed into a type of paid work characterized by feudal relations.[113] The concept of a 'culture of servitude' involving hierarchical relations in which workers are subordinated and employers dominate is used to encapsulate this legacy and

[107] Encarnación Gutiérrez Rodríguez, *Migration, Domestic Work and Affect: A Decolonial Approach on Value and the Feminization of Labor* (Routledge 2010) 89, 141–47.

[108] Aakanksha Sinha and others, 'Undervalued and Overrepresented: Voices of Migrant Domestic Workers in India' (2020) 7 Global Social Welfare: Research, Policy & Practice 285, 289; Aayush Rathi and Ambika Tandon, 'Platforms, Power, and Politics: Perspectives from Domestic and Care Work in India' (Centre for Internet & Society and Domestic Workers Rights Union Bengaluru 2021) 42; Neetha (n 43) 545. See further Chapter 5.

[109] Kimberlé Crenshaw, 'Demarginalizing the Intersection of Race and Sex: A Black Feminist Critique of Antidiscrimination Doctrine, Feminist Theory and Antiracist Politics' (1989) 1 University of Chicago Legal Forum 139, 149–66.

[110] Merike Blofield and Merita Jokela, 'Paid Domestic Work and the Struggles of Care Workers in Latin America' (2018) 66 Current Sociology 531, 537.

[111] Shreya Atrey, *Intersectional Discrimination* (OUP 2019) 33, 41.

[112] ILO, 'Report IV(1) 99th Session' (n 16) 1; Adelle Blackett, 'Introduction: Regulating Decent Work for Domestic Workers' (2011) 23 Canadian Journal of Women and the Law 1, 17. See also introduction, section 'Domestic work, gender, race and migration'.

[113] Ally (n 14) 24; Karolina Stefoni and Rosario Fernández, 'Mujeres Inmigrantes En El Trabajo Doméstico. Entre El Servilismo y Los Derechos' in Karolina Stefoni (ed), *Mujeres inmigrantes en Chile: ¿Mano de obra o trabajadoras con derechos?* (Ediciones Universidad Alberto Hurtado 2011) 47.

the resulting ongoing power relationships in Chile.[114] In India, domestic work has similarly been analysed as both reflecting and consolidating a 'culture of servitude ... in which social relations of domination / subordination, dependency, and inequality are normalized and permeate both the domestic and public spheres'.[115] While Britain is distinctive in having been a former colonizing power, the legacy of servitude is also relevant. The term 'domestic servant' was preceded by the category of 'menial servant' from the fifteenth century, which relates to those who both worked and lived within the home and 'were seen as having a private, personal relationship with their masters'.[116] This separate legal categorization saw domestic workers being increasingly disadvantaged compared to other sectors as regards collective bargaining processes and protective legislation, and continues to inform the structuring of approaches to domestic work regulation today.[117]

Manifestations of devaluation in domestic work regulation

The construction of the relationship as family-like and distinct from other forms of labour continues to provide the basis for domestic workers' exclusion from key protections. The representation of the domestic worker as being akin to a member of the employer's family is a central construction in the devaluation of domestic work.[118] This presentation tends to mask deeply unequal relationships and can be traced back to the personalized master–servant relationship of earlier eras.[119] A study from Kolkata (India) notes how employers struggle with the transition to a relationship founded on a wage contract, rather than one based on 'the rules of the rhetoric of love', which entails a hierarchical structure where the 'servant' or domestic worker falls at the bottom.[120] Correspondingly, a move to a rights-based approach counteracts the familial relation that keeps domestic workers in their allocated and devalued place. This can be illustrated by two recent examples of challenges to legislative exemptions that were premised on devaluation, which are introduced here and explored further in later chapters.

The first example is the UK's 'family worker exemption', which meant that minimum wage protection did not apply to live-in domestic workers where they were

[114] Rosario Fernández, 'Commodification of Domestic Labour, the Culture of Servitude and the Making of the Chilean Nation' (2018) 43 Österreichische Zeitschrift für Soziologie 49.

[115] Raka Ray and Seemin Qayum, *Cultures of Servitude: Modernity, Domesticity, and Class in India* (Stanford University Press 2009) 3.

[116] Einat Albin, 'From "Domestic Servant" to "Domestic Worker"' in Judy Fudge, Shae McCrystal, and Kamala Sankaran (eds), *Challenging the Legal Boundaries of Work Regulation* (Hart 2012) 232–35.

[117] ibid 235–41.

[118] See eg Abigail B Bakan and Daiva Stasiulis, 'Introduction' in Abigail B Bakan and Daiva Stasiulis (eds), *Not One of the Family: Foreign Domestic Workers in Canada* (University of Toronto Press 1997) 10–11; Ray and Qayum (n 115) 92–93; Stefoni and Fernández (n 113) 53.

[119] Albin (n 116) 234; Cox (n 85) 46; Blofield (n 3) 16–17.

[120] Ray and Qayum (n 115) 95–96.

considered to be 'treated as a member of the family'.[121] Both the statutory wording and case law that applied it to domestic workers relied directly on the trope of being 'like a member of the family' to deny access to one of the most basic labour rights.[122] The exemption was eventually repealed in April 2024 following a 2020 ruling that it was unlawful and constituted indirect sex discrimination because of its disproportionate impact on women workers.[123] Secondly, in South Africa, the groundbreaking 2020 Constitutional Court judgment *Mahlangu v Ministry of Justice* found domestic workers' exclusion from compensation for injury and death at work to be unlawful, violating rights to social security, equality, and human dignity.[124] It held that the exclusion demonstrated 'that not only is domestic work undervalued, it is also not considered to be *real work* of the kind performed by workers that do fall within [the statute's definition]'.[125] This is an example of a rights-based claim forming the basis for a challenge to the systematic devaluation of domestic work.

Another manifestation of devaluation stemming from the failure to recognize domestic work as equally valued to 'productive' work is the tendency to permit longer hours for domestic workers than those in other sectors.[126] While working hours have formally been equalized in South Africa, the other case study countries continue to treat it distinctly in some ways, such as the longer hours permitted for live-in domestic workers in Chile and the disapplication of maximum weekly hours in the UK. Again, this is an area where C-189 might be interpreted as allowing for differentiation in regulation, based on its reference to the 'special characteristics of domestic work' (Art 10). The original proposed wording was stronger, mandating 'measures to ensure' that hours etc. 'are not less favourable than those applicable to other wage earners'.[127] The distinction in the final wording reveals tension over the question of 'what "special characteristics of domestic work" would justify an exception to the principle of equal treatment'.[128]

This is not to downplay the importance of C-189's provisions. By mandating that some limits should apply, it took a vital step in counteracting the 'assumption that the boundarilessness of domestic workers' time should simply be normalized'.[129]

[121] National Minimum Wage Regulations 2015—SI 2015/621 s 57(3).

[122] Fredman and Fudge (n 96) 236–37; Sedacca (n 59).

[123] *Puthenveettil v Alexander & George & Secretary of State for Business, Energy and Industrial Strategy—Case Number 2361118/2013—judgment of 15 December 2020* (Employment Tribunal). See Chapter 5.

[124] *Sylvia Mahlangu & anor v Minister of Labour & ors* [2020] ZACC 24 (Constitutional Court of South Africa). See further Chapters 3 and 5.

[125] ibid [108].

[126] ILO, 'Report IV(1) 99th Session' (n 16) 49; Blofield (n 3) 65, 131.

[127] ILO, 'Report IV(2) 99th Session' (n 91) 419.

[128] Tonia Novitz and Phil Syrpis, 'The Place of Domestic Work in Europe: An Analysis of Current Policy in the Light of the Council Decision Authorising Member States to Ratify ILO Convention No 189' (2015) 6 European Labour Law Journal 104, 119.

[129] Blackett, *Everyday Transgressions* (n 14) 117.

Its stipulations for at least twenty-four hours' weekly rest and for on-call hours to be counted as working hours (Arts 10(2) and (3)) are both significant advances. At the same time, the reference to the 'special characteristics' of domestic work could be understood as legitimizing ongoing inequality and still reflecting, to some degree, the 'boundarilessness' of domestic workers' time[130] and the construction of tasks they complete as not being 'real work' of equivalent value to that taking place outside the home. The extended working hours often permitted for full-time domestic workers relate to both lack of accountability—for example, because there is often no record or oversight of hours worked—and devaluation, because the conflation of domestic work with work carried out for free by women in the family contributes to the expectation of unlimited hours, as further discussed in Chapter 6.

Devaluation is also reflected in the restrictiveness of visa regimes for migrant domestic workers, which use the group's supposedly 'low-skilled' status to deny opportunities for family reunification, labour mobility, and long- or medium-term residence.[131] This exclusionary impact can arise through diverse mechanisms, from the UK's specific visa for the domestic work sector with unfavourable terms, to the lack of any general work visa route in South Africa for those not deemed to be skilled, leaving many working irregularly. The concept of 'skill' must be problematized as it is used to deny rights available to other groups of workers,[132] acting as a conduit for gendered devaluation. Its denial in the context of domestic and care work 'continues to reinforce gendered perceptions of homecare as "wife-like" work' and the link to women's unpaid labour in the family.[133] However else it may be rationalized, the reality is that this differential protection 'perpetuates a subsidy from the poorest to those who have more'.[134] Where specific short-term visas are granted for the sector, these reinforce the idea that the worker does not come into the labour market more broadly but merely to serve a particular family,[135] intensifying the instrumentalization of domestic workers' movement in the service of employers and the host state.

Conclusion

This chapter has outlined the progressions and shortcomings in regulating domestic work in each of the case study countries, drawing out common themes including enforcement gaps, exclusions associated with a 'family-like' relationship,

[130] Adelle Blackett, 'The Decent Work for Domestic Workers Convention and Recommendation, 2011' (2012) 106 American Journal of International Law 778, 784.

[131] See Chapters 7 and 8.

[132] Catherine Briddick, 'When Does Migration Law Discriminate Against Women?' (2021) 115 AJIL Unbound 356, 359.

[133] Hayes (n 95) 52.

[134] Arriagada and Todaro (n 1) 153.

[135] ILO, 'Report IV(1) 99th Session' (n 16) 10.

extended working hours, and unfavourable migration regimes. Following this scene-setting, it explained the analysis of domestic workers' exclusion, drawing on feminist theory on the public/private sphere divide and on an intersectional approach that recognizes the compounded and structural nature of disadvantage faced by domestic workers. It argued that 'lack of accountability' applicable to the private sphere, meaning a lack of visibility, scrutiny, and regulation, is exemplified by the traditional treatment of domestic violence and marital rape in law. Non-interference in such matters does not reflect 'neutrality' by the state but rather grants substantial privatized powers to the more powerful party, traditionally the male head of household. By analogy, the complete exclusion of domestic work from labour inspections is not neutral or generally respectful of privacy, but reinforces the power of the already dominant party, the employer, by granting them latitude to continue mistreatment.

This chapter has also detailed how work in the private sphere is subject to 'devaluation' by being viewed as detached from production, with tasks in the home constructed as inherent to women and undeserving of economic reward. The marginalization of paid domestic work also stems from the prevalence of women who are disadvantaged through characteristics such as ethnicity and migration status, alongside the sector's historical association with slavery and servitude. Considering the ongoing representation of domestic workers as akin to family members, the chapter addressed manifestations of their exclusion through low pay, longer working hours, and unfavourable visa regimes, alongside some recent successful challenges to exclusionary measures in the UK and South Africa. The next chapter will explore how human rights cases on domestic violence have contested the idea of the private as an impermeable sphere, demonstrating the possibility of applying scrutiny to areas previously considered out of bounds. Subsequent chapters will examine the use of human rights law to counteract devaluation, advocating an intersectional approach that supports the extension of rights to domestic workers from which they have previously been excluded. The rights-based approach that the chapter advocates opposes a familial relation providing cover for failure to properly recognize and compensate work, since it not only makes the work more visible, but also challenges the assumption that affective relations can substitute for proper reward.

3

Domestic workers and human rights

Introduction

This chapter develops the argument that human rights law can have a positive role in progressing domestic workers' *inclusion*: the goal that they are covered by labour law standards, that those standards are properly enforced, and that workers are not deterred from enforcing rights—for example, because of vulnerabilities arising from immigration status. The chapter's primary focus is on normative considerations about how human rights should be understood, including the relevance of theories developed in more general contexts to the specific situation of domestic workers. It also includes some initial consideration of the extent to which human rights jurisprudence across the three regional human rights systems reflects the principles I advocate, which will be developed in more depth in later chapters. Table 3.1 below, prepared by the author, lists the main relevant conventions and bodies by region, including the acronyms I will use to refer to them.

The first part of the chapter argues that the values of labour law and human rights are primarily shared rather than in opposition to each other, beginning by tracing their post-war development. The section also considers critiques of human rights from a labour law perspective: the relative neglect of socio-economic rights, the charge that human rights are too individualistic to be of value to workers' rights, and the suggestion that a human rights framework relies too heavily on legalistic means, de-prioritizing workers' agency. I seek to respond carefully to these concerns, bearing in mind that threats to the legitimacy and ongoing relevance of the human rights project[1] call for a 'spirit of introspection and openness'.[2] Engagement with compelling criticisms of human rights can spur reform to better reflect the movement's core principles.[3] I argue that the current overemphasis on individualism is a historically contingent understanding, which is open to challenge and is not universally reflected in human rights jurisprudence, particularly outside

[1] Colm O'Cinneide, 'Rights Under Pressure' (2017) 2017 European Human Rights Law Review 43; Kathryn McNeilly, 'Are Rights Out of Time? International Human Rights Law, Temporality, and Radical Social Change' (2018) 28 Social & Legal Studies 817, 818.

[2] Philip Alston, 'The Populist Challenge to Human Rights' (2017) 9 Journal of Human Rights Practice 1, 4.

[3] Gráinne De Búrca, *Reframing Human Rights in a Turbulent Era* (OUP 2021) 4.

Human Rights and the Protection of Domestic Workers in Labour and Migration Law. Natalie Sedacca, Oxford University Press. © Oxford University Press 2026. DOI: 10.1093/9780198985266.003.0004

Table 3.1 Human rights conventions and bodies by region

Region	Main general human rights treaty	Body/ies responsible for interpreting/ enforcing
Americas (Organization of American States)	American Convention on Human Rights (ACHR).[a]	Inter-American Commission on Human Rights (IAComHR); Inter-American Court of Human Rights (IACtHR).
Europe (Council of Europe)	European Convention on Human Rights (ECHR).[b]	European Court of Human Rights (ECtHR).
Africa (African Union)	African Charter on Human and People's Rights (ACHPR).[c]	African Commission on Human and People's Rights (AComHPR); African Court on Human and People's Rights (ACtHPR).

[a] Organization of American States, 'American Convention on Human Rights, Nov 22, 1969, OASTS No 36, 1144 UNTS 123'

[b] Council of Europe, 'European Convention on Human Rights—Convention for the Protection of Human Rights and Fundamental Freedoms—Rome, 4.XI.1950 (ECHR)'

[c] Organization of African Unity, 'African Charter on Human and Peoples' Rights (Banjul Charter), June 27, 1981, OAU Doc CAB/LEG/67/3 Rev 5—1520 UNTS 217'

Europe. On the question of human rights as a judicialized/legalistic framework, I argue for a less prescriptive approach to what constitutes 'agency' that recognizes the constrained circumstances of domestic workers, before exploring the potential for human rights to address a range of abuses.

In the second section, I focus on universality as a normative feature of human rights that has significant value for addressing the position of domestic workers, who frequently fall outside the protection of labour law because of their work's association with the 'private sphere'. I examine tensions between universality and particularism, positing an intersectional perspective on human rights as a way of resolving these, and consider the significance of a failure to live up to universalistic principles on migrants' rights. The final part of the chapter sets out the scope and relevance of a human rights approach for domestic workers' inclusion. This encompasses the concept of the 'positive obligation', making human rights law increasingly pertinent in the regulation of private relationships, with ramifications for workers' rights, and feminist developments in relation to domestic violence progressing accountability for abuses that take place within the private sphere. The section also examines the application of an 'integrated approach' to human rights in allowing for an extension of protection for social and economic rights. Taking these critiques and considerations together, I set out the approach to human rights on which the book's argument is based, which centres positive obligations, views categories of rights holistically, draws on feminist critiques of lack of accountability in the private sphere, and holds to universalistic values.

Labour law and human rights: Shared or opposing values?

Overlapping values, shared history

Labour law and human rights have important shared values, as they are both fundamentally directed to addressing abuses and imbalances of power and inequalities. A useful way of understanding the goal of human rights is to 're-shape the distribution of power in a society' away from where 'the market or the distribution of coercive resources might otherwise deposit them', thus endeavouring to change 'long established patterns of domination and asymmetries of power'.[4] Labour law, meanwhile, may be classically understood as a counterweight to the inequality of bargaining power between employers and workers.[5] Labour law and human rights therefore converge in their orientation to addressing abuses and imbalances of power and inequalities, whether between the individual and the state, the worker and the employer, or resulting from racial, gender-based or other oppression.

The overlap in principles can be traced by looking to early, non-binding human rights instruments of the modern era, the Universal Declaration of Human Rights (UDHR),[6] and the American Declaration of the Rights and Duties of Man,[7] both of which include workers' rights. In the American Declaration, these encompass the right to work and fair remuneration and to leisure time at Articles XIV and XV. The UDHR contains several salient provisions at Articles 23 and 24, including the right to work, to free choice of employment, to just and favourable conditions and remuneration, to form and join trade unions, and to rest and leisure. By virtue of Article 2, the rights in the UDHR apply to all persons 'without distinction of any kind'. Although it has been proposed that the inclusion of workers' rights in Articles 23 and 24 UDHR was anomalous,[8] there are compelling reasons for viewing it as a principled convergence. According to Caffentzis, the UDHR represented an 'attempt to universalize workers' rights', stemming from the rooting of modern human rights in the alliance between Social Democratic and Communist forces, which had both opposed fascism and saw labour as 'the decisive force of material progress' despite other great differences.[9] The central role of labour movements

[4] Daniel M Brinks, *The Judicial Response to Police Killings in Latin America: Inequality and the Rule of Law* (CUP 2008).

[5] Brian Langille, 'Labour Law's Theory of Justice' in Guy Davidov and Brian Langille (eds), *The Idea of Labour Law* (OUP 2011) 105.

[6] United Nations, 'Universal Declaration of Human Rights (Adopted 10 December 1948) UNGA Res 217 A(III)'.

[7] 'American Declaration of the Rights and Duties of Man, OAS Res XXX Adopted by the Ninth International Conference of American States (1948) Reprinted in 'Basic Documents Pertaining to Human Rights in the Inter-American System OEA/Ser L V/II.82 Doc 6 Rev 1 at 17 (1992)'.

[8] Hugh Collins, 'Theories of Rights as Justifications for Labour Law' in Guy Davidov and Brian Langille (eds), *The Idea of Labour Law* (OUP 2011) 143.

[9] George Caffentzis, '"Workers' Rights Are Human Rights": The Scope and Limits of a Precarious Wageworker's Strategy' (2016) 19 WorkingUSA 25, 27.

in upholding human rights also points to a synergy between the fields. As Leary notes, threats to freedom of association tend to be 'the first sign of a deteriorating situation' vis-à-vis human rights in general, with union leaders 'the most frequent victims of repression' in authoritarian regimes, such that human rights and social justice must be seen as intricately related.[10]

The ILO's development has also reflected the strong relationship between human rights and social justice. Its original 1919 constitution centred on the proposal that labour must not be seen as a commodity, but was primarily focused on protecting social justice or welfare issues without creating a competitive disadvantage,[11] thus not yet clearly reflecting human rights principles. However, a shift to an approach based on human rights and equality took place with the 1944 Declaration of Philadelphia.[12] Alarm at the widespread use of forced labour in concentration camps led to a heightened recognition that human rights and human dignity are foundational to workers' rights.[13] Reflecting this understanding, the Declaration proclaimed that: 'all human beings, irrespective of race, creed or sex, have the right to pursue both their material well-being and their spiritual development in conditions of freedom and dignity, of economic security and equal opportunity'.[14] Vitally, both the Declaration of Philadelphia and the UDHR appear to be based on the assumption that social and economic rights are indivisible from their social and economic counterparts,[15] a position strongly supported in this book.

These categories, however, became increasingly divided in the Cold War context. Broadly speaking, Western capitalist states were willing to commit to civil liberties but not to social and economic rights, and the reverse position was taken by Eastern bloc countries.[16] The division eroded the ILO's links with human rights principles as it sought to avoid the controversy arising from their separation.[17] It was only much later that the ILO turned back to a human rights-centred approach with the 1998 Declaration on Fundamental Principles and Rights at Work, which recognized freedom of association and effective collective bargaining, elimination of forced labour and discrimination, and the effective abolition of child labour as

[10] Virginia A Leary, 'The Paradox of Workers' Rights as Human Rights' in Lance A Compa and Stephen F Diamond (eds), *Human Rights, Labor Rights, and International Trade* (University of Pennsylvania Press 1996) 22–23, 39–43.

[11] Lee Swepston, 'The International Labour Organization and International Human Rights System' in Scott Sheeran and Nigel S Rodley (eds), *Routledge Handbook of International Human Rights Law* (Routledge 2013) 340; Janice R Bellace and Beryl ter Haar, 'Perspectives on Labour and Human Rights' in Janice R Bellace and Beryl ter Haar (eds), *Research Handbook on Labour, Business and Human Rights Law* (Edward Elgar 2019) 7–13.

[12] Swepston (n 11) 341.

[13] Tonia Novitz, *International and European Protection of the Right to Strike* (OUP 2003) 99.

[14] ILO, 'Declaration of Philadelphia (General Conference, 10 May 1944)' Art 2(a).

[15] Novitz (n 13) 99.

[16] Roy J Adams, 'From Statutory Right to Human Right: The Evolution and Current Status of Collective Bargaining' (2008) 12 Just Labour 48, 50.

[17] ibid.

core rights,[18] with the right to a safe and healthy working environment added in 2022.[19] The ILO's 2019 recommendation of a Universal Labour Guarantee proposed the inclusion of these five rights alongside an adequate living wage and limitations on working hours.[20]

The Cold War and the split between categories of rights

The Cold War split led to the division of the comprehensive rights declared in the UDHR into the two separate binding international instruments of 1966, the International Covenant on Economic, Social and Cultural Rights (ICESCR)[21] and the International Covenant on Civil and Political Rights (ICCPR).[22] ICESCR only mandated steps to 'progressively realise' rights, making it less specific than the equivalent requirements in the ICCPR.[23] The divide gave rise to limitations in the enforceability of socio-economic rights: an Optional Protocol to ICESCR allowing for individual petitions was only adopted in 2008, and has only 29 state parties to date.[24] The regional systems, particularly the Inter-American and European, reflect this divide to some degree, with a main enforceable treaty that focuses primarily on civil and political rights, the ACHR and ECHR, respectively. Both regional systems have a separate social and economic rights instrument that is not subject to the same enforcement mechanisms. In the Americas, the relevant document is the Protocol of San Salvador,[25] and only two of the rights within it—to education and unionization—are actionable before the IACtHR.[26] In Europe, the European

[18] ILO, 'Declaration on Fundamental Principles and Rights at Work and Its Follow-Up' (86th ILC Session 1998); Janice R Bellace, 'From Workers' Rights to Human Rights at Work' in Janice R Bellace and Beryl ter Haar (eds), *Research Handbook on Labour, Business and Human Rights Law* (Edward Elgar 2019) 411–12.

[19] Anne Trebilcock, '2022 Amendments to the ILO Declaration on Fundamental Principles and Rights at Work' [2023] International Legal Materials 1.

[20] ILO, 'Work for a Brighter Future—Global Commission on the Future of Work' (ILO 2019) 39.

[21] United Nations, 'International Covenant on Economic, Social and Cultural Rights (Adopted 16 December 1966, Entered into Force 23 March 1976) 993 UNTS 3'.

[22] United Nations, 'International Covenant on Civil and Political Rights (Adopted 16 December 1966, Entered into Force 23 March 1976) 999 UNTS 171'.

[23] Virginia Mantouvalou, 'In Support of Legalisation' in Conor Gearty and Virginia Mantouvalou, *Debating Social Rights* (Hart 2010) 94; Colm O'Cinneide, 'Bringing Socio-Economic Rights Back to the Mainstream of Human Rights: The Case-Law of the European Committee of Social Rights as an Example of Rigorous and Effective Rights Adjudication' (2009) 13 Revista Europea de Derechos Fundamentales 259, 262–63.

[24] United Nations, 'Optional Protocol to the International Covenant on Economic, Social and Cultural Rights (Adopted 10 December 2008, Entered into Force 5 May 2013) 2922 UNTS 29'; O'Cinneide, 'Bringing Socio-Economic Rights Back to the Mainstream of Human Rights' (n 23) 263–64. By contrast, the ICCPR's Optional Protocol came into force in 1976 and has 119 state parties.

[25] Organization of American States, 'Additional Protocol to the American Convention on Human Rights in the Area of Economic, Social and Cultural Rights ("Protocol of San Salvador"), 16 November 1999, A-52'.

[26] Francesco Seatzu and Amaya Ubeda de Torres, 'The Social Charter of the OAS: A Step Forward in the Enforcement of Socioeconomic Rights in the Americas?' (2014) 32 Netherlands Quarterly of Human Rights 130, 146.

Social Charter (ESC)[27] protects a comprehensive series of social and economic rights, although states can decide to opt out of particular provisions and its enforcement mechanisms remain much more limited than the process of bringing claims to the ECtHR—for example, because compensation is not awarded to victims.[28] Furthermore, the Appendix to the ESC delineates many rights within it as applying only to foreigners that are 'nationals of other Parties lawfully resident or working regularly within the territory of the party concerned'.[29] The African system is distinctive, since the ACHPR includes social and economic rights to work, to health, and to education (Articles 15–17)—although still not the full range of social rights seen in instruments like ICESCR.[30]

The relative neglect of socio-economic rights should be understood not as an inherent feature of human rights but rather as the product of a particular, dominant Western conception.[31] The position I have stated is in opposition to critics who view the divide as 'no mere accident of politics but a structural feature of human rights with its orientation to formal matters of procedure over more substantive matters of redistribution'.[32] For example, Moyn argues that human rights are too weak to challenge inequality, since their economic and social aspects are focused on the achievement of minimal, subsistence levels, which do not require interference with historically high levels of inequality within or between states.[33] However, the specific, primarily US-based examples of theorists and approaches Moyn cites as suggesting a lack of attention to social and economic rights do not equate to 'the human rights movement' as a whole.[34] The critique of human rights as integrally unable to address distributional issues also downplays the work of grassroots movements that use human rights alongside broader redistributive claims.[35]

[27] Council of Europe, 'European Social Charter, 18 October 1961, ETS 35'. There is a revised version of the Charter dated 1996, but the UK has not ratified it.

[28] Tonia Novitz, 'Protection of Workers under Regional Human Rights Systems: An Assessment of Evolving and Divergent Practices' in Colin F Fenwick and Tonia Novitz (eds), *Human Rights at Work: Perspectives on Law and Regulation* (Hart 2010) 416–17.

[29] For a critique of these limitations, see Claudio Panzera, 'The Personal Scope of the European Social Charter: Questioning Equality' (2014) 24 Revista Europea de Derechos Fundamentales 51. On these limitations and exceptions to them, see Chapter 7.

[30] Takele Soboka Bulto, 'The Utility of Cross-Cutting Rights in Enhancing Justiciability of Socio-Economic Rights in the African Charter on Human and Peoples' Rights' (2010) 29 University of Tasmania Law Review 142; Rachel Murray, *The African Charter on Human and Peoples' Rights: A Commentary* (OUP 2019) 31–32.

[31] Felipe Isa, 'Cultural Diversity, Legal Pluralism, and Human Rights from an Indigenous Perspective: The Approach by the Colombian Constitutional Court and the Inter-American Court of Human Rights' (2014) 36 Human Rights Quarterly 722, 724.

[32] Guy Aitchison, 'Are Human Rights Moralistic?' (2018) 19 Human Rights Review 23, 34. Aitchison summarizes and responds to this criticism.

[33] Samuel Moyn, *Not Enough: Human Rights in an Unequal World* (Belknap Press of Harvard University Press 2018) 111–23, 145–47, 176.

[34] Julia Lemaitre, 'The View from Somewhere: On Samuel Moyn's Not Enough' (*LPE Project*, 9 July 2018) <https://lpeproject.org/blog/the-view-from-somewhere-on-samuel-moyns-not-enough/> accessed 25 August 2025.

[35] Paul O'Connell, 'Capitalism, Inequality, and Human Rights' (*LPE Project*, 4 June 2018) <https://lpeproject.org/blog/capitalism-inequality-and-human-rights/> accessed 25 August 2025.

The response to concerns about de-prioritization of some categories of rights should not be a rejection of the human rights project but a continued quest to strengthen the protection of social and economic as well as civil and political rights. While advocating for better realization of social and economic rights, it is crucial not to be dismissive of the value of civil and political rights, nor to optimistically view such rights as near universally achieved, which would risk an orientation that neglects the interests of women and minorities.[36] Additionally, a framework based on human rights can constitute one part of a broader contestation of inequality. Such a challenge will require the participation of a range of actors, including trade unions and others with a primarily redistributive focus, but organizations of this nature are more likely to be able to operate effectively and make demands for redistribution successfully under conditions where human rights, including civil rights such as freedom of assembly and association, are respected.[37] Expressed in Fraser's terms, justice requires cultural recognition and political representation as well as economic redistribution;[38] for domestic workers, this means that recognition of their status as workers rather than servants or family members, and of their need for a private life of their own, is crucial alongside distributional rights like better pay and benefits.

In sum, the divisions between labour rights and human rights, and the separation of human rights by category, are not inherent to either field but arose from specific contextual factors. The values of labour and human rights dovetail at a normative level and, having overlapped in their post-war foundational documents, have at least begun to return to this convergence in recent decades. The remainder of this section will explore further challenges to the normative congruence between these fields.

Individualism versus collective interests

A key criticism from a labour law perspective is the idea that human rights are too individualistic to be valuable to progressing workers' rights.[39] For example, Youngdahl argues that 'rights discourse individualizes the struggle at work' in contrast to the 'solidarity and community' of the union movement, and that rights

[36] Gráinne de Búrca, 'Not Enough: Human Rights in an Unequal World' (2018) 16 International Journal of Constitutional Law 1347, 1349–51.

[37] Margot E Salomon and Martin Scheinin, 'Samuel Moyn, Not Enough: Human Rights in an Unequal World' (2019) 32 Leiden Journal of International Law 609, 612.

[38] Nancy Fraser, 'From Redistribution to Recognition? Dilemmas of Justice in a "Post-Socialist" Age' [1995] New Left Review 68, 69; Nancy Fraser, *Scales of Justice: Reimagining Political Space in a Globalizing World* (Polity 2008) 15.

[39] For a partially overlapping discussion of the points in this and the next subsection, see Joe Atkinson and Natalie Sedacca, 'Realising Decent Work for Platform Workers: A Human Rights Approach' (2025) 16 Transnational Legal Theory 578, 590–96.

cannot provide an effective movement to take on power or motivate workers to make sacrifices for others.[40] The criticism is understandable based on mainstream approaches to human rights, which have often focused on creating 'a sphere of freedom for each individual person from the control of the state'.[41] Yet there are alternative foundations for understanding human rights that recognize social relationships and the need for positive action. A primarily individualistic model has arisen from a particular conception of human rights as influenced by (neo)liberalism, which emphasizes 'formal freedom', or the absence of interference, to the detriment of 'substantive freedom'.[42] Rather than accepting this vision as representative, it is crucial to take into account the debates *within* the field, to bear in mind the variability of the way rights are thought about and utilized.[43] Human rights can be conceptualized in a way that recognizes sociality and community, and the role of the state in intervening against power imbalances, instead of supporting individual liberty and agency at any cost, or setting a strict dichotomy between the two.[44] While most human rights are expressed as individual entitlements, this does not mean that they require 'atomistic individualism';[45] and claims by an individual to realize one of these rights by an individual can ultimately benefit groups.

The move beyond a solely individualistic approach is also reflected in human rights doctrine. The clearest example of eschewing a purely individualistic approach is found in the African system, since the ACHPR contains 'Peoples' Rights' at Articles 19–24, comprising collective rights such as equality, the free disposal of wealth and natural resources, development, peace and security, and a satisfactory environment. The IACtHR has also shown a shift to interpreting rights in a collective manner, partly based on the influence of indigenous peoples' philosophies.[46] In *Awas Tingni v Nicaragua,* which arose from an indigenous community's struggle for land tenure, the IACtHR departed from a traditional liberal perspective by holding that the right to property included 'the rights of members of the

[40] Jay Youngdahl, 'Solidarity First: Labor Rights Are Not the Same as Human Rights' (2009) 18 New Labor Forum 30, 31–35.

[41] Tonia Novitz and Colin F Fenwick, 'The Application of Human Rights Discourse to Labour Relations: Translation of Theory into Practice' in Colin F Fenwick and Tonia Novitz (eds), *Human Rights at Work: Perspectives on Law and Regulation* (Hart 2010) 14.

[42] Langille (n 5) 117–8.

[43] Colin F Fenwick and Tonia Novitz, 'Conclusion: Regulating to Protect Workers' Human Rights' in Colin F Fenwick and Tonia Novitz (eds), *Human Rights at Work: Perspectives on Law and Regulation* (Hart 2010) 590.

[44] Robin West, *Re-Imagining Justice: Progressive Interpretations of Formal Equality, Rights, and the Rule of Law* (Ashgate 2003) 6, 86; Iris Marion Young, *Justice and the Politics of Difference* (Paperback reissue, Princeton University Press 2011) 228–29; Natalie R Davidson, 'The Feminist Expansion of the Prohibition of Torture: Towards a Post-Liberal International Human Rights Law?' (2019) 52 Cornell International Law Journal 109, 133; Barrie Sander, 'Democratic Disruption in the Age of Social Media: Between Marketized and Structural Conceptions of Human Rights Law' (2021) 32 European Journal of International Law 159, 162.

[45] Jack Donnelly, *Universal Human Rights in Theory and Practice* (3rd edn, Cornell University Press 2013) 30.

[46] Isa (n 31).

indigenous communities within the framework of communal property'.[47] In turn, this perspective has influenced workers' rights cases. For example, *Five Pensioners v Peru*, in setting out the right to social security and a pension for retired employees, highlighted the importance of protecting a collective—in this instance, retired people.[48]

The position in the ECtHR is more complex: some decisions, particularly on the question of 'closed shops' in trade unions, can be criticized for their individualistic approach.[49] Yet there have also been other judgments recognizing workers' collective interests. For example, in *Demir and Baykara v Turkey*, in which civil servants challenged the denial of their right to join trade unions and bargain collectively, the court held that the right to collective bargaining had become part of Article 11 ECHR on freedom of association,[50] while *Enerji Yapi-Yol Sen v Turkey* made a similar finding regarding industrial action.[51] Some recent ECtHR cases against the UK have again been less accommodating of collective interests,[52] so the progression towards greater recognition has not been linear or complete. Nonetheless, the ACHPR, alongside a holistic view of the other regional courts' jurisprudence, demonstrates the potential for moving beyond a solely individualistic view of human rights.

Legalism/agency

Another salient critique is that a human rights framework is too closely based and reliant on legal routes to be valuable for workers' rights, and that it inappropriately de-prioritizes self-organization and collective action. Arthurs, for example, stresses the importance of non-legal means to the development of labour law and fears this form of mobilization would be undermined by a human rights approach, which would foreground courts in its place.[53] Maupain, Kolben and Gearty raise

[47] *Mayagna (Sumo) Awas Tingni Community v Nicaragua* IACtHR 31 August 2001, Ser C No 79; S James Anaya and Claudio Grossman, 'The Case of Awas Tingni v. Nicaragua: A New Step in the International Law of Indigenous Peoples' (2002) 19 Arizona Journal of International and Comparative Law 1, 1–4.

[48] *The 'Five Pensioners' v Peru* IACtHR 28 February 2003, Ser C No 98; Amaya Úbeda de Torres, 'Chapter 18 Workers' Rights' in Laurence Burgorgue-Larsen and Amaya Úbeda de Torres (eds), *The Inter-American Court of Human Rights: Case Law and Commentary* (OUP 2011) [18.07–18.08].

[49] *Sorensen and Rasmussen v Denmark* (2008) 46 EHRR 572; Virginia Mantouvalou, 'Is There a Human Right Not to Be a Trade Union Member? Labour Rights under the European Convention on Human Rights' in Colin F Fenwick and Tonia Novitz (eds), *Human Rights at Work: Perspectives on Law and Regulation* (Hart 2010).

[50] *Demir and Baykara v Turkey* (2009) 48 EHRR 54.

[51] *Enerji Yapi-Yol Sen v Turkey* [2009] ECHR 2251.

[52] Keith D Ewing and John Hendy, 'Article 11(3) of the European Convention on Human Rights' (2017) 4 European Human Rights Law Review 356. For example, a challenge to the ban on secondary strike action was unsuccessful—*RMT v United Kingdom* (2015) 60 EHRR 10.

[53] Harry Arthurs, 'Labour Law after Labour' in Guy Davidov and Brian Langille (eds), *The Idea of Labour Law* (OUP 2011) 24–27.

related concerns, positing that human rights are externally imposed and create a top-down or depoliticizing approach instead of drawing on collective mobilization.[54] Part of this critique is therefore that a human rights-based approach removes *agency* from workers, where agency is understood as worker mobilization and empowerment to transform working conditions.[55]

In responding, it can first be noted that judicial claims are not the only way to raise human rights questions. Complaints can be made to bodies that are not 'courts' in the strict sense, such as the European Committee of Social Rights (ECSR), which interprets the ESC. Human rights standards can also form the basis of grassroots activism and demands that challenge existing forms of power, with the appeal to human rights underscoring that entitlements being sought are urgent and not optional.[56] Secondly, judicial claims should not be viewed as inherently negative or depoliticizing, as they can play an important role as one part of the project of advancing workers' rights or otherwise addressing issues of inequality and abuses of power. Decisions by judicial bodies do not necessarily affect only individuals, and in some cases groups such as unions and NGOs pursue strategic litigation.[57] Findings in favour of the claimant in an individual case can have broader ramifications, potentially leading to more systematic reforms—particularly in systems that provide mechanisms for this, such as the IACtHR and the South African and Indian court systems—political discussion, further activism, and new legislation.[58] Legal mechanisms can be used alongside a range of other strategies, including collective organization and campaigning, to build improvements in workers' conditions. For example, independent unions representing 'gig economy' and other marginalized workers in Britain have successfully harnessed a strategy that entails the use of strategic litigation with social-movement style campaigning and more 'traditional' workers' actions such as strikes.[59] The availability of international mechanisms allows activists increased opportunities and resources and an alternative route where domestic routes fail, as well as raising their work's profile.[60]

[54] Francis Maupain, 'Is the ILO Effective in Upholding Workers' Rights? Reflections on the Myanmar Experience' in Philip Alston (ed), *Labour Rights as Human Rights* (OUP 2005) 139; Kevin Kolben, 'Labor Rights as Human Rights?' (2009) 50 Virginia Journal of International Law 449, 472; Conor Gearty, 'Against Judicial Enforcement' in Conor Gearty and Virginia Mantouvalou, *Debating Social Rights* (Hart 2010) 58. Gearty's critique relates specifically to judicial enforcement of social rights, rather than the broader concept of human rights.

[55] Arthurs (n 53) 24–27; Hila Shamir, 'A Labor Paradigm for Human Trafficking' (2012) 60 UCLA Law Review 76, 81–82.

[56] Aitchison (n 32) 35–37; Mantouvalou, 'In Support of Legalisation' (n 23) 108–9.

[57] Mantouvalou, 'In Support of Legalisation' (n 23) 126–27.

[58] ibid 125–30.

[59] Manoj Dias-Abey, 'Mobilizing for Recognition: Indie Unions, Migrant Workers, and Strategic Equality Act Litigation' (2022) 38 International Journal of Comparative Labour Law and Industrial Relations 137, 138–41.

[60] Par Engstrom and Peter Low, 'Mobilising the Inter-American Human Rights System: Regional Litigation and Domestic Human Rights Impact in Latin America' in Par Engstrom (ed), *The Inter-American Human Rights System: Impact Beyond Compliance* (Palgrave Macmillan 2019) 24–27.

In addition, the posited opposition between human rights and agency should not be overstated. A central aim of human rights is to empower individuals to make decisions aimed at fulfilling their dignity,[61] and the action of struggling for and institutionalizing a rights claim can be central to its validity.[62] Several critical race feminists have noted that the process of claiming or winning recognition of human rights may have a foundational power for minorities and marginalized groups seeking to have their voices heard in the context of exclusionary systems.[63] Williams argued that attaining rights can be empowering for 'the historically disempowered' since 'the conferring of rights is symbolic of all the denied aspects of their humanity',[64] and Matsuda that 'outsiders, including feminists and people of color, have embraced legalism as a tool of necessity'.[65] Particularly for an 'outsider', the action of claiming rights can entail the exercise of agency, which is salient for domestic workers who have been outsiders vis-à-vis the protections of mainstream labour law. Instead of drawing a sharp divide between organization based on solidarity versus rights, it is preferable to see the two approaches as strengthening each other through 'a skilful, strategic interweaving of these strands into a springboard for labor revitalization'.[66]

It is also vital to consider tangibly what agency means in any particular situation. Reliance only on collective action, without any framework for individual rights, comes up against the limitation that unions do not have universal coverage and their necessary focus on the interests of the majority of their members can leave minorities unprotected.[67] The need for a combination of tools to progress workers' rights rather than relying only on trade union representation is particularly important in the domestic work sector, where collective forms of organization are often harder to engage in because of factors such as isolation in the home, fears over migration status and a lack of time for organizing because of long working hours or funds to pay union fees.[68] The usual starting point for collective action

[61] Alicia Ely-Yamin, 'Empowering Visions: Toward a Dialectical Pedagogy of Human Rights' (1993) 15 Human Rights Quarterly 640, 644.

[62] Judy Fudge, 'Labour Rights as Human Rights: Turning Slogans into Legal Claims' (2014) 37 Dalhousie Law Journal 601, 604.

[63] Fulvia Staiano, 'Bringing Critical Race Theory to Europe: The Case of Immigrant Women' (2015) 8 European Journal of Legal Studies 73, 77.

[64] Patricia J Williams, *The Alchemy of Race and Rights* (Harvard University Press 1991) 153.

[65] Mari J Matsuda, 'When the First Quail Calls: Multiple Consciousness as Jurisprudential Method. (A Talk Presented at the Yale Law School Conference on Women of Color and the Law, April 16, 1988.)' (1992) 14 Women's Rights Law Reporter 297, 298.

[66] Lance Compa, 'Solidarity and Human Rights: A Response to Youngdahl' (2009) 18 New Labor Forum 38, 38–39.

[67] ACL Davies, 'Workers' Human Rights in English Law' in Colin F Fenwick and Tonia Novitz (eds), *Human Rights at Work: Perspectives on Law and Regulation* (Hart 2010) 177–78.

[68] Einat Albin and Virginia Mantouvalou, 'Active Industrial Citizenship of Domestic Workers: Lessons Learned from Unionizing Attempts in Israel and the United Kingdom' (2016) 17 Theoretical Inquiries in Law 321, 327–31; Zhe Jiang and Marek Korczynski, 'When the "Unorganizable" Organize: The Collective Mobilization of Migrant Domestic Workers in London' (2016) 69 Human Relations 813, 815–21; ILO, 'Making Decent Work a Reality for Domestic Workers: Progress and Prospects Ten Years after the Adoption of the Domestic Workers Convention, 2011 (No. 189)' (ILO 2021) 223. See further Chapters 4 and 6.

is a workplace with others alongside whom one could organize. By contrast, a domestic worker will often be in a workplace of one, without immediate colleagues, which creates inhibited circumstances for traditional organizing and claiming rights through mechanisms such as collective bargaining.[69] This means that a basic level of human rights protection is needed to facilitate workers being able to take part in collective action.

Davies and Freedland have usefully depicted labour law as 'a constant struggle to balance protection and agency',[70] signifying that regulation cannot be left simply to agency alone without any protective framework. The hindrances to domestic workers' collective organization create an enhanced need to strengthen the protective side of this equation and take steps to facilitate the exercise of agency by workers. As recognized during the ILO process leading to C-189, this requires specific legal rights that allow domestic workers to have time off and leave the workplace, in order to come into contact with others and access services.[71] This exemplifies the value of 'outside' or legalistic assistance as a precondition to meaningful involvement to counteract domestic workers' lack of bargaining power.[72] The contribution of NGOs may help to promote involvement and tackle 'the superior bargaining power of employers and the role of the state', and their role should not be dismissed simply because they are not traditional unions.[73] Recognizing the need for these additional mechanisms does not mean in any way that domestic workers are passive. Instead, it is an acknowledgement of the particular obstacles they face to organizing in traditional forms and of the unique circumstances of their work that is 'work like no other' as well as 'work like any other'. In these constrained circumstances, the exercise of agency can take on a range of forms, from taking part in self-help and community groups,[74] to leaving abusive workplaces despite the risk this can pose to a worker's immigration status, and exercising resistance individually at the workplace level.[75] By thinking less prescriptively about what agency means in the context of domestic work, it is possible to recognize the potential for a human rights-based approach to contribute to a framework for agency in highly challenging circumstances.

[69] Inga K Thiemann, 'Beyond Victimhood and Beyond Employment? Exploring Avenues for Labour Law to Empower Women Trafficked into the Sex Industry' (2019) 48 Industrial Law Journal 199, 214. Thiemann's focus is on sex workers who face additional challenges such as criminalization, but the point extends to others in the private sphere like domestic workers.

[70] Adelle Blackett, *Everyday Transgressions: Domestic Workers' Transnational Challenge to International Labor Law* (Cornell University Press 2019) 45; reference to Paul Davies and Mark Freedland, *Labour Legislation and Public Policy: A Contemporary History* (Clarendon Press 1993) 664.

[71] ILO, 'Report IV(2)—Decent Work for Domestic Workers—99th Session of the International Labour Conference' (2010) 159.

[72] Lisa Rodgers, *Labour Law, Vulnerability and the Regulation of Precarious Work* (Edward Elgar 2016) 174, 182.

[73] Albin and Mantouvalou (n 68) 323–28.

[74] ibid 323.

[75] Blackett (n 70) 43–44.

The potential for human rights to address a range of abuses

The protection of workers' rights as human rights can address a broad array of issues that take place at work or otherwise affect workers. This section outlines some of the main provisions of relevance to arguments in the book, which are elaborated further in its thematic chapters. While the UDHR is non-binding, the workers' rights entitlements in its Articles 23 and 24 are reflected at Articles 6–8 of ICESCR, which provide for the right to work, to just and favourable conditions at work and for several trade union freedoms, including the right to strike. The ACHPR contains an equivalent in Article 15, providing for 'the right to work under equitable and satisfactory conditions' as well as equal pay for equal work; the Indian constitution also contains a right to work (Article 41) and to just and humane working conditions (Article 42).[76] In the American and European systems, the right appears in the separate, less enforceable socio-economic rights instruments mentioned above, the Protocol of San Salvador and the ESC. Nonetheless, the IACtHR and ECtHR have made relevant findings encompassing aspects of the right to work through interpretations of other instruments;[77] and the right to freedom of association has been interpreted as protecting collective bargaining and industrial action.[78]

There are also civil and political rights that have great value for the protection of domestic and other workers' interests, including the right to private and family life, found at Article 17 of the ICCPR, Article 11 ACHR and Article 8 ECHR. There is no direct equivalent in the ACHPR, but the right is protected in the South African Constitution,[79] while in India, the Supreme Court has recognized privacy as a protected right via other constitutional provisions, including the guarantee of life and personal liberty.[80] In the ECtHR and IACtHR, the right has been broadly interpreted as encompassing rights to personal development, autonomy, and the establishment of relationships with others and the outside world.[81] Therefore, beyond issues like protecting workers from intrusive surveillance,[82] it is relevant to other key regulatory questions in domestic work including reasonable limitation of working time, since excessive and unregulated hours leave little or no time to engage in other activities or develop relationships.[83] The right is also undermined by

[76] The Constitution of India—as on May 2022.

[77] See subsection 'social and economic rights and the integrated approach' in this chapter, and Chapter 7.

[78] *Demir and Baykara v Turkey* (n 50); *Enerji Yapi-Yol Sen v Turkey* (n 51).

[79] The Constitution of the Republic of South Africa 1996, s14.

[80] *Justice KS Puttaswamy v Union of India* (2017) 10 SCR 569, Conclusions [3c].

[81] *Pretty v United Kingdom* (2002) 35 EHRR 1; *Artavia Murillo* et al *('in vitro fertilization') v Costa Rica* IACtHR 28 November 2012, Ser C No 257; *Atala Riffo and daughters v Chile* IACtHR 24 February 2012, Ser C No 239.

[82] See eg *Barbulescu v Romania* (2017) IRLR 1032 (ECtHR Grand Chamber).

[83] This builds on previous arguments such as Deirdre McCann, 'Decent Working Hours as a Human Right: Intersections in the Regulation of Working Time' in Colin F Fenwick and Tonia Novitz (eds), *Human Rights at Work: Perspectives on Law and Regulation* (Hart 2010). See Chapter 6.

visa regimes that fail to facilitate family reunification and therefore leave domestic workers separated from their families, potentially on a long-term basis.[84]

The prohibition on slavery and forced labour (Article 8 ICCPR, Article 6 ACHR, Article 4 ECHR and Article 5 ACHPR) has obvious salience to workers' rights. While it might be assumed that these protections relate only to addressing extreme violations, usually through criminal law measures, the book will explore the ways in which they have been interpreted to require broader and structural changes. For example, the IACtHR judgment in *Hacienda Verde v Brazil* set out the need to provide effective inspection mechanisms and other preventative strategies and to address 'structural historical discrimination' in order to address forced labour.[85] The Indian Constitution contains a prohibition on forced labour and trafficking at Article 23, which its Supreme Court has interpreted expansively, holding that any work for below minimum wage pay falls within its ambit and entitles a person to enforce their direct right to payment.[86]

The ability to challenge a range of abuses is important for increasing domestic workers' protection and challenging their exclusion. For example, unlimited and undefined working hours may arise in the context of a violation of the prohibition on slavery, servitude or forced labour, but where they are less severe and fall short of this standard, they may still breach other human rights provisions. Excessive hours will often leave insufficient time to spend with family members and therefore interfere with the right to a private and family life, as well as social and economic rights requiring reasonable limitation of working hours.[87] Strict immigration rules that make it difficult or impossible to change employer may or may not lead to situations that violate the prohibition on slavery, forced labour, and servitude, but where they do not, they may still amount to a violation of the right to work.[88]

Universality: Towards the inclusion of domestic workers?

I have argued that a key factor in domestic workers' exclusion from protective labour law standards and enforceability mechanisms is the location of their work in the private sphere, and consequently, their designation as outside the category of workers to whom protections apply. Labour law standards as formulated in domestic regimes are not necessarily inclusive of anyone who is carrying out work: they may apply contingently, depending on whether an individual meets

[84] See Chapter 8.

[85] *Workers of the Hacienda Verde Brasil Verde v Brazil* IACtHR 20 October 2016, Ser C No 337 [316–20].

[86] *People's Union for Democratic Rights v Union of India and Others* ('*Asiad Workers* case') (1982) 3 SCC 235 [5.3–5.9].

[87] See Chapter 6.

[88] See Chapter 7.

criteria such as being part of a 'productive' sector outside the home. By contrast, a central normative feature of human rights is universality, denoting the idea that everyone is entitled to their protection simply by virtue of being human.[89] This value is salient for questioning exclusions and progressing the inclusion of those who have fallen *outside* the protections of labour law.[90] Domestic workers clearly have a claim to human rights, since these apply to all humans,[91] regardless of where their work is performed.

The concept that human rights apply to all without distinction regardless of characteristics appears in the UDHR's Article 2, while both ICESCR and ICCPR proclaim in their preambles that 'these rights derive from the inherent dignity of the human person' and contain anti-discrimination provisions at Article 2(2) and 2(1) respectively. The requirement is that rights be guaranteed without discrimination based on a series of characteristics, including 'other status'. The regional instruments have similarly universalistic coverage in prohibiting discrimination regarding enjoyment of the rights within them, with the ACHR referring to 'other social condition' (Article 1(1)) and the ECHR and ACHPR to 'other status' (Article 14/Article 2). Importantly, 'other status' or 'condition' can encompass migration status. The Indian Constitution also includes anti-discrimination provisions at Articles 14 and 15(1). It is arguable that employment status itself can be a protected status under anti-discrimination provisions, such that exclusion from rights based on a particular labour market position would amount to discrimination.[92] The claim to universality therefore makes human rights law an important grounding for the rights of those left unprotected by labour law, through challenging any exclusion of domestic workers that entails lesser realization of human rights.

Tensions: Universality and particularism

It may be argued that the use of universalist language to defend particularist causes can be problematic when those causes conflict with universalism.[93] This would indicate a challenge in using universalistic values to bring domestic workers into the protective ambit of labour law, while also recognizing the distinctive nature of domestic work. Central to resolving this tension is Atrey's

[89] Donnelly (n 45) 10; Virginia Mantouvalou, 'Workers without Rights as Citizens at the Margins' (2013) 16 Critical Review of International Social and Political Philosophy 366, 378.

[90] Mantouvalou, 'Citizens at the Margins' (n 89) 367.

[91] Deirdre McCann and Jill Murray, 'Prompting Formalisation Through Labour Market Regulation: A "Framed Flexibility" Model for Domestic Work' (2014) 43 Industrial Law Journal 319, 328–29.

[92] Joe Atkinson, 'Employment Status and Human Rights: An Emerging Approach' (2023) 86 Modern Law Review 1166, 1187–91.

[93] Michael Ignatieff, *Human Rights as Politics and Idolatry* (Amy Gutmann ed, University Press 2011) 9.

proposition of an intersectional approach to human rights, which views difference as a 'unifying ground' for universality, rather than requiring common characteristics and homogeneity as its basis.[94] Through this understanding, difference can be addressed both by recognizing particular rights and entitlements of disadvantaged groups, and by 'the application of existing human rights to disadvantaged groups without discrimination'.[95] The latter route is particularly important for the extension of universal rights to domestic workers. It is based on understanding anti-discrimination requirements 'expansively and as a matter of substantive rather than formal equality already embedded in universality, to ensure that human rights actually apply to all, including those belonging to disadvantaged groups'.[96]

This approach is exemplified in the South African Constitutional Court's *Mahlangu* judgment on domestic workers' exclusion from compensation for death or injury in service, which identified intersectional discrimination based on both race and gender.[97] The judgment highlighted the value of an intersectional perspective in allowing for an understanding of structural concerns, 'which require courts to examine contextual factors including the oppression faced by Black women as a result of apartheid' as well as 'its capacity to shed light on the experiences and vulnerabilities of certain groups that have been erased or rendered invisible'.[98] This understanding was used alongside an interpretation of the human rights to social security, equality, and human dignity, to rule against the exclusion. The judgment uses intersectionality both as a way of *framing* rights that exist in the constitution and as a way of *evaluating* the way rights have been breached.[99] The distinctive characteristics of domestic workers thus do not undermine the entitlement to appeal to universality against their exclusion from rights that are intended to apply to all. An analogous approach can be used to formulate specific entitlements for domestic workers, where these are required to satisfy a human right of general application. An example would be a right to leave the home during breaks: the need for a special right relates to the fact that domestic workers may be required to stay in the employer's home during breaks. This is a particular exclusion that can be challenged through the application of the general right to a private and family life.

[94] Shreya Atrey, 'Beyond Universality: An Intersectional Justification of Human Rights' in Shreya Atrey and Peter Dunne (eds), *Intersectionality and Human Rights Law* (Hart 2020) 21–24.

[95] ibid 27.

[96] ibid.

[97] *Sylvia Mahlangu & anor v Minister of Labour & ors* [2020] ZACC 24 (Constitutional Court of South Africa).

[98] ibid [85–100].

[99] Shreya Atrey, 'Beyond Discrimination: Mahlangu and the Use of Intersectionality as a General Theory of Constitutional Interpretation' (2021) 21 International Journal of Discrimination and the Law 168, 172.

Universality and the weight added by categorization as a human right

The concept of universality can also describe a broad consensus around internationally recognized rights shared by most states and most 'cultures, regions and leading worldviews', resting on the generalized nature of 'the standard threats to human dignity posed by modern markets and modern states'.[100] The consensus is not absolute, and there are challenges to the legitimacy of the human rights project.[101] Even so, the moral weight added to a demand by its presentation as a human right is an important positive attribute,[102] which makes it more difficult to justify undermining or denying it in favour of business, economic or other interests,[103] allowing actors including local and transnational campaigners to 'appeal to widely endorsed international norms' that the state will often have agreed to be bound by.[104] This is important in counteracting the various explicit and implicit justifications for domestic workers' exclusion. The powerful rhetorical force in appealing to these standards was seen in the ILO process leading to the agreement of C-189.[105]

The importance of this moral counterweight also has a broader application beyond domestic workers. Neoliberal globalization (defined in Chapter 1) created severe challenges to the traditional industrial relations model at the foundation of labour law, with a strong tendency for workers' claims to be deprioritized in favour of economic interests.[106] The downward pressure exerted by this model manifests itself in increasing precarity across the labour market,[107] with the low pay and exclusion from labour rights that have long been an issue for domestic workers spreading to further sections of the workforce. For example, some of the challenges in labour rights protection in the 'gig economy' reflect the exclusions historically faced in domestic work.[108] This makes an orientation based on human rights salient to challenging exclusions that arise in other sections of the workforce—for example, through the proliferation of platform-based and other casualized forms

[100] Donnelly (n 45) 94.
[101] O'Cinneide, 'Rights Under Pressure' (n 1).
[102] Fudge, 'Labour Rights as Human Rights' (n 62) 609.
[103] Adams (n 16); Arthurs (n 53) 23; Bellace and ter Haar, 'Perspectives on Labour and Human Rights' (n 11) 12–13.
[104] Donnelly (n 45) 95.
[105] Blackett (n 70) 26. See Chapter 1.
[106] Philip Alston, 'Labour Rights as Human Rights: The Not So Happy State of the Art' in Philip Alston (ed), *Labour Rights as Human Rights* (OUP 2005) 5–8; Patrick Macklem, 'The Right to Bargain Collectively in International Law: Workers' Right, Human Right, International Right?' in Philip Alston (ed), *Labour Rights as Human Rights* (OUP 2005) 82; Sergio Gamonal C and César F Rosado Marzán, *Principled Labor Law: U.S. Labor Law through a Latin American Method* (OUP 2019) 33–34.
[107] Caffentzis (n 9) 25.
[108] Ruth Dukes, 'On Demand Work as a Legal Framework to Understand the Gig Economy' in Valerio De Stefano and others (eds), *A Research Agenda for the Gig Economy and Society* (Edward Elgar 2022).

of work.[109] Human rights thus not only have a role in repairing gaps in protection through which domestic workers have fallen, but, in addition, can potentially advance labour law protections for a wider and widening group of workers excluded from standardized employment contracts and rights. This demonstrates the central role of domestic workers' rights in the development of labour law, since the argument against their exclusion poses a challenge to a delimited view of labour law applicability that will exclude increasing numbers of workers in a deregulated economy.[110]

Universality and migrants' rights

In addition to the location of their work in the private sphere and the failure to recognize it as work, another central ground for the exclusion of many domestic workers is migration status. As noted in Chapter 2, domestic workers are frequently subject to restrictive visa regimes, with limited or no opportunities for extension or changing employer. Others—often as a result of these restrictions or a lack of available visa schemes—are in an irregular situation, lacking the correct legal authorization to remain and/or work in the host country. Both positions make it much more difficult to realize labour rights in practice, whether through collective action, individual complaints, or engagement with labour inspection bodies, meaning the exclusion should be open to challenge through the universalistic scope of human rights. The normative value that rights are owed to all humans has a clear role in challenging this ground of exclusion by critiquing the idea that rights can be contingent on citizenship.[111]

Human rights doctrine has not always lived up to universalistic principles, particularly in Europe,[112] with the ECtHR having often deferred to state sovereignty in cases involving migrants.[113] Gutiérrez Rodríguez notes how 'migration policies codify a field of exception to European universal human rights', maintaining a 'colonial logic' that separates full citizens from those at the margins.[114] This is clearly

[109] See eg Valerio De Stefano and Antonio Aloisi, 'Fundamental Labour Rights, Platform Work and Human Rights Protection of Non-Standard Workers' in Janice R Bellace and Beryl ter Haar (eds), *Research Handbook on Labour, Business and Human Rights Law* (Edward Elgar 2019); Atkinson and Sedacca (n 39).

[110] This formulation has been shaped by the comments of the first anonymous peer reviewer.

[111] Mantouvalou, 'Citizens at the Margins' (n 89) 367, 379.

[112] Graziano Battistella, 'Migration and Human Rights: The Uneasy but Essential Relationship' in Ryszard Cholewinski, Paul de Guchteneire, and Antoine Pecoud (eds), *Migration and Human Rights: The United Nations Convention on Migrant Workers' Rights* (CUP 2009) 49–50; Judy Fudge, 'Making Claims for Migrant Workers: Human Rights and Citizenship' (2014) 18 Citizenship Studies 29, 36.

[113] Marie-Bénédicte Dembour, *When Humans Become Migrants: Study of the European Court of Human Rights with an Inter-American Counterpoint* (OUP 2015) 127–28. See Chapter 8.

[114] Encarnación Gutiérrez Rodríguez, *Migration, Domestic Work and Affect: A Decolonial Approach on Value and the Feminization of Labor* (Routledge 2010) 72, 161.

a limitation from the perspective of progressing domestic workers' rights, although the ECtHR has shown a greater openness to the rights of migrants in some recent cases, where the applicants' irregular status was recognized as a vulnerability deserving of protection.[115] A universalistic understanding is more advanced in other regional systems. A 2003 IACtHR advisory opinion held that once an undocumented migrant is engaged as an employee 'they immediately become possessors of the labor rights corresponding to workers'.[116] This is highly significant as it means these rights are no longer conditional on having the correct immigration status,[117] exemplifying how a universalistic application of human rights can challenge migrant workers' exclusion from labour rights. The ACHPR contains specific protections for migrants in Article 12, while AComHPR guidelines have established that conditions of work of vulnerable and disadvantaged groups, including 'legal or illegal migrant workers', should not be inferior to those enjoyed by others.[118]

At the international level, the UN's specialist convention on migrants' rights allows for differentiation in some respects for authorized migrants versus those with irregular status, demonstrating some deference to state sovereignty.[119] Yet it still requires all migrants, including those who are irregular, to receive treatment no less favourable than nationals in relation to remuneration and key terms and conditions of work, such as hours, health and safety, and termination, and to have a right to take part in union meetings.[120] Given that only fifty-nine states in total, including one of the four case studies (Chile), have ratified this convention, this book focuses more on the generalist international treaties with higher ratification levels. These are generally expressed and interpreted in a universalistic way—for example, in the general comments of the committee monitoring ICESCR on the right to work.[121] Although not legally binding, such comments are of substantial interpretive value.[122]

[115] See eg *Siliadin v France* (2006) 43 EHRR 16. See Chapter 7.

[116] *Juridical Condition and Rights of the Undocumented Migrants, Advisory Opinion OC-18/03* IACtHR 17 September 2003, Ser A No 18 [136]; Dembour (n 113) 153–54.

[117] Virginia Mantouvalou, 'The Right to Non-Exploitative Work' in Virginia Mantouvalou (ed), *The Right to Work: Legal and Philosophical Perspectives* (Hart 2014) 57.

[118] AComHPR, 'Principles and Guidelines on the Implementation of Economic, Social and Cultural Rights in the African Charter on Human and Peoples' Rights, Adopted at the Forty-Seventh Ordinary Session Held in Banjul, the Gambia, from 12 to 26 May 2010' [59(i), 1(e)].

[119] UN General Assembly, 'International Convention on the Protection of the Rights of All Migrant Workers and Members of Their Families (Adopted 18 December 1990, Entered into Force 1 July 2003) 2000 UNTS 3'; Fudge, 'Making Claims for Migrant Workers' (n 112) 34–36.

[120] UN General Assembly (n 119) [Arts 25–26].

[121] See eg UNCESCR, 'General Comment No. 18 on the Right to Work (Art. 6 of the Covenant), 6 February 2006, E/C.12/GC/18' [12b, 18].

[122] Lottie Lane, 'The Horizontal Effect of International Human Rights Law in Practice: A Comparative Analysis of the General Comments and Jurisprudence of Selected United Nations Human Rights Treaty Monitoring Bodies' (2018) 5 European Journal of Comparative Law and Governance 5, 11.

Overall, divergences from the principles of universality are seen in some human rights mechanisms, primarily in the European region, but are not a generalized feature of the field. Although the interpretation of human rights has not always been in line with universalistic principles, this normative value remains of central importance. The way irregular migrants have mobilized on the basis of human rights shows that these rights 'are intrinsically *universalisable* in the sense of being open to being claimed by any purposive agent'.[123] When migrants make demands based on their entitlement to human rights, they utilize the contradiction between their normative coverage and practical application to challenge their exclusion.[124] This book argues in favour of deepening the inclusionary trend already seen in some jurisprudence and making it more consistent. Difficult as this may be politically in the current juncture, it is important to be clear that the partly exclusionary reading in the European context is not representative of the entire human rights field.

The scope and relevance of a human rights approach for domestic workers' inclusion

Human rights and the state—Development of the positive obligation

The development of the 'positive obligation'—the idea of human rights creating obligations on the state to regulate behaviour by private parties—is crucial in relation to the rights of workers beyond those in public sector employment. Critics of a human rights-based approach have argued that human rights are fundamentally geared towards limiting state power, and are therefore incompatible with the orientation of labour law, in which workers will often require state intervention to limit employers' actions and respond to private subordination.[125] While it is correct that the traditional remit of international human rights law has been the creation of legal obligations on states owed to those within their jurisdictions,[126] the move beyond a state-based paradigm is well-grounded in normative justifications. Amartya Sen has argued that '[d]evelopment requires the removal of major sources of unfreedom: poverty as well as tyranny, poor economic opportunities as well as systematic social deprivation, neglect of public facilities as well as intolerance or overactivity of repressive states'.[127] Developing Sen's

[123] Aitchison (n 32) 36–40.
[124] Fudge, 'Making Claims for Migrant Workers' (n 112) 41–42.
[125] See eg Kolben (n 54) 452.
[126] Robert McCorquodale and Rebecca LaForgia, 'Taking off the Blindfolds: Torture by Non-State Actors' (2001) 1 Human Rights Law Review 189, 189.
[127] Amartya Sen, *Development as Freedom* (OUP 1999) 3.

reasoning, Fredman argues for a nuanced view of freedom 'as enabling individuals to live lives that they value', including the state taking positive steps as necessary.[128]

The model of human rights advocated in this book draws on this conception, centring positive duties that are vital in applying human rights law to private employment relationships where the immediate source of rights violations is the private employer. This is already reflected to a significant degree in human rights jurisprudence. The international human rights framework requires states to 'respect, protect and fulfil' their obligations, including by active steps to ensure individuals' access to rights and through direct provision of resources where necessary.[129] The regional courts have increasingly recognized the relevance of human rights beyond state restraint by the recognition of positive duties, often referred to as 'the positive obligation' or 'due diligence'.[130] An early example is the ECtHR decision in *Marckx v Belgium* on the position of unmarried mothers, which held that the right to respect for private and family life did not only require non-interference by the state but could also entail positive obligations.[131] The concept of positive duties with regards to private actors was enunciated in the first contentious case heard by the IACtHR, *Velásquez Rodríguez v Honduras*, which arose from enforced disappearances carried out 'with the assistance or tolerance of the government'.[132] The court stressed the state's obligation to 'prevent, investigate and punish' human rights violations and held that illegal acts violating human rights, even if not directly attributable to a state, could lead to its international responsibility 'because of the lack of due diligence to prevent the violation or respond to it as required'.[133] The AComHPR has built on this approach in decisions such as *Zimbabwe Human Rights NGO Forum v Zimbabwe*.[134]

[128] Sandra Fredman, 'Poverty and Human Rights: A Peril and a Promise' in Dapo Akande and others (eds), *Human Rights and 21st Century Challenges: Poverty, Conflict, and the Environment* (OUP 2020) 224–32.

[129] UNCESCR, 'General Comment No 12 on the Right to Adequate Food (Art 11 of the Covenant), 12 May 1999, E/C.12/1999/5)' [15]; Asbjørn Eide, 'Economic, Social and Cultural Rights as Human Rights' in Asbjørn Eide, Catarina Krause, and Allan Rosas (eds), *Economic, Social and Cultural Rights: A Textbook* (2nd edn, Nijhoff 2001) 23–25.

[130] Some accounts analyse this through the concept of 'horizontal effects' of human rights, meaning their invocation in disputes between private parties, either directly when the right has a superior status (as EU law does in respect of its member states), or indirectly where it affects the court's interpretation of the right—Eleni Frantziou, 'The Horizontal Effect of Human Rights after Brexit: A Matter of Renewed Constitutional Significance' [2021] European Human Rights Law Review 365, 367–68; Lane (n 122). This book focuses instead on the 'positive obligation' pertaining to the obligation of states to regulate the relationship, including through legislative change and enforcement.

[131] *Marckx v Belgium* (1979) 2 EHRR 330 [8–19, 31].

[132] *Velásquez Rodríguez v Honduras* IACtHR 29 July 1988, Ser C No 4 [119].

[133] ibid [166, 172].

[134] *Zimbabwe Human Rights NGO Forum v Zimbabwe*—Communication No 245/02 [2006] ACHPR 73 (AComHPR) [142–64].

The positive obligation/due diligence has been central to the development of decisions on workers' rights. In *Cantoral Huamaní v Peru,* which arose from trade union leaders in the mining industry being arrested and subjected to extrajudicial execution, the IACtHR held that freedom of association gave rise to 'positive obligations, such as to prevent attacks on it, to protect those who exercise it, and investigate violence' that apply, including, where relevant, in relations between individuals.[135] Likewise, in *Wilson v UK,* the ECtHR found that the domestic legal position allowing employers to use financial incentives to persuade employees to give up their right to trade union representation amounted to a failure in the state's positive obligation to secure freedom of association.[136]

In the ECtHR, the positive obligation has also been relevant in cases relating to domestic workers. In the domestic servitude case *Siliadin v France,* the Court held that a violation of Article 4 ECHR had occurred because of the failure to provide 'practical and effective' protection through legislation requiring the 'penalisation and effective prosecution' of acts aimed at keeping an individual in slavery, servitude, or forced labour.[137] While it has been rightly noted that the positive obligation should not be overly reliant on coercive, criminal law-based duties,[138] the decision is still significant for its rejection of the way domestic courts had normalized devaluation in their attitude towards the case.[139] Elsewhere, the ECtHR has gone beyond criminalization to include other protective elements. In *Rantsev v Cyprus and Russia,* concerning a woman trafficked for sexual exploitation, it held that the 'artiste' visa scheme under which she had travelled fuelled dependency on the employer or agent, creating vulnerability to trafficking and failing to provide 'practical and effective protection'.[140] It therefore recognized how vulnerability to trafficking can stem from features of immigration law,[141] which is important in relation to restrictive visas in domestic work. These are examples of human rights law developing towards an approach that requires amendments to laws and practices that disadvantage workers, which is a promising direction for the protection of domestic workers' rights.

[135] *Cantoral Huamaní and García Santa Cruz v Peru* IACtHR 10 July 2007, Ser C No 167 [144].
[136] *Wilson v United Kingdom* (2002) 35 EHRR 523 (ECtHR) [47–48].
[137] *Siliadin v France* (n 115) [112, 148–49]. Similar findings were made in *CN v United Kingdom* (2013) 56 EHRR 24.
[138] See eg Liora Lazarus, 'Positive Obligations and Criminal Justice: Duties to Protect or Coerce?' in Lucia Zedner and Julian V Roberts (eds), *Principles and Values in Criminal Law and Criminal Justice* (OUP 2012); Laurens Lavrysen and Natasa Mavronicola (eds), *Coercive Human Rights: Positive Duties to Mobilise the Criminal Law under the ECHR* (Hart 2020).
[139] See Chapter 5.
[140] *Rantsev v Cyprus and Russia* (2010) 51 EHRR 1 [290–93].
[141] Cathryn Costello, 'Migrants and Forced Labour: A Labour Law Response' in Alan Bogg and others (eds), *The Autonomy of Labour Law* (Hart 2015) 218–19.

Human rights and the private sphere—The challenge to lack of accountability

Just as human rights law has advanced in relation to violations perpetrated by private *actors*, it has also advanced in responding to violations occurring in the private *sphere* of the home and family, as defined in Chapter 2. The early development of human rights law focused on ensuring the state did not intrude too heavily into the lives of citizens, viewing the private sphere as unsuitable for interference by the state.[142] Violence against women was not widely recognized as a human rights violation given its occurrence in private and perpetration by individuals rather than the state, and there was a failure to acknowledge its structural nature.[143] The shift that has gradually taken place in this area has necessitated a challenge to the public/private sphere divide.[144]

The 1979 Convention on the Elimination of All Forms of Discrimination against Women (CEDAW)[145] was significant for a renewed focus on women's rights, but did not specifically mention the private sphere or violence within it. A more significant change took place from the 1990s onwards, including the 1992 Recommendation of the CEDAW committee indicating that gender-based violence amounts to discrimination and violates human rights, and that states can be 'responsible for private acts if they fail to act with due diligence to prevent violations of rights or to investigate and punish acts of violence'.[146] Similar commitments were made in the 1993 UN Declaration on the Elimination of Violence against Women, and at a World Conference on Women held in Beijing in 1995.[147] The shift relied on a feminist adaptation of the IACtHR's 'due diligence' concept to understand that state failure to address violence against women in the private sphere could give rise to international responsibility, challenging the traditional understanding that such responsibility related only to state obligations in the public arena.[148] The commitment to addressing domestic violence was mirrored

[142] Ronagh JA McQuigg, 'Domestic Violence as a Human Rights Issue: Rumor v. Italy' (2015) 26 European Journal of International Law 1009, 1016.

[143] Jutta M Joachim, *Agenda Setting, the UN, and NGOs: Gender Violence and Reproductive Rights* (Georgetown University Press 2007) 122.

[144] Davidson (n 44) 117.

[145] UN, 'Convention on the Elimination of All Forms of Discrimination against Women (Adopted 18 December 1979, Entered into Force 3 September 1981) 1249 UNTS 13'.

[146] CEDAW Committee, 'General Recommendation No 19: Violence against Women—UN Doc A/47/38 (1992)' [7, 9, 24]. The human rights mentioned include the right to life, freedom from torture, inhuman and degrading treatment, liberty and security of person, equal protection under the law, health, and just and favourable conditions of work.

[147] United Nations, 'Declaration on the Elimination of All Forms of Violence against Women' (1993) A/RES/48/104, Arts 1 and 2; United Nations, 'Report of the Fourth World Conference on Women, Beijing, 4–15 September 1995' (1995) A/CONF.177/20/Rev1 [113–8].

[148] Elisabeth Jay Friedman, 'Gendering the Agenda: The Impact of the Transnational Women's Rights Movement at the UN Conferences of the 1990s' (2003) 26 Women's Studies International Forum 313, 320–1; Paulina García-Del Moral and Megan Alexandra Dersnah, 'A Feminist Challenge

in the decisions on several complaints brought to the CEDAW Committee in the early 2000s, which involved a direct challenge to the public/private sphere divide and criticism of the state party for declining to detain the perpetrator because it was seen as too invasive.[149]

Vital developments have also taken place in the regional systems. The 1994 Inter-American Convention on the Prevention, Punishment, and Eradication of Violence against Women (Convention of Belém Do Pará) confirmed that violence against women includes that occurring 'within the family or domestic unit or within any other interpersonal relationship', that all women have 'the right to be free from violence in both the public and private spheres', and that states must 'apply due diligence to prevent, investigate and impose penalties for violence against women'.[150] It thus encapsulated a feminist approach to due diligence and expressed it authoritatively through a binding legal instrument.[151] It was relied on in a 2000 IAComHR decision, *Maria da Penha v Brazil*, which held that the state's failure to prosecute the perpetrator of repeated serious domestic violence suggested state condonement of the violence, in breach of its international commitments.[152] Similar principles are found in other regional equivalents: the 2003 Maputo protocol for Africa,[153] and the 2011 Istanbul Convention for Europe.[154]

While the Istanbul Convention is more recent, the ECtHR has previously determined important cases challenging the public/private sphere divide. In *Bevacqua and S v Bulgaria* the Court criticized the state for treating domestic violence as a 'private matter', finding this 'incompatible with their positive obligations to secure the enjoyment of the applicants' Article 8 rights'.[155] It built on this development in *Opuz v Turkey*, which arose from serious violent incidents against the applicant, the killing of her mother, and major inadequacies in the proceedings against the perpetrator.[156] In finding violations of the right to life and the prohibition on torture, inhuman and degrading treatment, the ECtHR criticized the police for

to the Gendered Politics of the Public/Private Divide: On Due Diligence, Domestic Violence, and Citizenship' (2014) 18 Citizenship Studies 661, 665.

[149] Communication No: 5/2005, Goecke (deceased) v Austria (Views adopted on 6 August 2007, thirty-ninth session)—UN Doc CEDAW/C/39/D/5/2005 [12.1.5]; Communication No: 6/2005, Yildrim (deceased) v Austria (Views adopted on 61 October 2007, thirty-ninth session)—UN Doc CEDAW/C/39/D/6/2005 [12.1.5].

[150] Organization of American States, 'Inter-American Convention on the Prevention, Punishment, and Eradication of Violence against Women (Convention of Belém Do Pará) 1994', Arts 2, 3, 7.

[151] Elisabeth Jay Friedman, 'Re(Gion)Alizing Women's Human Rights in Latin America' (2009) 5 Politics & Gender 349, 361–62; Moral and Dersnah (n 148) 665–68.

[152] *Maria da Penha v Brazil,* Case No 12051, Merits Report No 54/01, IAComHR 16 April 2001 [55–56].

[153] African Union, 'The Protocol to the African Charter on Human and Peoples' Rights on the Rights of Women in Africa ('Maputo Protocol') 2003', Article 4(2).

[154] Council of Europe, 'Convention on Preventing and Combating Violence against Women and Domestic Violence ('Istanbul Convention')—CETS No 210, 2011' Art 4(1).

[155] *Bevacqua and S v Bulgaria* [2008] ECHR 498 [63, 83].

[156] *Opuz v Turkey* [2009] ECHR 870.

assuming the role of mediator, seeking to persuade victims to return to the home where they had suffered violence, reflecting the view of such matters as a 'family matter with which they cannot interfere'.[157] The observed domestic situation reflects a traditional understanding of privacy rights, with the primary objective being to refrain from disturbing the peace of the family unit, which is challenged by the finding of a violation.

Taken together, these developments at international and regional level indicate a shift. While previously human rights law had declined to provide remedies in relation to abuses taking place within the private sphere, there is now recognition that a failure by the state to prevent and punish violations can breach its positive duties. Dialogue between the two regional courts and the CEDAW committee has played a role in driving this transformation, exemplifying how a process of borrowing between judicial bodies contributes to a 'common law of human rights'.[158] For example, the court in *Opuz v Turkey* drew on CEDAW committee materials, including General Recommendation 19 and decisions on complaints, the principle of due diligence from *Velásquez Rodríguez,* the Belém do Pará Convention, and the findings in *Maria da Penha.*[159] The result is a rethinking of the public/private sphere from a human rights perspective, allowing for intervention in the interests of a party subjected to abuses within the home and family. This is important in and of itself for the challenge it poses to the problem of 'lack of accountability' for domestic workers. It also demonstrates that the potential for movement in other areas in which earlier human rights findings were inadequate, such as migrants' rights—indeed, as discussed in Chapter 7, a recent ECtHR case drew on *Opuz* to find a violation of Article 14 read with Article 4 in relation to irregular migrants.[160]

Social and economic rights and the integrated approach

The human rights model advocated in this book strongly defends the value of economic and social as well as civil and political rights, recognizing the interdependence between these categories. While some theorists argue that social and economic rights are too expensive and/or too difficult to realize, and therefore less concrete than civil and political rights and more of an ultimate goal,[161] these

[157] ibid [195].

[158] Olivier de Schutter, 'The Formation of a Common Law of Human Rights' in Emmanuelle Bribosia, Isabelle Rorive, and Ana Maria Correa (eds), *Human Rights Tectonics: Global Dynamics of Integration and Fragmentation* (Intersentia 2019) 3–5.

[159] *Opuz v Turkey* (n 156) [75–77, 83–86].

[160] *FM and others v Russia* App nos 71671/16 and 40190/18 (ECtHR, 10 December 2024).

[161] See eg Cass Sunstein, 'Against Positive Rights' (1993) 2 East European Constitutional Review 35; Onora O'Neill, *Towards Justice and Virtue: A Constructive Account of Practical Reasoning* (CUP 1996) 128–32.

assumptions are questionable in several ways.[162] The difficulties of full realization are not unique to social and economic rights, and do not justify treating them with lesser seriousness than civil liberties.[163] Relatedly, it is not possible to sharply delineate social and economic rights, as a certain degree of social protection is necessary in order to be able to enjoy civil and political rights, and it is overly simplistic to suggest that only social and economic rights are 'positive' rights requiring action or resources by the state.[164]

Since, as discussed above, stronger enforcement mechanisms primarily apply to civil and political rights, one important way to realize better protection of social and economic rights is through an 'integrated approach' to interpretation: one that combines a reading of 'certain socio-economic rights into a civil and political rights document'.[165] This approach has relevance in all the regional contexts, including the African system, despite its main instrument containing some social and economic rights.[166] For example, in the *SERAC* case regarding environmental degradation through oil spills, the AComHR 'read in' a right to housing or shelter that was not specifically provided for in the ACHPR, via existing provisions on the right to property, health, and protection of the family.[167]

The IACtHR saw an important 'turning point' in the 2009 case *Acevedo Buendía* et al *v Peru,* where it recalled the interdependence between categories of rights and referred to social and economic rights in a finding against the adoption of retrogressive steps regarding pensions.[168] Since 2017, it has developed a rich jurisprudence on workers' rights based on interpreting the requirement under Article 26 ACHR for state parties to adopt measures towards the full recognition of economic, social, educational, scientific, and cultural standards in the amended Charter of the Organization of American States.[169] This has been used to recognize, among others, rights not to be unjustly deprived of employment and

[162] Fenwick and Novitz, 'Conclusion: Regulating to Protect Workers' Human Rights' (n 43) 593.

[163] Amartya Sen, 'Elements of a Theory of Human Rights' (2004) 32 Philosophy & Public Affairs 315, 348; Stephen Marks, 'The Past and Future of the Separation of Human Rights into Categories' (2009) 24 Maryland Journal of International Law 209, 227–28.

[164] Marks (n 163) 221–34; Mantouvalou, 'In Support of Legalisation' (n 23) 98–107.

[165] Virginia Mantouvalou, 'Labour Rights in the European Convention on Human Rights: An Intellectual Justification for an Integrated Approach to Interpretation' (2013) 13 Human Rights Law Review 529, 536. An equivalent term (in Spanish) has also been used in reference to the IACtHR—Mónica Pinto, 'Los Derechos Económicos, Sociales y Culturales y Su Protección En El Sistema Universal y En El Sistema Interamericano' (2004) 40 Revista Instituto Interamericano de Derechos Humanos 26, 48.

[166] Takele Soboka Bulto (n 30).

[167] *Social and Economic Rights Action Center (SERAC) and Center for Economic and Social Rights (CESR) v Nigeria—Communication No 155/96* [2001] ACHPR 35 (AComHPR) [60].

[168] *Acevedo Buendía and others ('Discharged and Retired Employees of the Comptroller') v Perú* IACtHR 1 July 2009, Ser C No 210 [100–103]; Seatzu and de Torres (n 26) 147.

[169] OAS, 'Charter of the Organization of American States, 119 UNTS 3, Amended by Protocol of Buenos Aires, 721 UNTS 324, O.A.S. Treaty Series, No. 1-A, Entered into Force Feb. 27, 1970'; Julieta Lobato, 'Toward a Consolidated Case Law on Labour Rights in the Inter-American Human Rights System: The Case FEMAPOR and the Right to a Fair Remuneration' (2023) 9 International Labor Rights Case Law 252.

to equitable workplace conditions.[170] Furthermore, the IACtHR's recent Advisory Opinion on the right to care confirmed the application of these standards to care workers, including domestic workers.[171] The IACtHR's approach is promising for the protection of workers' rights, with examples discussed throughout the book, although it is not directly replicable in other regional contexts that lack an equivalent mechanism to Article 26.

Nonetheless, the ECtHR's jurisprudence also increasingly recognizes the social and economic aspects of claims brought under the Convention. Since 2002, it has shown greater willingness to take into account materials from the ILO and the ECSR when formulating judgments.[172] This is reflected in several union freedom of association cases such as *Wilson v United Kingdom*,[173] *Demir & Baykara*,[174] and *Enerji Yapi-Yol Sen*.[175] The integrated approach has also been used to apply social rights to individuals, particularly in *Sidabras v Lithuania* where the Court 'read in' a right to work by holding that a ban on former KGB agents accessing work in several areas of the private sector had an impact on 'the enjoyment of their respect for their 'private life' within the meaning of Article 8.[176] The ECtHR has retreated from an integrated approach in some subsequent cases, such as in *RMT v UK*, where it declined to consider whether the state complied with relevant standards of the ILO or the ESC with regards to collective action.[177] This book's approach is based on extending the recognition of social and economic rights that has been seen, at least to some degree, within all three regional human rights systems, and examining its salience for domestic workers' protection.

Conclusion

This chapter has explored the value of a human rights-based approach for progressing domestic workers' inclusion. I have argued that labour law and human rights have a shared orientation to addressing abuses and imbalances of power and traced the overlap between these areas, as well as the more holistic approaches to categories of rights, to the post-war context. I contended that an individualistic and

[170] *Lagos del Campo v Perú* IACtHR 31 August 2017, Ser C No 366 [141–8]; *Spoltore v Argentina* IACtHR 9 June 2020, Ser C No 404.

[171] *The Content and Scope of the Right to Care and Its Interrelationship with Other Rights—Advisory Opinion OC-31/25* IACtHR 12 June 2025, Ser A No 31 [219–226]. These paragraphs address the rights of paid carers, while the rights of unpaid carers are set out in [227–31].

[172] Mantouvalou, 'Is There a Human Right Not to Be a Trade Union Member?' (n 49) 442.

[173] *Wilson v UK* (n 136) [48].

[174] *Demir and Baykara v Turkey* (n 50).

[175] *Enerji Yapi-Yol Sen v Turkey* (n 51).

[176] *Sidabras and Dziautas v Lithuania* [2004] ECHR 395 [50]; Virginia Mantouvalou, 'Work and Private Life: Sidabras and Dziautas v Lithuania' (2005) 30 European Law Review 573.

[177] *RMT v UK* (n 52) [106]; Alan Bogg and KD Ewing, 'The Implications of the RMT Case' (2014) 43 Industrial Law Journal 221; de Schutter (n 158) 28–30.

restraints-based approach is neither the only way to understand human rights normatively, nor uniformly reflected in jurisprudence. Strong divergences are seen in the African regional system with its collective 'People's Rights' and the influence of indigenous thinking on the IACtHR's jurisprudence. Although not as consistently, the ECtHR has in some cases moved towards an approach that is more accommodating of collective interests. Regarding other critiques of human rights from a labour law perspective, I argued against overstating the apparent opposition between human rights and agency, noting the importance of individuals claiming rights as part of movements for improved conditions and regulations. Rather than imposing a set notion of what agency means from traditional industrial workplaces, understandings in the domestic work context should be more expansive and recognize the need for a protective framework that provides basic rights to facilitate self-organization. Furthermore, human rights are not only relevant to extreme forms of abuse but can also address more routine and structural matters like excessive working hours and a lack of opportunity to change employer.

Domestic workers have routinely been excluded from the protection of labour law by virtue of factors including the designation of their work as part of the 'private sphere' and therefore distinct from 'real work', and because of harsh visa regimes and the lack of rights afforded to migrant workers. The principle of universality is foundational to human rights law and is normatively significant for countering these exclusions of domestic workers from labour law's protection. An intersectional understanding of human rights is fundamental in addressing the tension between these universalistic values and the particularity of domestic workers' exclusion, as demonstrated in the *Mahlangu* case, while the inclusionary approach to the rights of irregular migrants in the IACtHR should be broadened. As identified in the final section, several developments in human rights law are pertinent to the exclusion of domestic workers: the positive obligation, which creates requirements on the state to prevent and punish rights-violating behaviour by private bodies; developments in addressing violence against women that have countered the idea of the private sphere as immune from scrutiny; and an 'integrated approach' to interpretation allowing for more enforceable civil and political rights instruments to be interpreted in a manner that protects social and economic interests.

These discussions create the foundation for the approach to human rights on which the analysis throughout this book is based: one that centres positive obligations as well as state restraint, gives proper weight to social and economic as well as civil and political rights, draws on feminist critique of the traditional lack of scrutiny of the private sphere, and holds to universalistic principles on the rights of marginalized groups including migrants. This framing is key to addressing the ongoing gaps in protection for domestic workers, both as an alternative justification where C-189 has not been ratified, and regarding discrepancies in entitlements and gaps in enforcement that remain where it has been. In the remaining chapters, I will use this understanding to elaborate human rights protections relevant to specific areas of exclusion affecting domestic workers.

PART 2

MANIFESTATIONS OF EXCLUSION AND THE HUMAN RIGHTS CHALLENGE

4

Labour in a private home

Enforcement, privacy, and human rights

Introduction

Working and often living in an employer's home, domestic workers face a range of violations, from a lack of privacy in accommodation and inadequate food, through risks to health and safety and susceptibility to abuse, violence, and harassment. This chapter examines the gap that often exists between the 'formal legal entitlements' of domestic workers and the treatment they receive in practice,[1] and its link to limitations in enforcement mechanisms. It is the first of the five issue-based chapters that draw in detail on my empirical research, citing interviews by the speaker's name or pseudonym,[2] and using this to critically analyse the impacts of the exclusion of private homes from labour inspection on workers' conditions and health and safety. Against this background, the chapter examines widespread justifications for excluding homes from inspection, which relate to conceptualization of the home as a private space that is not subject to ordinary regulation—a central example of the idea of 'lack of accountability' in the private sphere. Contrary to a conception of privacy that centres only on the employer's interest, I argue for an understanding that a home employing a domestic worker becomes a hybrid space where some degree of oversight must be expected. I support this view by reference to human rights provisions on the right to decent work, as well as the prohibition on forced labour, which requires a proactive and preventative approach. I then explore the implications of the right to private and family life, arguing that the protection of domestic workers' rights can amount to a 'legitimate aim' for some intrusion into privacy provided that any interference is carefully circumscribed.

[1] ILO, 'Report IV(1)—Decent Work for Domestic Workers—99th Session of the International Labour Conference' (2010) 89.

[2] For those cited by name, I give the full name on the first mention, followed by surname only for subsequent citations. The Appendix provides a list of all interviewees by name or pseudonym, and Chapter 1 provides background on the empirical work.

Human Rights and the Protection of Domestic Workers in Labour and Migration Law. Natalie Sedacca, Oxford University Press. © Oxford University Press 2026. DOI: 10.1093/9780198985266.003.0006

Overview of provisions on enforcement and inspection

Domestic workers' exclusion from enforcement measures is pronounced in the UK. The Health and Safety at Work Act 1974, s.51,[3] exempts those employed 'as a domestic servant in a private household' from its scope, including its provisions on inspections. Guidance from the Health and Safety Executive indicates that the term 'domestic servant' applies where a domestic worker is 'employed directly by the householder' and suggests several factors to help ascertain whether this is the case, such as having a contract with and being paid directly with the householder.[4] In EU labour law, a key directive on health and safety at work defines a worker as 'any person employed by an employer, including trainees and apprentices *but excluding domestic servants*'.[5] Other individual EU health and safety directives do not give any specific definition of workers, and it has therefore been widely assumed that they also exclude domestic workers.[6] While there is a convincing argument that this exclusion should be reconsidered since it is incompatible with the Court of Justice of the European Union's idea of health and safety as 'intrinsically linked to workers' dignity',[7] it remains the current position.

In the UK, domestic workers employed by households thus remain excluded from general inspection provisions. In interview, Avril Sharp of domestic worker NGO Kalayaan mentioned that the Gangmasters and Labour Abuse Authority (GLAA)—a public body that investigates reports of labour exploitation, human trafficking, and other offences—had stated that domestic workers were within their remit, potentially suggesting the development of an inspection process separate to the type excluded under health and safety legislation. However, Sharp went on to say that she did not think the GLAA were 'proactively developing any sort of procedure ... to ... conduct labour checks' in the way they did for other sectors, nor that many domestic workers had heard of the GLAA. This stands to reason, as the GLAA's remit only extends to inspection of licensed businesses, those operating without a licence, or 'circumstances where there is a risk of worker exploitation or other illegal activity'.[8] At most, this means they would inspect where worker exploitation is already alleged, rather than carrying out random or routine checks—but in any event, I am not aware of instances of the GLAA inspecting homes employing domestic workers. In addition, reflecting the government's 'hostile

[3] Applicable in England, Scotland, and Wales.

[4] Health and Safety Executive, 'Domestic Work' (*hse.gov.uk*, undated) <https://www.hse.gov.uk/domestic-work/> accessed 25 August 2025.

[5] Council Directive (EC) 89/391 on the introduction of measures to encourage improvements in the safety and health of workers at work [1989] OJ L 183 1989, Art 3(1). Emphasis added.

[6] Lisa Rodgers, *Labour Law, Vulnerability and the Regulation of Precarious Work* (Edward Elgar 2016) 180–81.

[7] Vera Pavlou, *Migrant Domestic Workers in Europe: Law and the Construction of Vulnerability* (Hart 2021) 109–11.

[8] GLAA, 'How We Inspect and Prosecute' (undated) <https://www.gla.gov.uk/our-impact/how-we-inspect-and-prosecute/> accessed 26 August 2025.

environment' policies, the GLAA has often sent reports on migrant workers' status to immigration enforcement.[9] Therefore, if such inspections were to take place, they could amount to a danger to workers with insecure immigration status.[10]

The UK has also failed to implement other measures that could assist enforcement of labour rights, including basic awareness-raising. In 2015, a government-commissioned independent review recommended commencing information meetings where domestic workers would be informed about their rights, noting that it was deeply unsatisfactory to rely on 'workers accessing information by making voluntary contact with any outside individual or organisation' given limitations on permission to leave the workplace and on access to phones and the internet.[11] The government has not implemented these meetings, meaning domestic workers are frequently left with inadequate information.[12] Of the twenty-one workers I interviewed, only two reported knowing where to get advice and assistance on their situation in the UK when they decided to escape.[13] On fleeing their employers, nine workers received assistance either from strangers they met in the street or from community members they did not know before leaving, while others made contacts in person or online before escaping or already knew people in the UK.[14] Conversely, the one worker who reported having received the information leaflet—'Juliana', who was on her second visit to the UK—said 'this is the leaflet that saved me' as it directed her to Kalayaan. The lack of enforcement through either inspection or basic awareness-raising measures in the UK generally leaves domestic workers with two extreme options: either withstand the situation or take the risk of escaping.

In India, since the household is not viewed as a workplace, it is not subject to provisions on labour inspection.[15] The Occupational Safety, Health and Working Conditions Code of 2020 defines 'industry' so as to exclude domestic workers from its provisions on health, safety, and conditions such as working hours.[16] The domestic worker's place of work therefore continues to be viewed as a private site and

[9] Labour Exploitation Advisory Group, 'Opportunity Knocks: Improving Responses to Labour Exploitation with Secure Reporting' (Focus on Labour Exploitation 2020) 36.

[10] See Chapter 7.

[11] James Ewins, 'Independent Review of the Overseas Domestic Worker Visa' (2015) 6, 36 <https://assets.publishing.service.gov.uk/media/5a806ecee5274a2e87db9c85/ODWV_Review_-_Final_Report__6_11_15_.pdf> accessed 17 July 2025.

[12] Avril Sharp, '12 Years of Modern Slavery: The Smokescreen Used to Deflect State Accountability for Migrant Domestic Workers' (Kalayaan 2024) 15–22.

[13] Natalie Sedacca and Avril Sharp, 'Dignity, Not Destitution: The Impact of Differential Rights of Work for Migrant Domestic Workers Referred to the National Referral Mechanism' (Kalayaan 2019) 17.

[14] ibid 18.

[15] Amrita Ghatak and Kingshuk Sarkar, 'Status of Domestic Workers in India: A Tale of Two Cities' (2022) 65 Indian Journal of Labour Economics 863, 864.

[16] With the exception of homes employing ten or more workers—The Occupational Safety, Health and Working Conditions Code— No 37 of 2020, s2(p)(ii)(iii); Shardha Rajam and Prabha Kotiswaran, 'Justice within the New Factory Gates: How to Hold RWAs Responsible for Workers' Welfare' (2025) 21 International Journal of Law in Context 176, 187. The Codes are pending implementation at the time of writing—see Chapter 2.

their labour as 'an informal voluntary arrangement'.[17] Even in most states that have made some labour laws such as the minimum wage applicable to domestic workers, enforcement continues to be problematic in the absence of a clear provision for inspection of the household or acceptance that it amounts to a workplace.[18] Limited exceptions have been noted in Rajasthan and Bihar states, but even here, labour department officials have taken the position that they could not investigate issues without receiving complaints.[19] Against this background, interview participants described a complete lack of inspection. For example, 'Meera' stated that inspection had been a 'demand by trade unions to a very, very large extent' but she did not think it was really instituted 'in formal terms'. Nalini Nayak of the Self-Employed Women's Association (SEWA) linked the issue to a lack of legislation, stating that 'as long as there's no legislation inspection doesn't apply at all', while Aditi Yajnik of SEWA further noted that the new Labour Code on health and safety had 'left out' domestic workers.[20] This suggests that, similarly to the UK, inspection mechanisms for domestic work in India are almost entirely lacking.

Interestingly, however, domestic work has been included within legislation from 2013 on sexual harassment, which sets out the employer's duty to provide a safe working environment and provides for complaint mechanisms, including local complaints committees for workplaces with fewer than ten workers.[21] Interviewees 'Meera', Supurna Banerjee, Samita Sen, and 'Gita' noted the significance of this inclusion for recognizing the household as a workplace. 'Gita' explained that, while many cases do not use the formal legal mechanisms and there is a reluctance to pursue claims because of the effect on the worker's reputation as 'difficult', the inclusion had been useful 'in that there is a language around it' and police and lawyers were more responsive to allegations. Yet several interviewees also noted limitations, including deficiencies in resourcing and a lack of awareness among workers. 'Meera' attributed many of these issues to the pandemic, noting that after 'really important work' done previously:

> with the Covid pandemic coming around, the momentum that had been built on the formation of these committees was ... lost ... a lot of women's organizations ... have observed ... that there are really no funds available to make these [local committees] work.

[17] Ghatak and Sarkar (n 15) 874.

[18] ibid 867.

[19] N Neetha, 'Minimum Wages for Domestic Work: Mirroring Devalued Housework' (2013) 48 Economic and Political Weekly 77, 83.

[20] See also Adwitiya Mishra and Aasheerwad Dwivedi, 'Labour Laws in India: History, Evolution and Critical Analysis' [2023] Labor History 1, 15.

[21] The Sexual Harassment of Women at Workplace (Prevention, Prohibition and Redressal) Act—Act No 14 of 2013 ss2(e) and (g), 19, 6. In practice, the local complaints committees have not always been set up—N Neetha, 'Misconstrued Notions and Misplaced Interventions: An Assessment of State Policy on Domestic Work in India' (2021) 64 Indian Journal of Labour Economics 543, 549.

By contrast to the UK and India, Chile is notable for having introduced a mechanism for 'inspection without entry to the home'. When a request is made to the employer in relation to domestic workers' labour conditions, they have a choice 'to accept their entry to the home or request the fixing of another date and time to attend the offices of the Labour Inspectorate with the required documentation'.[22] This is a favourable comparison to the countries lacking inspection. Yet the mechanism has limitations, most notably the lack of a power of entry to the home unless the employer permits this, reflecting the ongoing influence of the idea of the home as a private space rather than a workplace. My research also revealed a constraint on how the existing powers are utilized, with the vast majority of inspections regarding domestic work being driven by complaints rather than occurring randomly. According to José Francisco Castro in the Labour Ministry, whereas in other sectors, 'the relationship is approximately 70% of inspection by complaint at the national level, 30% by programme [i.e. random]', for domestic work 'inspection is basically by complaint', meaning few random inspections take place. Of the domestic workers interviewed, a couple reported using a complaints procedure, but none said they had been subject to a random inspection. As explained by worker 'Valentina': 'of course when they secured the laws ... they'd said that inspectors would come, but ... there's never an inspection'.

Several worker interviewees stressed the importance of providing information about rights. 'Josefa' mentioned the union's workshops about the 2015 reforms, while 'Romina' stated that 'the union for me is the best school to learn' about rights and how to respond to employers. Workers' accounts also showed the union's role as a social and accommodation space on free days and during periods of unemployment. The migrant rights organization where 'Catalina' was the coordinator played a similar role both in a recreational sense and for out-of-work periods. For example, 'Sara' explained that while she was not working, she was in the organization's building as it was a shelter house for migrants: 'I receive assistance, here they accommodate us ... and we feel like we're at home.' This role is significant since the difficulty of finding accommodation may otherwise disincentivize live-in domestic workers from leaving a job even if conditions are poor.

As explained by David Oddó Beas, head of the Juridical Department of the Labour Ministry, there are two mechanisms for dealing with concerns raised by a worker: a '*denuncia*' (complaint) relates to an issue that could end up in front of a court, such as (sexual) harassment or anti-union practices, whereas a '*reclamo*' (claim) is something simpler. Based on responses from some other interviewees, such as 'Catalina' and academic 'Rocío', the system for dealing with complaints

[22] Código del Trabajo—Edición actualizada al 8 de agosto de 2025 ('Labour Code—Chile 2025'), Art 146ter.

appeared to be reasonably effective.[23] Yet this procedure is only engaged where a worker makes an initial complaint, which amounts to a key limitation. As Ruth Olate, then secretary of the union SINTRACAP,[24] explained, it can be difficult for workers to proactively complain, as 'they can have anxiety' about attending the relevant office. In addition, a worker who complains may lose the chance for a reference—noted by 'Rocio' and exemplified by the domestic worker 'Isabella', who had made a complaint about one previous employer and had a dispute over wages with another, and said she now never received calls for jobs she applied for.

Having an inspection that is only or primarily complaints-led poses particular obstacles for migrant domestic workers, who often have difficulty accessing information about their rights.[25] Interviewees observed that the system could be challenging to access for migrant workers, who might not be familiar with cultural codes, and that this could be related to a recent decline in the number of complaints and claims.[26] This underscores the importance of random inspections in addition to complaints-led ones. As 'Nancy', Director of a university law clinic on migration, explained, the lack of active enforcement on the part of the state contributes to 'a super precarious situation for migrant women'.

Another potential issue for migrants without secure status is the fear that making a complaint or being subject to an inspection could be used against them. Castro said that domestic workers might be reluctant to complain if they 'have some migratory problem', but stressed that the Labour Department would not actually pass on information about it, because:

> the employer should comply with labour norms independently of the migratory situation of this worker ... even if they're in an irregular situation, the employer will be sanctioned, and that information stays inside the labour department and is not passed to the foreign office ... Because if one did that, there would be fewer complaints... from migrant workers.

He thus indicated that a 'firewall' existed between labour inspection and immigration. While some interviewees expressed doubt about whether this firewall was absolute,[27] none definitively stated that material would be passed between departments. The apparent existence of a firewall is positive in meaning that migrant workers can potentially complain even if their status is insecure.

[23] See further Cesar F Rosado Marzán, 'Of Labor Inspectors and Judges: Chilean Labor Law Enforcement after Pinochet (and What the United States Can Do to Help) Competition in the Global Workplace: The Role of Law in Economic Markets' [2009] Saint Louis University Law Journal 497.

[24] 'Sindicato de Trabajadoras de Casa Particular'—'union of (female) workers in private homes'. Olate sadly passed away in October 2024.

[25] Luis Eduardo Thayer Correa and Carlos Salvatore Durán Migliardi, 'Gobierno local y migrantes frente a frente: nudos críticos y políticas para el reconocimiento' [2015] Revista de CLAD 127, 144.

[26] Beas and 'Daniela'.

[27] 'Nancy' and 'Rocío' both alluded to the possibility of an information flow.

The position in South Africa is similarly one where inspection exists to some degree in the sector but has limitations. Several constitutional provisions provide a basis for enforcing domestic workers' rights: the rights to fair labour practices (which implies the need for enforcement mechanisms), to lawful, reasonable, and procedurally fair administrative action, and on access to the courts.[28] Effecting these rights, legislation empowers labour inspectors to 'promote, monitor and enforce compliance with an employment law' through measures including advice on rights and obligations, conducting inspections, and investigating complaints.[29] While inspectors can enter workplaces that are not homes 'without warrant or notice, at any reasonable time', they may only enter a home either with the owner/occupier's consent, or with written authorization from a labour court.[30] The Department of Labour views these limits as creating significant obstacles to regulation of domestic work, with employers often refusing entry to inspectors and even threatening their safety.[31] Echoing the concern about employer hostility and linking this to the racialization of domestic work, Yongeza Mbimbi from the Socio-Economic Rights Institute of South Africa (SERI) related an incident where the police were called after a white male employer assaulted a domestic worker and noted that 'the cops couldn't enter that house, you know, they were almost like powerless', going on to stress the difficulty of entering 'where the employers are ... in affluent spaces, and white'.

Some interviewees emphasized the need for a more proactive approach to inspections. Amy Tekié of IZWI Domestic Workers' Alliance noted that despite laws that are 'much better than in a lot of other countries', their impact was hindered because there was 'very little enforcement unless the domestic worker is the one that takes the step'. Thando George from SERI suggested that, once a domestic worker is registered for social security,

> perhaps a preliminary inspection... should be done just to ensure that the home is safe... that... a person is not risking their lives because they want to earn a living.

At the same time, resourcing was highlighted as a key challenge, both across the board and particularly for inspecting individual households.[32] Other interviewees viewed physical inspection as less important and suggested a focus on alternative measures. For example, Jane Barrett stated that while it might be necessary to

[28] The Constitution of the Republic of South Africa 1996, ss23(1), 33, 34; Pamhidzai Bamu, 'Nurturing a Culture of Compliance with Domestic Workers' Rights in South Africa' in Darcy Du Toit (ed), *Exploited, Undervalued and Essential: Domestic Workers and the Realisation of Their Rights* (Pretoria University Law Press 2013) 163.

[29] Basic Conditions of Employment Act—Act No 75 of 1997 (South Africa) ('BCEA'), s64.

[30] ibid, s65.

[31] Department of Labour, 'Adequacy of Resources for Effective Inspections to Be Conducted within the South African Labour Market' (Republic of South Africa 2017) 112.

[32] Barrett, Abigail Osiki, Fairuz Mullagee, and Mbimbi.

inspect physical conditions in 'extreme cases', it would more often be relevant to focus on questions like the monthly provision of pay slips.

Several interviewees pointed to the salience of the Commission on Conciliation, Mediation and Arbitration (CCMA), a dispute resolution mechanism aimed at improving accessibility for low-waged workers.[33] Marlese von Broembsen noted the advantage that the CCMA did not require legal representation, meaning workers are 'not disempowered like they are ... in a court', while Tekié pointed to its advantages for irregular migrants since it generally (with some exceptions) would not take an interest in a worker's migration status.[34] By contrast, she noted that 'we sometimes can't take cases to Department of Labour because they do work with Home Affairs, and we don't want to put the person's status in South Africa at risk'. This creates a significant limitation for irregular migrants, alongside the other issues of restricted inspection powers, lack of resources, and employer hostility.

Health, safety, and protection from violence and harassment

Contrary to 'the view of the domestic work environment as a "safe haven"', workers in reality face many risks to health and safety, which are exacerbated for those who live with their employers in accommodation which is 'unsuitable and unsafe'.[35] Lack of enforcement of labour rights leaves these situations unchallenged. A 2015 UK study noted some domestic workers having to share hotel rooms with their employers or sleep on the bathroom floor, alongside other serious labour abuses.[36] In my UK research, when workers were asked about reasons for leaving their original employer, there were reports of psychological abuse in thirteen cases, lack of food and drink in thirteen, lack of sleep and or rest breaks for twelve, physical abuse in eight, and being forced to work excessive hours in seven,[37] among other issues. 'Amy' gives an example of poor living conditions:[38]

> my salary is always delayed... I always begging her to give my salary, and I just sleeping in the floor of the living room, and I don't have a day off.

[33] Adelle Blackett and Thierry Galani Tiemeni, 'Regulatory Innovation in the Governance of Decent Work for Domestic Workers in South Africa: Access to Justice and the Commission on Conciliation, Mediation and Arbitration' (2018) 34 International Journal of Comparative Labour Law and Industrial Relations 203, 206.

[34] See Chapter 7.

[35] Rodgers (n 6) 181.

[36] Virginia Mantouvalou, '"Am I Free Now?" Overseas Domestic Workers in Slavery' (2015) 42 Journal of Law and Society 329, 344.

[37] Sedacca and Sharp (n 13) 17.

[38] Filipina domestic workers who chose to be interviewed in English rather than through a Tagalog interpreter sometimes made minor linguistic mistakes, which have been left in the quotations to reflect their original words.

Analogous issues arise in the South African context. A recent study involving interviews with over 100 workers found that a lack of privacy provisions, such as a requirement for a locked door on the worker's accommodation, can enable sexual harassment.[39] Alongside four direct accounts of sexual harassment, including a woman who was raped by her employer and infected with HIV, and two of being physically hurt, twenty-seven respondents had experienced shouting or foul language, and thirteen reported hearing clearly racist language.[40] My interviews further highlighted the issue of poor quality accommodation and safety risks for live-in domestic workers, with Mbimbi noting that, without regulation, these issues 'become entirely dependent on the will of the employers' and wrongly viewed as a matter of 'kindness' rather than of right. Interviewees mentioned examples from their organizations' work including 'a woman sleeping on a very, very thin mattress on the floor next to the car, like a metre away from the tyre of the car in the garage'[41] and workers living in a space that could only fit a double bed, leaving 'no demarcation between cooking space, sleeping space', being forced to sleep with a dog despite being scared of it, and getting dog bite injuries at work.[42]

A distinctive set of concerns about accommodation and working space arises in India, where domestic workers are often not permitted to use the same toilets as their employers, sit at the same tables, or share utensils—issues that are often understood as relating to caste hierarchy.[43] This causes pronounced problems where employers live in large housing blocks, as Anchita Ghatak explained:

> [M]any of these apartment buildings will probably have one or two toilets for staff, you know, like domestic workers, drivers, gardeners ... so they have to go wherever this other toilet is, which is usually in the basement or somewhere downstairs ... And if they have to go at night, what are the precautions? What kind of safety can they expect?

Praveena Kodoth noted how inspection would specifically help in this regard as a 'deterrent measure' that 'would really make employers think twice about the way they treat their domestic workers' by requiring them to show the provision of toilet access and decent living facilities. Banerjee similarly stressed how these points became a matter of employer goodwill rather than being recognized as health and safety measures in the absence of regulation, and linked susceptibility to verbal abuse and sexual harassment to 'that understanding that there is a certain invisibility of the workplace'.

[39] Solidarity Centre and IZWI, 'The Persistence of Private Power: Sacrificing Rights for Wages' (2021) 15.
[40] ibid 40–41.
[41] Tekié.
[42] George.
[43] Yajnik, Samita Sen.

Health and safety became even more of a concern during the Covid-19 pandemic, with workers susceptible to contracting the virus from employers returning from trips abroad, while also frequently lacking access to affordable healthcare.[44] At the same time, many felt compelled to conceal indications of the virus while at work, since employers' fears of infection often dovetailed with conceptions of domestic workers as 'dirty' and 'dangerous' outsiders.[45] The pandemic thus exacerbated pre-existing concerns related to questions of class and caste, with an intensification of avoidance measures based on social distancing, and some workers asked not to return at all.[46] Employers often required domestic workers to take protective measures, such as wearing masks and changing clothes, without doing the same themselves, with union representatives having to intervene on matters such as provision of soap and compliance with social distancing practices.[47] In interview, Banerjee highlighted the compulsion for some previously live-out domestic workers to stay with their employers, which 'made them especially precarious to, to health and safety problems'. Ghatak noted that some employers were open to helping domestic workers with buying sanitizers and masks, but this was 'unregulated' and 'very much dependent on what the employer feels she should provide and what the domestic worker is able to demand'.

Although magnified by notions of caste in India, in many respects these issues were mirrored across other countries. A report on the impacts in Latin America noted that domestic workers were exposed to the virus while commuting (where not living with their employers) and at the workplace, where employers failed to implement protective measures.[48] Despite needing to be in physical contact with others at work, many were not provided with adequate PPE, and testing has not always been available, even for those suffering Covid-19 symptoms.[49] In Chile, the first lockdowns took place in affluent areas where many domestic workers are employed; as they were denoted 'non-essential', many who usually worked on a live-out basis came under pressure to move in with their employers, sometimes leaving them unable to care for their own families.[50] Likewise in South Africa, many domestic workers who had been commuting to work were expected to 'lock down'

[44] Supurna Banerjee and Lauren Wilks, 'Work in Pandemic Times: Exploring Precarious Continuities in Paid Domestic Work in India' [2022] Gender, Work, and Organization 8.

[45] ibid 9.

[46] ibid 13–14.

[47] Srijani Datta and others, 'Domestic Workers from Margin to Center: Protest, Opportunity and Threat in Pandemic Politics' (2022) 26 Journal for Cultural Research 39, 56–57.

[48] Louisa Acciari, Juana del Carmen Britez, and Andrea del Carmen Morales Pérez, 'Right to Health, Right to Live: Domestic Workers Facing the COVID-19 Crisis in Latin America' (2021) 29 Gender and Development 11, 24; María Elena Valenzuela and Adriana Paz Ramírez, 'Strong and United: Facing up to the Pandemic' (IDWFED 2021) 6 ; ILO, 'Making Decent Work a Reality for Domestic Workers: Progress and Prospects Ten Years after the Adoption of the Domestic Workers Convention, 2011 (No 189)' (ILO 2021) 230.

[49] Acciari, del Carmen Britez, and del Carmen Morales Pérez (n 48) 24.

[50] Valenzuela and Paz Ramírez (n 48) 7; Acciari, del Carmen Britez, and del Carmen Morales Pérez (n 48) 19.

with their employers in March 2020, often sleeping in improvised spaces, with many reporting being unable to seek necessary medical treatment.[51] There was also a problem of double standards between workers and employers, with Fairuz Mullagee explaining that live-in domestic workers:

> weren't allowed to go home and see their families … as a worker, you could be infected by your employer's family, who come and go as they please, but you are expected to not infect the employers household…

In the UK, some live-in domestic workers reported being confined to their employers' homes and forbidden from leaving during lockdown.[52] Marisa Begonia, head of the Voice of Domestic Workers (a support network and campaign organization), reported dangers to health posed by a lack of protective equipment, with some workers making their own equipment from bin bags.[53] These problems were exacerbated by some employers' non-compliance with social distancing measures, such as reported examples of mass gatherings at times when these were banned, leading to workers being infected with Covid-19.[54]

These various examples exemplify how the right to health and decent work became 'a fight to stay alive' during the Covid-19 pandemic.[55] The control exercised over domestic workers during the pandemic, alongside disregard for their health and safety, both mirrored and enhanced pre-existing vulnerabilities. The general lack of regulation of work taking place in a private home became more dangerous in the pandemic context, leaving domestic workers dependent on the goodwill of employers to provide them with safe conditions and adequate PPE, and to follow social distancing guidelines. Having examined the safety issues that arise where inspection is lacking or constrained, I now turn to the link between these limitations and the 'lack of accountability' in the private sphere.

Privacy, limitations on enforcement, and lack of accountability

The argument for excluding domestic workers from inspection and other health and safety measures reflects the idea of family homes as subject to a lower degree of

[51] Solidarity Centre and IZWI (n 39) 30.

[52] Katherine Hearst, '"Like I'm in a Cage": Domestic Workers Trapped and Abused in Lockdown London | Middle East Eye' (14 June 2020) <https://bit.ly/3eQoPvR> accessed 25 August 2025.

[53] Amy Charlesworth, 'Locked In: The (In)Visibility of Migrant Domestic Workers during Covid-19' (*The Open University—Migrant Art Archive*, undated) <https://university.open.ac.uk/research-projects/migrant-art-archive/research/locked-in-the-invisibility-of-migrant-domestic-workers-during-covid-19> accessed 25 August 2025.

[54] May Bulman, 'The Domestic Workers Trapped in Homes Where Their Wealthy Employers Flout Lockdown Rules' (*The Independent*, 2 March 2021) <https://www.independent.co.uk/news/uk/home-news/domestic-workers-lockdown-rules-coronavirus-b1802525.html> accessed 25 August 2025.

[55] Acciari, del Carmen Britez, and del Carmen Morales Pérez (n 48) 26.

scrutiny than public workplaces. Rather than being neutral or respecting privacy in general, this reinforces a situation where domestic workers face poor or even abusive conditions without consequence. In some contexts, this is linked explicitly to constitutional ideas of privacy as applied to the employer's home, while in others it relates to a broader exclusion of domestic labour from categorization as 'real work'.

The desire to avoid labour inspection of homes employing domestic workers was a key reason for the UK government's refusal to support C-189.[56] In seeking to justify abstaining from a vote in ILO proceedings, the UK representative cited C-189's supposedly inflexible requirements, stating that it was not considered 'appropriate or practical to extend criminal, health and safety laws, including inspections, to private households employing domestic workers'.[57] During a subsequent parliamentary debate, a Minister argued that ratification would 'place a serious regulatory burden on individuals', creating a fear of liability and disincentivizing private employment of domestic workers, thus potentially forcing people into residential care.[58] Here, the argument goes further than the strict privacy point to suggest an exemption from regulatory frameworks is necessary to protect the rights of employers. Support for the choice to remain in one's own home is a relevant human rights consideration in relation to some but not all domestic workers, primarily those whose role includes caring for disabled or elderly persons.[59] However, this cannot justify an approach of underfunding care work provision while relying on the provision of services by workers whose own rights are violated in the process.[60]

In Chile, where measures for awareness-raising and dealing with complaints are more advanced, the remaining limitations regarding entry powers reflect the ongoing influence of the idea of the home as a private space rather than a workplace,[61] which relates to provisions on privacy and inviolability of the home.[62] Limits on inspection in South Africa are also related to privacy rights. S14 of the Constitution protects the right to privacy, including the right not to have one's person, home, or property searched, possessions seized, or privacy of communications infringed. However, the right has been interpreted in a nuanced way, with the Constitutional Court holding that the physical understanding of privacy needs to be considered

[56] Siobhán Mullally and Cliodhna Murphy, 'Migrant Domestic Workers in the UK: Enacting Exclusions, Exemptions, and Rights' (2014) 36 Human Rights Quarterly 397, 415.

[57] Quoted by Fiona Mactaggart, HC Deb 29 June 2011, vol 530, col 269.

[58] Edward Davey, HC Deb 29 June 2011, vol 530, col 290–91.

[59] United Nations, 'Convention on the Rights of Persons with Disabilities (Adopted 13 December 2006, Entered into Force 3 May 2008) 1249 UNTS 13', Art 19; Rosa Kornfeld-Matte, 'Report of the Independent Expert on the Enjoyment of All Human Rights by Older Persons—A/HRC/30/43' (UN Human Rights Council 2015) [74].

[60] See Chapters 1 and 6.

[61] This is evident in the process leading up to the enactment of Ley 20.786—Biblioteca del Congreso Nacional de Chile, 'Historia de La Ley N° 20.786', eg at 105.

[62] Constitución Política de la República de Chile—texto actualizado 22 January 2024, Arts 19(4) and (5).

against a more relational concept that affords higher protection from scrutiny to intimate relationships.[63] In *S v Jordan & ors*, the Court held that there was a range of factors distinguishing 'the core of privacy from its penumbra', including the nature of the relationship, with an invasion of a familial or otherwise 'intimate, meaningful and intensely personal relationship' indicating 'a violation close to the core of privacy', and the extent of interference with the body.[64] A labour inspection does not involve an invasion of the body, and it pertains to a relationship that is not familial even if it is often conceptualized that way—as discussed further in Chapter 5—suggesting that it would not fall at the 'core' of privacy. Likewise, in analysing constitutional rights violations in South Africa, there is an assumption that private property is not absolutely sovereign.[65] Privacy provisions therefore do not necessarily present a bar to inspection.

In India, the exclusion of the household from labour inspection has again been linked to the view of the household as 'essentially a private space' and domestic labour as an 'informal voluntary arrangement'.[66] The location of the work rather than its nature appears to distinguish domestic workers from the usual understandings of a 'worker', since those providing the same type of labour such as cleaning or cooking in external workplaces, e.g. offices and factories, enjoy greater protections of their labour rights.[67] The distinction is encapsulated in a comment from a Bangalore labour commissioner that 'one cannot disturb the privacy of households', reiterating the notion of households as entirely distinct from workplaces.[68]

In interviews, some participants accepted the view that the privacy of the home was paramount and justified limits, depicting labour rights as a secondary class. Castro (Chile), for example, said:

> Obviously, they are rights of different categories—on the one hand they're labour rights, but on the other hand [the employer's privacy rights are] fundamental rights of the person.

Others viewed the salience of privacy as being overstated. For example, Barrett (South Africa) saw the issue as a 'red herring' since inspectors could speak to employers or employees at the front gate to check on issues like payment of minimum wage, although she added that physical inspections could still be important

[63] Wessel le Roux, 'Advancing Domestic Workers' Rights in a Context of Transformative Constitutionalism' in Darcy Du Toit (ed), *Exploited, Undervalued and Essential: Domestic Workers and the Realisation of Their Rights* (Pretoria University Law Press 2013) 42.

[64] *S v Jordan & ors* [2002] ZACC 22 (Constitutional Court of South Africa) [80].

[65] Solidarity Centre and IZWI (n 39) 47.

[66] Ghatak and Sarkar (n 15) 874.

[67] Uday Shankar, 'Entitlements of Domestic Workers in India: Welfare or Right' in Upasana Mahanta and Indranath Gupta (eds), *Recognition of the Rights of Domestic Workers in India: Challenges and the Way Forward* (Springer 2019) 22–24.

[68] Neetha, 'Minimum Wages for Domestic Work' (n 19) 83.

for live-in workers and in extreme cases. Conversely, several participants across countries considered that homes employing domestic workers should be treated as other workplaces and that privacy could no longer be viewed in the same way once a person was employed in the home. In Chile, academic Arriagada said that inspections were needed to check timetables and conditions and that 'in this case entry into the privacy of the family is justified'. Another academic, 'Javiera', stated 'I don't think privacy can be invoked when privacy involves an abuse', going on to draw parallels to a situation of domestic violence.[69] Abigail Osiki (South Africa) similarly noted that:

> as soon as someone comes into your space to offer services... it kind of reduces your argument of my right to privacy, because then ... you're inviting a stranger to come work in your space

These observations challenge the presentation of the privacy of the employer and their home as a given or as inherently more important than workers' rights. They also problematize how a private space is defined, as further shown in the comment of Kodoth (India):

> That's very relational... For the domestic worker, it's not a private space. It's her place of employment ... I think that the private-public dichotomy's a non-starter

Notably, in India, Resident Welfare Associations (RWAs)—bodies that form within housing compounds to oversee issues such as infrastructure and services—were described as providing 'complete immunity for the residents' while workers were 'subject to constant surveillance',[70] while lacking any worker representation within them.[71] This demonstrates the contradictions of privacy being used as a means to reject any intrusion into employers' private lives, while intensive invasions of workers' privacy are deemed acceptable.[72] Instead, it should be accepted that a home employing a domestic worker is not solely private, but rather, becomes a hybrid space where some degree of oversight must be expected.

A further question that arises is whether, if some power of entry for inspection is provided, it should be modified from that applicable in other workplaces. Some interviewees considered any differentiation unnecessary, including Eunice Dhladhla of the South African Domestic Service and Allied Workers Union (SADSAWU), who stressed that while privacy should be respected, 'really it must be in law that ... the inspectors can go to each and every house to do the inspection'.

[69] See discussion of the parallel in Chapter 2.
[70] Banerjee.
[71] 'Gita'.
[72] Rajam and Kotiswaran (n 16) 181.

Academic Caamaño Rojo (Chile) likewise argued against modifying powers, referring to their existing limits:

> The labour inspection is not police, therefore... they're not going to do a ... break in to the home ... but a general view of work conditions, for example of the room ... that the remuneration is paid.

Congressman Giorgio Jackson similarly said that '[i]f we eliminated the distinction, I think it would be a great advance', but this view was predicated on inspections not being carried out randomly and only being complaint-led. Given the importance of proactive and random inspections, it is salient to bear in mind these quite extensive powers, which include entry to workplaces at any time of day or night, and sanctioning of those who prevent enforcement.[73]

Reflecting this, other participants expressed reservations about treating private homes in exactly the same way as other workplaces and pointed to the desirability of some form of modified power—for example, only applying during the day and with more delineated purposes. 'Nancy' (Chile) argued that inspectors should be able to, for example, interview with basic questions, inspect where domestic workers sleep, their hygiene and toilet conditions, ask conditions of an employer, and see a book or register of when the domestic worker comes and goes and when they go to sleep. Mullagee (South Africa) suggested the modification of arranging for the employer to be on site if the inspection takes place during working hours, when they might usually be at work, noting that 'it's not like a police raid into a private home. It has to be done with dignity for both the employer and the employee'.

Decisions around inspection do not relate to a simple binary between the privacy of the employer versus the labour rights of the worker: the worker's own privacy is also relevant, and workers as well as employers must be protected during inspection. This is reflected in concerns that immediate introduction of full inspection in Chile could have been unhelpful for domestic workers, as the less powerful party in the relationship. Sociologist 'Daniela' said there were dangers it could prejudice the situation, particularly where the person was a migrant worker, and stressed the need for more gradual change in this area:

> rather than immediate inspection, I would start with an immediate campaign around awareness that this is a job, that the worker is a worker, and that the employer is an employer, to start to normalise what the law is proposing.

Concerns about pressure on workers were mirrored elsewhere, including by 'Gita' in India, who noted that if a worker was surveyed in the employer's presence, she

[73] Rosado Marzán (n 23) 501–2.

was unlikely to say the truth because 'she is still beholden to ... what the employer thinks of her because her next work is dependent on the reputation she builds'. Sharp (UK) similarly observed that if inspections were to be introduced, it would be important to ensure they were not skewed by the worker being 'under the eye of the employer'. For example, rather than just asking the worker if they have possession of their passport or know where it is, she suggested they should be required to actually show they have it. Reforms to increase the strength of inspection powers therefore need to be accompanied by other enforcement measures and educational strategies if they are to protect workers' interests, as well as being carried out in a way that reflects specific vulnerabilities in the domestic work setting. Another concern about the effectiveness of inspections related to the South African 'context of structural unemployment where people want to keep their jobs' and may have a sense of loyalty to employers.[74] This underscores the importance of not relying solely on workplace-based interviews, but cross-referencing these materials with checking of documentation and allowing workers the opportunity for confidential reporting.

These concerns should not detract from the importance of effective inspection powers, but underscore the need for inspections to be carried out in a way that accounts for pressures on the worker and protects the privacy of all parties. They may need to be carried out in culturally sensitive ways as relevant to the context—for example, in India the entry of a 'whole army of men' when just the domestic worker and female employer are at home could be 'a little dicey' (Kodoth), meaning it could be necessary to have women inspectors on visits. Additionally, strengthened inspection powers should be introduced alongside other enforcement and educational measures if they are to protect workers' interests. This would include alternative accountability mechanisms requiring the input of information, whether through a duty of employers to register workers,[75] or the creation of a database for submission of information on domestic workers' receipt of the minimum wage, working hours, access to social security and/or training, and reports of abuse.[76] While such measures may not involve or focus on physical entry to the home, they nonetheless make the employer accountable in to the legal system[77] and therefore challenge the idea of the private sphere and events within it as being impermeable. They also allow for joint work with civil society, which may be important for practical reasons when the resources do not exist to increase state capacity sufficiently, as well as moving away from sole reliance on the state.

[74] Von Broembsen.

[75] Shankar (n 67) 33. Also mentioned as important by Barrett and von Broembsen (South Africa) and Yajnik (India). There is a duty to register domestic workers' employment contract in Chile: Labour Code—Chile 2025, Art 146ter.

[76] Upasana Mahanta and Indranath Gupta, 'Introducing the Status of Domestic Workers in India' in Upasana Mahanta and Indranath Gupta (eds), *Recognition of The Rights of Domestic Workers in India: Challenges and the Way Forward* (Springer 2019) 10–13.

[77] Shankar (n 67) 33.

Various interviewees in both South Africa and India stressed the crucial role of organizations including trade unions, in enforcing rights and empowering domestic workers. For example, Yajnik noted that:

> through unionising and organising and ... talking about the political and the social and the economic aspect of rights... we've tried to give an alternative space for education for women

At the same time, workers' isolation and conceptions of employers' privacy as a priority can act as a bar to effective organizing. Domestic workers, especially those who live with their employers, are frequently isolated and lack immediate colleagues in their workplace.[78] Several interviewees cited isolation and dispersal as a challenge to organizing.[79] The issue is also linked to the public/private sphere divide in that '[u]nions act in the public sphere, while domestic workers are consigned to the private sphere' of the household,[80] overlapping with challenges to inspection. In India, Banerjee mentioned countering this through finding 'local spaces within the community where domestic workers could get together'. But even this requires a dynamic where domestic workers have some time to leave the home, and a way to reach them.

Domestic workers' organizations have experienced difficulties in reaching live-in domestic workers whose employers often live in gated communities and restrict workers' mobility outside the home.[81] In some cases restricted access is directly linked to privacy considerations, as explained by the head of the National Domestic Workers' Federation in India: 'We can't get entry into flats because ... [employers] think we are infringing into their personal lives.'[82] Similar restrictions hinder organization in South Africa: provisions permitting union officials to enter work premises do not apply to private homes, while employers are not under an obligation to provide information to unions about disputes that have arisen in the household.[83] Interviewees described fear of employers as a challenge to organizing, variously mentioning recent difficult economic circumstances and workers' isolation.[84] Other obstacles mentioned were SADSAWU being outside of the main union federation for some time, hindering its ability to bring complaints to the Department of Labour and CCMA,[85] and the lack of a representative employer

[78] Zhe Jiang and Marek Korczynski, 'When the "Unorganizable" Organize: The Collective Mobilization of Migrant Domestic Workers in London' (2016) 69 Human Relations 813.

[79] Barrett (South Africa), Banerjee, and Kodoth (India).

[80] Einat Albin and Virginia Mantouvalou, 'Active Industrial Citizenship of Domestic Workers: Lessons Learned from Unionizing Attempts in Israel and the United Kingdom' (2016) 17 Theoretical Inquiries in Law 321, 331.

[81] Rina Agarwala and Shiny Saha, 'The Employment Relationship and Movement Strategies among Domestic Workers in India' (2018) 44 Critical Sociology 1207, 1215.

[82] ibid.

[83] Solidarity Centre and IZWI (n 39) 23.

[84] Barrett, Mullagee.

[85] Barrett, Dhladhla.

organization with which to bargain.[86] In this context, a 'floor' of enforcement, including the provision of information about rights and support organizations as well as ensuring workers have adequate time off during which they can leave the employer's home, is an important prerequisite to domestic workers' freedom of association. These questions and their relation to working time are discussed further in Chapter 6.

Enforcement and privacy: A human rights-based approach

ILO provisions support extending enforcement to domestic work, but they do not necessarily set out its precise parameters. C-189 provides for developing implementation of inspection and enforcement measures bearing in mind 'the special characteristics of domestic work' and with 'due respect for privacy' (Article 17). This leaves open the question of what exactly 'due respect for privacy' should entail, and to what extent inspections should be limited because of the 'special characteristics' of domestic work. Universalist and gender-sensitive protection is also mandated by ILO Convention 190 Concerning the Elimination of Violence and Harassment in the world of work (C-190),[87] which Chile, the UK, and South Africa have ratified. C-190 requires effective inspection and investigation of violence and harassment and appropriate preventative measures, including identification of sectors, occupations, and work arrangements where there is greater exposure to violence and harassment (Article 8). This is likely to include domestic work, in which five of the ten risk factors the ILO has identified as exposing workers to violence and harassment[88] are prevalent: situations that are not (properly) covered or protected by labour law and social protection; resource-constrained settings; unsocial working hours, such as evening and night work; working alone or in relative isolation; and working in intimate spaces and private homes. C-190 sets out a range of enforcement and remedies requirements, including appropriate and effective remedies, safe reporting, and empowering inspectorates to deal with violence and harassment (Article 10). An approach based on human rights law assists in providing further detail on the type of enforcement required, as well as addressing privacy concerns about inspection.

[86] Mullagee, George, von Broembsen, Barrett.

[87] ILO, 'C190—Convention Concerning the Elimination of Violence and Harassment in the world of work, 2019' (108th ILC Session 2019).

[88] ILO, 'Report V(1)—Ending Violence and Harassment against Women and Men in the World of Work—107th Session of the International Labour Conference' (2018) 29.

Decent work and the enforcement of labour rights

Human rights law creates a requirement to remedy the shortcomings in the labour enforcement machinery that were discussed in the empirical section of this chapter. At international level, the declaratory provisions on the right to work in just and favourable conditions in the Universal Declaration of Human Rights (UDHR) are reflected and expanded upon in Articles 6–8 of the International Covenant on Economic, Social and Cultural Rights (ICESCR),[89] ratified by all case study countries. General Comment 18 of the UN Committee on Economic, Social and Cultural Rights (UNCESCR), which interprets ICESCR, establishes the interdependence of Articles 6, 7, and 8 and the principle that the right to work entails a right to *decent work*.[90] This is reinforced in the ILO's Decent Work agenda, the goal of which is 'not just the creation of jobs, but the creation of jobs of acceptable quality', which protect rights, provide an adequate income, and are accompanied by social protection.[91] It was further cemented by the addition of the right to a safe and healthy working environment to the ILO's Fundamental Principles and Rights at Work in 2022, which followed recommendations by the Global Commission on the Future of Work.[92]

As noted in Chapter 3, the African regional system contains a right to work under equitable and satisfactory conditions within its key instrument, the African Charter on Human and People's Rights (ACHPR), at Article 15. Further detail is found in the African Commission on Human and People's Rights (AComHPR) Guidelines that require safe and hygienic working conditions alongside provisions on remuneration, rest, and limitation of working hours.[93] The right to decent work is mirrored at European regional level through provisions of the European Social Charter (ESC) on the right to just conditions of work (Article 2) and to safe and healthy working conditions (Article 3). For the Americas, relevant provisions are in Articles 6–8 of the Protocol of San Salvador, which Chile ratified in 2022.

The right to decent work creates a requirement for enforcement mechanisms, including a system of inspection. UNCESCR General Comment 23 on the right to just and favourable conditions of work (GC23) requires states to put a range of enforcement measures in place, including reparation, monetary damages and

[89] For the full citations of international and regional instruments, see Chapter 3.

[90] UNCESCR, 'General Comment No. 18 on the Right to Work (Art 6 of the Covenant), 6 February 2006, E/C.12/GC/18' [7–8].

[91] ILO, 'Decent Work—Report of the Director General to The International Labour Conference' (1999).

[92] ILO, 'Work for a Brighter Future—Global Commission on the Future of Work' (International Labour Office 2019). The point was also reiterated in 2024: ILO, 'Resolution Concerning Decent Work and the Care Economy—ILC.112/Resolution V—14 June 2024' [18].

[93] AComHPR, 'Principles and Guidelines on the Implementation of Economic, Social and Cultural Rights in the African Charter on Human and Peoples' Rights, Adopted at the Forty-Seventh Ordinary Session Held in Banjul, the Gambia, from 12 to 26 May 2010' [59(h)].

the establishment of 'a functioning system of labour inspectorates', which must be independent, adequately resourced, and have 'the authority to enter workplaces freely without prior notice'.[94] Likewise, Article 3 ESC requires not only the issuance of health and safety regulations, but also their enforcement by supervisory measures. The European Committee of Social Rights (ECSR) has further clarified the need for comprehensive and proactive measures. In its 2020 conclusions on the right to work, it highlighted the importance of regular workplace inspections and the need for monitoring whether or not complaints have been received.[95] Under-resourcing of enforcement mechanisms and a lack of proactive labour inspection are therefore contrary to the right to decent work.

Crucially, the comprehensive nature of labour inspection means that it must cover all sectors of the labour market. As well as requiring states to monitor 'all aspects of the right to just and favourable conditions of work for all workers, including workers in the informal economy, domestic workers and agricultural workers', UNCESCR has noted that 'certain workers, such as domestic workers, may require specific measures'.[96] The ECSR requires states to adopt and implement specific legal measures to protect domestic workers from forced labour and exploitation, given the risks of these violations occurring in the domestic environment, providing for inspectors to check all workplaces, including residential premises employing domestic workers.[97] In conclusions on the right to work, it has stressed the need for coverage of residential premises, criticizing systems that only allow prosecution following a prosecutor's involvement, or that rely on complaints being brought forward, and positing inspection measures as required for the prevention of forced labour and modern slavery.[98]

Exemptions of domestic work from labour inspection thus undermine protection of the right to decent work. Limitations are pronounced in the UK, where homes employing domestic workers are excluded from general health and safety provisions and the only potential enforcement takes place in response to complaints, and in most Indian states. The position is more nuanced in Chile and South Africa, as there is some mechanism for inspection, but the effectiveness of these measures is compromised for reasons including the lack of routine checks and the requirement for employer's consent to enter a home. Where inspections in the domestic work sector are mainly complaints-driven and require domestic

[94] UNCESCR, 'General Comment No. 23 on the Right to Just and Favourable Conditions of Work (Art. 7 of the Covenant), 27 April 2016, E/C.12/GC/23' [24, 54].

[95] ECSR, 'Conclusions 2020—Article 1, Right to Work'—Estonia [47] United Kingdom [46].

[96] UNCESCR (n 94) [54, 59].

[97] ECSR, 'Conclusions 2008, Statement of Interpretation on Article 1§2'; Virginia Mantouvalou, 'Human Rights for Precarious Workers: The Legislative Precariousness of Domestic Labor' (2012) 34 Comparative Labor Law & Policy Journal 133, 148.

[98] ECSR, 'Conclusions 2008' (n 97)—Albania [38] Austria [65–69] Estonia [47] United Kingdom [44–47]. The paragraph goes on to state that 'sufficient safeguards must be put in place to prevent risks of unlawful interferences with the right to respect for private life', on which see the below subsection 'Enforcement, inspection, and the right to a private and family life'.

workers to come forward the inspection system may not be effective and proactive enough to meet the requirements of the right to decent work.

Another vital characteristic of the type of labour inspection mandated in human rights law is separation from immigration enforcement. As per GC23, inspections 'should focus on monitoring the rights of workers and not be used for other purposes, such as checking the migration status of workers'.[99] This supports the use of 'firewalls' as a division between public bodies and immigration enforcement to avoid a situation where migrants avoid such services for fear of it leading to action against them.[100] Sharing information on migratory status is also contrary to a 1947 ILO Convention, which requires that other any duties given to inspectors must not interfere with effective labour enforcement.[101] Furthermore, C-190 requires member states to address violence and harassment in the world of work in relevant national policies, including those concerning migration,[102] while its accompanying recommendation stipulates the need to protect women migrant workers regardless of migration status.[103]

Allowing migrant workers to feel comfortable raising concerns about labour law violations creates a counterweight to the poor conditions and wages that stem from having a 'readily available pool of ... exploitable irregular migrant workers', and the risk that these workers are controlled by exploitative employers and traffickers.[104] In Chile, the indication that the Labour Inspectorate would not pass on information about migratory status suggests compliance with this requirement. In South Africa, information on status is more likely to be shared by the Department of Labour, although irregular migrant workers may be able to access the CCMA without putting their migration status at risk. In the UK, public bodies share information extensively with immigration enforcement, as part of the set of policies known as the 'hostile environment' discussed in Chapter 7. A separate set of issues arises in India, where the Inter-State Migrant Workers Act of 1979 puts the burden on recruiters and migrants to register, meaning that this rarely happens in practice.[105] Overall, where data about migration status is shared by inspectorates, this is contrary to the requirements of the right to decent work. The practice means that workers with irregular status, or uncertainty about their status, will be inclined to

[99] UNCESCR (n 94) [54].

[100] François Crépeau and Bethany Hastie, 'The Case for "Firewall" Protections for Irregular Migrants' (2015) 17 European Journal of Migration and Law 157, 158, 165; Linus Hermansson and others, 'Firewalls: A Necessary Tool to Enable Social Rights for Undocumented Migrants in Social Work' [2020] International Social Work 0020872820924454, 2.

[101] ILO, 'C-081—Convention concerning Labour Inspection in Industry and Commerce' (30th ILC Session 1947), Art 3(2).

[102] ILO, 'C-190' (n 87), Art 11.

[103] ILO, 'R-206—Recommendation concerning the elimination of violence and harassment in the world of work, 2019 (No. 206)' (108th ILC Session 2019) [10].

[104] Crépeau and Hastie (n 100) 167, 175.

[105] The Inter-State Migrant Workmen Act—Act No 30 of 1979 (India); Priya Deshingkar, 'Why Do Migrants Remain Excluded in Present-Day India and What Should We Do about It?' in Ashwani Kumar and RB Bhagat (eds), *Migrants, Mobility and Citizenship in India* (Routledge India 2022) 21.

avoid voluntary engagement with enforcement bodies, and would be put at risk by the proactive and routine inspection measures that are necessary to oversee basic labour rights.

Inspections and the integrated approach

Apart from the ACHPR, the above provisions stemming from labour and socio-economic rights instruments generally have limited justiciability and enforcement mechanisms,[106] making it important to address the corresponding justiciable civil and political rights that relate to labour law standards. Key among these is the prohibition on forced labour at Article 8 of the International Covenant on Civil and Political Rights (ICCPR), Article 6 of the American Convention on Human Rights (ACHR), Article 4 of the European Convention on Human Rights (ECHR) and Article 5 ACHPR. The European Court of Human Rights (ECtHR) judgment in *Rantsev v Cyprus and Russia*, introduced in Chapter 3, established the foundational point that in tackling trafficking, the state must take a 'comprehensive approach ... which includes measures to prevent trafficking and protect victims' and 'to put in place adequate measures regulating businesses often used as a cover for human trafficking' as well as punishing traffickers.[107]

An explicit link between labour inspections and the prevention of forced labour is established in the Inter-American Court of Human Rights (IACtHR) judgment *Hacienda Verde v Brasil*, which arose from the situation of over 100 workers recruited from poor parts of Brazil to work on a ranch under terrible conditions and prevented from leaving based on threats of violence.[108] The court held that the state had a duty to create conditions so that violations of the prohibition on slavery, servitude, trafficking, and forced labour did not take place—including by reducing the demand fuelling exploitation—and to address discrimination based on factors such as poverty and lack of employment opportunities, as well as providing preventative strategies.[109] Furthermore, the state's duty to prevent and investigate possible violations includes obligations to 'eliminate all legislation that legalizes or tolerates slavery and servitude', to 'conduct inspections or other measures to detect such practices', and to 'take measures to protect and assist victims'.[110] It thus establishes that the state's 'positive obligation' in relation to slavery, servitude, and forced labour requires a number of structural and preventative measures that pertain to

[106] See Chapter 3.
[107] *Rantsev v Cyprus and Russia* (2010) 51 EHRR 1 [284–85].
[108] *Workers of the Hacienda Verde Brasil Verde v Brazil* IACtHR 20 October 2016, Ser C No 337; Valentina Milano, 'Human Trafficking by Regional Human Rights Courts: An Analysis in Light of Hacienda Brasil Verde, the First Inter-American Court's Ruling in This Area' [2018] Revista Electrónica de Estudios Internacionales (REEI) 15–16.
[109] *Hacienda Verde v Brazil* (n 108) [316–38].
[110] ibid [319].

the right to decent work, including the establishment of a proactive regime to enforce rights. The judgment refers to its requirement of comprehensive measures as being 'in line with the holistic approach' in *Rantsev*.[111] The key point running through both is that the state's duties in relation to forced labour and trafficking are not only about reactive steps such as criminalizing perpetrators, but also include preventative elements and reform to legal systems to prevent systemic violations developing. The ECSR has also made this link clear by referring to the need for regular workplace inspections in order to prevent forced labour and exploitation, especially in high-risk sectors,[112] while the ILO's 2014 forced labour protocol requires preventative measures, including the strengthening of labour inspection.[113]

The recent jurisprudence of the IACtHR based on the interpretation of Article 26 ACHR on the 'progressive development' of economic, social and cultural rights[114] is also relevant to the right to decent work. In *Spoltore v Argentina*, concerning an occupational disease claim by a retired worker who had suffered from two heart attacks, the court identified preventing accidents and occupational disease as a core part of the right to fair and satisfactory working conditions.[115] It emphasized the requirement for work to be performed under 'conditions, including a system of fair wages, that ensure life, health and a decent standard of living for the worker and his family', including in retirement, while also referring to several other instruments on conditions at work, including the ICESCR and the UNCESCR's General Comments 18 and 23.[116] This is significant since it shows that the court's interpretation of the right to work can move beyond access to work and employment stability, to encompass the question of decent work.[117]

A further elucidation of the link to labour enforcement came in the 2020 *Fireworks Factory* case, which arose from a 1998 explosion in a fireworks factory in Brazil that left 64 persons dead and six survivors.[118] Highlighting the centrality of Article 45(b) of the Amended Charter of the Organization of American States alongside ILO and international human rights materials, the IACtHR used this to recognize the right to just and favourable conditions of work.[119] By failing to

[111] Milano (n 108) 20.
[112] ECSR (n 95) Estonia [47] United Kingdom [46].
[113] ILO, 'P-029—Protocol of 2014 to the Forced Labour Convention, 1930' (103rd ILC Session 2014) Art 2(c)(ii).
[114] Franz Christian Ebert, 'A Regional Revitalisation of Labour Rights? The Emerging Approach of the Inter-American Court of Human Rights' in Brian Langille and Anne Trebilcock (eds), *Social Justice and the World of Work: Possible Global Futures* (Bloomsbury 2023) 229. See Chapter 3.
[115] *Spoltore v Argentina* IACtHR 9 June 2020, Ser C No 404; Renan Kalil and Mauro Pucheta, 'DISPATCH No 32—Argentina: The Right to Fair and Satisfactory Working Conditions through the Lens of the Inter-American Court of Human Rights' (*Comparative Labor Law and Policy Journal*, 2021) <https://cllpj.law.illinois.edu/content/dispatches/2021/Dispatch-No.-32.pdf> accessed 25 August 2025.
[116] *Spoltore v Argentina* (n 115) [86–96].
[117] Kalil and Pucheta (n 115) 8. On access to work, see Chapter 7.
[118] *Employees of the Fireworks Factory of Santo Antônio de Jesus and their families v Brazil* IACtHR 15 July 2020, Ser C No 407.
[119] ibid [155–68].

oversee adequate workplace conditions despite awareness of the victims' special situation of vulnerability, it held that the State had contributed to increasing structural discrimination while failing to ensure the right to just and favourable conditions of work.[120] Remedies included the requirement to implement 'a systemic policy of regular inspections of places that make fireworks' to check health and safety conditions and compliance.[121] These obligations were reinforced the following year in the *Miskito Divers* case, where the authorities were criticized for failing to monitor and oversee dangerous working conditions and take effective steps to prevent accidents.[122] In both cases, the court emphasized the workers' vulnerability based on structural factors—being poor and primarily Afro-descendent women and girls in the *Fireworks Factory*, and a marginalized indigenous group without access to other sources of income in the *Miskito Divers*—as requiring a high standard of protection and leading to violations of Article 24 ACHR, the right to equal protection before the law.[123] By analogy, domestic workers, who are structurally disadvantaged, primarily women and frequently migrants and/or racialized minorities, would attract a similar requirement for protection of their conditions through proactive enforcement mechanisms.

Although there is no direct equivalent of Article 26 ACHR in the other regional systems, the IACtHR's judgments have a potential broader relevance since they mirror obligations in the international social and economic rights instruments,[124] and because of the Court's ongoing 'central role in the normative construction and evolving interpretations of international human rights standards'.[125] The right to decent work is already included in the ACHPR, and in the European context, related obligations can be derived from the prohibition on forced labour, which requires the establishment of effective inspection mechanisms, as set out earlier in this section. Failures to set up a functioning and proactive inspection system that includes the domestic work sector can facilitate forced labour and servitude by making it difficult to detect poor conditions that may lead to these forms of exploitation.

Enforcement, inspection, and the right to a private and family life

The requirements that inspectors be able to enter workplaces freely and without prior notice are contentious for domestic work because it takes place in a private home, as discussed in the section 'Privacy, limitations on enforcement, and lack of

[120] ibid [174, 201].
[121] ibid [287].
[122] *Miskito Divers (Lemoth Morris* et al*) v Honduras* IACtHR 31 August 2021, Ser C No 432 [77].
[123] *Fireworks Employees v Brazil* (n 118) [197–99]; *Miskito Divers* (n 122) [52, 104–7].
[124] Ebert (n 114) 233.
[125] Par Engstrom, 'The Impact of the Inter-American Human Rights System beyond Latin America' in Armin von Bogdandy and others (eds), *The Impact of the Inter-American Human Rights System: Transformations on the Ground* (OUP 2024) 101.

accountability' in this chapter. The importance placed on the privacy of the family home is also reflected in C-189's references to the 'special characteristics of domestic work'. It is undeniable that extending inspection powers to private homes has the potential to infringe on an employer's right to private and family life. Yet while the location of the work in a private home is a relevant consideration, it should not be viewed as an *absolute* bar to entry without prior consent, bearing in mind that a home employing a domestic worker is no longer only a private home but also a workplace. Workers' rights—particularly where they are understood as human rights, and therefore as having a 'fundamental moral importance'[126]—are not automatically 'trumped' by the employer's right to a private life. Human rights cases on domestic violence have shown an increasing scrutiny of abuses that take place in the 'private sphere' of the home and family, shifting from an earlier deference to the private domain.[127] If it is sometimes appropriate for the state to intervene within an actual family unit, then, by analogy, interference in a unit that consists of a family and a domestic worker cannot be completely precluded.

Furthermore, the right to private and family life does not support such a stark interpretation of the employer's entitlements as would be required to entirely prevent the entry of labour inspectors. Each iteration of the right (ICCPR Article 17, ACHR Article 11, and ECHR Article 8) refers to privacy/private life, family, home and correspondence, so clearly encompasses protection against arbitrary state actions such as searches of the home, separation of children from their parents, and reviews of correspondence. The right extends beyond this to subject matter as diverse as reputation, reproductive rights, and the treatment of prisoners, as well as surveillance and searches of the home.[128] While broad in scope, the right to private and family life is, crucially, a qualified right, meaning an individual's home, private life, or correspondence is not immune from *any* interference, but specifically from *arbitrary* interference. Examining the constitutional protection of privacy, the South African Constitutional Court has recognized that 'as a person moves into communal relations and activities such as business and social interaction, the scope of personal space shrinks accordingly'.[129]

The Inter-American Commission on Human Rights (IAComHR) has described arbitrariness as manifesting 'elements of injustice, unpredictability and unreasonableness'.[130] In weighing an interference on the right to private life with

[126] Janice R Bellace, 'Human Rights at Work: The Need for Definitional Coherence in the Global Governance System' (2014) 30 International Journal of Comparative Labour Law and Industrial Relations 175, 178.

[127] See Chapter 3.

[128] Lucas Lixinski, 'Comparative International Human Rights Law: An Analysis of the Right to Private and Family Life across Human Rights "Jurisdictions"' (2014) 32 Nordic Journal of Human Rights 99, 104.

[129] *Bernstein and Others v Bester NO and Others* [1996] ZACC 2 (Constitutional Court of South Africa) [67].

[130] *X and Y v Argentina, Case No 10506, Merits Report No 38/96* IAComHR 15 October 1996 [92].

the protection of another right, the IACtHR has found it necessary to analyse: '(i) the level of harm to one of the rights at stake ... (ii) the importance of ensuring the contrary right, and (iii) whether ensuring the latter justifies restricting the former'.[131] The ECtHR has also developed a detailed test. To justify interference with Article 8 ECHR, a measure must pursue one of the 'legitimate aims' set out at Article 8(2): national security, public safety, the country's economic well-being, prevention of disorder or crime, protection of health or morals, or protection of the rights and freedoms of others. In addition, it must have a basis in domestic law and must be 'necessary in a democratic society', meaning it corresponds to a 'pressing social need' and is proportionate to the legitimate aim pursued.[132]

Providing for inspections of homes that employ domestic workers is related to the legitimate aim of protecting 'the rights and freedoms of others', namely of those workers. Studies of locations where there is no or very limited provision for inspection discussed above demonstrate how severe labour abuses frequently go undetected unless the domestic worker takes the drastic and risky step of leaving their employer, or otherwise feels empowered to complain directly. Consequently, there is a 'pressing social need' to improve the rights of domestic workers, as per the ECtHR proportionality test. The question of whether less restrictive measures could have been used to achieve the same aim can be relevant in considering proportionality.[133] The availability of some other measures is unlikely to negate the need for some power of entry to homes, given the shortcomings in enforcement regarding matters such as the physical working and living conditions of domestic workers where this power is lacking.

The precise way an inspection takes place will be crucial to the determination of whether it is a proportionate means to meet the legitimate aim of protecting workers' rights. As per recent conclusions of the ECSR, inspections of homes employing domestic workers 'must be clearly provided for by law and sufficient safeguards must be put in place to prevent risks of unlawful interferences with the right to respect for private life'.[134] The UN Human Rights Committee's General Comment 16 on the right to privacy under Article 17 ICCPR states that home searches 'should be restricted to a search for necessary evidence and should not be allowed to amount to harassment'.[135] By analogy, any inspections of the home as a workplace should be confined to reviewing what is necessary to confirm

[131] *Artavia Murillo* et al *('in vitro fertilization') v Costa Rica* IACtHR 28 November 2012, Ser C No 257 [274]. This case addressed the right to life as the other right to be 'balanced' against privacy.

[132] *Leander v Sweden* (1978) 9 EHRR 433 [50]; *Pretty v United Kingdom* (2002) 35 EHRR 1 [70]; Marta Otto, *The Right to Privacy in Employment: A Comparative Analysis* (Bloomsbury 2016) 82.

[133] Eva Brems and Laurens Lavrysen, '"Don't Use a Sledgehammer to Crack a Nut": Less Restrictive Means in the Case Law of the European Court of Human Rights' (2015) 15 Human Rights Law Review 139.

[134] ECSR, 'Conclusions 2020' (n 95) Albania [38].

[135] UNHCHR, 'General Comment No 16: Article 17 (Right to Privacy)—32nd Session of the Human Rights Committee (8 April 1988)—UN Doc HRI/GEN/1/Rev.9 (Vol I)'. [8].

compliance with relevant labour and human rights standards: each step must relate to the aim of protecting the worker's rights. The level of intrusiveness of an interference is of clear relevance in determining its proportionality. In *Sidabras v Lithuania,* the ECtHR accepted that limitations on employment available to former KGB agents pursued a legitimate aim, but held that the severity of the restrictions and the ambiguity as to their effect made it 'impossible to ascertain any reasonable link' to such aims and meant that they were not proportionate.[136] It is therefore vital to show a direct connection between labour inspections and their protective aim, and for the content of a labour inspection to be regulated in detail, with guidance on what can and cannot be examined within the home. Conversely, if a high level of discretion were to be granted to inspectors, this could create difficulties for 'consistency and equity of treatment across enterprises and over time'[137] and would make the power less likely to be proportionate.

Bearing this in mind, an inspection of a home employing a domestic worker could properly entail asking questions of the employer and the worker, seeing records of the hours worked and accounts to show payments, and inspecting the conditions in which the worker sleeps (where they are live-in) and works, including access to toilets and other facilities, as these are all directly relevant to workers' rights. However, it would not grant a general power to search through the employing family's private correspondence and belongings,[138] which would be disproportionate and open to abuse. In addition, inspections at night should not be carried out as part of a random inspection process (although they might be appropriate in response to specific complaints of abuse happening at night, with proper safeguards in place).

Safeguards are also needed to ensure the inspection benefits the domestic worker. My empirical research, alongside other materials, reveals concerns that such a benefit would not be automatic, particularly if inspections were introduced in isolation. Consequently, inspections should be part of a range of measures aimed at increasing both parties' awareness of rights and workers' capacity to challenge against any violations. These would also include providing workers with written information and information meetings about their rights and relevant trade unions and community organizations in a language they understand well, raising employers' awareness of their responsibilities, requiring employers to complete online or written information about the conditions of work, hours, and payments, and creating accessible complaint mechanisms where these do not already exist. During an inspection, domestic workers would need to be spoken to

136 *Sidabras and Dziautas v Lithuania* [2004] ECHR 395 [59–61].

137 Michael J Piore and Andrew Schrank, 'Toward Managed Flexibility: The Revival of Labour Inspection in the Latin World' (2008) 147 International Labour Review 1, 8.

138 Unless there was reasonable suspicion that a criminal offence had been committed to which such documents would be relevant—in which case the authorities would need to obtain a search warrant following the normal procedures, and with the normal safeguards applying.

independently of their employer, and checks made to ascertain that they actually have access to their documents, including passports in the case of migrant workers. Finally, and crucially, inspections must be strictly separated from immigration enforcement, without which they will be a danger to workers without secure immigration status.

Conclusion

Effective enforcement of labour rights is crucial to ensure that any legal reforms intended to benefit domestic workers actually improve their conditions. Within the case study countries, the situation varies between some inspection mechanisms in Chile and South Africa, compared with much more limited provision in the UK and India. Where some measures exist, they tend to be constrained by the lack of a power of entry, resourcing issues, and reliance on complaints rather than proactive programmes. While observing such limitations, it is important to recognize that all accountability measures represent progress against the idea of a private sphere immune from scrutiny, provided they do not put migrant workers at risk by sharing details with immigration enforcement.

The exclusion of domestic workplaces from inspection is a function of 'lack of accountability', resting on the idea of the private home as distinct from and subject to a lower degree of scrutiny than public workplaces, and the work performed there as separate from 'real work'. While the employer's privacy is often presented as contrary to permitting a power of entry, I have argued that the right to private and family life should not be understood as an absolute bar. Instead, determining whether an interference is justified depends on the aim it pursues and the question of whether it is proportionate to that aim. The aim of improving domestic workers' rights is a compelling one since, without this, workers face poor conditions that include inadequate accommodation, lack of food, drink, and rest, abuse and harassment that can take physical, verbal, and sexual forms, and dangerous exposure during the Covid-19 pandemic. Furthermore, an effective monitoring system that extends to all sectors is required to fulfil the socio-economic right to decent work and as a measure to prevent forced labour.

At the same time, the proportionality of the measures is central. Any power of entry for inspection must be strictly delineated for two reasons. First, to prevent it interfering with privacy in a disproportionate way, it must be confined to measures needed to check the worker's rights and well-being, rather than granting sweeping powers to inspectors. Secondly, to ensure it is actually effective and beneficial to workers, it must be clearly separated from immigration control and form one part of a range of measures that include promoting awareness of rights, facilitating workers' participation in trade unions and community organizations, and requiring employers to submit information about working conditions. While other measures of this nature are necessary, they will not be adequate to prevent abuses in all cases without any recourse to inspection, as some unscrupulous employers may ignore rules despite being well-informed about them. Conversely, for employers who follow requirements and provide decent working conditions, the occurrence of inspection as a simple verification process should be no more than a formality.

5

The devaluation of domestic work

Regulatory reform and challenges to the perception of a 'family-like' relationship

Introduction

In Chapters 1 and 2, I noted that the devaluation of domestic work stems from gendered tropes, including the perception of a 'family-like' relationship, overlapping with marginalization based on factors like race/ethnicity, caste, migration status, and class. This chapter expands that argument, examining the construction of paid domestic workers as akin to members of the family that employs them—which I refer to as 'the familial discourse'—in light of material from the case study countries. Through engagement with my empirical research, it demonstrates that while the discourse is complex and some workers may identify with it, its overall impact is to perpetuate devaluation—for example, in stifling demands for improved working conditions and extracting additional work. It also examines how a lack of recognition of skills and complexity contributes to devaluation, and assesses the concept of 'social reproduction' as a route towards better valuation of domestic work.

The chapter assesses the extent of domestic workers' exclusion from key relevant rights, particularly minimum wage coverage, which apply in other sectors, starting from the expectation that better regulation of these areas to include domestic workers generally counters devaluation. It identifies three broad trends: the relatively strong regulatory framework with countervailing factors maintaining devaluation in Chile and South Africa; regulation that varies between states in India, with a familial discourse overlaid by caste and class; and devaluation based on an exemption from minimum wage that existed for some live-in domestic workers until recently in the UK. The final section explores the role and potential of human rights law in counteracting the devaluation of domestic work. Beyond equalization with existing frameworks based on anti-discrimination provisions, it examines the right to a living wage and to fair pay derived from social rights instruments, setting out a feminist approach to these rights that can properly account for the value of domestic work.

Human Rights and the Protection of Domestic Workers in Labour and Migration Law. Natalie Sedacca, Oxford University Press. © Oxford University Press 2026. DOI: 10.1093/9780198985266.003.0007

Discourses in the devaluation of domestic work

The familial discourse and its impacts

The familial discourse is a central construction in the devaluation of domestic work, acting to mask deeply unequal relationships and recreating master–servant relationships of earlier eras.[1] Asked to reflect on this theme, my interviewees across case studies pointed to the role of the familial discourse in allowing employers to take advantage of workers and making them feel indebted (UK and Chile) and to extract more work from them or to present relationships of servitude as based on mutual trust (South Africa and India). For example, Dhladhla (South Africa) stated that she understood the discourse as 'a bribe', which was used to try to stop workers making demands, such as for payment of the living wage or social security entitlements. Other participants pointed to the problematic nature of compliance with basic rights depending on employers' goodwill.[2] As stated by Yajnik (India):

> it's a thing that most ... of the employers use. Will you charge this much money if you do this in your own house? Is this not your own house as well?

This points to the familial discourse as, at least in some cases, a conscious tactic.[3] In Chile, Arriagada described the conception of the worker as a family member as 'a big lie ... used to abuse the worker' and to encourage them to stay despite lack of pay when the family is in bad economic conditions. By contrast, some respondents had more favourable understandings of the discourse. George (South Africa) viewed it as associated with the sharing of tasks between the worker and family members, which she related to some Black employers having less of a distance from domestic workers:

> I've seen it as a positive because even when domestic workers are released from work, they go home with packages and food parcels, old furniture, so there is this sense of wanting to still preserve their life, even after they no longer work with you

[1] See eg Raka Ray and Seemin Qayum, *Cultures of Servitude: Modernity, Domesticity, and Class in India* (Stanford University Press 2009); Einat Albin, 'From "Domestic Servant" to "Domestic Worker"' in Judy Fudge, Shae McCrystal, and Kamala Sankaran (eds), *Challenging the Legal Boundaries of Work Regulation* (Hart 2012) 234; Rosie Cox, 'Gendered Work and Migration Regimes' in Liam Leonard (ed), *Transnational Migration, Gender and Rights* (Emerald 2012) 46.

[2] See eg Tekié and Mbimbi, South Africa.

[3] Ethnographic studies elsewhere have likewise seen the conflation with family members as 'opportunistic'—Adelle Blackett, *Everyday Transgressions: Domestic Workers' Transnational Challenge to International Labor Law* (Cornell University Press 2019) 72. This does not mean that all employers who refer to domestic workers as family members do so in this deliberate way.

Yet even in this description, a discretionary nature is evident. The benefits mentioned remain dependent on an employer's goodwill and financial situation, as further noted by 'Gita' (India):

> Someone who's doing better financially will take this a little further and maybe take care of your children's education ... someone who ... is not financially well, they will limit it to good behaviour, or maybe a meal in a month

Alongside other participants in India, 'Gita' explained how the familial discourse had traditionally been associated with long-term service under old feudal arrangements. The apparent altruism of providing for workers beyond payment of their wages can also strengthen relationships of dependency, loyalty, and subservience.[4] Unlike *exchanges* of gifts, which anthropologists have identified as having a social as well as material significance, gifts within domestic work are unusual in being given one way only, thus cementing the worker's subordination and the employer's superiority.[5] Despite the discretionary and non-reliable nature of these benefits, their existence often reinforces employers' opposition to law or policy regulating domestic work, based on the idea that it is unnecessary since workers are already taken care of.[6] Yet one of the contradictions of the familial relationship is that the apparent obligations it generates can be 'readily dispensed of when [they become] too costly'.[7]

A relationship of this nature can be described as 'benevolent maternalism': one that is based on gifts and favours alongside a protective treatment of the worker, who is related to as child-like.[8] Sen (India) noted such infantilization:

> A domestic worker is usually older than the children of the household, but they're lower in status. So the normal status considerations that order the family does not apply ... not everybody, but a lot of children learn from the youngest possible age the power they have over domestic servants.

Many domestic workers appear to see through the familial discourse. In the Chile interviews, this point was expressed not only by workers who were broadly

[4] Jacklyn Cock, *Maids and Madams: Domestic Workers under Apartheid* (Rev edn, Women's Press 1989) 82; Padmaja Barua, Anne Waldrop, and Haldis Haukanes, 'From Benevolent Maternalism to the Market Logic: Exploring Discursive Boundary Making in Domestic Work Relations in India' (2017) 49 Critical Asian Studies 481, 488.

[5] Judith Rollins, *Between Women: Domestics and Their Employers* (Temple University Press 1985) 190–1.

[6] Divya Ravindranath and others, 'Employer Practices and Perceptions on Paid Domestic Work: Recruitment, Employment Relationships, and Social Protection' (ILO 2022) 19.

[7] Ray and Qayum (n 1) 110.

[8] Barua, Waldrop, and Haukanes (n 4) 486.

negative about their relationship with their employers, such as 'Francisca', but interestingly also by those who reported generally good relationships with their employers. 'Sara', for example, stated that there was a lot of respect, and that she felt valued, but with regards to her employers calling her a family member, said, 'it doesn't seem to me because ... I'm a housekeeper and I can never be family ... of theirs'. By contrast, some workers may view the familial presentation as a way to feel safer or more respected with their employer, as noted by Kodoth (India):

> It's not just strategic ... there is a real sense in which .... they're also conveying that... I was not just a servant... I had this relationship, and I meant a great deal to them ...

As she went on to explain, this presentation 'really goes against a rights discourse'. Therefore, while recognizing the subtleties and nuances in the ways that workers relate to the familial discourse, this should not detract from its overarching role in reinforcing devaluation, and the centrality of a rights-based framework in the shift away from this.

Devaluation and non-recognition of skill and complexity

Other than direct references to 'family-like' relationships or affective ties, devaluation also manifests itself through requirements on domestic workers to perform a range of tasks, which are often not clearly defined, without recognition of their complexity or the skills required.[9] This dovetails with the conflation of domestic workers' labour with work performed by women for free in the family home, discussed in Chapter 2. The concept of 'low-skilled workers' and the designation of domestic workers as such is problematic, overlapping with the gendered, racialized, and class-based devaluation of their work.[10] It also contrasts sharply with the demands and expectations often made by employers, particularly when a domestic worker is caring for young children. For example, one employer interviewed in Busch's study of nannies viewed the role as requiring a range of attributes, including 'warmth, patience, domestic skill and intelligent conversation (in a second or third language)'.[11]

[9] Encarnación Gutiérrez Rodríguez, *Migration, Domestic Work and Affect: A Decolonial Approach on Value and the Feminization of Labor* (Routledge 2010) 89–92, 110. See also Chapter 1.
[10] See Chapters 1 and 2.
[11] Nicky Busch, 'The Employment of Migrant Nannies in the UK: Negotiating Social Class in an Open Market for Commoditised In-Home Care' (2013) 14 Social & Cultural Geography: Gendered Spaces of Commoditised Care 541, 549.

A number of domestic worker interviewees pointed to the complexity of the various tasks they were expected to do together, and/or their undefined nature. 'Josefa' (Chile), for example, said that one person needs to 'do all the things in the house, to be with the children, do cleaning, ironing, the other'. At the same time as being devalued because of the assumption of straightforwardness, there is an added element that makes it even more demanding: as the work is being done for someone else's family, the consequences of something going wrong are more severe than for someone looking after their own child ('Catalina', Chile). Yet the complexity of these tasks is not recognized in pay structures. As noted by Mullagee (South Africa):

> The problem ... is that there's just one minimum wage. It is not a sector that is graded in terms of skill level ... There's no separate wage for ... more experienced or ... specific skills like care work or cooking ...

Nayak (India) made a related point on the problem of calculating the domestic worker's minimum wage based on that of an unskilled worker:

> the work that a lot of domestic workers do, particularly if they are cooking, if they are looking after an old patient, if they're looking after a child, a baby... those are skills, and therefore they should get the wage of a skilled worker

Another issue noted in India was the lack of wage progression for years of experience,[12] particularly during or following the Covid-19 pandemic, where many workers were forced to switch household and therefore to 'start from zero' in terms of their pay.[13] This points to the need for recognition of distinct tasks or skills as an antidote to the familial discourse, and as deserving of enhanced levels of pay.[14] There are some risks of differentiated wages leading to reflections of other hierarchies: in Karnataka, which has higher rates for housework with childcare than for cleaning only, task-based differentiations have been found to reinforce class and caste-based hierarchies.[15] Yet overall, it is important that the range of task requirements is at least considered in determining pay, while not being the only such factor.

[12] 'Meera', Kodoth, 'Gita'. See also Samita Sen and Nilanjana Sengupta, *Domestic Days: Women, Work, and Politics in Contemporary Kolkata* (OUP 2016) 106–7.

[13] Kodoth.

[14] Darcy Du Toit and Elsabé Huysamen, 'Implementing Domestic Workers' Labour Rights in a Context of Transformative Constitutionalism' in Darcy Du Toit (ed), *Exploited, Undervalued and Essential: Domestic Workers and the Realisation of Their Rights* (Pretoria University Law Press 2013) 111.

[15] N Neetha, 'Minimum Wages for Domestic Work: Mirroring Devalued Housework' (2013) 48 Economic and Political Weekly 77, 80.

Valuation through social reproduction

Beyond the skills question, another potentially important tool for recognizing the value of domestic work and understanding the connected nature of public and private spheres is the concept of social reproduction. This concept includes a range of actions, including the care and birth of children, day-to-day recreation of conditions needed to support life, and looking after older and disabled people,[16] which 'produce and reproduce labor-power' (i.e. the 'capacity to work').[17] Social reproduction theory underscores the fact that without reproductive labour, including that which takes place in the private sphere, the labour power necessary for all other work and 'productive' activities to run the broader economy would not be available. This helps bring to the forefront a large part of the contribution of domestic work. However, it does not provide a complete picture of all the value such work generates, which is not only economic but also relates to the regeneration of communities and social bonds[18] and enhancing children's rights through quality childcare.[19]

A further proviso is that domestic work may go beyond any predetermined or set amount of work required to reproduce the labour of the group of workers making up a household. Domestic workers' tasks sometimes significantly exceed what employers would do for themselves, and can also be about reproducing a given lifestyle and social standing.[20] An example of work beyond necessity is seen in the description provided by 'Joana' (UK worker participant) of being constantly asked to find items for members of her employing family:

> They want the socks, give me the socks. They want their charger, give me the charger... Everything they want... I tell them—your clothes is... in your cabinet, but they want me to bring to them.

Likewise, 'Daniela' (Chile) pointed to the way that domestic workers are used to support a particular class-based culture and way of life, so that the employers can take part in activities like hosting friends, going out to eat and travelling, while having someone at their service. The widespread employment of domestic

[16] Joanne Conaghan, 'Labour Law and Feminist Method' (2017) 33 International Journal of Comparative Labour Law 93, 14–15.

[17] Matthew Carlin and Silvia Federici, 'The Exploitation of Women, Social Reproduction, and the Struggle against Global Capital' (2014) 17 Theory & Event 6.

[18] Ania Zbyszewska and Supriya Routh, 'Challenging Labour Law's "Productivity" Bias Through a Feminist Lens: A Conversation' in Alysia Blackham, Miriam Kullmann, and Ania Zbyszewska (eds), *Theorising Labour Law in a Changing World: Towards Inclusive Labour Law* (Hart 2019).

[19] Sandra Fredman, 'Care as a Constitutional Value' (2024) 22 International Journal of Constitutional Law 741, 746.

[20] Bridget Anderson, 'Just Another Job? Paying for Domestic Work' (2001) 9 Gender and Development 25, 25–28; Nimushakavi Vasanthi, 'Addressing Paid Domestic Work: A Public Policy Concern' (2011) 46 Economic and Political Weekly 85, 87.

workers, even in contexts where women's external labour force participation is low, including India, further underscores how the work's role can go beyond providing support for working families.[21]

Accordingly, domestic workers may contribute in ways that are less tangible to identify in terms of economic value than supporting others to be able to go to work, including the creation of leisure time for the employers and the reproduction of cultural norms. Understanding these other facets helps to move away from a romanticized notion of household work as intrinsically contributing to a social good;[22] indeed, social reproduction when conceptualized broadly can encompass the reproduction of culture and ideology.[23] The output of domestic work is not solely relevant to processes that can be easily understood as 'valuable' in a normative sense, such as childcare, but it must still be recognized as creating *value*—just as the assessment of productive work as 'valuable' does not depend on its normative value.

Devaluation versus inclusion: Wage and social security coverage

Following the discussion of discourses that reinforce devaluation, this section moves to examine how such understandings interact with regulatory frameworks in domestic work. One of the clearest legal manifestations of devaluation is the exclusion of domestic workers from entitlements applicable in other sectors to the minimum wage or relevant social security provisions, reflecting the failure to treat their work as 'real work'. This section examines the degree of movement away from such exclusionary provisions in the case study countries and the extent to which this move counteracts the familial discourse that devalues domestic work.

Chile and South Africa: A strong regulatory framework with countervailing factors

Chile was the earliest of the case study countries to equalize domestic workers' minimum wage with that of other workers, based on the principle of non-discrimination.[24] A 2008 law provided for an increase, initially to 75 per cent of that applicable in other sectors, with progressive equalization to 100 per cent

[21] Anderson (n 20) 27; Ray and Qayum (n 1) 9.

[22] Kathi Weeks, *The Problem with Work: Feminism, Marxism, Antiwork Politics, and Postwork Imaginaries* (Duke University Press 2011) 124; Zbyszewska and Routh (n 18) 259–60 (Zbyszewska).

[23] Shirin Rai, *Depletion: The Human Costs of Caring* (OUP 2024) 14.

[24] Lorena Poblete, 'The ILO Domestic Workers Convention and Regulatory Reforms in Argentina, Chile and Paraguay: A Comparative Study of Working Time and Remuneration Regulations' (2018) 157 International Labour Review 435, 450.

by 2011.[25] However, the monthly minimum wage is based on an eight-hour day, whereas live-in domestic workers are permitted to work longer hours than this,[26] meaning a degree of distinction remains. In 2015, a law passed alongside ratification of C-189 took further steps to address devaluation through prohibiting 'payment in kind'—deductions from the wage to account for the provision of food and accommodation—and the unilateral reduction of remuneration as a consequence of a shorter working week.[27] With these reforms already in effect at the time of my interviews, union General Secretary Ruth Olate pointed to an ongoing campaign for an increase in unemployment insurance. This initiative has since been successful, with legislation in 2020 incorporating domestic workers into unemployment insurance provisions applicable to other workers,[28] leading to better protection against dismissal and unemployment, in the context of the Covid-19 pandemic.[29]

South Africa has also seen progressive equalization of the minimum wage, although this was completed more recently than in Chile. From 2002, a specific minimum wage for domestic workers was established by the Sectoral Determination process, which is used for sectors viewed as 'vulnerable' where employers and/or workers are not organized to use the other methods of bargaining council agreements or statutory council agreements.[30] The process of setting wages that led to Sectoral Determination 7 of 2002[31] involved a series of hearings organized by the Employment Conditions Commission, with representatives from labour, business, government, and researchers, which is 'a participative process' although not a negotiation forum as such.[32] Subsequently, in 2018, a National Minimum Wage Act came into force, under which the stipulated wage for domestic workers was initially 75 per cent of the otherwise applicable wage, and was equalized with other workers as of February 2023.[33]

Coverage of unemployment, maternity, and sickness benefits was extended to domestic workers through the Unemployment Insurance Amendment Act of 2003,

[25] Ley No 20.279—Reajusta Monto del Ingreso Mínimo Mensual 2008; Lidia Casas and Helena Olea, 'Trabajadoras de Casa Particular—Invizibiladas y Discriminadas' in Centro de Derechos Humanos (ed), *Informe Anual sobre Derechos Humanos in Chile 2014* (Ediciones Universidad Diego Portales 2014) 150.

[26] Poblete (n 24) 450–1. See Chapter 6 on subsequent changes to working time.

[27] Ley No 20.786—Modifica la Jornada, Descanso y Composición de la Remuneración de los Trabajadores de Casa Particular, y Prohíbe La Exigencia de Uniforme en Lugares Públicos 2014, third transitory article. The legislation was implemented in 2015 alongside ratification of C-189.

[28] Ley 21.269—Incorpora a los Trabajadores de Casa Particular al Seguro de Desempleo de la Ley 19.728 2020.

[29] ILO, 'Making the Right to Social Security a Reality for Domestic Workers: A Global Review of Policy Trends, Statistics and Extension Strategies' (ILO 2022) 40.

[30] Debbie Budlender, 'The Introduction of a Minimum Wage for Domestic Workers in South Africa' (ILO 2016) 2–4.

[31] Reference in Chapter 2.

[32] Barrett.

[33] National Minimum Wage Act—Act No 9 of 2018; Candice James, Fairuz Mullagee, and Abigail Osiki, 'Domestic Workers in South Africa: Inclusion Under the Compensation for Occupational Injuries and Diseases Act' (2023) 96 The Thinker 13, 15.

but in practice, entitlement relies on the employer registering the worker, which many fail to do,[34] while those working fewer than 24 hours per month with a particular employer are outside its scope.[35] However, until 2020, domestic workers remained excluded from the Compensation for Occupational Injuries and Diseases Act (COIDA).[36] This was successfully challenged in the Constitutional Court case *Mahlangu v Minister of Labour*, which was brought by the daughter of a domestic worker who had tragically drowned in her employer's pool,[37] and is discussed further in the human rights section below. The Court's order finding the law to be constitutionally invalid applies retrospectively from 27 April 1994, the date of South Africa's interim constitution.[38]

Broadly speaking, these regulatory reforms help to recognize domestic work as work and move away from the devalued, familial understanding. In Chile, the academic 'Rocio' traced a shift away from the conflation of domestic workers with family members to a 1998 law that gave domestic workers maternity protection,[39] stating that this established the idea that this was a job like others by 'putting the contractual logic in relations of affect'. The language of rights is posed here as a direct challenge against affective relations; even where regulatory reforms such as minimum wage inclusion suffer from practical shortcomings, their communicative value in establishing a worker's identity is still significant.

Participants in Chile similarly stressed the communicative importance of the 2015 reforms. Academic Jose Luis Ugarte, despite being critical of the limitations in the law and its practical impacts, noted that 'the idea of making the situation of these workers politically visible emerged with force ... the theme came into the public arena for the first time', while 'Daniela' said the law had brought up questions among workers about how to empower themselves and to create more effective inspection and better awareness of rights. This suggests that changes based on the visibilization of domestic work have had some concrete effects, rather than being merely symbolic, because the message about the value of domestic work can lead to a shift in power dynamics. Domestic worker 'Camila' indicated that improved basic standards of rights provided greater confidence at challenging poor conditions, stating:

> Yes, it's changed a lot ... in what we can work and what we cannot do in the work... before we were very sacrificing... little money... very low salary... now

[34] ILO, 'Making Decent Work a Reality for Domestic Workers: Progress and Prospects Ten Years after the Adoption of the Domestic Workers Convention, 2011 (No. 189)' (ILO 2021) 127. This was also mentioned by several interviewees.

[35] ILO, 'Making the Right to Social Security a Reality' (n 29) 36.

[36] Act No 130 of 1993.

[37] *Sylvia Mahlangu & anor v Minister of Labour & ors* [2020] ZACC 24 (Constitutional Court of South Africa) [7].

[38] ibid [129, 131].

[39] Ley No 19.591—Modifica el Código del Trabajo en Materia de Protección a la Maternidad 1998.

> no, because now at least we have a salary that's a bit higher and we can say no to our boss.

While the increase in laws casting domestic work *as work* and protecting rights generally supports a move away from the familial discourse, countervailing factors remain. These include migration status, with migrant domestic workers potentially more willing than nationals to view themselves as 'like a member of the family' in the interests of their sense of belonging or to process their situation, and employers similarly viewing migrant workers as more loving and submissive.[40] The academic 'Francisco' gave the example of an Ecuadorian migrant domestic worker who had irregular status and was unable to see her children, who was working:

> without a contract, in conditions ... of intense subordination, working sixteen hours, with changes in hours ... And however she understood ... that she was part of the family of the employer.

He described this as a survival strategy, linked to a conception of a 'trajectory of migration as associated with sacrifice' whereby migrant domestic workers may substitute attachment to their employing family when separated from their own. Such attachment was suggested by the Bolivian domestic worker 'Michelle', who talked about extra hours she was expected to work:

> My work was heavy but ... I am always one of those people that needs to work. And I also have a large heart ... I am really sentimental.

Notably, while she understood more or less that the family saw her as a member, because she and her husband had treated them with so much affection, this took place in the context of a non-formalized relationship, where the employer had refused to give her a contract or document confirming her position on termination. This suggests a correlation between affective ties and additional work being done without reward.

The impact of visa regimes and assumptions about migrants can therefore undermine the potential of progressive legislation to destabilize the familial relationship. Relatedly, in South Africa, several participants indicated that the law had not gone far enough to challenge the understanding of the domestic worker as family member, with distinctions based on race and class, and increasingly also on migration, playing a crucial role in reinforcing devaluation. As explained by Mullagee, the 2002 Sectoral Determination 7:

[40] Rosario Fernández, 'Commodification of Domestic Labour, the Culture of Servitude and the Making of the Chilean Nation' (2018) 43 Österreichische Zeitschrift für Soziologie 49, 57. See also Chapter 7.

> intends to professionalise the sector and ... expect employers to recognise and value workers as workers rather than the house help doing you a favour and you doing them a favour by paying them a wage ... but ... the law hasn't gone far enough to change that relationship.

This largely relates to failures in the enforcement framework: Dhladhla stated that although the laws are 'very good' for domestic workers, many employers do not want to comply. While unions have a crucial role in enforcing payment of the minimum wage, there are also pitfalls of relying on them, given low unionization rates (Tekié). Apart from being a feature of 'lack of accountability' as discussed in Chapter 4, enforcement failings must also be understood in light of the devalued view of domestic workers, which arguably makes non-compliance seem acceptable to so many employers. George linked the prevalence of Black women in domestic work with the failure to follow the progressive regulatory framework:

> It isn't a coincidence that it's a woman of a particular race ... of particular class. And so it becomes easy to not comply or to turn a blind eye because you don't value the person who's doing the work

George further explained that, because many domestic workers lack formal education, 'employers understand this, that whether I pay you minimum wage or not, chances are you won't get any other work'. Relatedly, Mbimbi linked the familial discourse to legacies of apartheid, which mean 'the work that particularly Black women do is not seen as real work' since 'Black people are undermined in general, and then Black women are undermined more'. These issues are especially pronounced for irregular migrants, whose desperation means that they 'can work for months without being paid'.[41] Furthermore, despite the inclusion of domestic workers in COIDA since the 2020 ruling, numbers of successful claims to date were low, with technical difficulties of registering noted as an obstacle.[42] Beyond compliance questions, several interviewees stressed that the minimum wage was not the same as a living wage. While equalizing the minimum wage of domestic workers with other sectors was a vital step, participants noted that it was not enough to provide a decent standard of living, particularly when supporting an extended family.[43] Even where higher 'going rates' were set in neighbourhood WhatsApp groups, there was often a lack of reference point based on the cost of living.[44]

[41] Mullagee.
[42] Tekié, Mullagee, George, Mbimbi, von Broembsen.
[43] George, von Broembsen.
[44] von Broembsen.

In summary, while the relatively strong regulatory frameworks in South Africa and Chile thus have a clear role in counteracting the devaluation of domestic work, countervailing factors based on race, migration status, and class continue to exist.

India: State-based regulation and informal negotiation

The situation regarding minimum wage provision for domestic work in India is complex. As a starting point, domestic work is designated as a personal service provided by the home and therefore outside the ambit of labour laws, as indicated by the Supreme Court in several cases.[45] Any modifications to this apply on a state-by-state basis.[46] Early notifiers of minimum wages were Karnataka (2004), Andhra Pradesh and Bihar (2007) and Rajasthan (2008); by 2024, a total of sixteen states and two union territories had extended minimum wage coverage to domestic workers.[47] Yet even where a minimum wage exists, this is set specifically for the sector and frequently undervalues domestic work, including in comparison to male-coded household occupations like driving and gardening, and equivalent work performed in non-domestic settings such as office cleaning.[48] Yajnik noted that in states with minimum wages for domestic workers, the rate 'is so low that it actually is beyond the unskilled category', demonstrating the complexity of calculating rates, particularly for live-out workers. This is not universally the case: Banerjee raised Kerala as an example of good practice, noting that it had combined a compulsory minimum living wage with recognition that some middle-class employers have limited capacity to pay, in response to which, 'they have also provided for a state subsidy ... the two amounts together ensure that the workers get a living wage'.

While positive, this appears to be contingent and region-specific:

> Kerala is a very, very different case compared to the rest of the country ... There's actually a very high demand for domestic workers ... [because of which] there's a lot more dignity and respect given to that sector ('Meera')

[45] *Bangalore Water-Supply & Sewerage vs R Rajappa & Others* [1978] AIR 548, 50–51; *Mgt of Som Vihar Apt Owners Housing vs Workmen, Indian Engg & General Mazdoor* (2002) 9 SCC 652 [7]; *Arun Vihar Residents Welfare vs State of UP And 2 Others* (2019) 10 ADJ 51 [23].

[46] Srijani Datta and others, 'Domestic Workers from Margin to Center: Protest, Opportunity and Threat in Pandemic Politics' (2022) 26 Journal for Cultural Research 39, 42.

[47] ILO, 'Making Decent Work a Reality' (n 34) 106; Sophy K J, 'Paid Domestic Work as Work-Dynamics of Theory and Regulation in India' (2024) 10 Journal of National Law University Delhi 53, 70.

[48] Neetha (n 15) 80; Ravindranath and others (n 6) 47; Samita Sen, 'Regulating Wage, Realizing Rights: Domestic Workers in India' in Pedro Ramos Pinto and Massimo Asta (eds), *The Value of Work Since the 18th Century: Custom, Conflict, Measurement and Theory* (Bloomsbury 2023) 133.

It is yet to be seen whether the system of state-level discretion will be superseded by the new federal Labour Codes.[49] The 2019 Code on Wages makes no direct reference to domestic workers, except in one paragraph stating that requirements to maintain a register, display notices, and issue wage slips do not apply to those employing up to five persons for agriculture or a domestic purpose.[50] While this could suggest that its provisions are otherwise applicable to domestic workers, they rely on a definition of 'employee' that requires, inter alia, that a person be 'employed on wages by an establishment', and there is significant doubt over whether this would include private households.[51] In a response to a Parliamentary Question, the Minister of Labour and Employment stated that since domestic work is performed in households, adding it to the schedule of employment was a matter for states rather than central government.[52] This suggests that the current system of distinct regulatory frameworks across states may continue to apply and potentially reinforces the focus of labour law on industrial settings.[53] However, in the 2025 decision *Malik v Uttarkhand*, the Supreme Court observed that the 2019 Code 'introduces provisions to address the issue of minimum wages for domestic workers.[54] Even if *obiter* because the case primarily related to trafficking, this could be helpful in bolstering the argument for domestic workers' inclusion, particularly given its comments on the 'indispensable' nature of domestic workers' contributions.[55]

As regards social security, the Unorganised Workers' Social Security Act 2008 includes coverage of domestic workers within a broad definition of 'self-employed workers', but has been criticized for its general focus on welfare and poverty reduction rather than setting up concrete social security schemes.[56] Interviewees mirrored this critique, for example stating, 'there's no real social security ... those are just very generalised schemes ... that are available to all poor, not because you're a domestic worker'.[57] Others pointed to the challenges of coverage when a worker has more than one employer.[58] There was some hope that the new E-Shram

[49] See generally Adwitiya Mishra and Aasheerwad Dwivedi, 'Labour Laws in India: History, Evolution and Critical Analysis' [2023] Labor History 1; Supriya Routh, *Labour Justice: A Constitutional Evaluation of Labour Law* (CUP 2024).

[50] The Code on Wages—No 29 of 2019, s50.

[51] ibid s5; Saurabh Bhattacharjee, 'Universalization of Minimum Wages as a Pipe Dream: Many Discontents of the Code on Wages, 2019' (2020) 16 Socio-Legal Review 1, 5–11.

[52] Government of India Minister of Labour and Employment, 'Unstarred Question No 2463 to Be Answered on 01.08.2022' <https://sansad.in/getFile/loksabhaquestions/annex/179/AU2463.pdf?source = pqals> accessed 25 August 2025.

[53] Shardha Rajam and Prabha Kotiswaran, 'Justice within the New Factory Gates: How to Hold RWAs Responsible for Workers' Welfare' (2025) 21 International Journal of Law in Context 176, 187.

[54] *Ajay Malik v State of Uttarakhand and Anr* [2025] INSC 118 [51].

[55] ibid [38–39].

[56] Act No 33 of 2008; Uday Shankar, 'Entitlements of Domestic Workers in India: Welfare or Right' in Upasana Mahanta and Indranath Gupta (eds), *Recognition of the Rights of Domestic Workers in India: Challenges and the Way Forward* (Springer 2019) 26–28.

[57] Nayak.

[58] 'Meera' and 'Gita' (India); also mentioned by Abigail Osiki (South Africa).

portal—a database of unorganized workers through which social security is to be provided[59]—could increase coverage, although a lack of clarity remained as to what it entitled domestic workers to.[60]

The familial discourse in India is overlaid by caste and class, with domestic work primarily performed by poorer women and those from disadvantaged caste groups.[61] Traditionally, there was a divide between cooking, which was associated with higher castes, viewed as more respectable, and better paid, versus cleaning, particularly of toilets, which was allocated to those of lower castes.[62] The role of task separation by caste within domestic work appears to be declining, but not to have disappeared. As explained by Banerjee, there was a move to 'less and less of task differentiation and more and more of feminisation'—although there continued to be a niche group of upper caste Brahmins engaged in cooking, particularly for festivals. Despite the decline in differentiation *between* tasks, the move to domestic work as a 'caste-based' occupation and its complex interplay with class relations contribute to continued devaluation and low wages.[63]

In the absence of a national regulatory framework and with many domestic workers not formally unionized, informal networks often have a significant role in setting wages, which can include asking for annual increments and even social boycotts of homes known to be mistreating domestic workers.[64] There is some hesitancy about moving to a more formalized system: 'Meera' stressed the idea of the minimum wage as a floor rather than a ceiling, and the importance of organizing to ensure the ability to negotiate higher wages, particularly for live-out work. She therefore questioned whether:

> by pushing for a minimum, are you not driving down wages of workers who perhaps earn more than that is also the question, right? How do we then build in the question of experience?

Nonetheless, Sen noted the importance of the minimum wage entitlement in establishing the status of domestic work as work, explaining that the domestic workers' movement:

> demanded inclusion in the minimum wage schedule, not so much for improvement in their wage level, but because it's one way to establish their worker identity[65]

[59] Kuldeepsingh Rajput and S Irudaya Rajan, 'Visibilising Invisible Population: E-Shram Portal and Essentiality of Internal Migration Database in India' (2023) 9 Journal of Social Inclusion Studies 82, 85.
[60] 'Meera' and 'Gita'.
[61] Datta and others (n 46) 43.
[62] Sen and Sengupta (n 12) 99.
[63] Sen and 'Gita'.
[64] Ghatak.
[65] See also Rina Agarwala and Shiny Saha, 'The Employment Relationship and Movement Strategies among Domestic Workers in India' (2018) 44 Critical Sociology 1207, 1219.

The ability of some workers to negotiate higher rates of pay does not detract from the importance of a statutory minimum, but rather means this should be understood as a floor on which to build and a basis for mobilization.[66] Relying only on informal negotiations can lead to precarious outcomes, particularly during crises and for those in weaker negotiating positions. The Covid-19 pandemic precipitated a significant fall in wages for several reasons, including not only a drop in the number of hours worked or households worked for but also a decline in the actual rates of remuneration, which was possible because of the lack of codification of wages.[67] In the post-pandemic situation, the setback had normalized but previous gains from years of experience with an employer had been lost: As 'Gita' explained:

> that setback still holds as a group level, and also there's a setback at the individual level [because when domestic workers move employer they tend to start from the bottom rate]

Overall, the devaluation of domestic work is reflected in the lack of any minimum wage in some states, and, to a degree, in the low level of wages set in others. Informal negotiations play a role that is important in the absence of regulation, but is also precarious, particularly in crisis contexts.

The UK: Devaluation and the 'family worker exemption'

Whereas a lack of national regulation and low set wage levels can be seen to implicitly reinforce devaluation, the UK situation until April 2024 explicitly recreated the conception of a 'family-like' relationship through a legislative exclusion from minimum wage entitlement known as the 'family worker exemption'. From its initial introduction in 1998, the National Minimum Wage was disapplied from 'work relating to the family household', namely where a worker lived in the employer's family home and was 'treated as a member of the family' in relation to living accommodation and meals, and the sharing of tasks and leisure activities.[68] The provision strikingly relied on the familial discourse to designate the work performed as 'not work' and therefore exempt from payment of the minimum wage.[69]

[66] Gautam Bhan and others, 'Deficits in Decent Work: Employer Perspectives and Practices on the Quality of Employment in Domestic Work in Urban India' (ILO 2022) 37.

[67] Kinjal Sampat, Antara Rai Chowdhury, and Gautam Bhan, 'Recovery as Resilience: Domestic Work and Workers in the Aftermath of COVID-19' (2022) 57 Economic and Political Weekly 34, 36–37.

[68] Originally in National Minimum Wage Regulations 1999—SI 1999/584, Reg 2(2); subsequently National Minimum Wage Regulations 2015—SI 2015/621, Reg 57(3).

[69] Natalie Sedacca, 'Domestic Workers, the "Family Worker" Exemption from Minimum Wage, and Gendered Devaluation of Women's Work' (2022) 51 Industrial Law Journal 771. The discussion of the exemption throughout this chapter draws on this article.

Rather than being intended for domestic workers, the exemption was directed towards au pairs, who were imagined as young, without dependents, in the UK for cultural reasons, and working no more than five hours per day.[70] Even this understanding is highly gendered, and no longer reflects the reality for many au pairs, particularly as the sector has become less regulated.[71] The exemption is even more ill-suited to the type of domestic workers this book focuses on—those engaged to provide for household needs, usually on a full-time basis—yet in some cases it worked precisely to deny such workers their entitlement to minimum wage protection. Lawyer Carita Thomas discussed the cynical way the exemption was used against workers:

> it's such a complicated concept, they are clearly not being treated as family members ... but they have human hearts and empathy, and often relationships with children that are very hard to break.

She noted that one of her clients had been 'smiling in photos of ... a day trip' and that it had been problematic to see this used against him: 'victims are allowed to smile, it doesn't negate the exploitation'.

An example of employers succeeding in such an approach is the Court of Appeal case *Nambalat v Taher*,[72] in which two domestic workers unsuccessfully appealed a finding that the family worker exemption applied to them.[73] The Court refused to accept that a 'broad equivalence' of work between the worker and family members was needed for the exemption to apply, holding that '[a] person receiving free accommodation and meals may be expected to perform more household duties for the family than other family members'.[74] This shows a circularity in applying the definition, since other family members, such as dependent children, would usually also be provided with 'free accommodation' without being expected to serve the family on a full-time basis or more in return. The Court of Appeal also found that it had been appropriate for the tribunal to consider the time a domestic worker spent with children 'beyond the scope of her duties' in assessing whether she was treated as a member of the family.[75] This had the 'perverse effect' of meaning that undertaking additional tasks was used to negate the entitlement to pay,[76] reflecting the

[70] Lord Sainsbury of Turville, HL Deb 02 March 1999, vol 597, col 1621–32; Margaret Hodge, HC Deb 25 February 1999, vol 326 col 634–35. See also Chapter 1, section 'Defining domestic work'.

[71] Rosie Cox, 'Gender, Work, Non-Work and the Invisible Migrant: Au Pairs in Contemporary Britain' (2018) 4 Palgrave Communications 1, 3; Busch (n 11) 547.

[72] *Nambalat v Taher and another Chamsi-Pasha and others v Udin* 2013 ICR 1024 (CA).

[73] *Julio & Others v Jose & Others* [2012] ICR 487 (EAT); see Sedacca, 'Family Worker Exemption' (n 69) 785–86.

[74] *Nambalat v Taher* (n 72) [42].

[75] ibid [19–20].

[76] Jenny Moss, 'Migrant Domestic Workers, the National Minimum Wage and the "Family Worker" Concept' in Rosie Cox (ed), *Au Pairs' Lives in Global Context: Sisters or Servants?* (Palgrave Macmillan 2015) 78.

gendered idea of such household work as not real work. In other sectors, the idea of additional time an employee spent beyond their duties being used to reduce their wage entitlement would be likely to be seen as absurd.

While other such challenges went in the worker's favour,[77] each such case turned on specific facts that were often extreme and supported by strong independent evidence, meaning that the overall impact of the exemption was to create uncertainty and a problematic blurring of boundaries.[78] As Sharp explained: 'the kind of grey area ... reinforces any statements made by unscrupulous employers, who are trying to get out of ... their legal responsibilities'. Sharp also pointed to a contradiction with the immigration rules: to enter or remain in the UK on an Overseas Domestic Worker Visa, the entry clearance officer had to be satisfied that the worker would be paid in compliance with the National Minimum Wage.[79] Noting that Kalayaan had seen applications refused by the Home Office for non-compliance with that requirement, she continued:

> But the thing that always strikes me is it's the domestic worker who is penalised for it ... it's not issued, their visa, and they become undocumented and all the issues that that throws up... There are—as far as I'm aware ... no repercussions for the employer.

The visa conditions therefore failed to provide much-needed protection to domestic workers while the exemption remained in place. The impetus to the eventual repeal of the exemption was an Employment Tribunal decision in 2020 that the exemption was unlawful and indirectly discriminatory, which is discussed in the human rights section below. Even after this, the exemption was only repealed on 1 April 2024 following a review by the Low Pay Commission and successful civil society campaigning.[80] The slowness of the government's response following the judgment reflects a lack of priority given to addressing devaluation in domestic work. There are ongoing issues over the calculation of hours worked for minimum wage purposes, and enforcement remains a significant challenge given the harsh visa regime.[81] Likewise, migrant domestic workers remain excluded from non-contributory benefits as a result of the 'no recourse to public funds' condition,

[77] See eg *Taiwo v Olaigbe; Onu v Akwiwu* [2016] UKSC 279.

[78] Sedacca, 'Family Worker Exemption' (n 69) 786–88.

[79] Home Office, 'Immigration Rules (UK)—Updated 5 October 2020' <https://www.gov.uk/guidance/immigration-rules> accessed 22 November 2020, R159A(v). This is also found in the updated version: Home Office, 'Immigration Rules (UK)—Updated 13 August 2025' <https://www.gov.uk/guidance/immigration-rules> accessed 22 August 2025, Appendix Overseas Domestic Worker, ODW 5.5.

[80] The National Minimum Wage (Amendment) Regulations 2024—SI 2024/75; Natalie Sedacca, 'The Family Worker Exemption Revisited: A Sustained Campaign against the Devaluation of Domestic Work' (*UK Labour Law*, 17 November 2023) <https://uklabourlawblog.com/2023/11/17/the-family-worker-exemption-revisited-a-sustained-campaign-against-the-devaluation-of-domestic-work-by-natalie-sedacca/> accessed 28 April 2025.

[81] See Chapters 6 and 7.

while the non-renewable six-month limit to most visas means workers would not have sufficient time to build up contributory benefits.[82] Nonetheless, the repeal of the exemption demonstrates the eventual prevalence of an approach based at least partly on legal rights over the devalued familial discourse.

Human rights law and the challenge to devaluation

Having discussed reforms in the case study countries and countervailing factors that can maintain devaluation, this section moves to examine the salience of human rights law, including the role of anti-discrimination provisions in equalizing frameworks, and the potentially more far-reaching effect of the right to a living wage and to fair pay.

Disparate impacts and discrimination

A clear avenue for challenging exclusion from minimum wage frameworks and social security benefits is equality law, particularly via indirect discrimination, where an apparently neutral provision, criterion, or practice has a disproportionately negative effect on members of a particular group that cannot be justified by a legitimate aim. The composition of the domestic work sector means exclusionary provisions will often have a disparate and negative impact on women, either in general or of a specific (e.g. ethnic) characteristic. Therefore, much depends on the assessment of the legitimate aims that such provisions seek to further. This section examines several cases finding exclusionary regimes towards domestic workers to be discriminatory and demonstrates that, while the outcome of each was of assistance to domestic workers, their implications for the proper valuation of domestic work vary depending on the court's evaluation of reasoning and purported justifications.

A strong recognition of the value of domestic work is found in the South African *Mahlangu* judgment that the exclusion of domestic workers from COIDA was constitutionally invalid based on human rights obligations on social security, equality, and human dignity.[83] In the analysis on social security, it held that 'no legitimate objective is advanced' by the exclusion, which, on the contrary, 'has a significant stigmatising effect which entrenches patterns of disadvantage based on race, sex and gender'.[84] The judgment aptly contextualizes the link between the situation of Ms Mahlangu as an individual domestic worker and the broader, ongoing structural disadvantage dating back to apartheid, treating intersectional discrimination

[82] See Chapters 7 and 8.
[83] *Mahlangu* (n 37).
[84] ibid [64].

as a central concept in guiding the interpretation of other rights and analysing claims involving multiple grounds.[85] Consequently, beyond finding this specified exclusion unlawful, it may lay the groundwork for findings of discrimination in future cases where the disparate impact is less straightforward to prove.[86]

By contrast, other cases finding exclusionary frameworks to be unlawful have given more weight to potential justifying factors. In the UK, the impetus for the repeal of the family worker exemption was the 2020 Employment Tribunal ruling in *Puthenveettil v Alexander*.[87] This arose from the situation of a domestic worker paid substantially below the minimum wage, whose employers raised the exemption in defence against her claim.[88] The Claimant's successful generalized challenge was premised on the incompatibility of the family worker exemption with anti-discrimination law because it primarily and adversely affects women.[89] Once the disparate impact on women had been established, the ET examined two legitimate aims that had been suggested to justify this: first, reflecting 'the unusual working relationship which exists when a live-in worker is or is treated as a member of the family', and secondly, 'encouraging and/ or not discouraging parents from seeking to return or from returning to work'.[90] It swiftly dismissed the first suggested aim for failing to show a real need,[91] which was important in counteracting the idea that a lack of wages could be justified simply because of an 'unusual' relationship. Regarding the second, it concluded that support for working families could amount to a legitimate objective of supporting mothers to work, but that there was a lack of evidence to show it had been adopted, let alone that it was proportionate given its very serious impact and the availability of other, less discriminatory, means of meeting these policy objectives.[92]

Although the ultimate outcome was valuable from the standpoint of domestic workers' rights, viewing the suggested aim as legitimate could potentially allow the rights of one group of workers to be compromised to meet those of another group if stronger evidence on proportionality were provided. Similar concerns have arisen about a judgment of the Court of Justice of the European Union regarding the exclusion of domestic workers in Spain from unemployment protection.[93]

[85] Shreya Atrey, 'Beyond Discrimination: Mahlangu and the Use of Intersectionality as a General Theory of Constitutional Interpretation' (2021) 21 International Journal of Discrimination and the Law 168, 172–74. See also Chapter 3.

[86] ibid 175.

[87] *Puthenveettil v Alexander & George & Secretary of State for Business, Energy and Industrial Strategy*—Case Number 2361118/2013—judgment of 15 December 2020 (Employment Tribunal).

[88] ibid [9].

[89] ibid.

[90] ibid [76].

[91] ibid [78, 85].

[92] ibid [88–100].

[93] *Case C-389/20, CJ v Tesorería General de la Seguridad Social (TGSS)* [2022] Celex 62020CJ0389 (CJEU). This book does not generally focus on EU law since none of the case study countries are current EU member states, but this decision merits mention given the overlap in themes.

The Spanish government put forward various justifications for the exclusion, including the view of domestic work as involving 'high levels of employment with a low level of skill and therefore of pay' and the non-business nature of the employer. In response, the Court held that these were 'in principle legitimate social policy objectives' but took issue with a lack of evidence about the consistency and appropriateness of the measures to meet the aims.[94] Therefore, as with *Puthenveettil*, justifications that implied a devaluation of domestic work were accepted as legitimate, failing only at the proportionality stage,[95] in contrast with the stronger recognition of the value of domestic work in *Mahlangu*.

In addition, while *Puthenveettil* was crucially important as a move away from blatant discrimination and devaluation of domestic work, it equalizes with a national minimum wage that is still below a real living wage.[96] This demonstrates a limitation of anti-discrimination law where it leads to equivalence with a minimum wage that is still low or where there are problems in its calculation. Similarly, the requirements of ILO Convention 189 for domestic workers to enjoy minimum wage coverage *where such coverage exists*, and for remuneration to be established without sex-based discrimination (Article 11), rely on the existing minimum wage framework being adequate.

The right to a living wage and to fair pay

By contrast, a generalized, freestanding requirement for pay that is both adequate for a decent standard of living and 'fair' arises from social rights instruments. Article 7 of the International Covenant on Economic, Social and Cultural Rights (ICESCR) states that remuneration must provide workers, as a minimum, with 'Fair wages and equal remuneration for work of equal value without distinction of any kind', including equality of conditions and pay between genders, and a 'decent living for themselves and their families'.[97] This encompasses three interlinking elements: fairness, equality, and provision for a decent standard of living. General Comment 23 (GC23) of the UN Committee on Economic, Social and Cultural Rights (UNCESCR) clarifies that a 'decent living' should be assessed with regard to factors such as 'the cost of living and other prevailing economic and social conditions', allowing workers to enjoy an adequate standard of living, and that minimum

[94] ibid [53–71].

[95] By contrast, the Advocate General's opinion found such justifications to be based on gender stereotypes—Elisa Chieregato, 'The Role of EU Law in Challenging the Unjustified Differential Treatment of Domestic Workers: An Analysis of the Court of Justice Decision in "CJ v Tesoreria General de La Seguridad Social (TGSS) (C-389/20)"' (2022) 47 European Law Review 827, 832–33.

[96] The Real Living Wage Foundation calculates the living wage as £12.60 UK-wide and £13.85 in London, whereas the statutory National Living Wage from April 2025 for those aged 21 and over is £12.21 throughout the country.

[97] Full references for this and other human rights instruments are in Chapter 3.

wages must be set in line with these goals.[98] Accordingly, where a minimum wage exists but is not set at a high enough level to meet such needs, as seen in the empirical material (e.g. in South Africa), there may still be a failure to meet the standard.

Turning to 'fair pay', GC23 clarifies that this is not a static notion but one that:

> depends on a range of non-exhaustive objective criteria, reflecting not only the *output of the work* but also the *responsibilities of the worker*, the *level of skill and education required* to perform the work, the *impact of the work on the health and safety* of the worker, *specific hardships* related to the work and the *impact on the worker's personal and family life*.[99]

To understand what this means for fair pay in domestic work, it is instructive to examine each of these factors using a feminist perspective and in light of the empirical material. First, 'output' is a factor that risks devaluing domestic work if understood as direct economic productivity, but the social reproduction approach allows for modifications to this approach. Recent contributions that have made a strong case for greater valuation of care and other 'essential work' in assessing value include Bueno's proposal to centre human capabilities in assessing the social value of work[100] and Fredman's suggestion of recognizing care as a constitutional value.[101] For remuneration to be 'fair' according to de Schutter, the UN special rapporteur on Extreme Poverty and Human Rights, it must reflect the work's contribution to society, based on categories deemed 'essential' such as food production and retail, health care, retail, and transport.[102] These conceptions are most relevant to aspects of domestic work that involve care or are otherwise recognizable as 'essential', including the nurturing of children or the care of older people. Other parts of the work's output, such as reproducing the employer's way of life by facilitating leisure time and the culturally appropriate functioning of the household, are less obviously within these 'essential' or caring categories. However, as argued in the subsection on social reproduction in this chapter, they must still be recognized as outputs for the non-tangible goods they provide to employers.

The second and third factors—responsibilities, and requisite skill and education—also require consideration based on feminist critique that rejects the notion of household work as 'simple' or 'unskilled' labour. GC23 acknowledges

[98] UNCESCR, 'General Comment No. 23 on the Right to Just and Favourable Conditions of Work (Art. 7 of the Covenant), 27 April 2016, E/C.12/GC/23' [18–21].

[99] ibid [10]. Emphases added.

[100] Nicolas Bueno, 'The Value of Work in Labour Law' in Nicolas Bueno, Beryl ter Haar, and Nuna Zekic (eds), *Labour Law Utopias: Post-Growth & Post-Productive Work Approaches* (OUP 2024) 125–26.

[101] Fredman (n 19).

[102] Olivier de Schutter, 'Report of the Special Rapporteur on Extreme Poverty and Human Rights—The Working Poor: A Human Rights Approach to Wages—UN Doc A/75/175' (UN General Assembly 2023) [49–54].

this to an extent, stating that the fairness assessment 'should also take into account the position of female workers, particularly where their work and pay has traditionally been undervalued'.[103] Bearing in mind the material discussed above, this value assessment must properly account for the range of distinct skills and activities involved in domestic work. GC23 further states that where minimum wages are set at industry level, 'the work performed in sectors predominantly employing women, minorities or foreign workers should not be undervalued compared with work in sectors predominantly employing men or nationals'.[104] This suggests that equal pay assessments should not be confined to comparisons within an organization, which limits their utility for domestic workers who are employed in individual households, since there is often no comparator working for the same employer on a higher wage.[105] Rather, they should also examine more structural discrepancies that leave feminized sectors facing systemic low pay, as further highlighted in the direct stipulation for domestic workers to enjoy conditions including 'minimum wage coverage where this exists, remuneration established without discrimination based on sex, and social security'.[106]

The final three factors mentioned in the fairness paragraph of GC23—hardships and impact on health and safety and the worker's personal and family life—also point towards a higher stipulation for a fair wage for domestic work. Chapter 4 demonstrated the extensive risks to health and safety and specific hardships involved in domestic work, including a lack of privacy, heightened risk of sexual harassment and abuse, isolation, and adversities including exposure to contagion and containment to employers' homes during the Covid-19 pandemic. The impact on personal and family life is also pronounced, with excessive hours commonly leaving workers with too little time for family life, leisure activities or the development of social relationships, while exclusionary provisions on family reunification mean that migrant domestic workers are often separated from their family members while working.[107]

In sum, when analysed against the empirical material on domestic work using a feminist perspective that brings the value of household labour to the forefront, these factors support not only the equalization of domestic workers' wages with general minimum wage levels, but also the right to higher pay where the adjusted salary does not meet other criteria of fairness or provide sufficiently for a decent standard of living. Most commonly, stipulated rates above a basic minimum come from collective bargaining, which should be encouraged and facilitated for domestic workers. However, bearing in mind the constraints on organizing and the

[103] UNCESCR (n 98) [10].
[104] ibid [23].
[105] On the right to equal pay for women in EU law and its limitations, see Alan Bogg and others, *Human Rights at Work: Reimagining Employment Law* (Hart 2024) 178–79; Fredman (n 19) 769.
[106] UNCESCR (n 98) [47f].
[107] See Chapters 6 and 8.

lack of a representative employer organization with which to bargain, this should not be a precondition for negotiating and setting a stipulated wage for the sector above the general minimum. Such processes can also be facilitated through legislative reform or other specific wage-setting processes that exist—for example, the Sectoral Determination process in South Africa.

The right to a living wage and fair pay in regional systems

In the African system, the African Charter on Human and People's Rights stipulates at Article 15 'the right to work under equitable and satisfactory conditions' and equal pay for equal work. In *Ernest Karatta v Tanzania,* the African Court on Human and People's Rights noted the 'substantive congruence' between this provision and ICESCR Articles 6 and 7,[108] indicating inclusion of the right to a living wage and to fair pay. The African Commission's Principles and Guidelines on economic, social, and cultural rights also indicate that Article 15 includes State obligations to 'ensure the right of everyone to equitable and satisfactory conditions of work, including ... fair remuneration'.[109] Furthermore, the Maputo Protocol provides for the right to equal remuneration for jobs of equal value, the establishment of protection and social insurance for women working in the informal sector, and the necessary measures to recognize the economic value of women's work in the home.[110]

A provision on remuneration providing 'dignified and decent living conditions' and 'fair and equal wages for equal work' is found in the Protocol of San Salvador, Article 7(a). There is also a relevant stipulation in the European Social Charter Article 4(1), which provides for workers' right to remuneration, giving them and their families a decent standard of living, although the Article's contents refer more to a decent standard of living and equal pay for work of equal value than to broader distributional questions of fairness.[111] In interpreting this right, the European Committee of Social Rights previously required the minimum wage to be set at 68 per cent of the national average and reduced this to 60 per cent from the late 1990s, with some leeway to make up the difference to 50 per cent through benefits.[112] The reliance on benefits to make up a living wage can be viewed as conceptually

[108] *Ernest Karatta and others v United Republic of Tanzania* App no 002/2017 (ACtHPR, 30 September 2021) [100].

[109] AComHPR, 'Principles and Guidelines on the Implementation of Economic, Social and Cultural Rights in the African Charter on Human and Peoples' Rights, Adopted at the Forty-Seventh Ordinary Session Held in Banjul, the Gambia, from 12 to 26 May 2010' [59(h)].

[110] African Union, 'The Protocol to the African Charter on Human and Peoples' Rights on the Rights of Women in Africa ('Maputo Protocol') 2003', Article 13.

[111] Hugh Collins, 'Fat Cats, Production Networks, and the Right to Fair Pay' (2022) 85 Modern Law Review 1, 4.

[112] Zoe Adams and Simon Deakin, 'Article 4—The Right to a Fair Remuneration' in Niklas Bruun and others (eds), *The European Social Charter and the Employment Relation* (Hart 2017) 199–207.

problematic because they do not play the same role as a fair wage in building the worker's self-esteem and dignity,[113] and poses particular issues for domestic workers, who are often excluded from access to public funds (e.g. because of their migration status). In any event, the UK has been repeatedly found in breach of the requirement since the early 1990s, largely because of an overreliance on benefits in making the overall wage up to 60 per cent of the average.[114]

The European Convention on Human Rights (ECHR) and the American Convention on Human Rights (ACHR) do not contain an equivalent right to decent work. However, the Inter-American Court of Human Rights (IACtHR) has 'read in' this provision, including a right to a fair wage, using an integrated approach under Article 26 ACHR.[115] *FEMAPOR v Peru* concerned a failure to comply with a Supreme Court order ('amparo') fixing methods of calculating pay increases in the case of over 4,000 maritime and port workers who had been dismissed on economic grounds.[116] The IACtHR held that the right to work encompassed obtaining a fair wage, drawing *inter alia* on provisions in Articles 45(b) and 34(g) of the Amended Charter of the Organization of American States, requiring States to respect and guarantee those rights to allow 'levelling the unequal relation that exists between workers and employers and the access to fair wages and safe working conditions'.[117] This judgment could have broader ramifications regarding the sufficiency of remuneration, in the private as well as the public sector.[118] It might be used to question whether the minimum wage in Chile, calculated on a monthly basis, is adequate for domestic workers given their longer working hours. More recently, the IACtHR's Advisory Opinion on the right to care emphasized the 'undeniable social value' of caring activities and confirmed the applicability of all guarantees deriving from the right to work to paid care work.[119]

Also notable for a strong 'integrated approach' is the 1982 *Asiad Workers* case in the Indian Supreme Court, which links non-payment of the minimum wage to forced labour.[120] While primarily addressing a specific form of forced labour called 'begar', it holds that the Constitution makers intended a much broader prohibition, which encompasses economic compulsion 'to provide labour or service even though the remuneration received for it is less than the minimum wage' within

[113] Collins (n 111) 4.
[114] Adams and Deakin (n 112) 207–10.
[115] See Chapter 3.
[116] *The National Federation of Maritime and Port Workers (FEMAPOR) v Peru* IACtHR 1 February 2022, Ser C No 448 [1–44].
[117] ibid [108].
[118] Franz Christian Ebert, 'A Regional Revitalisation of Labour Rights? The Emerging Approach of the Inter-American Court of Human Rights' in Brian Langille and Anne Trebilcock (eds), *Social Justice and the World of Work: Possible Global Futures* (Bloomsbury 2023) 231.
[119] *The content and scope of the right to care and its interrelationship with other rights— Advisory Opinion OC-31/25* IACtHR 12 June 2025, Ser A No 31 [215–19].
[120] *People's Union for Democratic Rights v Union of India and Others* ('*Asiad Workers* case') (1982) 3 SCC 235, 26.

the term 'force'.[121] The Indian Constitution also provides a definition of the living wage, with Article 43 providing that the State shall:

> endeavour to secure, by suitable legislation or economic organisation or in any other way, to all workers, agricultural, industrial or otherwise, work, a living wage, conditions of work ensuring a decent standard of life and *full enjoyment of leisure and social and cultural opportunities*.[122]

In 1957, the tripartite Indian Labour Conference specified five norms for calculation of wages, including the nutritional and clothing requirements of an average family, rental costs, and items such as fuel and lighting.[123] Subsequently, the 1992 *Reptakos Brett* case added the requirement for 25 per cent of the minimum wage to cover children's education, medical costs, recreation including festivals and ceremonies, and provision for factors such as old age and marriages.[124] This is noteworthy for its expansive approach to a living wage and the range of goods expected to be included.[125] However, it has not generally assisted domestic workers to date, with the sector either excluded from a minimum wage altogether or subjected to a lower level. Accordingly, this is an example where the right to fairness and pay equality between men and women remains important in establishing that the same norms apply to women's work.

The link with forced labour is also relevant in the European Court of Human Rights (ECtHR) context, with several cases referring to underpayment or non-payment of persons held in domestic servitude as background to findings of a breach of Article 4 ECHR on forced labour. The domestic servitude case *Siliadin v France* concerned a Togolose national brought to France aged fifteen who—contrary to promises of education and formalization—had her passport taken from her and became a 'housemaid', working long hours seven days a week with few exceptions, almost always without pay.[126] The domestic decisions strongly reflect devaluation, with the Versailles Court of Appeal confirming the first instance finding that 'carrying out household tasks and looking after children throughout the day could not by themselves constitute working conditions incompatible with human dignity, this being the lot of many mothers'.[127] The applicant's submissions challenged that by referring to Council of Europe criteria on domestic slavery as including the 'absence of remuneration or remuneration that was disproportionate

[121] ibid 26–31.
[122] Emphasis added. See also the discussion in Bogg and others (n 105) 171.
[123] Jehosh Paul, 'What Exactly Are the Current Norms for Calculating the Minimum Wage in India?' (2023) 4 Indian Public Policy Review 57, 60–61.
[124] *Workmen Represented by Secretary vs Management of Reptakos Brett and Co* [1992] AIR 504.
[125] This approach has not been incorporated into the new Labour Codes—Bhattacharjee (n 51) 15–16.
[126] *Siliadin v France* (2006) 43 EHRR 16 [10–15].
[127] ibid [44].

to the services provided', and, in finding that her treatment amounted to forced labour and servitude, the ECtHR noted the lack of payment among other factors.[128] Therefore, despite a primary focus on the lack of appropriate criminal legislation and the question of whether the labour was freely performed or coerced,[129] the finding against the state implies a rejection of the domestic courts' views that reinforced devaluation.

Similarly, in another domestic servitude case, *CN v UK*, the applicant had her passport taken from her on arrival in London, was warned about being arrested, and was placed with an elderly couple for whom she was almost permanently on call every day and night.[130] She was found to have received no significant payment for her labour, but the police viewed this as 'no more than an absence of "honour among thieves"'—an assumption which, she submitted, 'betrayed a fundamental disregard of the ILO's key indicators of forced labour and a troubling ignorance of the vulnerabilities of illegal immigrants'.[131] The ECtHR held that the absence of a distinct offence of servitude prevented domestic authorities from giving due weight to relevant factors, including the failure of a relative to keep wages for her as agreed.[132] Again, therefore, while the primary outcome related to criminal law remedies, the case contains recognition of the role that withholding of wages plays in domestic servitude and forced labour. Furthermore, in *Chowdury & ors v Greece*, the fact that migrant workers recognized they were unlikely to ever receive their wages if they stopped working was held to negate any voluntary agreement to the poor conditions they worked in.[133] That case also involved threats to the workers and being surrounded by armed guards, making it difficult to 'separate the structural and individual coercion' on which the finding is based.[134]

From the ECtHR cases to date, it is unclear whether the issues relating to non- or low payment alone would have been adequate to establish an Article 4 breach, without additional factors such as confinement, passport confiscation, or threats. However, these decisions indicate at least the potential to develop a more structural reading of the prohibition on forced labour, in line with the IACtHR approach discussed in Chapter 4, which encompasses positive obligations to pass and enforce preventative legislation. Furthermore, the recent case of *FM v Russia* demonstrated how frameworks with a disproportionate impact in making a particular group susceptible to forced labour can give rise to a violation of Article 14, which prohibits discrimination in relation to other rights, read with Article 4.[135]

[128] ibid [93–148].
[129] Virginia Mantouvalou, *Structural Injustice and Workers' Rights* (OUP 2023) 121.
[130] *CN v United Kingdom* (2013) 56 EHRR 24 [5–9].
[131] ibid [10, 49–50].
[132] ibid [80].
[133] *Chowdury and Others v Greece* App no 21884/15 (ECtHR, 30 March 2017) [96–97]; Mantouvalou (n 129) 122–23.
[134] Maayan Niezna, 'Consent to Labour Exploitation' (2024) 53 Industrial Law Journal 3, 27.
[135] *FM and others v Russia* App nos 71671/16 and 40190/18 (ECtHR, 10 December 2024) [340–44]. For a detailed discussion of the case, see Chapter 7.

This will often be relevant to legislative provisions and enforcement gaps that leave domestic workers without access to a fair or living wage, given the concentration of their impact on (minoritized) women. A broader understanding of Article 4 would also be in line with the ILO's recognition of a link between underpayment or withholding of payments and forced labour or economic coercion, mirroring the approach in the *Asiad Workers* case.[136] As Drew has argued, the strengths of this approach lie in its potential for a 'more sensitive and protective identification of forced labour' compared with market-based understandings that fail to account for a background of economic compulsion.[137] Although not every violation of the right to decent work reaches the threshold of forced labour, systemic violations such as widespread non-payment of the minimum wage can facilitate forced labour and servitude.[138]

Another potential route to challenging non-payment of wages is through the entitlement to peaceful enjoyment of possessions in ECHR Protocol 1, Article 1.[139] For this purpose, the term 'possessions' is determined independently from classifications in domestic law, and is not limited to owning physical goods,[140] having been found relevant to confiscation of earnings in *Paulet v UK*.[141] Therefore, the failure to pay a fair or living wage to domestic workers could be within the ambit of the right and could give rise to a violation, particularly when read with Article 14.[142] Taken together, these provisions should be understood as creating a requirement to repeal or amend laws that facilitate systemic violations of the right to decent work, which include both statutory exclusions from payment and laws that set the minimum wage at a level below a 'fair' wage adequate for a decent standard of living.

Conclusion

Drawing on empirical material from across the case study countries, this chapter has explored how the familial discourse that represents domestic workers as 'like a

[136] ILO, 'Indicators of Forced Labour' (ILO 2012); Sandhya Drew, 'Safe in Leicester Town? Law's Reach to Those Working for Less Than the National Minimum Wage' [2025] Industrial Law Journal dwaf004, 11–15.

[137] Drew (n 136) 15–17.

[138] Klara Skrivankova, 'Between Decent Work and Forced Labour: Examining the Continuum of Exploitation' (Joseph Rowntree Foundation 2010) 4; Kate Roberts, 'Rights Not Rescue: Lessons from Migrant Domestic Workers in the UK and Their Struggle for Systems Change' (2020) 15 Anti-Trafficking Review 167, 170.

[139] Mantouvalou (n 129) 131–34.

[140] *Öneryildiz v Turkey* (2005) 41 EHRR 20 [124].

[141] *Paulet v United Kingdom* (2015) 61 EHRR 39 [6–11, 65–68].

[142] This argument is made regarding exclusion from the minimum wage by Mantouvalou (n 129) 132. See further Chapter 7.

member of the family' creates feelings of indebtedness and allows employers to extract additional work from workers. While domestic workers may appreciate additional goods that they are provided with as a result of this discourse, these benefits nonetheless remain discretionary and precarious, while reproducing inequality between the worker and the employer. Meanwhile, the concept of a family-like relationship facilitates non-recognition of the varied and complex skills and responsibilities involved in household work. Social reproduction theory is an important route to recognizing how domestic work contributes to economic value by facilitating employers' labour market participation, but a modified understanding of this concept is necessary to ensure that the contribution to less tangible goods such as employers' leisure time and the reproduction of a particular way of life is also accounted for.

The chapter has analysed regulatory reforms to domestic work through an extension of minimum wage and social security entitlements as having an important role in counteracting the familial discourse and devaluation. Yet even in the countries where the regulatory process is more advanced—Chile and South Africa—there remain influential countervailing factors, such as the impact of migration status in making workers more susceptible to viewing themselves as akin to family members as a survival strategy, and devaluation based on race making non-compliance seem more acceptable to employers. Such factors are similarly likely to persist in the UK following the recent repeal of the 'family worker exemption' from minimum wage, given the ongoing restrictive migration regime. In India, the lack of any minimum wage in some states and the low level of rates in many others continues to reflect devaluation, leaving informal negotiations playing an important role, but one that is precarious in crisis context such as the Covid-19 pandemic.

Against this background of incomplete reform to counter devaluation, human rights law has an important role in supporting the recognition of the value of domestic work and demands for equalization with existing minimum wage and social security entitlements. Across several jurisdictions, anti-discrimination law has been used to challenge frameworks excluding domestic workers from minimum wage or social security coverage. While these cases have all been of practical utility, their normative significance for recognizing the value of domestic work has varied depending on the way that each court treated potential justifying factors. Whereas the anti-discrimination framework and provisions of C-189 are limited to equalizing with existing provisions on minimum wage, the right to fair pay and to a living wage based on ICESCR have potentially broader ramifications in requiring that pay is fair and provides an adequate standard of living to domestic workers and their families. The right to a fair wage, read in light of the empirical material and feminist critique, requires acknowledgement of the varied outputs of domestic work that go beyond classic social reproduction theory, alongside the complexity of responsibilities often involved in the role, which this chapter has explored. It should also reflect the significant hardships, risks to health and safety, and impact on personal and family life experienced by domestic workers. In the next chapter, this final factor will be explored in more detail through an analysis of working time and the excessive hours faced by many, particularly live-in, domestic workers.

6
Working time
The challenge of regulating hours in domestic work

Introduction

This chapter examines the regulation of working time, which is a persistent challenge in the domestic work sector. Live-in domestic workers in particular frequently undertake very long hours without defined breaks, reflecting a lack of effective enforcement of standards and, in some jurisdictions, formal exemptions from working hours regulations applicable in other sectors. Live-out workers may have more delineated hours but often combine these with other commitments, including care and housework for their own families. In 2020, an ILO report found that half of the 108 countries it examined had set weekly hours limits for domestic work that were at least equal to those applying in other sectors, while 19 per cent of countries had longer weekly hours and 28 per cent did not impose such limits.[1] However, the distribution of domestic workers across these countries means that 48.9 per cent of all domestic workers have no limits on their working hours, and even where limits have formally been set, compliance is often lacking in practice.[2]

The obstacles to regulating working hours relate to both the 'lack of accountability' and 'devaluation' frameworks of analysis. They demonstrate a lack of scrutiny in the private sphere because hours are frequently uncontrolled and unmonitored, with a reluctance to keep proper records of time worked. In addition, they reflect devaluation because they are linked to the work's conflation with the unpaid labour that women traditionally provided for free in the family household and the low social value consequently assigned to it.[3] The view of domestic work as inherent to women and its conflation with unpaid labour in the home obscures the recognition of additional time spent with members of the employing family as overtime that should be limited and properly accounted for. The difficulties in

[1] ILO, 'Making Decent Work a Reality for Domestic Workers—Progress and Prospects Ten Years after the Adoption of the Domestic Workers Convention, 2011 (No. 189)' (ILO 2021) 72.
[2] ibid 72, 150–51.
[3] Mignon Duffy, 'Doing the Dirty Work: Gender, Race, and Reproductive Labor in Historical Perspective' (2007) 21 Gender & Society 313, 330; Kamala Sankaran, 'Domestic Work, Unpaid Work and Wage Rates' (2013) 48 Economic and Political Weekly 85. See further Chapter 2.

Human Rights and the Protection of Domestic Workers in Labour and Migration Law. Natalie Sedacca, Oxford University Press. © Oxford University Press 2026. DOI: 10.1093/9780198985266.003.0008

regulating hours, particularly for live-in work, relates to an assumption that the worker is 'someone whose time is at the disposal of the employer almost wholesale', resulting in what Mundlak has called a 'boundaryless relationship'.[4] Blackett uses the similar concept of the 'boundarilessness' of domestic workers' time to discuss the expectation of 'servants' being constantly available to perform duties for their 'masters'.[5]

The next section of this chapter examines the legal position in the case study countries, beginning with South Africa, which has the strongest framework for regulating the hours of both live-in and live-out workers but ongoing shortcomings in implementation. It then considers Chile, where reforms in 2015 have shortened hours but still left a distinction between live-in and live-out arrangements. It examines weaker frameworks in the UK, with its specific legal exemptions for 'domestic servants', and India, where a lack of regulation of working hours at national level reflects broader exclusions from labour law. Noting that across all the studies, live-in domestic workers can face an expectation of uncontrolled hours and constant availability, it goes on to critically examine the justifications offered for these arrangements, and the impact of extended hours on domestic workers' private and family lives.

The human rights section sets out the social and economic rights framework relevant to the limitation of working time before focusing primarily on the salience of the right to private and family life, which brings the matter within the more justiciable sphere of civil and political rights. I argue that viewing the question of working hours through this lens is especially pertinent in domestic work regulation because it underscores the need for time away from work, regardless of whether the worker has periods of 'downtime' during the day. The section draws on regional human rights jurisprudence to support this broad understanding of the right to private and family life before analysing implicit and explicit justifications for limiting this right in the domestic work sector, including cultural expectations of constant availability and the notion of supporting working families. While accepting that the latter can amount to a legitimate aim, it argues that measures taken to pursue it are unlikely to be proportionate where they have a significant negative effect on the human rights of domestic workers. It also highlights the availability of other measures that states could use to support these aims and address work-family reconciliation, including improved publicly-funded childcare services and working time reform.

[4] Guy Mundlak, 'Recommodifying Time: Working Hours of "Live in" Domestic Workers' in Joanne Conaghan and Kerry Rittich (eds), *Labour Law, Work, and Family: Critical and Comparative Perspectives* (OUP 2005) 129–30.

[5] Adelle Blackett, 'The Decent Work for Domestic Workers Convention and Recommendation, 2011' (2012) 106 American Journal of International Law 778, 784.

Legal frameworks for regulating domestic workers' hours

Across the case study countries, the strongest formal framework regarding domestic workers' hours, regardless of live-in or live-out status, is found in South Africa. According to the 2002 Sectoral Determination, an employer may not require or permit a domestic worker to work more than forty-five hours in any week, nine hours in any day if they work for five days or less, and eight hours if they work for more than five days.[6] Any overtime must be agreed between the parties and is limited to fifteen hours per week, while workers cannot work more than twelve hours, including overtime, on any day, and must be paid at a higher rate for overtime or compensated by additional time off.[7] There are also restrictions on the use of standby, requirements for meal intervals and rest periods, and limits on work on Sundays and public holidays.[8] However, there are significant shortcomings in compliance. In interviews conducted in 2004–05, Ally found that many workers continued to work twelve hours per day, seven days per week.[9] More recently, a study of over 100 live-in domestic workers conducted by the NGOs Solidarity Center and IZWI referred to the frequent expectation for them to be available 'at any time of day or night', such that having their own familial duties is seen as a conflict of interest.[10] This concern was mirrored in my interviews, with George stating:

> [M]any of them end up working around the clock. So if you are within your employer's vicinity ... if something happens, they need you in the middle of the night, they call you, so, lines get very blurry between the rights and how they're enforced

Several interviewees indicated that limiting working hours and accessing leave that is set out as an entitlement in the Sectoral Determination was often, in practice, a matter of negotiation. According to Osiki, particularly for live-in domestic workers, access 'just depends on the personal agency of the domestic worker in question', but overall, they 'tend to work longer hours, have less time for their family ... there's less distinction between their private and their work life'. As to the scale of such non-compliance, Tekié stated that there was no systemic study of the numbers that were working more than eight to nine hours but that 'anecdotally, it's very clear that it's ... probably most domestic workers who come to [domestic

[6] Basic Conditions of Employment Act—Act 75 of 1997—Sectoral Determination 7: Domestic Worker Sector [updated to 26 November 2014] 2002 [10].

[7] ibid [11–12].

[8] ibid [14–18].

[9] Shireen A Ally, *From Servants to Workers: South African Domestic Workers and the Democratic State* (Cornell University Press 2009) 80.

[10] Solidarity Center and IZWI, 'The Persistence of Private Power: Sacrificing Rights for Wages' (2021) 22–23. See also LN Maqubela, 'Mothering the "Other": The Sacrificial Nature of Paid Domestic Work within Black Families in the Post-Apartheid South Africa' (2016) 14 Gender & Behaviour 7214.

worker organization IZWI], I would say more than 50% are'. This suggests that significant compliance issues exist despite the protective framework, which are especially stark for live-in workers and underscore the 'constant negotiation' that takes place to control working time.[11]

Chile similarly has comprehensive regulation, but this distinguishes between categories of domestic workers. For live-out domestic workers, the 2014 amendments introduced a general weekly limit of forty-five hours, to be distributed over no more than six days, and the possibility to agree in writing up to an extra fifteen hours of work per week to be paid at a higher rate.[12] This is similar to the situation for all domestic workers in South Africa, and contrasts favourably with a previous much higher working week of seventy-two hours.[13] It created a position broadly in line with workers in other sectors, who were subject to a forty-five-hour weekly limit distributed over five or six days.[14] Further legislation passed in 2023 reduces the usual maximum to forty hours weekly for live-out domestic workers as well as other workers,[15] and will be progressively implemented by 2028.[16] Relevant to both live-in and live-out workers, the 2015 reforms prevented unilateral reduction of remuneration as a result of the decreased working week or increased rest days it implemented,[17] which is important in ensuring the changes benefit workers and properly value domestic work.

However, live-in domestic workers are not subject to the same limits or a fixed timetable. Instead, they are normally expected to have a total of twelve hours' daily rest, including nine continuous hours between days.[18] This leaves open the possibility of being expected to work during the twelve hours of rest, reflecting a resistance to defining hours as precisely as for other sectors.[19] As regards rest days, live-in workers have an entitlement to Sundays, Saturdays, and public holidays off as a starting point, but the exact regulations around these vary. The entitlement to Sundays cannot be waived; for Saturdays, the entitlement can be accumulated,

[11] Adelle Blackett, *Everyday Transgressions: Domestic Workers' Transnational Challenge to International Labor Law* (Cornell University Press 2019) 62.

[12] Ley No 20.786—Modifica la Jornada, Descanso y Composición de la Remuneración de los Trabajadores de Casa Particular, y Prohíbe La Exigencia de Uniforme en Lugares Públicos 2014, unitary article para 3(a)–(d).

[13] Rosario Fernández, 'Commodification of Domestic Labour, the Culture of Servitude and the Making of the Chilean Nation' (2018) 43 Österreichische Zeitschrift für Soziologie 49, 55.

[14] Código del Trabajo (Labour Code of Chile)—Edición actualizada al 3 de Mayo de 2021, Arts 22, 28. The older version is cited here because of the subsequent changes.

[15] Ley No 21.561—Modifica el Código del Trabajo con el Objeto de Reducir la Jornada Laboral 2023, Art 1(1) and (19).

[16] Dirección del Trabajo, 'Dictamen 81/02 - 01.02.2024' <https://www.dt.gob.cl/legislacion/1624/articles-125559_recurso_1.pdf> accessed 4 June 2025, 1(b). A 'Dictamen' is an administrative act that specifies the meaning and scope of norms—José Luis Ugarte Cataldo, 'Inspección del Trabajo en Chile: Vicistudes y Desafíos' (2008) 6 Revista Latinoamericana de Derecho Social 187, 191.

[17] Ley 20.786—2014, third transitory article.

[18] Código del Trabajo—Edición actualizada al 8 de agosto de 2025 ('Labour Code—Chile 2025'), Art 149(e).

[19] Fernández (n 13) 55.

fragmented, or changed for another day in the same month, and for public holidays, it can be changed for another day during the following ninety days.[20] The provision for days off is a significant positive attribute, particularly bearing in mind that some other sectors of workers, such as those in establishments and businesses that attend directly to the public, can be exempted from provisions on Sunday rest.[21] However, it could still leave a standard working week of sixty hours (twelve hours multiplied by five days). The recent legislation mentioned above has added the right to two days freely available per calendar month to be absent from labour, which can be accumulated within a three-month period by mutual agreement.[22]

There has been concern over the 2015 reforms leaving some distinctions between live-in and live-out workers intact. Law 20.786 faced criticism, including during parliamentary discussions, for not going far enough to remedy inequalities because of the extended timetable during the week for live-in workers, with the unions originally arguing for the same limits to apply as for live-out workers.[23] In interviews, Olate observed that some difference in limitations could be rationalized based on the fact that live-out workers have to commute to and from their workplace. Others criticized the extended working week for live-in domestic workers, with Ugarte and Caamaño Rojo arguing that all should have exactly the same limits. A key reason that was given to explain the lack of a fixed timetable was the expectation of constant availability for live-in domestic workers. As Olate expressed it: 'we know the hour that we wake up but not the hour when we go to sleep', a point echoed by domestic workers 'Francisca' and 'Michelle'. These points demonstrate the impact of the ongoing expectation of constant availability, and the need for effective enforcement procedures.

Interviewees mentioned some instances of non-compliance with the limits as they stood at the time of my research. For example, live-in worker 'Sofia' had originally been told her schedule would be Monday to Friday but had ended up working on Saturdays too, and having to be back at the employer's home at 8pm on Sundays to start work again. Even for live-out workers, Gallego mentioned that they would often still be paid per day rather than have a fixed number of hours such as 9am to 7pm. A more prevalent theme in the interviews than non-compliance per se was the negative impact of the ongoing longer hours permitted for live-in workers, with several worker interviewees mentioning the lack of respect for timetables in this context.[24] 'Constanza', for example, said her relationship with her employer was generally 'fantastic ... harmonious ... As long as we're not discussing the specific

[20] Dirección del Trabajo, 'Dictamen 4268/68—30.10.2014' <https://www.dt.gob.cl/legislacion/1624/w3-article-104299.html> accessed 3 June 2025.
[21] Labour Code—Chile 2025, Art 38.
[22] Ley No 21.561—Modifica el Código del Trabajo con el Objeto de Reducir la Jornada Laboral, Art 1(19); Labour Code—Chile 2025, Art 150(d).
[23] Biblioteca del Congreso Nacional de Chile, 'Historia de La Ley N° 20.786' 64–71.
[24] 'Sofia', 'Romina' (live-out, previously live-in), and 'Constanza' (live-in).

issue of finishing time, and timetable'. Likewise, 'Rocío' explained that 'for the majority of people, if a domestic worker puts limits on their hours, they'll find it super rude', stressing how it could be difficult to negotiate or decline working hours while a person is in the household, and perhaps is being asked to work extra because of a family birthday.

An unequal position for domestic workers regarding working time is formalized in the UK. Regulation 19 of the Working Time Regulations (WTR) excludes persons 'employed as a domestic servant in a private household' from a number of its key provisions, most notably the maximum average working week of forty-eight hours, and also limits on night work, requirements for additional breaks where the pattern of work puts health and safety at risk, and specific provisions for workers aged fifteen to seventeen.[25] As discussed in Chapter 4, the definition of 'domestic servant' encompasses domestic workers 'employed directly by the householder'. While workers in other sectors can individually opt out of the forty-eight-hour weekly limit, the situation for domestic workers is distinctive as the whole category is opted out without individual choice for the worker. Formally, other parts of the WTR are applicable to domestic workers, including for a daily rest period of at least eleven consecutive hours, a twenty-four-hour rest period generally each week, and a rest break of at least twenty minutes per six hours worked.[26] However, without a weekly maximum, this still allows for a very lengthy working week,[27] meaning that, even before enforcement issues are factored in, excessive hours are a significant problem. The official government page tells domestic workers that their employer must 'not force you to work excessive hours',[28] without indicating what level would be excessive or mentioning overtime, and seemingly implying that excessive hours may be worked as long as they are not 'forced'.

Since the WTR derives from the EU's Working Time Directive,[29] it is salient to briefly address the compatibility of these carve outs with EU law. The Working Time Directive refers to the EU's health and safety directive, which excludes domestic servants;[30] the exclusion has been interpreted as allowing domestic workers to be excluded from working time protection.[31] This interpretation has been

[25] SI 1998/1833, which applies in England, Scotland, and Wales. The disapplied regulations are: 4(1) and (2); 5A(1) and (4); 6(1), (2), and (7); 6A, 7(1), (2), and (6); and 8. For Northern Ireland, the equivalent is Reg 23 of the Working Time Regulations (Northern Ireland) 2016, SI 2016/49 and the disapplied regulations are: 4(1) and (2); 6(1) and (4); 7(1), (2) and (6); and 9(1), (2), and (6).

[26] SI 1998/1833 Regs 10(1), 11(1) and (2), 12(1) and (3).

[27] Jill Murray, *Transnational Labour Regulation: The ILO and EC Compared* (Kluwer Law International 2001) 199–200.

[28] GOV.UK, 'Overseas Domestic Worker Visa' (*GOV.UK*) <https://www.gov.uk/overseas-domestic-worker-visa/your-employment-rights> accessed 3 June 2025.

[29] Directive 2003/88/EC of the European Parliament and of the Council of 4 November 2003 concerning certain aspects of the organisation of working time 2003.

[30] Council Directive (EC) 89/391 on the introduction of measures to encourage improvements in the safety and health of workers at work [1989] OJ L 183 1989, Art 3(1). See Chapter 4.

[31] Tonia Novitz and Phil Syrpis, 'The Place of Domestic Work in Europe: An Analysis of Current Policy in the Light of the Council Decision Authorising Member States to Ratify ILO Convention No.

convincingly challenged in academic literature,[32] and the European Commission has stated that such exemptions are not consistent with the Working Time Directive unless transposition of its provisions is ensured by collective agreements.[33] Yet the Commission has been slow to take infringement proceedings on this matter,[34] and had not done so by the time of the UK's exit from the EU.[35]

There are also issues in the UK around 'on-call' time, namely hours where the worker is on standby and available to work. The pronounced difficulties defining and measuring such time for live-in domestic workers—who are both at 'home' and at their workplace—create a strong argument that all their 'on-call' time should be counted as working time,[36] but the UK has been resistant to this. Under the WTR Regulation 2(1), working time is defined as periods during which a person is working, at their employer's disposal, and carrying out activities or duties. Pre-Brexit judgments of the Court of Justice of the European Union generally defined an 'on-call' period as working time where it required physical presence at the workplace, or a quick response from the worker where they were not at the workplace,[37] but these principles were not consistently applied in domestic decisions.[38] Furthermore, for the purpose of National Minimum Wage calculations, 'on-call' time is only classed as work where the worker is not at home, and is 'awake for the purpose of working', even if they sleep at or near the place of work.[39] This was interpreted strictly in the 2021 Supreme Court case *Mencap v Tomlinson Blake* regarding care workers' 'sleep-in shifts'. Despite the care workers needing to listen out for issues that arose during the night, the Court held that their time was not included in working time calculations unless they actually answered an emergency call.[40] Although not relating directly to live-in workers, the

189' (2015) 6 European Labour Law Journal 104, 110–12; Lisa Rodgers, *Labour Law, Vulnerability and the Regulation of Precarious Work* (Edward Elgar 2016) 180–81.

[32] Vera Pavlou, *Migrant Domestic Workers in Europe: Law and the Construction of Vulnerability* (Hart 2021) 110–11; Kirsten Scheiwe, 'Domestic Workers, EU Working Time Law and Implementation Deficits in National Law—Change in Sight?' (European University Institute Department of Law 2021) EUI Working Paper LAW 2021/03.

[33] European Commission, 'Report on the Implementation by Member States of Directive 2003/88/EC Concerning Certain Aspects of the Organisation of Working Time' (2017) COM(2017) 254 final.

[34] Scheiwe (n 32) 15.

[35] On the status of EU law post-Brexit, see eg Emily Hancox, 'Interpreting the Post-Brexit Legal Framework' (2021) 80 Cambridge Law Journal 428; Sylvia de Mars, 'A Little Less Liable? Enforcing Post-Brexit EU Law in the UK' (2023) 48 European Law Review 151.

[36] Deirdre McCann and Jill Murray, 'The Legal Regulation of Working Time in Domestic Work—International Labour Office Conditions of Work and Employment Series No. 27' (9 September 2010) 5, 28–32 <https://papers.ssrn.com/abstract = 1794171> accessed 4 July 2025.

[37] Case C-303/98 *SIMAP v Conselleria de Sanidad y Consumo de la Generalidad Valenc* [2000] ECLI ECLI:EU:C:2000:528 (CJEU); Case C-518/15 *Ville de Nivelles v Rudy Matzak* [2018] ECLI ECLI:EU:C:2018:82 (CJEU); Leszek Mitrus, 'Defining Working Time versus Rest Time: An Analysis of the Recent CJEU Case Law on Stand-by Time' (2023) 14 European Labour Law Journal 35, 36–37.

[38] Lisa Rodgers, 'The Notion of Working Time' (2009) 38 Industrial Law Journal 80.

[39] National Minimum Wage Regulations 2015—SI 2015/621, Reg 32.

[40] *Royal Mencap Society v Tomlinson-Blake* [2021] UKSC 8.

decision further underscores the devaluation and differential treatment of care work.[41]

These various weaknesses and areas of uncertainty in the regulations have serious ramifications for domestic workers. In interview, Sharp said the 'number one complaint at Kalayaan' was that, because of the nature of the work in a private household, reported hours were 'far in excess of the hours that they agree in their contract, with no reflection in their pay . . . working "on-call" through the night' and workers felt they had no choice other than compliance. She indicated that this was a particular issue where caring responsibilities are involved, including children or elderly people who needed support at night, where there is 'the tendency . . . for employers to forget that this is work'. The reasons domestic worker interviewees gave for leaving their original employers included being forced to work excessive hours in seven cases, and having excessive work (in the sense of tasks to complete) in five. 'Maria', for example, stated:

> I take care for the parents of my employer and the sister of my employer and my madame . . . So call me help . . . the other one will call me do this do this, do that. And I don't have enough sleep.

The worker 'Joana', cited in Chapter 5 in relation to the expectation to fetch items for members of the employer's family, explained how she was then punished for an inability to keep up with the demanding tasks: 'one time my female employer she angry with me too much because . . . I didn't finish all my works . . . she hurt me, she slapped me . . . '. The interviews thus convey a sense of domestic workers being given unending tasks from an undefined number of people, sometimes going beyond housework and care to include being at their beck and call. Interviewees 'Katalina' and 'Marina' also mentioned being sent to clean the house of a friend of a relative in addition to their main tasks, which clearly reflects devaluation. Since it is not seen as 'real' work, there is an idea that domestic workers can be called on at will to give extra help, including to people beyond their main employing family, without recognizing this, putting limits on it, or paying overtime.

These concerns are reiterated by a survey of 200 domestic workers conducted by the Voice of Domestic Workers in 2023, in which 55 per cent of the respondents had left their original employer and reported on conditions with their new employer, 27 per cent reported being 'on-call' twenty-four hours a day, 26 per cent that they were not given rests or break periods, and 5 per cent not being given a day off from work.[42] Similarly, a survey conducted in 2022–23 among ninety-seven

[41] LJB Hayes, 'Discrimination by Legal Design? UK Supreme Court in Mencap v Tomlinson-Blake Finds Care Workers Are Not Protected by Minimum Wage Law for Sleep-in Shifts' (2022) 51 Industrial Law Journal 696.

[42] Marissa Begonia and Matt Reynolds, 'Domestic Work Is Work—Findings from a Survey of 200 Overseas Domestic Workers in the UK' (The Voice of Domestic Workers and London School of

primarily migrant domestic workers with a range of employment statuses identified 24 per cent as working more than forty hours per week and 10 per cent as working between twelve and twenty-four hours per day,[43] while in another project on Latin American domestic workers in the UK, ten of twelve interviewees reported working twelve hours or more per day.[44] These findings underscore the impact of the limited and unclear regulation of working hours, alongside the restrictive visa discussed in Chapter 7.

In India, regulation on working hours is currently lacking at federal level, as with other areas of labour law for domestic workers. Working time is addressed in two of the new Labour Codes in slightly different ways. First, the Code on Wages, which may apply to domestic workers,[45] provides that where minimum wage rates have been fixed under the code, the appropriate government may also fix the number of hours and provide for a day of rest in every seven-day period.[46] However, more stringent limiting provisions, including a maximum eight-hour working day, six-day week, and requirement to pay extra wages for overtime, appear in the Occupational Health and Safety Code,[47] which is not applicable to domestic workers.[48] States that have notified minimum wages for domestic workers either define or assume a usual maximum working day of eight hours, with overtime to be paid for work beyond this.[49] However, none of the notifications provide for rest breaks and it is unclear who is responsible for paying any overtime where the worker works for more than one household.[50] The latter point is particularly salient because much domestic work in India is based on an individual attending multiple homes once or twice in a day to perform a specific task, meaning that shifts at each workplace are short but intense, and complex scheduling is required.[51] Most workers in this situation have no formal provisions for days off and

Economics) <https://www.thevoiceofdomesticworkers.com/_files/ugd/6608f3_2227eb51bc6641aa9989ddc0cf8d22bc.pdf> accessed 3 June 2025.

[43] Selim Yilmaz and Caroline Emberson, 'Exploring the Nature of Labour Exploitation among Domestic Workers in the UK' (University of Nottingham Rights Lab 2023).

[44] Dolores Modern and Luísa Calvete Portela Barbosa, 'Behind Closed Doors—Experiences of Latin American Domestic Workers in the UK' (Latin American Women's Rights Service 2023) 12.

[45] See Chapter 5.

[46] The Code on Wages—No 29 of 2019, s13.

[47] The Occupational Safety, Health and Working Conditions Code—No 37 of 2020, ss25–27.

[48] See Chapter 4.

[49] N Neetha, 'Minimum Wages for Domestic Work: Mirroring Devalued Housework' (2013) 48 Economic and Political Weekly 77, 81; Uday Shankar, 'Entitlements of Domestic Workers in India: Welfare or Right' in Upasana Mahanta and Indranath Gupta (eds), *Recognition of the Rights of Domestic Workers in India: Challenges and the Way Forward* (Springer 2019) 26.

[50] Neetha (n 49) 82.

[51] Samita Sen and Nilanjana Sengupta, *Domestic Days: Women, Work, and Politics in Contemporary Kolkata* (OUP 2016) 101–2; Bino Paul GD, Venkatesha Murthy R, and Susanta Datta, 'Working & Living Conditions of Women Domestic Workers: Insights from a Survey' (2018) 53 Indian Journal of Industrial Relations 390, 392–93.

must individually negotiate any leave required,[52] and the struggle to complete tasks across a range of households often leaves no time for rest and leisure.[53]

Interviewees pointed to the challenges of this working arrangement, particularly where workers are expected to visit each home they work in twice per day, also adding up to long working hours.[54] Several linked the problem of long hours across multiple homes to low rates of pay, indicating that rather than needing specific regulation of working hours, the key issue was to have better rates so that it was not necessary for workers to work in as many homes.[55] Yajnik stated that, while the union would try to raise the importance of workers getting rest:

> a lot of workers don't really prefer that. They would rather have more houses to go and work in ... the idea of rest and leisure is really absent.

This reinforces the view that for those working across multiple homes, a more straightforward or realistic way to address the number of hours worked would be through an increase in the pay per household visited. Banerjee pointed to an existing trend in this direction for people she worked with or knew in her area, because:

> [D]uring the pandemic their workloads increased in the existing houses ... so maybe they were working four houses, but they've reduced the houses and negotiated for a higher wage and a little bit more time in these houses.

By contrast, live-in domestic workers do not have the degree of control to determine workload by varying how many houses they visit in a day, meaning that this arrangement raises more direct and pronounced issues of excessive working hours without proper rest breaks or time off. An ILO study of internal migrants from the Jharkhand area to Delhi showed that many workers either mentioned being forced to work long hours, or simply took it as a given that their working day would be sixteen to eighteen hours as live-in workers.[56]

As with the other case studies, interviewees often noted the tendency towards much longer hours for those workers who lived with their employers. Nayak explained that for live-in workers, 'nobody has any control on the way they work and the number of hours they work', contrasting this with many workers' preference 'to work only on specific jobs, and not one worker do all kinds of jobs in the home'.

[52] Sen and Sengupta (n 51) 122.

[53] Nioshi Shah and Ravikant Kisana, '"Even If I Die I Won't Get a Holiday": Daily Indignities and Vulnerabilities of Women Domestic Workers in Pune, India' (2021) 27 Asian Journal of Women's Studies 295, 302–5.

[54] Nayak, 'Gita'.

[55] Nayak, Kodoth, 'Gita'.

[56] ILO, 'Indispensable yet Unprotected: Working Conditions of Indian Domestic Workers at Home and Abroad' (ILO 2015) 41.

The link between the lack of regulation and the gendered, affective nature of the work was also highlighted: Banerjee pointed to the situation of comparable male household workers, such as gardeners and drivers: 'their hours are so much more regulated. There is so much less questions around affect in these labour relationships'. She indicated that this was a reason why 'feminist organising is an important part of rights building'. This further underscores how excessive and unregulated hours relate to the devaluation of feminized domestic work.

Justifications and critiques of extended working hours

A key justification offered for allowing extended hours relates to the role of domestic workers in supporting families and women in the workplace. In declining to support Convention 189 (C-189) at the ILO, the UK representative argued that provision for 'on-call' time or standby periods to be counted as working time could not be accepted since they would risk 'bringing... uncertainty into the family home and compromising the benefits of domestic work to families, women in the workforce and communities ...'.[57] This signals a commitment to maintaining an exclusionary approach that prioritizes the employer's needs over the worker's, justified by reference to its role in supporting women's labour force participation. It mirrors the purported justifications previously offered for the now repealed 'family worker exemption' from the National Minimum Wage relating to 'unusual working relationships' and encouraging or not discouraging parents from returning to work, as discussed in Chapter 5.

In Chile, in response to the question of why demand for constant availability persists, structural labour market issues also emerged as significant, given the long working hours that had remained the norm for work outside the home.[58] During the debate on the legislative changes introduced in 2015, domestic workers' unions argued for more stringent limits on working time, but the ensuing debate saw references made to the flexibility needed 'to attend to particular needs of the family'.[59] A Chilean ex-minister stated in an interview for a previous study that limiting domestic workers' working day was difficult because this would be at the expense of other women who worked.[60] These issues were mirrored in my interviews.

[57] 'Record of Proceedings, ILC, 100th Session, Eighteenth Sitting, 15 June 2011, 25(Rev.)' 20.

[58] A 2017 study found 83.6 per cent of men and 63.5 per cent of women worked over 40 hours per week in Chile, the highest in a regional comparison: Pamela Merino-Salazar and others, 'Work and Health in Latin America: Results from the Working Conditions Surveys of Colombia, Argentina, Chile, Central America and Uruguay' (2017) 74 Occupational and Environmental Medicine; London 432, 435.

[59] Biblioteca del Congreso Nacional de Chile (n 23) 67–74, 137–38.

[60] Lidia Casas and Helena Olea, 'Trabajadoras de Casa Particular—Invizibiladas y Discriminadas' in Centro de Derechos Humanos (ed), *Informe Anual sobre Derechos Humanos in Chile 2014* (Ediciones Universidad Diego Portales 2014) 134.

Academic 'Javiera' explained that 'always more Chilean women are entering the labour market … probably with longer working days'. As noted by lawyer 'Alicia', it follows that 'domestic workers are making up for a deficiency of the Chilean labour system': the fact that people work long hours, which are incompatible with school timetables.

Accordingly, the requirement for domestic workers to complete excessive hours compensates for a lack of broader reforms to address work–family reconciliation. At the same time, these structural labour market issues are not the only reason for the long hours requirements. Other interviews demonstrated how the issue also relates to cultural expectations about the way services are provided in the home, which links to the 'boundarilessness' of domestic workers' time.[61] 'Daniela' noted that the role domestic workers play in reproducing a particular way of life and cementing the employer's status meant that 'if you limit the hours, you limit the point'. Relatedly, Arriagada also spoke of a 'cultural brake' on the use of publicly-provided services, despite quite a large output during the second Bachelet government (from 2014 to 2018), and 'Rocío' pointed to an ongoing tendency among upper-class families to have many children 'so they are very dependent on domestic workers'. Giving a worker's perspective that illustrates a similar point, 'Francisca' explained how it had been difficult for her employers to adapt to the changes in working hours:

> because they no longer had their worker there on Saturday … Because they weren't used to having to take things off the table, to clean, to tidy, to wash, so it was difficult for them.

The requirement for extended and uncontrolled hours is therefore, at least in part, attributable to cultural expectations. A subsequent study carried out in 2020–21 in Chile found that employers were drawn to Filipina domestic workers 'because they present the possibility of total availability and devotion', with an increasing expectation of emotional attachment and companionship.[62] One employer interviewed in that study complained that the worker went straight to her room when finishing work, rather than being available for conversations,[63] suggesting a strong expectation of availability that goes beyond allocated tasks. Similar issues exist in the UK, since the work completed by live-in domestic workers may go beyond what is necessary to support families or women's participation in work outside the home.[64] Relatedly, Tekié (South Africa) took the view that the outstanding issues about

[61] See introduction to this chapter for references; I have adopted Blackett's spelling of the term.

[62] Carol Chan and Rosario Fernández-Ossandón, '"Compañerismo": Care and Power in Affective Labor Relations' (2023) 49 Critical Sociology 707, 713–15.

[63] ibid 715.

[64] See Chapter 5 and this chapter's section 'Legal frameworks for regulating domestic workers' hours'.

complying with working time limits related to 'professionalisation' and 'the sense of this person is not here to meet my every need'. In India, the smooth running of a middle-class home has been described as requiring 'constant vigilance and care', including stringent requirements relating to food preparation,[65] with employment of domestic workers viewed as a way to (partially) buy out of the extensive stresses that these standards require.[66] Accordingly, the expectation of constant availability cannot be seen as straightforwardly or exclusively linked to the requirements of working families, but also has a cultural element.

The impact of working hours on domestic workers' private and family lives

Regardless of the justifications put forward for them, excessive and extended working hours have significant ramifications for domestic workers' private and family lives. This is especially challenging for those with no set limit on working time, whereas it should (subject to compliance) be less of an issue for those who have a direct upper limit of weekly and daily hours, as for all domestic workers in South Africa and live-out domestic workers in Chile. The position of live-in workers in Chile offers a middle ground, with requirements on daily rest and days, but no fixed timetable. In my interviews, I examined the extent to which these limits were seen as adequate to protect private and family life.

The responses broadly suggested that the additional rest days resulting from the new legislation had made a positive difference to the private and family lives of domestic workers. 'Francisca' (live-in) said that the change 'was a relief especially for those who work and have children' and that having the Saturday off 'was a liberation', thus raising the issue of family life. Relatedly, Olate took the view that live-in workers now had enough time for their family lives: 'Because live-in workers work from Monday to Friday, they can visit their family on the weekends.' Others, however, felt that having weekends off did not allow sufficient time for a family life. Domestic worker 'Constanza' when asked about the subject, replied, 'There's no family life—almost nothing' and said there was almost no time to do anything other than work, seeing this as inherently linked to live-in domestic work and the lack of time this left for other activities. Likewise, 'Catalina' stated that 'although they have two days free, a family life isn't constructed in two days'. This suggests that the partial restriction of working time is a positive change, but one that does not necessarily go far enough for domestic workers.

[65] Raka Ray and Seemin Qayum, *Cultures of Servitude: Modernity, Domesticity, and Class in India* (Stanford University Press 2009) 74–75.

[66] Shirin Rai, *Depletion: The Human Costs of Caring* (OUP 2024) 84–86.

The interviews also demonstrated that 'dead' hours during the day, which are sometimes used to rationalize extended hours, did not help domestic workers but instead made the experience more frustrating. 'Francisca' explained:

> It's a very long day ... at times there are dead hours ... when I have nothing to do and I would love to be in my house or work in a place where you work to a certain hour and then go.

This shows the importance of countering an assumption that limits to working time exist solely because of the effort of performing the work itself. Instead, they should be understood as related to a need to ensure time for activities outside of the employer's home and their work, be they related to family relationships or otherwise.

Given the very long hours involved in live-in work, another way of maintaining relationships would be to have a family member living with the domestic worker, or able to stay with them at their place of work, but this is often precluded or constrained by the rules employers set.[67] In South Africa, Mbimbi mentioned that there were examples of domestic workers living with a young child, around five or six years old, but that as they got older, they were more likely to have to go and stay with a relative. Moreover, sometimes domestic workers are not even permitted to have partners staying for occasional visits, reflecting an 'absolutist conception of private property' where the employer assumes that owning the accommodation gives them a prerogative over whether others can live there.[68] As Tekié explained:

> very many either housing complexes or individual employers will ... prevent workers from having visitors in their staff quarters. Sometimes they'll say you can have visitors, but ... not overnight .... Sometimes no visitors at all.

She went on to mention a pending challenge to this that her organization was bringing. Interviewees stressed how seriously these issues could affect family life, with George referring to a relationship that broke up because the domestic worker could not have a partner visit on the weekend or get time off to visit them. Dhladhla also vividly expressed the challenges that arise:

> to be at work and look only after your madam's work, forgetting about your family, it affects a lot because at the end, when things get bad, you'll go back to

[67] See also Chapter 8, section 'Practical barriers to family (re)unification and limits on access to social rights'.

[68] Solidarity Center and IZWI (n 10) 23.

> your family .... Find that the family now is fighting all alone ... Maybe they see you once a month, or maybe once after two months ... it breaks the family.

Furthermore, excessive hours combined with a lack of employer respect for workers' family life can affect even the ability to keep up a relationship remotely. In the UK, Sharp said that the excessive hours worked have 'a huge impact on [domestic workers'] ability to maintain contact with their ... families back home'. The time difference between the UK and countries such as the Philippines was one issue, meaning some workers had to 'call at unreasonable hours' or be limited only to messages, but there were also 'unscrupulous employers' that did not allow workers to access mobile phones or the internet, and sometimes made deductions from pay when workers call home.

Another way of maintaining relationships over a longer distance is for workers to have extended periods of leave on a less frequent basis to enable them to visit them. The interviews demonstrated that this was a prominent and sometimes preferred model for internal, often inter-state, migrants in India. 'Meera' stated that it was rare for live-in domestic workers to have a 'weekly off' (a phrase used to indicate a weekly rest period) and that they tended to take time off bunched around festivals, which some found preferable if they did not have their own room in the employer's home and lacked places to go during time off. Ghatak similarly noted that for inter-state migrants, 'there's usually a negotiation with the employer that you'll get a month off to come home' with the employer paying the train fare. In these cases, the worker maintains intermittent time and a connection with their family in the place of origin, but this is likely to be at the expense of building new social connections and other aspects of a private life in the place where their work is located. Conversely, several interviewees mentioned that those who work on a live-out basis often view their own childcare and housework duties as a constraint on the amount of work they can take on, but without time for their own rest and leisure being factored in.[69] Kodoth, for example, noted that 'I don't remember domestic workers talking about time for themselves, for leisure or anything. It was always another obligation that they had to meet.' This is a pronounced example of how the 'second shift' of unpaid work by women combines with paid work to limit opportunities for the worker's own private life,[70] meaning that a simple distinction between 'leisure' and 'work' is inadequate to understand women's experiences.[71]

[69] 'Meera', Yajnik, Kodoth.

[70] Kirsten Scheiwe, 'It's about Time: Gender, Justice and Working Time Regulation in Employment and Care Work' in Brian Langille and Anne Trebilcock (eds), *Social Justice and the World of Work: Possible Global Futures* (Bloomsbury 2023) 315.

[71] Mundlak (n 4) 127.

The impact of working hours on ability to organize collectively and challenge abuse

The interviews also pointed to ways in which excessive working hours and a lack of entitlement to time off outside the workplace for live-in workers undermine the ability to organize and challenge abuse. As Ghatak (India) noted:

> organising any group of marginalised women, I think, always comes up with its own challenges ... for them to have time to come for the activities to come for regular meetings

In the UK, although Kalayaan and the Voice of Domestic Workers both have a long-term working relationship with the major trade union Unite,[72] domestic workers with the severest conditions can struggle to participate. As expressed by Thomas:

> joining unions is a really great thing if you have freedom of movement and, and sort of self-determination over your time ... But ... the people who would often need it the most probably do not have that

Having this opportunity tends to be particularly difficult for migrant domestic workers. In Chile, Olate noted that the union she led had about 500 members, and the federation it is part of around 2,000, out of a total of around 300,000 domestic workers in Chile, with particularly low representation among migrant workers, 'not because we don't want to have migrants, but because they haven't arrived', as Olate explained. The domestic workers I interviewed at the migrant rights organization had a range of reasons for not being union members, including having initially joined a union but not kept it up because of the distance and the travel there ('Michelle'). In South Africa, several interviewees pointed to difficulties in organizing as a result of long working hours, including both interviewees from SERI. For example:

> with our workshops, we need to convene on weekends ... And then we found that even on Saturdays, many of them need to maybe leave after twelve or after a certain time because they need to report to work (George)

Dhladhla took a more positive angle in stating that 'reasonable employers who understand that a worker needs to take a day off if they ask ... so that they can participate in their union'. Yet this still involves a degree of reliance on the employer's

[72] More recently, a domestic workers' branch was set up in February 2025.

goodwill, reiterating that workers need a degree of determination over their own time to be able to fully participate in unions or other organizations. Even beyond affecting organizing, working hours can prevent workers from being able to address abuse directly. As explained by Tekié:

> [W]e've had cases of workers who are being assaulted by their employers, but because they're not allowed to leave their place of employment even during their off hours, then they're not able to report it, right? So then the exploitation continues.

In sum, lengthy and unregulated working hours often have detrimental effects both on workers' capacity to develop and sustain a private and family life outside work, and on their potential to assert their rights and organize for improved conditions. This is vital to bear in mind as part of the human rights analysis.

Human rights and the regulation of working hours

Working hours that exceed normal limits or are not properly regulated are contrary to social and economic rights stipulations, including the right to 'rest, leisure and reasonable limitation of working hours and periodic holidays with pay' in the International Covenant on Economic, Social and Cultural Rights (ICESCR), Article 7(d). General Comment 23 of the UN Committee on Economic, Social and Cultural Rights indicates that 'the general daily limit (without overtime) should be eight hours'.[73] Any exceptions should be 'extremely limited and subject to consultation with workers and their respective organizations', while weekly limits should be set by legislation and applicable across all sectors and work types;[74] the Comment explicitly references domestic workers' right to normal working hours and daily and weekly rest equal to other workers.[75]

At regional level, ICESCR Article 7 is mirrored in Article 15 of the African Charter on Human and People's Rights (ACHPR),[76] while in the other two regional regimes the equivalent appears in the separate social and economic rights instrument. For the Americas, the Protocol of San Salvador provides for a reasonable limitation of daily and weekly working hours.[77] The European Social Charter (ESC) also includes a provision on 'reasonable daily and weekly working hours' at Article 2(1), which has been interpreted as meaning that daily working time

[73] UNCESCR, 'General Comment No. 23 on the Right to Just and Favourable Conditions of Work (Art 7 of the Covenant), 27 April 2016, E/C.12/GC/23' [35].

[74] ibid [35–37].

[75] ibid [47(f)].

[76] See Chapter 5.

[77] Organization of American States, 'Additional Protocol to the American Convention on Human Rights in the Area of Economic, Social and Cultural Rights ("Protocol of San Salvador"), 16 November 1999, A-52', Art 7(g).

exceeding twelve hours or more than sixty hours per week is 'unreasonable'.[78] However, the UK has not accepted this provision. This reflects a limitation of the ESC's 'á la carte' approach, which allows individual states to determine the provisions they accept.[79] Other than the African region, the enforcement provisions for the economic and social rights instruments at international and regional levels are limited, particularly as regards ICESCR. This is one of the reasons it is salient to consider working time from the perspective of more enforceable human rights instruments.

Working time and the right to private and family life

The proper regulation of working time impacts the extent to which time is available for private and family life.[80] Excessive working hours can therefore be understood as a violation of the right to private and family life where they leave inadequate time to lead one's private life, spend time with family, or develop relationships outside of work. As the empirical material shows, excessive hours often have a direct impact on family life—for example, by leaving domestic workers insufficient time to maintain their relationships with these relatives in person and sometimes to communicate by other means. If there is no set limit to the working day or week, or even the continuous free period guaranteed is too limited, it is difficult to combine the role with caregiving or other significant non-work activities, including the formation of new family relationships.

An understanding of working time limits as engaging the right to private and family life brings the matter within the more justiciable sphere of civil and political rights. This may help to avoid its marginalization, adding a 'rhetorical force' to the entitlement.[81] An emphasis on working hours can also counteract a tendency to focus only on the most severe forms of abuse or to view forced labour as exceptional and sharply delineated from other forms of work.[82] Instead of seeing

[78] Magdalena Butrymowicz and Robert Tabaszewski, 'Article 2: The Right to Just Conditions of Work' in Carole Nivard (ed), *The European Social Charter: A Commentary: Volume 2, Preamble, Part I and Part II (Articles 1 to 10)* (Brill 2023) 102–3.

[79] Stefan Clauwaert, 'The Charter's Supervisory Procedures' in Niklas Bruun and others (eds), *The European Social Charter and the Employment Relation* (Bloomsbury 2017).

[80] Klaus Lörcher, 'Article 2: The Right to Just Conditions of Work' in Niklas Bruun and others (eds), *The European Social Charter and the Employment Relation* (Bloomsbury 2017) 167. This section builds on and develops arguments I put forward in Natalie Sedacca, 'Migrant Domestic Workers and the Right to a Private and Family Life' (2019) 37 Netherlands Quarterly of Human Rights 288.

[81] Deirdre McCann, 'Decent Working Hours as a Human Right: Intersections in the Regulation of Working Time' in Colin F Fenwick and Tonia Novitz (eds), *Human Rights at Work: Perspectives on Law and Regulation* (Hart 2010) 526.

[82] For criticism of focuses on extremes, see eg Klara Skrivankova, 'Between Decent Work and Forced Labour: Examining the Continuum of Exploitation' (Joseph Rowntree Foundation 2010) 18; Virginia Mantouvalou, 'Legal Construction of Structures of Exploitation' in Hugh Collins, Gillian Lester, and Virginia Mantouvalou (eds), *Philosophical Foundations of Labour Law* (OUP 2018) 188–89.

phenomena such as forced labour as exceptional, this highlights how the inadequate regulation of working hours creates vulnerability to forced labour. For example, the regulation of mandatory overtime is a key shared focus between the limitation of working time and the question of forced labour, as demanding additional hours is both a significant risk to family life and potentially an indicator of an abusive employment relationship.[83]

Viewing the question of working hours through the prism of the right to a private and family life centres the idea that limits to working time exist in order to have time to carry out activities and create a sphere of life separate from work. A related way to express this is that '[p]ersonhood also requires restrictions on working time', including by allowing for leisure time that provides the foundation for being an autonomous decision maker.[84] Consequently, an approach drawing on the right to private and family life underscores the need for proper rest periods, whether or not the working day consists of back-to-back tasks. Crucially, this includes time that can be spent away from the employer's household. This approach is a counterweight to one of the potential limitations of C-189 introduced in Chapter 2: the fact that it allows for differentiation in the regulation of working time, allowing for the 'special characteristics' of domestic work (Article 10). The reference to 'special characteristics' within the provision does not necessarily mean that domestic workers should have less rest time overall—it could, for example, be interpreted as requiring sensitivity to the preferences of domestic workers and their organizations, as further explored in the subsection 'Conclusion and implications for labour standards' later in this chapter—but there is a risk of it being viewed in a rights-restrictive way without further definition.

Notably, several comments made in the ILO session leading up to C-189's adoption reflected the view that domestic workers' entitlement to rest time should be curtailed because they are (apparently) not constantly engaged in tasks throughout their time at work.[85] These arguments are premised on viewing working time limits as existing mainly because of the effort of performing the work itself, neglecting the broader need for the worker to have time for activities outside the employer's home. They can also be linked to the view of the domestic worker as akin to a member of the employing family, which means additional time spent in the employer's household is not necessarily viewed as work. To counteract this view, it is helpful to understand working time limits as founded on the right to private and family life. As McCann has argued, working time should be viewed

[83] McCann, 'Decent Working Hours as a Human Right' (n 81) 519–21.

[84] Joe Atkinson, 'Human Rights as Foundations for Labour Law' in Hugh Collins, Virginia Mantouvalou, and Gillian Lester (eds), *Philosophical Foundations of Labour Law* (OUP 2018) 133.

[85] ILO, 'Report IV(2)—Decent Work for Domestic Workers—99th Session of the International Labour Conference' (2010) 152–54.

as 'at least in part, time spent away from a life centred or shared elsewhere', including workers' own domestic and care responsibilities.[86] This means that even if domestic workers have periods of 'downtime' during the day, or periods when they are 'on-call' but not actively engaged in work, the accumulated working hours will still be an interference with their right to a private and family life if they do not have sufficient time that they are entitled to spend away from work. The role of legal intervention is therefore to ensure domestic workers' private and family lives are not undermined by the drive to protect the family life of the employer, as the dominant party in the relationship.[87]

A right to private and family life exists in the international, Inter-American and European regional systems and the South African constitution, and has been recognized by the Indian Supreme Court,[88] while there is also a right to protection of the family in the ACHPR Article 18, which includes a positive obligation to assist the family towards meeting its needs and interests.[89] A broader understanding of the right to private and family life as encompassing limitations on working hours is in line with the Inter-American Court of Human Rights (IACtHR) and European Court of Human Rights (ECtHR) jurisprudence. For example, in *Pretty v UK*, a case on assisted dying, the ECtHR indicated that private life is a 'broad term not susceptible to exhaustive definition' that 'protects a right to personal development, and the right to establish and develop relationships with other human beings and the outside world' as well as personal autonomy'.[90] The IACtHR endorsed these principles in *Atala Riffo v Chile*, which arose from the applicant's loss of care and custody of her children because of her sexual orientation.[91] Excessive hours that leave domestic workers little or no time to engage in other activities impact negatively on their autonomy, development and opportunities to build relationships with others beyond their employers, and therefore on their right to a private life. This impact is intensified by the isolated nature of the work, since most domestic workers will not have colleagues at their workplace with whom to develop relationships or organize collectively; time outside of the workplace is required in order to facilitate these connections.

Infringements of the right to private and family life may arise in circumstances that fall short of the high threshold required to show forced or compulsory labour. In *Tibet Menteş v Turkey*, a group of workers in an airport duty-free shop whose schedules required them to work twenty-four hours continuously, followed by

[86] Deirdre McCann, 'The Role of Work/Family Discourse in Strengthening Traditional Working Time Laws: Some Lessons from the on-Call Work Debate Work, Family and the Law' (2005) 23 Law in Context: A Socio-Legal Journal 127, 130–3.

[87] McCann and Murray, 'The Legal Regulation of Working Time' (n 36) 13.

[88] See Chapters 3 and 4.

[89] *Kenneth Good v Republic of Botswana—Communication No 313/05* [2010] ACHPR 106 (AComHPR) [212]; Rachel Murray, *The African Charter on Human and Peoples' Rights: A Commentary* (OUP 2019) 461–63.

[90] *Pretty v United Kingdom* (2002) 35 EHRR 1 [61].

[91] *Atala Riffo and daughters v Chile* IACtHR 24 February 2012, Ser C No 239 [3, 135, 162].

twenty-four hours of rest, failed in their claim that the lack of adequate overtime compensation paid to them amounted to a violation of Article 4 of the European Convention on Human Rights (ECHR), the prohibition on forced labour.[92] The ECtHR held that they had willingly accepted this arrangement and there was no evidence of any mental or physical coercion,[93] thus focusing only on the question of consent. In third party submissions, the European Trade Union Confederation argued that the question should be examined under Article 8 to determine 'whether the excessive working hours had constituted an unjustified interference with the applicants' private lives'.[94] The judgment did not address this point directly, which is disappointing, although the outcome might have been different had this formed part of the applicants' case. Therefore, there is still the potential for a claim based on Article 8 ECHR where elements of forced labour are missing despite excessive hours being worked, which would allow for a move beyond a narrow reading based only on consent. Furthermore, since the excessive hours for domestic workers disproportionately affect women, provisions facilitating these hours are likely to give rise to a violation of Article 14 ECHR taken with Article 8, and the equivalent anti-discrimination provisions in the other regional systems (Article 1(1) ACHR and Article 2 ACHPR).

Assessing justifications for interference with the right to private and family life

As discussed in Chapter 4, the right to private and family life is a qualified right, making it relevant to consider whether the excessive, unregulated working hours can be justified. Since this is a discussion of a positive obligation on the state, it might be assessed via a less stringent 'fair balance' test rather than a structured proportionality analysis in the ECtHR.[95] Nonetheless, stricter scrutiny is undertaken where a case involves disparate impact by a factor such as race or gender,[96] which is salient here given the concentration of women in domestic work; I therefore use the proportionality test to structure this section's analysis. The first question is what, if any, legitimate aim is pursued by the various distinctions in working hours seen across the case study countries, including the disapplication of maximum hourly limits in the UK, the continued permissibility of a longer week for live-in domestic

[92] *Tibet Menteş & others v Turkey* [2017] ECHR 936.
[93] ibid [10, 68–69].
[94] ibid [66].
[95] Dimitrios Kagiaros, 'Vulnerability as a Path to a "Social Minimum"? An Analysis of ECtHR Jurisprudence' in Frans Pennings, Toomas Kotkas, and Ingrid Leijten (eds), *Specifying and Securing a Social Minimum in the Battle against Poverty* (Hart 2019) 250.
[96] Helena Wray, *Article 8 ECHR, Family Reunification and the UK's Supreme Court: Family Matters?* (Hart 2023) 53–63. See Chapter 8, subsection 'Restrictions on family reunification and the right to family life'.

workers in Chile, and the lack of national regulation in India. My empirical research revealed two distinct, although potentially overlapping, rationalizations for live-in domestic workers' extended hours. One is that they are a consequence of structural issues arising from a labour market where long hours are the norm, while the other relates to some employers' cultural expectations of a particular way that a service in the home is provided, which entails constant availability.

The ECHR sets out specific 'legitimate aims' for an interference at Article 8(2), while the test the IACtHR has developed requires considering the level of harm to a right, importance of ensuring the contrary right, and whether the latter is enough to justify the former.[97] It is difficult to see how the strand of justifications that relate to cultural expectations of constant availability could meet any of the legitimate aims in Article 8(2), or to be important enough to limit rights to a private and family life in the IACtHR test. The idea of having a worker always at an employer's service is an arrangement associated with legacies of servitude,[98] rather than the kind of positive social purpose that would justify an interference with rights. Relatedly, the 'unusual working relationship' was held not to amount to a legitimate aim in the *Puthenveettil* tribunal judgment in the UK;[99] although this was under a separate legislative framework, the reasoning is still of interest as regards how the weight of different justifications is understood.

It is a more complex and nuanced question to address the objectives relating to labour market participation by parents, particularly women. In Article 8(2) terms, this aim could be viewed as a subset of 'the economic wellbeing of the country' given that in some cases, the extended hours of domestic workers facilitate the parents being able to fulfil their own work duties. They could alternatively be viewed as protecting the 'rights and freedoms of others' in the sense of allowing parents leisure time, albeit at the expense of the same rights for the domestic worker. The justification therefore potentially amounts to a legitimate aim, making it necessary to consider whether it satisfies the proportionality (or fair balance) test. Alongside other studies, my empirical material demonstrates that the lack of stringent restrictions on working hours significantly impacts the rights of domestic workers, including both their right to private and family life and their potential to assert other rights through organizing, necessitating a very compelling justification for the interference.

This point was mirrored by the finding in *Puthenveettil* that, if an aim seeks to facilitate the return to work by one category of workers by denying a statutory right to another category, 'one would expect, or indeed require, some degree of

[97] See Chapter 4, subsection 'Enforcement, inspection, and the right to a private and family life'.

[98] Lorena Poblete, 'The ILO Domestic Workers Convention and Regulatory Reforms in Argentina, Chile and Paraguay: A Comparative Study of Working Time and Remuneration Regulations' (2018) 157 International Labour Review 435, 446.

[99] *Puthenveettil v Alexander & George & Secretary of State for Business, Energy and Industrial Strategy*—Case No 2361118/2013— judgment of 15 December 2020 (Employment Tribunal) [85].

cogent evidence on proportionality and the balance of competing interest'.[100] Here, the justification relies on the labour market participation of some women coming at the expense of other women,[101] or realizing the rights of one group of workers by denying basic rights to another. It is difficult to rationalize objectively why the rights of one set should be prioritized in this way. Put differently, the private and family life of domestic workers should not be 'jeopardized by the drive to sustain the family life of the dominant party to the wage-work bargain'.[102] A key problem with accepting that support for families justifies extended hours for domestic workers is that it obscures critical engagement with the reasons such long hours are required. These include the way standards of 'normal' working time have been organized around the idea of an 'unencumbered male worker',[103] denying the interconnections and mutual dependence between the work and family spheres.[104] Responding to this problem with an expectation for extended hours in paid domestic work arguably perpetuates the culture of long working hours by offering a partial mitigation, rather than a more substantive solution. The benefits of this workaround are limited to those who can afford to employ domestic workers, deflecting some of the negative consequences of long hours to another worker, without providing generalized solutions.

It is also relevant that there are other means the state could use to support working families and women's participation in the workforce that would not have the same negative effect on domestic workers' human rights, such as better public childcare and addressing the problem of long hours in other workplaces.[105] For example, Busby has proposed the development of a specific right to provide care alongside paid employment, requiring the needs of those providing care to be centred.[106] Proper recognition of the value of reproductive and care work would require broader working time norms 'on the assumption that all workers engage in domestic labour for others', rather than relegating this to an unpaid responsibility for women.[107] Alongside improved provision of public support for care and

[100] ibid [97].

[101] Casas and Olea (n 60) 134.

[102] Deirdre McCann and Jill Murray, 'Prompting Formalisation through Labour Market Regulation: A "Framed Flexibility" Model for Domestic Work' (2014) 43 Industrial Law Journal 319, 331.

[103] Ania Zbyszewska, *Gendering European Working Time Regimes: The Working Time Directive and the Case of Poland* (CUP 2016) 31–32.

[104] Joanne Conaghan, 'Work, Family and the Discipline of Labour Law' in Joanne Conaghan and Kerry Rittich (eds), *Labour Law, Work, and Family: Critical And Comparative Perspectives* (OUP 2005) 27–32.

[105] Novitz and Syrpis (n 31) 105. On public childcare and other support measures for working families, see also Sophie Goossens and Annick Masselot, 'A Race against Time: The Dynamics of Work–Life Balance Policies' [2025] Action publique. Recherche et pratiques 33.

[106] Nicole Busby, *A Right to Care? Unpaid Work in European Employment Law* (OUP 2011) 11.

[107] Judy Fudge, 'Feminist Reflections on the Scope of Labour Law: Domestic Work, Social Reproduction and Jurisdiction' (2014) 22 Feminist Legal Studies 1, 20. For a related argument, see Joan Williams, *Unbending Gender: Why Family and Work Conflict and What to Do about It* (OUP 2000) 4–5.

socially reproductive tasks, this would allow a reconciliation of work and family/ care-based tasks that did not depend on excessive hours by paid domestic workers and had broader reach beyond those employing them.

The ECtHR often finds states to have a wide margin of appreciation in relation to the provision of services that have significant financial resourcing implications,[108] which would be relevant to arguments around better public support for care and childcare. However, the point being made in this analysis is slightly distinct from the line of case law that seeks, for example, a redistribution of resources to help individuals facing destitution,[109] or to increase the autonomy of disabled persons.[110] Rather than raising a direct claim for the state to provide resources, here the demand is to curtail excessive working times, supported by the assertion that the state would have alternative options to meet the objective of work-family reconciliation. Frameworks permitting excessive hours interfere with rights to develop, establish, and maintain relationships for domestic workers, which should be understood as reducing the state's margin of appreciation in this area. It is disproportionate to expect domestic workers to bear the consequences of an unsustainable long-hours culture by sacrificing their own private and family lives.

Conclusion and implications for labour standards

This chapter has explored the legislative frameworks regulating working hours, from the spectrum of a regulated forty-five-hour working week limit for all domestic workers in South Africa with compliance shortcomings, to a general lack of regulation of the sector in India. In between these two positions, Chile has introduced an equal position for live-out domestic workers with other sectors, but ongoing extended hours for those who live with their employers, while the UK has a broader exemption of domestic workers from weekly limits and other regulation. By allowing for extended working hours, these exceptions have an impact on domestic workers' ability to socialize, form new relationships, and maintain existing ones, thus interfering with their right to private and family life. The chapter has argued that this interference cannot be justified based on expectations of constant availability for service in the home. While support for working women and families is a stronger potential justification, it needs to be weighed against the severe impact of measures taken to pursue it on domestic workers' private and family lives.

[108] Janneke Gerards, 'The ECtHR's Response to Fundamental Rights Issues Related to Financial and Economic Difficulties: The Problem of Compartmentalisation' (2015) 33 Netherlands Quarterly of Human Rights 274.

[109] On this line of case law, see Colm O'Cinneide, 'A Modest Proposal: Destitution, State Responsibility and the European Convention on Human Rights' (2008) 5 European Human Rights Law Review 583; Kagiaros (n 95).

[110] See eg *Sentges v Netherlands* App no 27677/02 (ECtHR, 8 July 2003); Gerards (n 108) 281–82.

If, as I argue, excessive working hours for the domestic work sector violate the right to private and family life, this creates a positive obligation on the state to repeal or amend the legislative framework that creates this position, replacing it with a system that provides for adequate time off that can be spent outside the employer's home. To determine the precise nature of the frameworks, more detailed labour law provisions will be needed to add specificity to human rights within domestic systems.[111] This demonstrates the complementary nature of the relationship between the fields, as a human rights-based approach places a demand on labour law for greater inclusivity and universality, as against the exemption of domestic workers from its protection, and adds weight to its claims. Once the value and universality of a claim are recognized and the issue brought within the scope of protection, greater specificity can be introduced through labour law standards.

As part of this process, consultation with domestic workers and their representatives could determine whether it was in workers' interests to have the option of variation of hours on a daily or weekly basis. Building on the ILO maxim that domestic work is both 'work like any other and work like no other',[112] this recognizes both the need for limits on hours worked to allow domestic workers to partake in life outside of work, like any other worker, and the potential need for adjustments to protect this right in the specific circumstances of domestic work. For example, domestic workers who are working away from their families may also need the option of working some longer weeks with appropriately paid overtime and then spending extended periods travelling home,[113] as an alternative option where family reunification is not (yet) possible and existing annual leave entitlements are not sufficient to cover this. Such variation should be in line with the UNCESCR's stipulation that any exceptions to the daily eight-hour limit be 'strictly limited and subject to consultation with workers and their representative organizations' and that where weekly variations exist the hours should meet standards 'when averaged over a period of time'.[114] Therefore, alternatives would need to be subject to defined boundaries and safeguards to ensure that variations are not excessive and are only implemented where genuinely voluntary on the part of the worker.

Basing these standards on a clear understanding of the need to protect domestic workers' right to a private and family life provides a vital framing concept to the discussions. For countries that have already ratified C-189, this foundation

[111] McCann, 'Decent Working Hours as a Human Right' (n 81) 527; Janice R Bellace and Beryl ter Haar, 'Perspectives on Labour and Human Rights' in Janice R Bellace and Beryl ter Haar (eds), *Research Handbook on Labour, Business and Human Rights Law* (Edward Elgar 2019) 14.

[112] ILO, 'Report IV(1)—Decent Work for Domestic Workers—99th Session of the International Labour Conference' (2010) 12–13.

[113] Dorothee Frings, 'Transnational Domestic Work and Right to Family Life in International and European Law' in Maria Kontos and Glenda Tibe Bonifacio (eds), *Migrant Domestic Workers and Family Life: International Perspectives* (Palgrave Macmillan 2015) 45.

[114] UNCESCR (n 73) [35–57].

provides clarification that any distinctions from ordinary working time regulation are not about preserving a privileged position for the employer whereby their right to a private and family life is protected at the worker's expense, but aimed at ensuring domestic workers' rights are promoted in a meaningful way. For those that have not yet ratified C-189, it points to existing obligations under human rights law to secure frameworks ensuring domestic workers are not required to work unlimited and/or excessive hours.

PART 3

MIGRATION REGIMES AND HUMAN RIGHTS

7

Restrictive migration regimes, labour mobility, and rights at work

Introduction

Migration for domestic work is often a survival strategy in response to factors like gendered discrimination, poverty, and lack of employment opportunities, and provides a major benefit of valuable work for host countries.[1] Yet restrictive migration regimes frequently curtail this survival strategy or mean that it takes place in conditions of hostility. This chapter addresses how migration regimes shape domestic workers' labour market access and mobility between jobs, and rights at work. It discusses the specific, restrictive scheme for domestic workers in the UK, before examining the regime in Chile, both at the time of my research and following subsequent changes. It then examines how the general labour migration rules in South Africa are exclusionary towards domestic workers, albeit with special exemption permits existing for specified countries. In the context of internal migration in India, there are no directly comparable visa restrictions, but practical constraints on mobility can arise from factors such as precarious housing and a lack of local networks.

In varying ways, the restrictiveness of migration regimes plays a role in pushing workers towards irregular statuses, or ambiguous states of 'semi-legality', as the second section explores. Examples include the denial of a right to work to some domestic workers awaiting a determination of their status as trafficking victims in the UK; the imposition of more restrictive visa conditions in Chile since 2021; the frequent uncertainties associated with the special exemption permit regime in South Africa; and the parallel though distinct issue of labelling as 'doubtful' individuals and families suspected not to have citizenship in India. Addressing the labour rights consequences for workers who are irregular or have uncertain status, the section notes the harsh situation in the UK as a result of policies known as the 'hostile environment', which are designed to make life impracticable for such workers. It compares this with more complex positions in Chile and South Africa, where labour rights apply in principle to migrants regardless of status, but legal ambiguities and practical constraints can make it difficult to realize these.

[1] See Chapter 1.

Human Rights and the Protection of Domestic Workers in Labour and Migration Law. Natalie Sedacca, Oxford University Press. © Oxford University Press 2026. DOI: 10.1093/9780198985266.003.0010

The final section discusses measures that restrict or prevent access to the labour market as an infringement on the right to gain a living by freely chosen work, examining how the regional human rights systems have 'read in' this entitlement to civil and political rights instruments, including the right to a private and family life. I argue for potential justifications for such interferences based on migration control to be treated with great caution, particularly when differential treatment is based on apparent levels of skill and thus reflects the devaluation of domestic workers. Furthermore, very restrictive schemes may go beyond violating the right to work and may also breach the prohibition on forced labour, meaning no justification is possible. I further explore how the right to decent work supports a series of core standards that apply to all workers, regardless of migration status, which has been reflected in the Inter-American and African systems. While the European system is more complex on this matter, judgments relating to forced labour and servitude increasingly recognize irregular status as a factor driving violations, which calls for the amendment of frameworks that create this susceptibility to abuse.

Restrictive migration regimes and labour market access and mobility

The UK has had a specific visa scheme for overseas domestic workers since 1998.[2] Originally, the visa allowed workers to change employer (although only within the domestic work sector), renew their visa, apply for their dependants to join them in the UK, and ultimately apply for settlement after five years.[3] In 2012, a set of changes led to a much more restrictive visa that was tied to the employer that brought the worker to the country and not extendable beyond six months, with rights to settlement and family reunification removed. An independent review of this system by the barrister James Ewins in 2015 raised substantial concerns about the impact of the new, restrictive visa on domestic workers' fundamental rights. It found that the inability to change employer leads to a lack of bargaining power, a sense of 'being "owned" by an employer, or at least being trapped', and the risk of creating a large class of undocumented workers who lack legal protection.[4] Academic research similarly raised significant concerns that the restrictive

[2] Before 1998, domestic workers could only come to the UK under a 'concession' with an employer they had already spent at least twelve months working for, to whom their employment status was tied—Siobhán Mullally and Cliodhna Murphy, 'Migrant Domestic Workers in the UK: Enacting Exclusions, Exemptions, and Rights' (2014) 36 Human Rights Quarterly 397, 408–9.

[3] ibid 409. The visa also required, and continues to require, the worker to have already worked for the employer that brought them to the UK for at least a year before arriving.

[4] James Ewins, 'Independent Review of the Overseas Domestic Worker Visa' (2015) 22 <https://assets.publishing.service.gov.uk/media/5a806ecee5274a2e87db9c85/ODWV_Review_-_Final_Report__6_11_15_.pdf> accessed 17 July 2025.

visa was driving abuse and irregularity.[5] Ewins' recommendations to address these issues included an unconditional right to change employer, without the need to prove abuse, and the right to apply for visa extensions of up to twelve months each, up to a maximum of two-and-a-half years.[6]

Following the Ewins review, limited changes were made to the Overseas Domestic Worker Visa (ODWV) in 2016: a formal right to change employer was reintroduced, but only during the initial six-month validity period, with the government rejecting the recommendation of a right to renew the visa.[7] This partial change has been inadequate to address the identified problems, given how difficult it is for a domestic worker leaving a role to find a new position with only a short time remaining on their visa, meaning it remains very difficult to change employers or challenge abuse.[8] Additionally, the ODWV is issued with no recourse to public funds (NRTPF), meaning the holder is prevented from claiming most state benefits except in very limited circumstances.[9] My interviews highlighted the ongoing difficulties caused by the scheme, which remains highly restrictive. Discussing the theoretical possibility of changing visas within the original six-month period, Thomas said she was unable to remember a client taking advantage of this. She indicated that the length of the visa was the main obstacle to workers changing employer, alongside other aspects of 'the political landscape ... generally a hostile environment to migrants'. Likewise, Sharp emphasized the inadequacy of being able to change within the initial six months only, stating that workers frequently lack information about their rights and many escape without their passports, which can take weeks to replace and without which they cannot prove their right to work. In this respect, she considered the situation was better for those on a diplomatic visa.[10]

Since 2016, domestic workers who are conclusively identified as survivors of trafficking or 'modern slavery' can apply for two years further leave to remain.[11]

[5] An example based on empirical findings is Virginia Mantouvalou, '"Am I Free Now?" Overseas Domestic Workers in Slavery' (2015) 42 Journal of Law and Society 329.

[6] Ewins (n 4) 34–35.

[7] Avril Sharp, '12 Years of Modern Slavery: The Smokescreen Used to Deflect State Accountability for Migrant Domestic Workers' (Kalayaan 2024) 15. The current rules are in Home Office, 'Immigration Rules (UK)—Updated 13 August 2025' <https://www.gov.uk/guidance/immigration-rules> accessed 22 August 2025, Appendix Overseas Domestic Worker.

[8] Virginia Mantouvalou and Natalie Sedacca, 'Trapped in Cycles of Exploitation: The UK Overseas Domestic Worker Visa 10 Years On' (*UK Labour Law*, 6 April 2022) <https://uklabourlawblog.com/2022/04/06/trapped-in-cycles-of-exploitation-the-uk-overseas-domestic-worker-visa-10-years-on-by-virginia-mantouvalou-and-natalie-sedacca/> accessed 25 August 2025; Sharp (n 7) 19.

[9] Colin Yeo, 'What Is the No Recourse to Public Funds Condition?' (*Free Movement*, 20 February 2025) <https://freemovement.org.uk/what-is-the-no-recourse-to-public-funds-condition/> accessed 28 August 2025.

[10] A separate scheme allowing the worker to be sponsored for an initial two-year period, extendable for two years at a time to a maximum of five years, for work in diplomatic households—Home Office, 'Workers and Temporary Workers: Guidance for Sponsors - Sponsor an International Agreement Worker—Version 04/25' (2025) 12.

[11] Home Office, 'Immigration Rules' (n 7), Appendix Domestic Worker who is a Victim of Modern Slavery. For a definition of 'modern slavery', see Chapter 2. Other possible routes to remain are

This route still only allows work as a domestic worker in a private or diplomatic household and precludes access to public funds. As Thomas explained in interview, the continued lack of labour mobility through preventing a change of sector can be retraumatizing for workers who have suffered abuse in a domestic setting. She further noted that the NRTPF condition means that workers are left with little choice about the work they accept because they lack a safety net, while Sharp similarly highlighted this condition as a problem, alongside difficulties of having to show self-sufficiency to be granted the visa. More broadly, Sharp observed that it was inadequate for the extension to the ODWV to be available beyond six months only in the case of modern slavery and trafficking victims, creating a 'protection gap' since 'not all abuse meets that threshold'.

In addition to the ODWV and related schemes, on which my research focuses, other migration routes for domestic work include free movement for European Union/European Economic Area nationals who arrived before 2021, the Health and Care Worker Visa for domiciliary care workers arriving post 2022, and initial arrival on a six-month visitor visa followed by irregularity.[12] While those who benefit(ed) from freedom of movement do not face direct visa-based restrictions on changing employer, they often have other disadvantages, including language barriers and low qualification levels.[13] The Health & Care Worker Visa is also a highly restrictive scheme that is dependent on employer sponsorship.[14] The position of irregular migrants is discussed in the next section.

In Chile, domestic workers migrate under the general immigration system, which was regulated by Pinochet-era Decree Laws[15] at the time of my research in 2019. The main relevant visa types, in ascending order of the level of rights attached, comprised: visa subject to contract of work, under which permission to stay is conditioned on a contract with an employer; temporary visa; and visa of permanent residence.[16] Workers from other parts of Latin America and the Caribbean often arrived as tourists and subsequently regularized their status after obtaining

discretionary leave, for which the current provisions are in the Nationality and Borders Act 2022, s65, or a claim for asylum or humanitarian protection.

[12] Nando Sigona and others, 'Irregularised Migrants Doing Domestic Work in the United Kingdom' (I-CLAIM 2025) 6–7.

[13] Thomas.

[14] Inga Thiemann and others, 'UK Agriculture and Care Visas: Worker Exploitation and Obstacles to Redress' (Modern Slavery & Human Rights Policy and Evidence Centre 2024) 35–36; Adis Sehic, Dora-Olivia Vicol, and Andrei Savitski, 'The Forgotten Third: Migrant Care Workers' Views on Improving Conditions in England's Adult Social Care Sector' (Work Rights Centre 2024) 12–14.

[15] Decreto Ley No. 1.094, Establece Normas sobre extranjeros en Chile 1975; Decreto Supremo No. 597 de 1984—Aprueba nuevo reglamento de extranjería; Rodrigo Sandoval Ducoing, 'Una nueva Política Migratoria para los trabajadores migrantes en Chile' (2016) 4 Relaciones Laborales y Derecho del Empleo 1, 12–13.

[16] Luis Eduardo Thayer Correa and Carlos Salvatore Durán Migliardi, 'Gobierno local y migrantes frente a frente: nudos críticos y políticas para el reconocimiento' [2015] Revista de CLAD 127, 133; Ducoing (n 15) 18–19.

a contract.[17] While awaiting regularization, payment of social security contributions could be delayed because of complexities in the process of obtaining an identity card.[18] 'Alicia' noted that this drove precarity because in practice workers had to start working immediately, while 'Rocio' observed that employers did not always keep promises to help workers regularize. 'Maria', a domestic worker from Peru, described the process of changing from tourist to work visa as 'a bit tedious', involving getting up at 4 a.m. or 5 a.m. to stand in line, although she stated that it had subsequently improved.

Once obtained, the 'visa subject to contract' only authorized work for the employer with whom the worker signed the contract; if and when that employment ended, the worker had to obtain a new contract and present it to the Department of Foreigners and Migration within thirty days, with a request to change employer, or their visa would expire.[19] Two full years of work on the 'visa subject to contract' basis were needed to meet subsequent residency requirements,[20] which could lead migrants to accept precarious roles and positions.[21] My research highlighted some difficulties caused by these requirements,[22] including workers withstanding poor conditions or remaining in an irregular status rather than having to register a new contract within thirty days,[23] and the fact that changing employer would delay a worker in their progress towards a more secure status.[24] 'Isabella', a domestic worker from Colombia, stated that when she had been on a 'visa subject to contract':

> if you... recruited me and you were an abuser... I endured it. Now... if I decide that you're maltreating me I can go... Before no, because I lose all my rights[25]

'Isabella' also explained the complexity of changing employer while on a 'visa subject to contract', involving visits to the embassy, the civil register, and the civilian police: 'you have to do an impressive number of laps'.

[17] 'Nancy', Arriagada.

[18] Paulina Granados Zambrano, María Fernanda Toledo Badilla, and Nicolás Rivera González, 'Documento de Trabajo N° 63: Caracterización de La Población Inmigrante En El Sistema de Pensiones y Seguro de Cesantía' (Superintendencia de Pensiones, Chile 2019) 41.

[19] Lidia Casas and Helena Olea, 'Trabajadoras de Casa Particular—Invizibiladas y Discriminadas' in Centro de Derechos Humanos (ed), *Informe Anual sobre Derechos Humanos in Chile 2014* (Ediciones Universidad Diego Portales 2014) 126.

[20] Decreto Supremo No. 597 de 1984, Art 40.

[21] Claudia Mora and Eduardo A Undurraga, 'Racialisation of Immigrants at Work: Labour Mobility and Segmentation of Peruvian Migrants in Chile' (2013) 32 Bulletin of Latin American Research 294, 306.

[22] See also Rosario Fernández, 'Commodification of Domestic Labour, the Culture of Servitude and the Making of the Chilean Nation' (2018) 43 Österreichische Zeitschrift für Soziologie 49, 52.

[23] 'Catalina'.

[24] 'Nancy'.

[25] While the definitive visa she subsequently obtained gave 'Isabella' scope to change employer, she did not feel overall that her conditions had improved as she was suffering ongoing difficulties with formalization.

Although it could be challenging to change employer during this initial period, the situation improved once the two-year 'visa subject to contract' was completed. Granados Zambrano noted that many immigrants who were 'highly educated' would use the contract and identity card gained while doing domestic work to 'move to the work they want'. A system where those who begin in domestic work subsequently have the option to move to other work sectors and visa schemes contrasts favourably, from a workers' rights perspective, with the more severe restrictions seen in the UK. Furthermore, as a result of a residence agreement implemented in 2009 by the regional trading bloc MERCOSUR,[26] nationals of Brazil, Uruguay, Paraguay, Argentina, and Bolivia can apply for a less restrictive visa from within Chilean territory.[27] The two Bolivian domestic workers I interviewed had both initially had a MERCOSUR visa and found this advantageous because it was quick to obtain,[28] could be secured without a contract, and allowed changes of employer.[29]

Several interviewees referred to what was at the time a proposed reform to migration law, noting particular concerns about its role in ending the possibility of changing migration status from tourist to resident. This would mean it was only possible to request a working visa from outside of Chile, so workers who had entered as tourists would need to go back to their country of origin to regularize—a suggestion that Jackson viewed as 'a little absurd'. Echoing a reference in government documents to a 'dizzying growth in migration' putting institutions under strain,[30] Beas gave a partial justification of the proposal as providing more control in relation to people who arrive and stay on despite not finding a job. Contrastingly, most interviewees were more sceptical about ending the possibility of changing status, believing it would remove flexibility and lead to an increase in irregular work and a decline in rights. Another issue expressed by 'Nancy' was that the proposed points-based system, prioritizing those with professional or technical qualifications, would be difficult for domestic workers to access.

The new migration law was passed in 2021 and has borne out many of these apprehensions, including by ending the possibility of moving from tourist to resident status.[31] A subsequent decree law of May 2022 established that the 'Legal

[26] The name translates as 'the common market of the South;' for the residence agreement, see: 'Agreement on Residence for Mercosur Member States' Nationals 2002—Unofficial Translation from the Spanish Version Prepared by Diego Acosta and Victoria Finn'. Chile is an associate rather than a full member of MERCOSUR.

[27] International Organisation for Migration, 'Evaluación Del Acuerdo de Residencia Del MERCOSUR y Su Incidencia En El Acceso a Derechos de Los Migrantes' (2018) 34–35.

[28] 'Sara'.

[29] 'Michelle'—who also noted a disadvantage that the fees for a MERCOSUR visa were higher than for other types.

[30] Minister of the Interior and Public Security, Chile, 'Minuta: Reforma Migratoria y Política Nacional de Migraciones y Extranjería (2018)' 1 <https://cdn.digital.gob.cl/filer_public/d2/39/d239d0df-c4e9-488e-a36f-8b1ac2ca00ef/nueva_ley_de_migracion.pdf> accessed 17 July 2025.

[31] Ley No 21.325—Ley de Migración y Extranjería 2021; Mayra Feddersen and Antonio Morales, 'How Do Migratory and Labor Policies Interact to Regulate Migrant Workers?' (2024) 51 Revista Chilena de Derecho 159, 164–65.

remunerated activities' work category requires a work contract with at least three months' duration signed by an employer and public notary, with the foreign worker to sign in the consulate, and their work activities being consistent with the employer's declaration to the tax authorities.[32] These requirements could be difficult for domestic workers to comply with, bearing in mind the way that jobs in the sector have generally been obtained after entering the country, raising concerns of a rise in clandestine entry.[33] The law also opens the way to a more 'skills-based' determination of migrants' entry, allowing the National Migration Service to draw up a national policy determining the number and types of visas that are most needed to meet the country's social and economic needs.[34] It has a somewhat contradictory nature, since its more restrictive approach goes alongside certain reforms to promote migrants' rights,[35] including equality before the law, labour rights and social rights, and family reunification.[36] Under the 'legal remunerated activities' category, the end of the contract that serves as the basis for granting the visa will not generally be a reason for revocation and workers can change employers without needing to report this.[37] Therefore, for those who are able to meet the more stringent requirements initially, this is likely to be advantageous compared to the previous 'visa subject to contract'. In addition, a new visa type has been introduced for victims of the crime of trafficking, certified by the Public Prosecutor's office.[38] However, especially given significant challenges to identifying and prosecuting labour trafficking cases in Chile,[39] this may not be sufficient to mitigate the more restrictive aspects of the new system.

In South Africa, there are limited formal labour migration routes for domestic workers. Its migration framework, including the Immigration Act of 2002 and a 2017 White Paper on International Migration, have prioritized attracting 'highly skilled migrants' to the country.[40] A general work visa will only be issued where the Department of Labour has reviewed a job offer and agreed that the employer has adequately attempted to find a similarly qualified South African national or permanent resident.[41] This results in an exclusionary scheme for those, like domestic

[32] Decreto 177—Establece las subcategorías migratorias de residencia temporal 2022, Art 17.

[33] Luis Eduardo Thayer Correa and others, 'El Estado En Su Frontera: Arbitrariedad e Ilegalidad En Las Políticas Migratorias Recientes En Chile' (2022) 68 Diálogo Andino 167, 168.

[34] Ley 21.325 Art 161–2.

[35] Pablo Ignacio Roessler Vergara and others, 'Relational Inclusion of Migrants in Chile: Towards a Statistical Measurement Model' (2022) 13 Migraciones Internacionales 3 <https://doi.org/10.33679/rmi.v1i1.2465> accessed 18 July 2025.

[36] Ley 21.325 Arts 13–19. See further Chapter 8.

[37] Decreto 177, Art 19.

[38] ibid, Arts 41 and 42.

[39] Carol Chan and Natalie Gomez, 'Challenges to Addressing Trafficking into Forced Labor in Chile: A Legal Culture Perspective' (2023) 79 Crime, Law, and Social Change 395, 412–14.

[40] Immigration Act—Act No 13 of 2002 (South Africa) 2002; Tara Polzer Ngwato, Amy Tekié, and Kimani Ndung'u, 'Migrant Domestic Workers in the SADC Region: Intersecting Decent Work with Safe, Orderly and Regular Migration' (ILO 2022) 72.

[41] Fatima Khan and Sally Hurt, 'Temporary Residence' in Fatima Khan (ed), *Immigration law in South Africa* (Juta and Company 2018) 103.

workers, who are deemed to be 'low-skilled',[42] restricting access to work permits and driving high levels of irregularity.[43] However, the government has at different times granted 'special exemptions' to nationals of Zimbabwe, Lesotho, and Angola under s31(2) of the Immigration Act 2002, under which a foreigner or category of foreigners can be granted residence as justified by special circumstances.[44] Interviewees explained that these permits have been relevant to domestic workers from the specified countries, particularly Zimbabwe,[45] while also highlighting the difficulties that limited visa options posed to domestic workers, particularly those from countries not covered by special exemptions. Tekié stated that while the permits had been helpful for some Zimbabweans, Malawians had 'a lot of problems with documentation', lacking an avenue for regularization, meaning 'they tend to be very vulnerable in terms of exploitation, and employers can take advantage of that'. Apart from the special exemptions, other potential options include entering on a ninety-day visitor permit and overstaying or leaving when it expires and returning later (a form of circular migration), or holding an asylum seeker permit, which may cover the right to work.[46]

While some interviewees were in favour of extending visa schemes to cover domestic workers, this was not universal. Osiki expressed concerns about the prospect, given high levels of unemployment and the view of domestic work as 'not a critical skill'. However, she also noted that:

> when the domestic work sector becomes professionalised the way it should be beyond just seeing the women as doing normal woman's work at home… there might be a visa category for them

Contrastingly, Barrett referred to the ongoing projects for reform in this area as introducing 'a points system on top of the scarce skills system'. She expressed the concern that it would be just as exclusionary since points would be based on criteria such as education and financial independence, on which basis it would be difficult for domestic workers to qualify. The proposals have subsequently been published as a White Paper, which includes the objective of 'creating legal labour migration pathways through strong bi-and multilateral partnerships with SADC

[42] Jennifer N Fish, 'Rights across Borders: Policies, Protections and Practices for Migrant Domestic Workers in South Africa' in Darcy Du Toit (ed), *Exploited, Undervalued and Essential: Domestic Workers and the Realisation of Their Rights* (Pretoria University Law Press 2013) 236.

[43] ibid 237; Zaheera Jinnah, 'Negotiated Precarity in the Global South: A Case Study of Migration and Domestic Work in South Africa' (2020) 2020 Studies in Social Justice 210, 218–19.

[44] Shingirai Nyakabawu, 'Legal Violence: Waiting for Zimbabwe Exemption Permit in South Africa' (2022) 8 Journal of Law, Society and Development 1, 9.

[45] Barrett, Tekié, Mullagee.

[46] Vusilizwe Thebe and Pamela Maombera, 'Negotiating the Border: Zimbabwean Migrant Mothers and Shifting Immigration Policy and Law in South Africa' (2019) 62 African Studies Review 134, 141–42; Jinnah (n 43) 218.

[Southern African Development Community] Member states and beyond'.[47] It remains to be seen how far that will address the limited routes available to domestic workers.

In India, to briefly address international migration from neighbouring countries, there is an 'open border' between Nepal and India, allowing citizens to go and work in the other country without requiring a visa or permit, as a result of a Treaty made in 1970.[48] Conversely, new migrants from Bangladesh, unless classed as refugees, generally do not have any legal migration pathway and are therefore likely to have irregular status.[49] However, the more prevalent issue in the domestic work context is internal migration.[50] For internal migrants in India, there are no direct constraints on labour mobility arising from visa regimes. For example, a study of migrants to Kolkata from nearby districts noted that, while workers could be dismissed for trivial reasons, they also sometimes left jobs without notice in the interests of improved pay and conditions.[51] This would generally be much more difficult for a worker on a restrictive visa, or one with irregular status, showing improved mobility compared to this. Yet some internal migrants, particularly those who cross state boundaries, face practical constraints on their labour mobility. For example, 'Gita' explained that internal migrants are much more likely to have to pay for informal rental housing, which creates pronounced pressures. While other expenses can often be deferred:

> house rents are something it's very hard to get any sort of break with, so it's also what beholds you to your employer that you cannot afford to suddenly lose your work

This illustrates how insecurities in areas external to the workplace, like housing (even where not employer-provided), can make it more difficult to move jobs because of the risks involved in not being able to pay rent. This is exacerbated where domestic work is the household's more stable income, creating additional pressure to remain in a job. As noted by 'Gita':

[47] Department of Employment and Labour, 'White Paper on National Labour Migration Policy for South Africa, May 2025—Notice 3234 of 2025' 86.

[48] Jagannath Adhikari and others, 'Labour Migration from Nepal: Trends and Explanations' in S Irudaya Rajan (ed), *Migration in South Asia: IMISCOE Regional Reader* (Springer International 2023) 68–69.

[49] Silvia Tieri, 'Migration, Borders, and Security Discourses in the Time of COVID-19: The Case of Migration from Bangladesh to India' (European University Institute—Robert Schuman Centre for Advanced Studies, Global Governance Programme 2021) RSC PP 2021/10.

[50] Deepita Chakravarty and Ishita Chakravarty, *Women, Labour and the Economy in India: From Migrant Menservants to Uprooted Girl Children Maids* (Routledge 2016) 3–6; RB Bhagat and Ashwani Kumar, 'Internal Migration and Citizenship in India: An Emerging Perspective' in Ashwani Kumar and RB Bhagat (eds), *Migrants, Mobility and Citizenship in India* (Routledge India 2022).

[51] Samita Sen and Nilanjana Sengupta, *Domestic Days: Women, Work, and Politics in Contemporary Kolkata* (OUP 2016) 138.

> male household members are in sectors of work which are not as regular, so even if there's no contract in domestic work, it's still regular waged work... So it's women's responsibility that you don't lose your job. And that's... plays on their mind constantly

Banerjee referred to other obstacles for internal migrants, including 'less access to local networks', making workers, particularly those who are live-in, 'more and more vulnerable to ... the employer's terms and conditions', as well as difficulty navigating the city for rural migrants, particularly from another state, to negotiate. Furthermore, she noted that 'the Inter-State Migrant Workers Act needs to be extended ... it covers ... I think about 10% of the migrant population'. The legislation she referred to is intended to protect the conditions and interests of workers who cross state borders.[52] Deficiencies in coverage arise in part because the legislation applies only to establishments that employ, and contractors that engage, at least five inter-state workers, leaving a gap regarding most domestic workers employed privately by households.[53] While it could in principle assist those employed via labour contractors, this does not function well because of the proliferation of sub-agents and a lack of proper registration,[54] while intra-state migrants are excluded in any event.[55] Additionally, a lack of enforcement and the onus placed on recruiters and migrants for registration means it is generally ineffective.[56] In the absence of effective regulation, internal migrant workers can thus be more susceptible to exploitation despite being, formally speaking, citizens with the right to work.

Migration regimes and the construction of irregularity

Following the discussion of how restrictive migration schemes affect labour mobility, this section moves to address these regimes' role in pushing migrants towards irregularity, and how this in turn affects migrant domestic workers' ability to realize their rights. 'Irregular' status refers to a lack of permission to remain and/or work in the host country; the term 'undocumented' is also sometimes used to denote this, but is less accurate as irregular migrants may possess documents of some

[52] The Inter-State Migrant Workmen Act—Act No 30 of 1979 (India); name amended to refer to 'Workers' in 2011: ILO, 'Indispensable yet Unprotected: Working Conditions of Indian Domestic Workers at Home and Abroad' (ILO 2015) 54.

[53] ILO (n 52) 55.

[54] ibid.

[55] Indrani Mazumdar and N Neetha, 'Crossroads and Boundaries: Labour Migration, Trafficking and Gender' (2020) 55 Economic and Political Weekly 66, 67.

[56] Bhagat and Kumar (n 50) 6; Priya Deshingkar, 'Why Do Migrants Remain Excluded in Present-Day India and What Should We Do about It?' in Ashwani Kumar and RB Bhagat (eds), *Migrants, Mobility and Citizenship in India* (Routledge India 2022) 6.

sort, though not the ones required by immigration regulations.[57] While often assumed to denote clandestine entry, many irregular migrants have initially entered the host country lawfully and subsequently lost their status, for example when a visa expires, which can arise from overly expensive and complex processes.[58] 'Irregular' status is thus frequently created by the immigration laws and policies that states implement.[59] Moreover, there is not a simple binary between 'regular' and 'irregular' status, as migrants can also experience legally ambiguous states of what Kubal has called 'semi-legality'[60] and Menjívar has referred to as 'liminal legality': a status 'in between' regular and irregular status.[61] Both these terms are used in the analysis below.

A salient example of the law producing liminal legality is the position of migrant domestic workers in the UK who are waiting for identification of their status as a victim of 'modern slavery' or trafficking. The determination is made by a body called the National Referral Mechanism (NRM) and has two stages: the initial 'Reasonable Grounds Decision' (RGD) determining whether there are reasonable grounds to believe the person is a victim of slavery or trafficking, and the 'Conclusive Grounds Decision' (CGD) regarding whether there is enough evidence, on the balance of probabilities, to determine that they are a victim.[62] Workers frequently wait many months or even years for a CGD,[63] meaning that their rights during this waiting period are highly consequential. As of 2016, the position is that if a domestic worker receives a positive RGD during the validity of their initial six-month visa, they will have permission to work until twenty-eight days after the CGD. However, if the visa has already expired by the time of receiving a positive RGD, they have no right to work in that period.[64]

[57] UN High Commissioner for Human Rights, 'Behind Closed Doors: Protecting and Promoting the Human Rights of Migrant Domestic Workers in an Irregular Situation—Report No HR/PUB/15/4' (2015) 1.

[58] UN High Commissioner for Human Rights, 'The Economic, Social and Cultural Rights of Migrants in an Irregular Situation—HR/PUB/14/1' (United Nations 2014) 3–4; Monish Bhatia, 'Reproductive Injustice in Britain: Punishing Illegalized Migrant Women from the Global South and Separating Families' (2023) 30 Identities 471, 476.

[59] Bridget Anderson, 'Migration, Immigration Controls and the Fashioning of Precarious Workers' (2010) 24 Work, Employment and Society 300, 311.

[60] Agnieszka Kubal, 'Conceptualizing Semi-Legality in Migration Research' (2013) 47 Law & Society Review 555, 557.

[61] Cecilia Menjívar, 'Liminal Legality: Salvadoran and Guatemalan Immigrants' Lives in the United States' (2006) 111 American Journal of Sociology 999, 1000.

[62] On the NRM's background and decision-making process, see Virginia Mantouvalou, 'The UK Modern Slavery Act 2015 Three Years On' (2018) 81 Modern Law Review 1017, 1026–30; Alan Bogg and others, *Human Rights at Work: Reimagining Employment Law* (Hart 2024) 164.

[63] The median waiting time at the end of December 2024 was 630 days: Home Office, 'Modern Slavery: National Referral Mechanism and Duty to Notify Statistics UK, End of Year Summary 2024' (*GOV.UK*, 6 March 2025) <https://www.gov.uk/government/statistics/modern-slavery-nrm-and-dtn-statistics-end-of-year-summary-2024/modern-slavery-national-referral-mechanism-and-duty-to-notify-statistics-uk-end-of-year-summary-2024> accessed 16 July 2025. From my role as a Kalayaan trustee I am aware of efforts to accelerate this process in 2025, but further figures are not yet available.

[64] Immigration (Variation of Leave) Order 2016—SI 2016/948, Reg 3.

This uneven provision creates a class of individuals who are entitled to remain in the country for their trafficking claims to be determined, but are prohibited from working, thus finding themselves in a 'liminal' state. My research with Kalayaan in 2018 involved interviewing twenty-one workers in this interim position: all had received a positive RGD and were awaiting a CGD, of whom eleven had permission to work while waiting and ten did not.[65] The findings revealed the arbitrariness of the factors determining whether a worker has permission to work while in the NRM, since delays in receiving the RGD had arisen from factors that were generally beyond workers' control, including a lack of information about rights and the need to obtain visa information when an employer had retained the worker's passport.[66]

The research also highlighted the detrimental impact of lacking permission to work, which occurs over an extended period given the frequent long wait for a CGD. While workers without the right to work were receiving the available state support available (at the time, £35 per week), several mentioned that the money was not enough to live on and that they had to rely on community networks, friends, or a food bank for financial support. Left without the means to meet their basic needs, those denied permission to work were often pushed into informal working, which was mentioned by five interviewees (of ten in that position). One mentioned occasionally doing friends' nails for tips ('Amy'), while the other four were performing domestic work—one on an hoc basis ('Joana') and in the other three cases for people they were living with. All these workers stated that they would be too afraid to complain if they experienced any abuse since they were working without permission. One such worker, 'Nicky', who was not paid at all for her work, just receiving free meals and accommodation, said that despite this, 'I help out every day because, because I'm there every day'. The other two reported being paid £100–£120 per week, and likewise indicated they were working every day, for example:

> if I see something to clean … like toilet… even they don't ask me to, but I'm shy, I'm ashamed because my free accommodation, free food … so I should be work ('Natasha')

The lack of permission to work thus paradoxically leads to an absence of leisure time since the individual feels indebted to the person providing them with accommodation, despite being pushed into this situation by their lack of options for regular work. The results also highlighted negative emotional impacts on those

[65] The results were published in a co-authored policy report: Natalie Sedacca and Avril Sharp, 'Dignity, Not Destitution: The Impact of Differential Rights of Work for Migrant Domestic Workers Referred to the National Referral Mechanism' (Kalayaan 2019). See further Chapter 1, section 'Researching domestic workers' exclusion'.

[66] ibid 17–19.

denied permission to work,[67] alongside problems caused to families including debt and inability to afford education and related costs, housing or other bills, for example:

> … this coming June it's like the starting of the school. They need some stuff for school, uniforms, and they need to pay the bills last year but I don't have ('Elena')

Therefore, the denial of permission to work in the NRM has stark implications, not only for the workers but also for their families' needs. In addition, the UK's legal framework makes it particularly difficult for irregular migrants to access labour rights. The 'illegality doctrine', which provides a defence in private law actions (e.g. tort and contract) where there has been unlawful conduct by the claimant that closely relates to their claim, has often obstructed irregular migrants from being able to claim basic labour rights.[68] In *Zarkasi v Anindita,* for example, a domestic worker was barred from bringing a claim including unlawful deduction of wages because it was held that she was working without permission and had knowingly participated in deception.[69] In the subsequent case of *Hounga v Allen,* a claimant who had been working without permission was successful in a tort claim under anti-discrimination law,[70] but restrictive rules on bringing claims in contract law remained intact.[71] There was something of a shift in the successful claim for unpaid wages by a migrant domestic worker who had lost permission to work in *Okedina v Chikale,* but this hinged on specific rationales, including the Claimant's lack of awareness of her irregular status,[72] which meant she had not committed a criminal offence based on the law at the time, whereas the employer had.[73]

On current law, it is likely that a claimant in a similar position to Ms Okedina would commit the offence of 'illegal working' that was introduced in 2016. This directly criminalizes any individual who works without the correct authorization, exposing them to imprisonment or a fine, and to confiscation of their earnings as 'proceeds of crime'.[74] This is one aspect of the set of policies known as the hostile environment, which were mainly introduced through the Immigration Acts of

[67] ibid 27–28.

[68] Bogg and others, *Human Rights at Work* (n 62) 158–59; Jack Beadsworth, 'The Migrant Personal Work Relation: A New Category of Employment' (2025) 54 Industrial Law Journal 211, 231.

[69] *Zarkasi v Anindita & Anor* [2012] ICR 788 (EAT) [5]; Mullally and Murphy (n 2) 29; Alan Bogg, 'Okedina v Chikale and Contract Illegality: New Dawn or False Dawn?' (2020) 49 Industrial Law Journal 258, 264.

[70] *Hounga v Allen and another* [2014] UKSC 47.

[71] Alan Bogg, 'Irregular Migrants and Fundamental Social Rights: The Case of Back-Pay under the English Law on Illegality' in Bernard Ryan and Rebecca Zahn (eds), *Migrant Labour and the Reshaping of Employment Law* (Hart 2023) 204.

[72] *Okedina v Chikale* [2019] EWCA Civ 1393 [2–3, 14, 48].

[73] Bogg, 'Okedina v Chikale and Contract Illegality' (n 69) 259–63.

[74] Immigration Act 2016, s34; ACL Davies, 'The Immigration Act 2016' (2016) 45 Industrial Law Journal 431, 438.

2014 and 2016 and accompanying policy documents, with the aim of obstructing irregular migrants from living, working and accessing benefits and services in the UK.[75] The hostile environment has seen the regular seizure of cash including wages in 'illegal work' raids by Immigration Enforcement,[76] alongside an intensification of data sharing with the Home Office by other bodies including labour inspectorates.[77] This creates well-grounded fears for migrants, especially those with irregular status, that reporting concerns or engaging with such bodies could lead to immigration enforcement against them.[78] Employers can take advantage of these fears and the migrants' precarious position through violations of workplace rights.[79] The government elected in 2024 has signified its intention to maintain a similar approach, noting in its 2025 White Paper that it will continue 'to surge resource into illegal working'.[80] The position therefore remains one of directly creating susceptibility to exploitation for migrant workers with irregular or precarious status.

In Chile, the recent tightening of the immigration system has similarly created conditions that could drive irregularity. The heightened conditions imposed on regular migrants make them 'susceptible to falling into irregular status' and becoming subject to deportation.[81] Having not identified material directly about the impact of 2021 reforms on domestic workers at the time of writing, it is salient to consider the parallel issue of Venezuelan and Haitian migrants, who had special requirements imposed on them for consulate-issued visas from 2018 and 2019 respectively, with a high refusal rate.[82] Del Real's research on Venezuelan migrants found that, since most visa categories require proof of continuous formal employment or economic self-sufficiency, those who change employers or leave their jobs

[75] Frances Webber, 'On the Creation of the UK's "Hostile Environment"' (2019) 60 Race & Class 76. Webber points out that there were earlier antecedents to many aspects of the hostile environment. I have addressed the impact of the hostile environment on migrant women, including domestic workers, in Natalie Sedacca, 'Migrant Work, Gender and the Hostile Environment: A Human Rights Analysis' (2024) 53 Industrial Law Journal 63.

[76] David Bolt, 'An Inspection of the Home Office's Approach to Illegal Working—August–December 2018' (Independent Chief Inspector of Borders and Immigration 2019) 50, 73; Beadsworth (n 68) 231–2.

[77] Alison Harvey and Zoe Harper, *A Guide to the Immigration Act 2016* (Bloomsbury Professional 2017) 275–76; Sedacca (n 75) 71–72.

[78] Hannah Lewis and Louise Waite, 'Migrant Illegality, Slavery and Exploitative Work' in Gary Craig and others (eds), *The Modern Slavery Agenda: Policy, Politics and Practice* (Policy Press 2019) 231.

[79] Stuart N Hodkinson and others, 'Fighting or Fuelling Forced Labour? The Modern Slavery Act 2015, Irregular Migrants and the Vulnerabilising Role of the UK's Hostile Environment' (2021) 41 Critical Social Policy 68, 78; Sigona and others (n 12) 12.

[80] Home Office, 'Restoring Control over the Immigration System (White Paper, CP 1326, 2025)' [229].

[81] Thayer Correa and others, 'El Estado En Su Frontera' (n 33) 167–68.

[82] Luis Eduardo Thayer Correa, 'Closed Doors and Open Footprints: Undocumented Migration, Precarious Trajectories, and Restrictive Policies in Chile' (2021) 12 Migraciones Internacionales 13–15 <https://doi.org/10.33679/rmi.v1i1.2270> accessed 23 July 2025; Deisy Del Real, 'Gradations of Migrant Legality: The Impact of States' Legal Structures and Bureaucracies on Immigrant Legalization and Livelihoods' [2024] International Migration Review 01979183231223700, 10–11.

experience difficulties in renewing their status.[83] During these 'liminal periods' without formal employment, interviewees could not obtain or renew Chilean identity documents and were therefore treated as irregular and excluded from job opportunities and government assistance.[84]

In Chile, irregular migrant workers are in principle entitled to the same labour rights as other workers,[85] with the relatively favourable position reflected in the understanding that employers should meet labour standards regardless of the worker's migration status, discussed in Chapter 4. However, unlike some other South American countries such as Argentina and Bolivia, Chile has not explicitly provided for back payments of wages and other labour rights for undocumented migrants,[86] meaning shortcomings in protection remain. The 2021 legislation reiterates that foreigners are entitled to the same labour rights as Chilean nationals, 'without prejudice to the requirements and sanctions established by law for certain cases' and that employers should comply with their legal obligations regardless of the worker's migratory condition.[87] At the same time, it has established a new set of sanctions applicable both to irregular migrants and those employing them, which could increase risk to such migrants.[88] Sanctions apply to carrying out remunerated activities without authorization, which appears under the sub-header 'less serious infringements', and the employment of foreigners without authorization under 'serious infringements'.[89] However, the legislation also provides that migrants working without authorization will not be sanctioned for that fact where they make a complaint against their employer for not complying with immigration, labour, or other legislation, meaning that a degree of protection is retained, and the sanctions are not of a criminal nature, with confirmation that irregular migration does not amount to a crime.[90]

Another example of a liminal status is the situation of migrants in South Africa on special exemption permits for nationals of particular countries such as Zimbabwe. Difficulties associated with this route include the wait for a decision on granting the permits, a lack of options to renew or apply for permanent residence, and frequent policy changes and uncertainty about the scheme's form and continuation.[91] Drawing on Menjívar's concept of 'liminal legality', Nyakabawu has described the impact of this uncertainty on Zimbabwean migrants as 'legal

[83] Del Real (n 82) 11–17.
[84] ibid 18.
[85] Ducoing (n 15) 15.
[86] Diego Acosta, *The National versus the Foreigner in South America: 200 Years of Migration and Citizenship Law* (CUP 2018) 128.
[87] Ley 21.325, Art 14.
[88] Jorge Chuaqui, *The Quality of Life in Chile: Historic Definitions, Current Challenges and Future Possibilities*, vol 1 (Emanuel Arredondo, Laura Moreau, and James Linn eds, Garth University Consortium Publishers 2024) 36.
[89] Ley 21.325, Arts 109, 117.
[90] ibid, Arts 117, 9.
[91] Nyakabawu (n 44) 2–4; Polzer Ngwato, Tekié, and Ndung'u (n 40) 72.

violence', since they 'were not necessarily illegal in South Africa while waiting for [the Zimbabwe Exemption Permit] but were in a precarious legal existence that affected their livelihoods as they had little or no access to economic opportunities'.[92] My interviews also highlighted the risks created by the uncertainty around the scheme. Mullagee explained that workers in this situation could initially open a bank account with their passport, but that:

> if there's any problem, they just kind of shut you off, and so then you don't have access to your money either... migrant domestic workers have to operate under the radar and that's the reality... It's a hard and ugly reality.

In South Africa, the employment of an irregular migrant constitutes an offence by the employer rather than the worker[93] and an employee working without a valid permit is still entitled to enforce any claim based on statute or the employment relationship against the employer.[94] The 2008 *Discovery Healthcare* case confirmed that migrant workers with expired permits were still entitled to employment protection, noting that otherwise, unscrupulous employers could employ foreign nationals and then refuse to pay them or otherwise take advantage of their situation.[95] As with Chile, this is a protective position that compares favourably to the explicit denial of rights in the UK. In practice, however, workers can still bear much of the risk in this situation, since being identified in the process of reporting the employer for any breaches could lead to their dismissal and deportation.[96] My research highlighted how irregular migrant workers are exposed to abuse, being formally entitled to protection of labour law but often not aware of this or with difficulties in enforcing it in practice. As George explained,

> many of the migrant domestic workers aren't even aware that the law applies to them, so many will take years of abuse, years of poor pay... it's always easy for the employers to either not comply with minimum wage regulations, to make them work extra hours... So they generally feel disrespected and... undermined

In this context, migrant workers are often conceptualized as more compliant and less likely to complain, which is sometimes manifested in employers preferring migrant workers because of the idea that they will work harder. Dhladhla observed that employers:

[92] Menjívar (n 61) 1000; Nyakabawu (n 44) 4.
[93] Immigration Act 2002, s38.
[94] Employment Services Act—Act No 4 of 2014 (South Africa) 2014, s8(2).
[95] *Discovery Health Limited v CCMA & Others* (2008) ILJ 1480 (Labour Court of South Africa) [24–32].
[96] Laura Griffin, 'Unravelling Rights: "Illegal" Migrant Domestic Workers in South Africa' (2011) 42 South African Review of Sociology 83, 91.

> take it as a game. That if they find ... migrant workers, they are using them, saying that they are hard workers just because they are afraid to demand the minimum wage

Dhladhla also observed that some migrant workers 'are afraid to join the union', while von Broembsen noted that there could be a sense of 'competition' between South African unionized workers and migrants who are less likely to be unionized.

There is somewhat better potential for irregular migrant workers to enforce their rights through the CCMA, introduced in Chapter 4, which is not primarily focused on migration issues. Tekié noted that despite some exceptions and instances of discrimination and abuse towards migrants, for the most part the CCMA would say 'this isn't Home Affairs, we're ... concerned only with labour issues', adding that workers could even file a CCMA complaint with an expired passport. Yet there could still be some risk to irregular migrant workers in doing so. Barrett noted that if the Department of Home Affairs 'gets wind of the fact that there is an undocumented migrant, they can ... trigger deportation'. She also noted another concern that the employer could get annoyed and 'settle in accordance with the ruling of the CCMA, but then fire the domestic worker because they are an undocumented migrant'. The recent White Paper on labour migration refers to the role of both the CCMA and Labour Court in 'assisting workers regardless of their migratory status to pursue their rights' and calls for further measures to strengthen its engagement with irregular as well as regular migrant workers, such as capacity building for mediators and judges.[97] This signals an intention to move towards a situation where better enforcement of rights is possible.

In India, there is no direct equivalent relating to visa schemes creating irregularity, but internal migrants can face practical challenges in accessing social rights, particularly when crossing state lines.[98] Furthermore, restrictions in citizenship law can create broader difficulties in proving status[99] in ways that also raise the spectre of 'liminal legality'. In 2003, a National Register of Indian Citizens was established, with a mandate for officials to go house-to-house to collect information and, during the verification process, enter 'doubtful' as the status for individuals or families suspected not to have citizenship.[100] While intended for the whole country, to date this has been implemented in the Eastern State of Assam, in response to concerns of large-scale unauthorized migration.[101] Those labelled as

[97] Department of Employment and Labour (n 47) [5.3.6.7].

[98] Rameez Abbas, 'Internal Migration and Citizenship in India' (2016) 42 Journal of Ethnic and Migration Studies 150. See Chapter 8.

[99] ibid 152.

[100] Citizenship (Registration of Citizens and Issue of National Identity Cards) Rules—G.S.R. 937(E) 2003 [3–4]; Mohsin Alam Bhat, 'Doubtful Citizens: Irregularization and Precarious Citizenship in Contemporary India' in Michelle Foster, Jaclyn Neo, and Christoph Sperfeldt (eds) *Statelessness in Asia* (CUP 2024) 211.

[101] Bhat (n 100) 211. The government has recently allocated substantial funds to updating the National Population Register database, viewed by some as a first step towards a nationwide National

'doubtful' must adduce documentary evidence to prove their status, which is problematic in a context where universal documentation is far from the norm,[102] especially as strict standards are applied, and minor errors such as inconsistencies in dates and spellings can be used to deem persons to be foreigners.[103] This has been found to disproportionately affect socially marginalized people and women, who are more likely to be illiterate and to lack access to documentation that would be gained through formal work, as well as other evidence such as property deeds.[104] Those who cannot dispel their 'doubtful' status, apart from losing voting rights and potentially facing deportation, may also be barred from accessing welfare benefits and food aid.[105] This, in turn, is likely to heighten their dependency on employers and susceptibility to exploitation.

Human rights, access to the labour market, and decent work for irregular migrants

Restrictive immigration regimes and the status of irregularity can breach numerous different human rights, including those discussed in Chapter 8. This section focuses on two of the most pertinent issues that are foundational to rights at work: the right to gain a living by freely chosen work, and the salience of the right to decent work to all migrants regardless of status.

The right to gain a living by freely chosen work: Tied visa schemes and other restrictions on access

Article 6 of the International Covenant on Economic, Social and Cultural Rights (ICESCR) defines the right to work as including 'the right of everyone to the opportunity to gain his living by work which he freely chooses or accepts'.

Register of Citizens—Buddhadeb Halder, 'Doubtful Citizenship: Data and Division in India's New Citizenship Laws' (2021) 54 PS: Political Science & Politics 638.

[102] Tieri (n 49) 15; Ishita Chakrabarty, 'The Greys between Citizenship and Foreignness: The Inherent Flaws within India's Citizenship Legislation' (2023) 37 Journal of Immigration Asylum and Nationality Law 166, 182–83. These sources also examine the recent Citizenship Amendment Act, Act 47 of 2019, which allowed non-Muslims from neighbouring Muslim-majority countries (Afghanistan, Bangladesh, and Pakistan) an expedited route to naturalization.

[103] Trisha Sabhapandit and Padmini Baruah, '"Untrustworthy and Unbelievable": Women and the Quest for Citizenship in Assam' (2021) 3 Statelessness & Citizenship Review 236, 253; Bhat (n 100) 216.

[104] Sabhapandit and Baruah (n 103); Bhat (n 100) 222.

[105] Silvia Masiero, 'A New Layer of Exclusion? Assam, Aadhaar and the NRC' (*South Asia@LSE* -, 12 September 2019) <https://blogs.lse.ac.uk/southasia/2019/09/12/a-new-layer-of-exclusion-assam-aadhaar-and-the-nrc/> accessed 26 July 2025; Anindita Chakrabarty, 'Structural Intersections, Hierarchical Citizenship and Criminalization of the Migrant in Assam' (2024) 32 Critical Criminology (Richmond, B.C.) 339, 350.

Conceptually, this can be understood as the 'negative' component of the right to work, namely protection against state interference in being able to seek employment or being coerced into employment, while other elements are the 'positive' aspect of the right to have employment, and the requirement of decent work.[106] Measures that restrict migrants' access to the labour market, for example through ties to a particular employer or sector, are relevant to this negative aspect of the right to work. General Comment 18 of the UN Committee on Economic, Social and Cultural Rights (UNCESCR) on Article 6 indicates that 'the labour market must be open to everyone under the jurisdiction of States' parties', prohibiting discrimination on grounds including 'national or social origin'.[107] It notes a specific legal obligation on state parties to refrain from 'denying or limiting equal access to decent work for all persons, especially disadvantaged and marginalized individuals and groups, including prisoners or detainees, members of minorities and migrant workers'.[108] It thus provides for a comprehensive application of the right to work to migrants.[109]

Article 15 of the African Charter on Human and People's Rights (ACHPR) provides a close equivalent at regional level, stating the right of every individual 'to work under equitable and satisfactory conditions',[110] with decisions of the African Commission on Human and People's Rights (AComHPR) indicating that this also encompasses the negative aspect of the right to work.[111] For example, the AComHPR found violations in the case of a magistrate who was sentenced by a military tribunal and not reinstated after his release, contrary to a government amnesty,[112] and where the closure of a newspaper as a result of government

[106] Guy Mundlak, 'The Right to Work: Linking Human Rights and Employment Policy' (2007) 146 International Labour Review 189, 192–93; Virginia Mantouvalou, 'The Right to Non-Exploitative Work' in Virginia Mantouvalou (ed), *The Right to Work: Legal and Philosophical Perspectives* (Hart 2014).

[107] UNCESCR, 'General Comment No 18 on the Right to Work (Art. 6 of the Covenant), 6 February 2006, E/C.12/GC/18' [12(b)].

[108] ibid [23].

[109] The UK has reserved the right to interpret Article 6 as not precluding 'restrictions, based on place of birth or residence qualifications, on the taking of employment in any particular region or territory', but such reservations should be understood narrowly in light of 'the overall object and purpose of ICESCR to protect human dignity'—Colm O'Cinneide and Cathryn Costello, 'The Right to Work' in Cathryn Costello, Michell Foster, and Jane McAdam (eds), *The Oxford Handbook of International Refugee Law* (OUP 2021) 958.

[110] Women's equality of access to employment and freedom to choose their occupation is also separately protected—African Union, 'The Protocol to the African Charter on Human and Peoples' Rights on the Rights of Women in Africa ('Maputo Protocol') 2003', Art 13.

[111] Rachel Murray, *The African Charter on Human and Peoples' Rights: A Commentary* (OUP 2019) 387–90.

[112] *Pagnoulle (on behalf of Mazou) v Cameroon Communication No 39/90* 2000 AHRLR 57 (AComHPR) [29]; Manisuli Ssenyonjo, 'The Protection of Economic, Social and Cultural Rights under the African Charter' in Danwood Mzikenge Chirwa, and Lilian Manka Chenwi (eds), *The Protection of Economic, Social and Cultural Rights In Africa: International, Regional and National Perspectives* (CUP 2016) 113–14.

legislation prevented the complainants and their employees from working.[113] The Commission has also applied these principles in complaints arising from restriction of access in relation to migration, including in the context of mass expulsions from Angola.[114] A further salient decision arose from the tightening of nationality requirements in Côte d'Ivoire, which led to some persons from the Dioula ethnic group being denied certain benefits and services including identity cards.[115] The discriminatory and arbitrary denial of nationality was held to violate Article 15, which included 'the prerogative to access employment as a source of income and to benefit from the same treatment as persons in a work situation and in similar circumstances'.[116]

In the other regional systems, the right to work is not directly protected in the main enforceable instrument, appearing instead in the San Salvador Protocol Articles 6–7, and the European Social Charter (ESC) Articles 1–4. Yet both regional courts have made relevant findings using the 'integrated approach' to interpretation discussed in Chapter 3. In the Inter-American Court of Human Rights (IACtHR) case *Lagos del Campo v Peru*, a union organizer who had been dismissed for complaining about work conditions was found to have been subject to a violation of the right to stable employment.[117] Reiterating the interdependence and indivisibility between categories of rights, the Court recognized the right not to be unjustly deprived of employment, as well as referring to provisions on fair salaries, employment opportunities, and employment conditions.[118] The analysis relied on Article 26 of the American Convention on Human Rights (ACHR) to draw on regional social and economic rights instruments.[119] This was a vital step in enhancing the justiciability of social and economic rights and the protection of workers' rights,[120] which laid the groundwork for the recognition of a right to decent work in the cases discussed in Chapter 4.

In the ECtHR, relevant cases have primarily hinged on Article 8 of the European Convention on Human Rights ('ECtHR'), the right to a private and family life. For example, in *Sidabras and Dziautus v Lithuania*, two former KGB agents challenged limitations on employment available to them, which prevented them from

[113] *Zimbabwe Lawyers for Human Rights & Associated Newspapers of Zimbabwe v Republic of Zimbabwe—Communication No 284/03* 2009 AHRLR 235 (AComHPR) [179].

[114] *Institute for Human Rights and Development in Africa v Angola—Communication No 292/2004* 2008 AHRLR 43 (AComHPR) [43, 76]; Ssenyonjo (n 112) 113.

[115] *Open Society Justice Initiative v Côte d'Ivoire (Communication 318/06)* [2015] ACHPR 1 (AComHPR) [3–9].

[116] ibid [176–77].

[117] *Lagos del Campo v Perú* IACtHR 31 August 2017, Ser C No 366.

[118] ibid [141–48].

[119] 'American Declaration of the Rights and Duties of Man, OAS Res XXX Adopted by the Ninth International Conference of American States (1948) Reprinted in Basic Documents Pertaining to Human Rights in the Inter-American System OEA/Ser L V/II.82 Doc 6 Rev 1 at 17 (1992)', Art XIV; *Lagos del Campo v Perú* (n 117) [144]. See Chapter 3.

[120] Franz Christian Ebert and Charlotte Fabricius, 'Strengthening Labor Rights in the Inter-American Human Rights System' (2019) 4 International Labor Rights Case Law 179, 183.

accessing a number of areas of work within the private sector, as a violation of Article 8.[121] The ECtHR reiterated 'that "private life" is a broad term not susceptible to exhaustive definition', holding that this was affected by comprehensive bars on employment in the private sector.[122] Similarly, in *Campagnano v Italy* the ECtHR found that restrictions on a bankrupt person carrying out certain professions 'undoubtedly [fell] within the sphere of her private life',[123] indicating that Article 8 requires justifications of 'class based prohibitions on work'.[124] Additionally, where a dismissal or disciplinary action 'has severe consequences on a person's ordinary private life', compliance with Article 8 will also require a justification following the proportionality test.[125]

It is therefore relevant to consider the justifications for restrictions on labour market access and choice of work for domestic workers, such as those discussed earlier in this chapter. In some cases, the reasons for restrictions are ostensibly worker protective, but this is not borne out in practice. For example, the UK government's initial reasons for not allowing general extensions of the ODWV were based on the view that this would 'increase the risk of abuse', while limiting permission to work for domestic workers awaiting a decision on their trafficking status to those who receive an RGD during the validity of their initial six-month visa apparently relates to encouraging early reporting of abuse.[126] However, my empirical work, far from suggesting that workers receiving a later decision had made a conscious decision to delay reporting, showed that the delay was affected by numerous factors often beyond their control. The arbitrary nature of the distinction, alongside the serious nature of its impacts, makes the restrictions less likely to be considered proportionate. Furthermore, the assumption that the right to extend the visa would make workers less likely to report abuse is highly dubious, since it contradicts the Ewins review as well as research by NGOs and academics.[127]

More generally, justifications for limiting the negative aspect of the right to work based on migration control should be treated with great caution, particularly where they arise from differential treatment based on the classification of migrant workers' apparent levels of skill. The concept of 'low-skilled workers' and the designation of domestic workers as such is problematic, overlapping with the gendered, racialized, and class-based devaluation of their work. It contrasts sharply with the demands and expectations often made by employers, particularly when a domestic worker is caring for young children.[128] Labour migration policies

121 *Sidabras and Dziautas v Lithuania* [2004] ECHR 395.
122 ibid [34, 43, 47].
123 *Campagnano v Italy* (2005) 48 EHRR 43 [54].
124 Rory O'Connell, 'The Right to Work in the ECHR' [2012] European Human Rights Law Review 176, 188.
125 *Denisov v Ukraine* [2018] ECHR 1061; Hugh Collins, 'An Emerging Human Right to Protection against Unjustified Dismissal' (2021) 50 Industrial Law Journal 36, 40–41.
126 James Brokenshire MP, HC Deb 25 April 2016, vol 608, col 1189.
127 Ewins (n 4); Sharp (n 7); Mantouvalou, 'Am I Free Now?' (n 5).
128 See Chapters 2, 5, and 6.

that admit migrants based on concepts of 'skill' or 'talent' tend to favour male-dominated work sectors,[129] with less advantageous schemes for migrant workers deemed 'low-skilled' reflecting the lesser value attached to them and gendered segregation in the labour market.[130] Devaluation takes place not only on gendered grounds, but also more broadly as a response to movement of people who are conceptualized as not performing the most 'desirable' and sought-after forms of labour. Gender thus works alongside other categories of distinction—including race/ethnicity and class—to recreate hierarchies among migrants, underscoring the importance of an intersectional understanding of devaluation.[131]

Across the international migration regimes, the explicit or implicit classification of domestic workers as 'low-skilled' has a prominent role in shaping the limited options available to this group. The changes to the ODWV in the UK arose in the context of a move to a 'points-based' system, which designates certain forms of migrants as 'low-skilled workers' carrying out work 'of little economic value'.[132] This understanding made it appear anomalous to permit the entry of domestic workers,[133] whose admission to the UK was rationalized as taking place on an exceptional basis to make it 'attractive to wealthy transnational migrants' who could bring their existing staff with them when they moved.[134] Therefore, domestic workers are essentially constructed as appendages to wealthy employers. In South Africa, the notion of skill is also significant in leading to domestic workers being generally excluded from labour migration schemes, which are designed to prioritize those with 'critical skills' or filling jobs for which a suitable South African national or permanent resident cannot be recruited.[135] Accordingly, the legitimacy of migration control as a reason for restricting labour mobility should not be taken as a given but carefully scrutinized, particularly given the severe impact of restrictions on migrants' access to rights at work.

Furthermore, some restrictive visa schemes that limit choice of work may violate the prohibition on forced labour, meaning that no justification is possible. By preventing labour mobility, these schemes undermine 'a key element of what makes

[129] Désirée Lim, *Immigration and Social Equality: The Ethics of Skill-Selective Immigration Policy* (OUP 2023) 121–23.

[130] Daiva Stasiulis, 'Gender Perspectives on Citizenship Rights and Social Protection for Migrants' in Marco Giugni and Maria Grasso (eds), *Handbook of Citizenship and Migration* (Edward Elgar 2021) 240.

[131] Antje Ellermann, 'Discrimination in Migration and Citizenship' (2020) 46 Journal of Ethnic and Migration Studies 2463, 2464; Daiva Stasiulis, Zaheera Jinnah, and Blair Rutherford, 'Migration, Intersectionality and Social Justice (Guest Editors' Introduction)' (2020) 2020 Studies in Social Justice 1.

[132] Mullally and Murphy (n 2) 411.

[133] Bridget Anderson, 'Nations, Migration and Domestic Labor: The Case of the UK' (2014) 46 Women's Studies International Forum 5, 11.

[134] Judy Fudge and Kendra Strauss, 'Migrants, Unfree Labour, and the Legal Construction of Domestic Servitude' in Cathryn Costello and MR Freedland (eds), *Migrants at Work: Immigration and Vulnerability in Labour Law* (OUP 2014) 161.

[135] Khan and Hurt (n 41) 102–3.

wage labour "free" (to the extent that it can be considered free, given the economic imperative to sell one's labour power),[136] while exacerbating the worker's dependency on the employer and often making it difficult to leave since their continued sponsorship is necessary for the right to remain in the country.[137] An example is seen in *Rantsev v Cyprus* relating to the 'artiste' visa that owners of establishments obtained on behalf of workers, being required to make a deposit in advance for repatriation expenses and to notify the Immigration Officer if an artiste missed work or otherwise breached their contract.[138] The ECtHR held that the restrictive terms of the visa created dependency on the employer or agent, driving susceptibility to trafficking and failing to provide 'practical and effective protection'.[139] As Mantouvalou has noted, while the ODWV is not precisely as restrictive as the visa in *Rantsev*, it nonetheless creates very significant obstructions to labour mobility, such that its terms arguably violate Article 4 of the European Convention on Human Rights (ECHR).[140] These arguments take on further salience in relation to irregular migrants, whose situation of dependency is heightened.

The human rights of irregular migrants at work

Contrary to frameworks that deny rights to irregular migrants, the right to just and favourable conditions of work under Article 7 ICESCR supports a series of minimum standards that apply to all, regardless of migration status, work sector, or other difference. UNCESCR's General Comment 23 makes it clear that access to remedy should be available for all violations of the right and should not be denied on the grounds that the affected person is an irregular migrant'.[141] This position is mirrored in the Americas by the IACtHR's Advisory Opinion on the rights of Undocumented Migrants.[142] This states that, although there is no obligation to offer employment to undocumented migrants, once they are engaged in a job 'they immediately become possessors of the labor rights corresponding to workers and may not be discriminated against because of their irregular situation'.[143] The

[136] Maayan Niezna, 'Paper Chains: Tied Visas, Migration Policies, and Legal Coercion' (2022) 49 Journal of Law and Society 362, 363.

[137] Cathryn Costello, 'Migrants and Forced Labour: A Labour Law Response' in Alan Bogg and others (eds), *The Autonomy of Labour Law* (Hart 2015) 210.

[138] *Rantsev v Cyprus and Russia* (2010) 51 EHRR 1 [113–17].

[139] ibid [290–93].

[140] Virginia Mantouvalou, *Structural Injustice and Workers' Rights* (OUP 2023) 125–26.

[141] UNCESCR, 'General Comment No. 23 on the Right to Just and Favourable Conditions of Work (Art. 7 of the Covenant), 27 April 2016, E/C.12/GC/23' [57]. The Migrant Workers Convention (ratified by Chile) also provides for treatment no less favourable than nationals regarding remuneration and other conditions and terms of employment, including for irregular migrants—UN General Assembly, 'International Convention on the Protection of the Rights of All Migrant Workers and Members of Their Families (Adopted 18 December 1990, Entered into Force 1 July 2003) 2000 UNTS 3', Art 25.

[142] *Juridical Condition and Rights of the Undocumented Migrants, Advisory Opinion OC-18/03* IACtHR 17 September 2003, Ser A No 18.

[143] ibid [135–36].

IACtHR has reiterated the principle of equal protection and non-discrimination irrespective of migratory status in *Girls Yean & Bosico*.[144] A similarly universalistic framing applies to the right to decent work in the ACHPR. AComHPR guidelines indicate that that states must ensure equality and non-discrimination in access to decent work and ensure 'conditions of work to members of vulnerable and disadvantaged groups that are not inferior to those enjoyed by other employees', a category that is defined as including 'legal or illegal migrant workers'.[145]

The position in the European system is somewhat more complex. First, regarding social rights, the Appendix to the ESC states that the rights at Articles 1–17 apply only to those who are 'lawfully resident or working regularly within the territory'. Meanwhile, Article 19 ESC provides a series of rights for migrant workers and their families, such as to decent remuneration and to protection against expulsion, which are phrased as applying to those 'lawfully within their territories', thus suggesting a lack of protection for those without status. Yet the European Committee of Social Rights (ECSR) has shown some openness to rights applying to irregular migrants in particular circumstances. For example, in *CEC v Netherlands*, it determined that the right to social and medical assistance applied to adult migrants in an irregular situation because receiving necessary food, water, clothing, and shelter was closely connected to fundamental rights and human dignity.[146] Interestingly, it found the state had not proven that denial of emergency shelter was 'absolutely necessary' to achieve its migration-related policies,[147] which is a high bar for the state to meet. Workplace violations against irregular migrants can also infringe fundamental rights and dignity, meaning they also have the potential to give rise to exceptions to the ordinary exclusion of irregular migrants.

Relatedly, the ECSR has raised concerns about the offence of illegal working in the UK for 'prohibiting undocumented workers from claiming rights at work for fear of being arrested and deported' and requested further information about discrimination against migrants in employment.[148] Since this offence prevents migrants from accessing their wages and even permits them to be seized as 'proceeds of crime', the right to peaceful enjoyment of possessions under ECHR Article 1, Protocol 1, is also relevant, particularly when taken together with the Article 14 prohibition on discrimination as regards other ECHR rights.[149] In the successful challenge to confiscation of wages in *Paulet v UK*, the ECtHR found that a 'reasonable relationship of proportionality' needed to exist between the means

[144] *The Girls Yean and Bosico v Dominican Republic*, IACtHR 8 September 2005, Ser C No 130 [155].

[145] AComHPR, 'Principles and Guidelines on the Implementation of Economic, Social and Cultural Rights in the African Charter on Human and Peoples' Rights, Adopted at the Forty-Seventh Ordinary Session Held in Banjul, the Gambia, from 12 to 26 May 2010' [59(i), 1(e)].

[146] ECSR, 'Complaint No 90/2013 – Conference of European Churches (CEC) v. the Netherlands—Decision on the Merits of 9 July 2014' [74–75].

[147] ibid [113–21].

[148] ECSR, 'Conclusions XXII-1 (2020)—the United Kingdom' (2021) 8.

[149] Mantouvalou, *Structural Injustice and Workers' Rights* (n 140) 131–33. See also Chapter 5.

(confiscating wages) and the aim they pursued, rather than requiring the affected person to bear an 'individual and excessive burden'.[150] The proportionality of the illegal working offence is questionable since it arises in the context of 'hostile environment' legislation that aims to make life unsustainable for migrants.[151] To the extent that the policy has an overarching aim of encouraging irregular migrants to leave the UK voluntarily, there is little evidence that it achieves this; rather, the Home Office remains committed to it because of a contention that it is 'the right thing to do' and what the public finds acceptable.[152]

In general, the ECtHR has not recognized the labour rights of irregular migrants as clearly as the IACtHR.[153] Nonetheless, it has increasingly acknowledged the susceptibility to exploitation caused by irregular status as a factor in cases regarding servitude, trafficking, and forced labour under Article 4 ECHR. In the cases about domestic servitude and forced labour discussed in Chapter 5, the applicants' irregular migration status was central to the findings of violations. For example, in *Chowdury,* the ECtHR referred to the applicants' vulnerability as irregular migrants 'at risk of being arrested, detained and deported', who 'probably realised that if they stopped working they would never receive their overdue wages' in support of its finding that they had been subject to trafficking and forced labour.[154] The ECtHR has gone further in recognizing the need for legal frameworks to address abuses arising from irregular status in the 2024 decision *FM & ors v Russia.*[155] This concerned women from Kazakhstan and Uzbekistan who were recruited to work in grocery shops in Moscow with a promise of good salaries and normal working conditions and then subjected to a situation of servitude, including overwork, deprivation of sleep and food, being confined in the shops and forced to drink alcohol, beatings, and sexual violence.[156] Their identity documents were seized, leaving them in an irregular situation where they were fearful of the police.[157] In its findings on the state's violations of its positive obligation, the ECtHR not only discussed the criminal law but also referred to the lack of possibility of regularizing residence in Russia for (potential) victims of trafficking illegally present in the country, and the fact that providing assistance to such individuals was punishable

[150] *Paulet v United Kingdom* (2015) 61 EHRR 39 [64–65].
[151] Hodkinson and others (n 79); Mantouvalou, *Structural Injustice and Workers' Rights* (n 140) 133.
[152] David Bolt, 'An Inspection of the "Hostile Environment" Measures Relating to Driving Licences and Bank Accounts—January to July 2016' (Independent Chief Inspector of Borders and Immigration 2016) [7.7–7.8]; National Audit Office, 'Report by the Comptroller and Auditor General—Home Office Immigration Enforcement—HC 110 Session' (2020) [2.9].
[153] For critique of the ECtHR's approach see Marie-Bénédicte Dembour, *When Humans Become Migrants: Study of the European Court of Human Rights with an Inter-American Counterpoint* (OUP 2015), ch 5.
[154] *Chowdury and Others v Greece* App no 21884/15 (ECtHR, 30 March 2017) [97–100]. See also *Zoletic and Others v Azerbaijan* App no 20116/12 (ECtHR, 7 October 2021) [193].
[155] *FM and others v Russia* App nos 71671/16 and 40190/18 (ECtHR, 10 December 2024).
[156] ibid [1, 232].
[157] ibid [265, 232].

by administrative and criminal sanctions.[158] It notably found a violation of Article 14 taken with Article 4 in light of the disproportionate impact of the state's poor anti-trafficking efforts on 'female foreign migrant workers in an irregular situation'.[159] This element of the decision built on previous cases, including *Opuz v Turkey*,[160] to indicate that such discrimination need not be intentional.[161] The case is therefore significant for showing 'how the right not to be discriminated against under Article 14 ECHR can be successfully utilized by undocumented migrants or migrants with insecure migration status'.[162] Bearing in mind the continuum between work that falls below the standards of decent work and forced labour, as discussed in Chapter 5, it is arguable that the prohibition on forced labour necessitates amending legal frameworks that deny labour rights to irregular migrants.

Conclusion

Across the case study countries where international migration plays a prevalent role in domestic work, migrant workers face a series of restrictions to changing employers freely and realizing their labour rights. These include the lack of a general migration pathway and uncertainties caused by special exemption permit regimes in South Africa, constraints on changing employer during the initial two-year period in Chile, and the highly restrictive scheme with limited and inadequate concessions for trafficking victims in the UK. In India, internal migrants face practical obstacles to mobility and realization of rights, with legislation on inter-state migrants proving inadequate to ensure protections. Barriers to changing employers through restrictive migration regimes can lead to violations of not only the negative aspect of the right to work but also the prohibition on forced labour, given the situation of dependency they create on the employer. Migration regimes should therefore be amended to ensure both that workers have an unrestricted right to change employer and that this is effective in practice, removing barriers such as the generally non-extendable six-month time limit in the UK. Beyond this, there is an argument that even sectoral limitations should be removed, since the right to gain a living by 'freely chosen work' implies not being tied to a particular type of role.[163]

158 ibid [291].
159 ibid [344].
160 *Opuz v Turkey* [2009] ECHR 870. See discussion in Chapter 3.
161 *FM v Russia* (n 155) [341].
162 Vladislava Stoyanova, 'F.M. and Others v Russia: The Role of the Prohibition on Discrimination for Migrant Victims of Slavery' [2025] European Human Rights Law Review 239, 244.
163 Additionally, the UN Special Rapporteur on Trafficking has also identified sectoral restrictions as a risk factor for trafficking—Siobhán Mullally, 'Migrant Domestic Workers and Trafficking in Persons: Prevention, Rights Protection and Access to Justice—Report of the Special Rapporteur on Trafficking—UN Doc A/HRC/59/56' (UN General Assembly 2025) [57(g)].

The myriad ways in which statuses of irregularity and semi-legality are created in domestic work include a lack of options for legal migration, regularization and extension, bureaucratic requirements that are challenging to comply with, and the imposition of rules such as denial of a right to work to some workers awaiting a determination of their trafficking status. Workers lacking status frequently suffer restrictions in the realization of their labour rights, even when these are in principle guaranteed, with especially pronounced and deliberate obstacles seen in the context of the UK's 'hostile environment'. A universalistic reading of human rights law requires all workers to have their right to just and favourable conditions at work protected, with this position already accepted by UNCESCR, IACtHR, and AComHPR. This universalistic position should be extended to other contexts, including the European system, since without it, domestic workers are left unprotected. There have been tentative steps in this direction in recent European regional developments, particularly the *FM v Russia* decision, which went beyond the criminal law framework to examine how a lack of opportunities for regularization and the criminalization of support for irregular migrants facilitated forced labour and servitude. This is crucial, since responses that are limited only to measures such as criminalizing trafficking will not be sufficient to address the issue;[164] conversely, if the linkages between 'migration status, access to safe migration routes, and the enjoyment of rights' are recognized, human rights norms have the 'potential to be transformative'.[165] I recognize that the impetus towards a further protection of migrants' rights may be tempered by the concern to protect sovereignty, but have proposed that arguments on that basis should be carefully scrutinized, particularly when they arise from skills-based criteria that perpetuate the devaluation of domestic work. In Chapter 8 on family reunification, I develop this argument further, calling for the analysis of justifications for any restrictions to give proper weight to structural factors driving large-scale migration for domestic work and the harm caused by separation.

[164] Hila Shamir, 'A Labor Paradigm for Human Trafficking' (2012) 60 UCLA Law Review 76; Costello (n 137) 217–225.

[165] Mullally and Murphy (n 2) 426.

8

Wanting the work but not the worker

Barriers to family reunification

Introduction

Much of the discussion on domestic work emphasizes the worker's role in supporting, sustaining, and reproducing their employers' family life. A comprehensive approach to rights in domestic work requires a shift of focus to centre the worker's own potential for contact and cohabitation with their family. This chapter addresses the restrictions migrant domestic workers face in accessing family reunification—the opportunity for family members to join migrants in their destination country—both directly as a result of visa regimes and indirectly through practical barriers that make it difficult to sustain a family life in practice. The next section begins by examining the immigration law position in the three countries where international migration is prevalent: broadly speaking, a bar on bringing dependents for the main domestic worker visa in the UK, a more permissive system in Chile particularly since 2021, and limited possibilities for family reunification in South Africa. It analyses these provisions alongside empirical material on their impact, including the distress that can be caused by long-term separation from family members. It then examines practical barriers that migrant workers—including internal migrants in India—face through a lack of access to social rights, such as education and welfare support, which may be necessary to sustain family life.

The second section outlines how social rights provisions are relevant to addressing the practical barriers internal and international migrants face to family reunification. It then examines the protection of family reunification under international and regional human rights obligations, particularly the right to private and family life. It traces the identification of an obligation on the state to promote the development of the family unit in the Inter-American Court of Human Rights (IACtHR), with similar rights recognized by the African Commission on Human and People's Rights (AComHPR). It then assesses the situation in the European Court of Human Rights (ECtHR), which has often been reluctant to find that restrictions of family reunification in the migration context violate the right to private and family life because of its deference to state sovereignty considerations. It analyses exceptions to this general rule and the stricter scrutiny undertaken in cases that involve potential discriminatory access to rights, which will often be

Human Rights and the Protection of Domestic Workers in Labour and Migration Law. Natalie Sedacca, Oxford University Press. © Oxford University Press 2026. DOI: 10.1093/9780198985266.003.0011

relevant to restrictions on domestic workers. It finishes by proposing a 'contextualized proportionality analysis' when examining provisions that restrict access to family reunification, namely one that takes into account the structural factors driving large-scale migration for domestic work and the serious harm caused by long-term family separation.

Restrictions on access to family reunification for international migrants

The UK has pronounced restrictions in this area, since its specific visa for domestic work precludes family reunification. Following the introduction of the original visa scheme in 1998, domestic workers were able to apply for their dependents to join them in the UK, but with the change to the short-term, non-renewable visa in 2012, this possibility was removed.[1] The Immigration Rules Appendix for the current Overseas Domestic Worker Visa (ODWV) states that the route does not permit dependents;[2] in any event, the six-month limit would make it difficult to bring family members, particularly children. Likewise, the rules on the two-year visa available to domestic workers identified as victims of modern slavery make no reference to dependents and preclude a route to settlement,[3] while the potential for care workers on the Health and Care Worker visa to bring dependents was abolished in 2024.[4]

The possibility of bringing dependents exists for two specific sub-groups of domestic workers: those who are on the old Domestic Workers in a Private Household route, having arrived before the visa changes on 6 April 2012, and workers in homes of diplomats under the 'Temporary Work—International Agreement' route. In both cases, these are subject to strict criteria. For the former, the decision-maker must be satisfied of adequate maintenance and accommodation for the applicant, worker, and any other dependents, while for diplomatic visas, financial requirements apply to those who have not already been in the UK for at least a year.[5] Given the prevalence of low wages in domestic work, these conditions will often be difficult to meet. Even for those who manage to obtain indefinite leave to

[1] Siobhán Mullally and Cliodhna Murphy, 'Migrant Domestic Workers in the UK: Enacting Exclusions, Exemptions, and Rights' (2014) 36 Human Rights Quarterly 397, 412. See Chapter 7.

[2] Home Office, 'Immigration Rules (UK)—Updated 13 August 2025' <https://www.gov.uk/guidance/immigration-rules> accessed 22 August 2025, Appendix Overseas Domestic Worker Visa.

[3] ibid, Appendix Domestic Worker Who Is a Victim of Modern Slavery.

[4] CJ McKinney and Melanie Gower, 'Changes to Legal Migration Rules for Family and Work Visas in 2024' (House of Commons Library 2024) <https://commonslibrary.parliament.uk/research-briefings/cbp-9920/> accessed 14 March 2025.

[5] Home Office (n 2), Appendix Domestic Workers in a Private Household, DW 20.1; Appendix Temporary Work—International Agreement, IA 29.1.

remain or citizenship in the UK, there is still a financial eligibility requirement in order to sponsor a spouse or partner, currently set at £29,000, having risen sharply from £18,600 in 2024.[6] With only around 50 per cent of UK employees overall, and 36 per cent of women employees, earning enough to meet this threshold,[7] it is likely to be beyond the reach of many domestic workers.

In interview, while mentioning that those who secure other forms of protection such as asylum will have better prospects of bringing family members to the UK, Thomas confirmed the difficulties for those on a domestic worker visa. Although domestic workers can be very used to being apart from their family, 'it doesn't mean they don't feel that isolation and separation keenly'. Even visits to home countries were difficult for domestic workers on low wages: 'it's a luxury, that you would do after working extraordinarily hard, you might be able to afford it once a year if you're lucky … I've had clients that *live* for that visit.' Similarly, Sharp stated that 'we have a lot of emotional appointments where workers find it very distressing … having been so far away from their family'. The interviews therefore highlight the distress caused by the restrictive visa and limited possibilities for family reunification.

In Chile, at the time of my empirical research, there was no substantive right to family reunification, contrary to regional trends.[8] Instead, the right had primarily been protected through judicial decisions,[9] or through the MERCOSUR residence agreement for citizens of Argentina, Bolivia, Brazil, Paraguay, and Uruguay, subject to documentation requirements.[10] Earlier research found family reunification difficult to access for those who lacked permanent residence, job stability, or a place to live, with such difficulties partially offset 'where migrants have a higher level of education, more stable work and better pay', such as among Argentinian migrants.[11] For populations from Peru and Bolivia, whose migration

[6] CJ McKinney, Melanie Gower and Terry McGuinness, 'Research Briefing: The Financial (Minimum Income) Requirement for Partner Visas' (2025) 7. For critique see Benedict Douglas, 'Love and Human Rights' (2023) 43 Oxford Journal of Legal Studies 273, 291–97.

[7] Nuni Jorgensen, 'Family Fortunes: The UK's New Income Requirement for Partner Visas—Updated 1 August 2024' (*Migration Observatory*, 1 February 2024) <https://migrationobservatory.ox.ac.uk/resources/commentaries/family-fortunes-the-uks-new-income-requirement-for-partner-visas/> accessed 25 August 2025.

[8] Decreto Ley No. 1.094, Establece Normas sobre extranjeros en Chile 1975; Diego Acosta, *The National versus the Foreigner in South America: 200 Years of Migration and Citizenship Law* (CUP 2018) 154.

[9] Juan Carlos Ferrada Bórquez and others, 'La "Reagrupación Familiar" Como Concepto y Límite a Los Poderes Del Estado de Chile En Materia Migratoria' (2021) 34 Revista de derecho (Valdivia) 225, 226; Kamila Ignacia Jalaf Varas, 'La reunificación familiar de personas migrantes en Chile: análisis de jurisprudencia de la Corte Suprema entre 2020 a 2022' (Universidad de Chile 2024) 45 <https://repositorio.uchile.cl/handle/2250/202212> accessed 18 March 2025.

[10] 'Agreement on Residence for Mercosur Member States' Nationals 2002—Unofficial Translation from the Spanish Version Prepared by Diego Acosta and Victoria Finn', Article 9(2). See Chapter 7.

[11] Carolina Stefoni, 'Transformaciones Sociales a Partir de Nuevos Procesos Migratorios' in Luis García-Corrochano and others, *Generación de diálogo Chile-Perú Perú-Chile. Documento 4. Aspectos migratorios* (Konrad Adenauer Stiftung 2013) 18.

was concentrated in more precarious sectors of the labour market, however, the presence of minors was low.[12]

Examining these issues in the domestic work context, my interviews indicated that family reunification was usually only possible quite a long time after initial migration. Interviewees explained that in most cases, domestic workers lived with their employers when they first migrated[13] and consequently arrived alone, given the difficulty of having family members with them when working on a live-in basis.[14] Few employers would accept a live-in worker with children, and to accept a worker bringing a partner was only common in a larger home with several roles.[15] After living with their employer for the first years, those who are more aware of their rights would seek to move to live-out work once they had moved to a more secure form of visa, in order to be able to bring family members.[16] 'Catalina' gave a higher estimate of the time delay: 'People stabilise themselves first ... working live-in for five, six years' before looking for live-out work and bringing their family. Practical financial barriers to bringing family members were also noted. The domestic worker 'Isabella' from Colombia said that she was not able to bring her spouse to live with her because of the cost, while 'Sara' from Bolivia said the issue was 'that it's also on average more difficult to find work here for a man', which would affect her sons.

The legal position on family reunification has subsequently changed with Chile's 2021 migration law, which provides residents the right to request reunification with spouses or persons in an equivalent relationship, parents, minor children, and some older children, such as those with disabilities.[17] The provisions on family reunification have been criticized—for example, for lacking clarity on age requirements and on the cost of relevant visas, thus allowing fluctuation in prices.[18] However, the changes represent an advance overall, since they establish a clearer right to family reunification[19] and allow dependents to carry out paid activities on the same basis as holders of temporary residence permits.[20] There is also a provision for a freestanding visa for children and adolescents, to be granted irrespective of their parents' or guardians' immigration status.[21] Even before these

[12] ibid.

[13] Mentioned by several interviewees including Arriagada, 'Nancy', and 'Catalina'.

[14] 'Francisco'.

[15] 'Rocio'.

[16] Arriagada. She said the exceptions, who might be able to bring children with them, are likely to be those who already have a job offer or relatives in Chile.

[17] Ley No 21.325—Ley de Migración y Extranjería 2021, Art 19.

[18] Jorge Vásquez, Victoria Finn, and Sebastián Umpierrez de Reguero, 'Cambiando la cerradura. Intenciones legislativas del proyecto de ley de migraciones en Chile' [2021] Colombia Internacional 57, 74–75.

[19] Jalaf Varas (n 9) 24.

[20] Ley 21.325, Art 17; Mayra Feddersen and Antonio Morales, 'How Do Migratory and Labor Policies Interact to Regulate Migrant Workers?' (2024) 51 Revista Chilena de Derecho 159, 167.

[21] Ley 21.325, Art 41.

changes, the potential for at least some workers to access family reunification demonstrated the benefits of a system that gives a pathway to migration on a more extended basis compared with the UK's very short-term visa.

By contrast, as set out in Chapter 7, South Africa lacks a labour migration pathway for most domestic workers. For irregular migrants, there is by definition no regular route to family reunification, meaning that the domestic worker either remains separated from family, or the family members living with them are also irregular (unless they obtain migration status separately). Only two visa categories explicitly allow for a right to bring family members: the business visa and critical skills visa,[22] neither of which is relevant to most domestic workers. While nationals of Zimbabwe, Lesotho, and Angola may be regularized through special exemption permits, these are of limited assistance regarding family reunification, being difficult to extend to a spouse or children.[23] Many therefore rely on irregular, informal networks to facilitate their children's entry.[24] By contrast, reunification rights apply to those recognized as refugees, whose spouse, dependent children, and destitute, aged, or infirm family members are also categorized as refugees, although there is still no specific system set up to facilitate their reunification.[25]

My interviews reflected a variation as to whether migrant domestic workers had their family members with them. As Barrett indicated,

> a lot do have families, I mean, many have lived here for decades. But ... there are also large numbers who are here on their own and the whole family is ... back in Zimbabwe.

In parallel with the Chilean situation, family reunification in South Africa is sometimes more viable later in the migration progress, as explained by George:

> There are many who come to South Africa with their families. It's not always the entire family, so some will maybe come with their spouse or their partner and some of the children will stay at home with grandmothers ... And then when they're better positioned, they will bring their children.

[22] Immigration Act—Act No 13 of 2002 (South Africa) 2002, ss15 and 19(4); Fatima Khan and Sally Hurt, 'Temporary Residence' in Fatima Khan (ed), *Immigration Law in South Africa* (Juta and Company 2018) 107.

[23] Shingirai Nyakabawu, 'Legal Violence: Waiting for Zimbabwe Exemption Permit in South Africa' (2022) 8 Journal of Law, Society and Development 1, 16.

[24] Zaheera Jinnah, 'Negotiated Precarity in the Global South: A Case Study of Migration and Domestic Work in South Africa' (2020) 2020 Studies in Social Justice 210, 219.

[25] Refugees Act—Act No 130 of 1998 (South Africa), ss1(ix) and 3(c); Jean Chrysostome Kanamugire, 'Family Reunification for Refugees: A Comparative Study' (2021) 10 Perspectives of Law and Public Administration 50, 52.

As she went on to note, those who are separated 'miss out ... on the day-to-day life' such as knowing their child is safe, helping with their homework, and generally making connections. Furthermore, the disruption to family life can be significant, as workers who have children abroad might 'only see them once a year'.[26] Conversely, migrant workers whose family members are with them in South Africa often lack a regular status, making their situation very precarious. As explained by Mullagee, 'there are cases where ... children were born here and now they are being evicted from the country. These kids know no other place.'

Practical barriers to family (re)unification and limits on access to social rights

Whereas the other three countries have specific international migration regimes that facilitate or limit family reunification procedures, the situation in India is distinctive. As noted in Chapter 7, rather than specific visa schemes, there is a free movement agreement with Nepal and a lack of regular migration pathway with Bangladesh, but the prevalent type of migration for domestic work is internal. There are no specific legal restrictions on bringing family members in the internal migration context, given the Constitutional right for all citizens to 'reside and settle in any part of the territory of India'.[27] Yet in practice, there have been inadequacies in the extension of social rights such as housing, healthcare, education, and maternity benefits, at least for circular migrants.[28] These issues can affect the practicability of migrant domestic workers bringing their family members to live with them.

For live-in domestic workers, it is generally difficult to bring family members to live at the destination. Sen explained that in this case:

> the norm is single women's migration. It is rarer to have whole families migrate when the woman takes up ... live-in jobs ... this pattern tends to be more interstate rather than intra-state migration

However, she also noted that the 'expanding market' meant that a lot of 'migrations are now led by domestic work' with a family migrating together and sustaining itself from the woman's earnings at first, until 'eventually the man also finds something'. While this demonstrates the greater flexibility that exists when there are no formal visa restrictions, challenges still arise because of the cost and availability

[26] Mbimbi.

[27] The Constitution of India—as on May 2022, Art 19(1)(e).

[28] Harsh Mander and others, 'Stolen Citizenship, Stolen Freedoms' [2019] Esclavages & Post-esclavages<https://journals.openedition.org/slaveries/602> accessed 26 March 2025.

of housing, as discussed in Chapter 7. A related issue is exclusion from social security and healthcare, which is 'not very good or portable in the country'.[29] Such rights are often lost when crossing a state boundary unless the worker can provide evidence of their new address, which is often difficult because of informal arrangements, and requires the worker to give up residency in their home state, which is not necessarily attractive or viable for short-term or circular migrants.[30] In 2019, the 'One Nation, One Ration Card' Scheme was established to allow portability of access to subsidized foodgrains, an important aspect of welfare provision, but its implementation to date has been inconsistent, with only Delhi making serious progress in relation to inter-state migrants.[31] Processes for obtaining the ration card vary between states, and new migrant workers in a city may lack the connections needed to secure one.[32]

That said, in 2021, the Supreme Court directed all remaining states to implement the scheme and put in place appropriate measures for distributing food rations to migrant labourers.[33] In interview, 'Meera' pointed to the potential of the new E-Shram portal in improving welfare access for internal migrants:

> so the Government of India has ... created this huge database of informal workers in which domestic workers have been registered in very, very, very large numbers ... But again, the question is what kind of schemes will be available ... which respond to you know their entitlements as workers

Reinforcing this sense of tentative optimism, research showed that by 2023 more women workers had registered on E-Shram than men, while also noting that registration on the portal was not a full answer to the challenge of including such workers.[34] Overall, this new system may help to address the limitations on the portability of rights that have created a practical barrier to family reunification in India.

It is also pertinent to examine such factors in relation to the other case studies, since they add to the challenges already posed by international migration regimes. Echoing the points made regarding India, Dhladhla (South Africa) noted that live-in domestic workers are unable to share the employer-provided accommodation with family members unless the employer permits this. She pointed out that it is difficult even for South Africans to bring family members because of the difficulty

[29] Yajnik.

[30] Pankhuri Agarwal, 'State-Migrant Relations in India: Internal Migration, Welfare Rights and COVID-19' (2022) 52 Social Change 239, 241.

[31] Chinmay Tumbe and Rahul Kumar Jha, 'One Nation, One Ration, Limited Interstate Traction: Migration and PDS Portability in India' (2024) 9 Urbanisation 87.

[32] Agarwal (n 30) 249.

[33] *Bandhua Mukti Morcha v Union of India—Writ Petition (Civil) No 6 of 2020—order of June 29, 2021* [80].

[34] Kuldeepsingh Rajput and S Irudaya Rajan, 'Visibilising Invisible Population: E-Shram Portal and Essentiality of Internal Migration Database in India' (2023) 9 Journal of Social Inclusion Studies 82, 86–90.

staying at the employer's property, but that it was even worse for international migrant workers, asking 'Where are they going to stay?' Housing issues were also raised as a deterrent to reunification in Chile, thus potentially acting as a countervailing factor to its relatively permissive framework in immigration law. Olate said none of her union's members had brought relatives, describing this as arising from material conditions: 'we know there are many families without anything, who are crowded'. This is quite striking, although she had also noted a relatively low migrant membership. It is likely to reflect barriers that exist for migrants in accessing good quality accommodation, such as the need for permanent residency to apply for subsidies.[35]

Another issue raised by Mullagee (South Africa) was that, where migrant workers have family members with them but lack status, it can be difficult to access medical facilities and schools for migrant children. This issue has also affected some migrants with asylum seeker permits,[36] and those on the Zimbabwe Exemption Permit, particularly in 2017–18 when there was a gap between a previous scheme expiring and receipt of new permits.[37] Despite the government instructing learning institutions to continue giving and receiving services until new permits were provided, some declined to await a decision on permits, meaning children were forced to withdraw.[38] A High Court judgment in 2019 indicated that all children are entitled to basic education regardless of immigration status, deeming clauses in previous policy documents that allowed children to be excluded based on lack of identity documents or migration status to be unconstitutional.[39] While a crucial ruling, practical difficulties in accessing education appear to persist.[40]

A similar position of access in principle but not always in practice exists in Chile. A Ministry of Education Instruction in 2005 provides for all migrant children to access primary and secondary schools.[41] However, access is restricted through factors including the need for documentation, such as a national identity card that is required for grades to be registered.[42] Likewise, in the UK, local education

[35] Juan Correa and Pablo Flores, 'Migración, acceso a la vivienda y a la ciuadad' in Nicolás Rojas Pedemonte and José Tomás Vicuña (eds), *Migración en Chile: evidencia y mitos de una nueva realidad* (LOM Ediciones 2019) 175; Ley 21.325 Art 18.

[36] Vusilizwe Thebe and Pamela Maombera, 'Negotiating the Border: Zimbabwean Migrant Mothers and Shifting Immigration Policy and Law in South Africa' (2019) 62 African Studies Review 134, 144.

[37] Nyakabawu (n 23) 10.

[38] ibid 10–11.

[39] *Centre for Child Law & Others v Minister of Basic Education & Others (2840/2017)* [2019] ZAECGHC 126 (High Court) [90–101].

[40] Sarah Blessed-Sayah and Dominic Griffiths, 'Equity Not Equality: The Undocumented Migrant Child's Opportunity to Access Education in South Africa' (2024) 76 Educational Review (Birmingham) 46, 49.

[41] Chile—Ministry of Education, 'Oficio Ordinario No 07/1008 (1531)' (2005); Marcia Vera Espinoza and others, 'Towards a Typology of Social Protection for Migrants and Refugees in Latin America during the COVID-19 Pandemic' (2021) 9 Comparative Migration Studies 52, 59.

[42] Philip Alston, 'Report of the Special Rapporteur on Extreme Poverty and Human Rights on His Mission to Chile—UN Doc A/HRC/32/31/Add.1' (UN General Assembly 2016).

authorities have a duty to provide school places to children residing temporarily or permanently in the area, with the implication that evidence of residence is needed, which is likely to pose a problem for irregular migrants.[43] From 2016 to 2018 there was a concerning practice of the Department for Education sharing pupils' nationality and country of birth data with the Home Office, which risked deterring those with precarious status from enrolling.[44] This ended as a result of campaigning,[45] but other aspects of the hostile environment for irregular migrants, as discussed in Chapter 7, remain in place.

Access to welfare benefits is also a central issue, which can determine the viability of supporting a family. This is particularly true where the ability to work is affected by an emergency, which came to the fore in the Covid-19 pandemic. In Chile, for example, a series of protection measures were implemented, such as the 'Emergency Family Income' directed at families working in the informal sector.[46] Since they required a Chilean identification card and inclusion in a registry of homes, they were inaccessible to irregular migrants, those with expired identification documents, and those who had started but not yet completed the regularization process.[47] In South Africa, restrictions on claiming Covid-19 social relief grants aimed at redressing poverty and hunger went further in excluding special exemption permit holders and asylum seekers with valid permits, while being open to citizens, permanent residents, and refugees.[48] However, the High Court held these limits to be unlawful, noting that the excluded groups would not have escaped the negative consequences, such that a person's immigration status would become irrelevant, and ordered an extension of the schemes.[49] Even after this ruling, migrants continued to experience practical barriers, including difficulty verifying income when working in the informal sector and the exclusion of children based on a lack of a birth certificate.[50]

[43] Stefano Piemontese and Nando Sigona, 'The Legal and Policy Infrastructure of Irregularity: United Kingdom' (I-CLAIM 2024) 17.

[44] ibid.

[45] Liberty, 'Department for Education ENDS Collection of Children's Nationality and Country of Birth Data' (*Liberty*, 9 April 2018) <https://www.libertyhumanrights.org.uk/issue/department-for-education-ends-collection-of-childrens-nationality-and-country-of-birth-data/> accessed 29 March 2025.

[46] Luisa Feline Freier and Marcia Vera Espinoza, 'COVID-19 and Immigrants' Increased Exclusion: The Politics of Immigrant Integration in Chile and Peru' (2021) 3 Frontiers in Human Dynamics 3–4 <https://www.frontiersin.org/journals/human-dynamics/articles/10.3389/fhumd.2021.606871/full> accessed 27 March 2025.

[47] ibid 4.

[48] *Scalabrini Centre of Cape Town and Another v Minister of Social Development and Others* [2020] ZAGPPHC 308 (High Court) [12–14].

[49] ibid [24–25].

[50] Jonas Nzabamwita and Mulugeta Dinbabo, 'International Migration and Social Protection in South Africa' (2022) 8 Cogent Social Sciences 13–16 <https://doi.org/10.1080/23311886.2022.2144134> accessed 27 March 2025.

The UK's position on access to social welfare is harsher, as restrictions extend beyond irregular migrants to those on a valid visa through the No Recourse to Public Funds (NRTPF) condition introduced in Chapter 7. A procedure exists for NRTPF to be lifted where there is a risk of destitution, but this is primarily aimed at persons holding other forms of leave to remain—for example, based on family life. For migrants on working visas, 'particularly compelling circumstances' are required to lift the condition.[51] This criterion generally will not be met where 'an applicant has been granted permission on the basis they can maintain themselves and their family members without access to public funds and their circumstances change and they can no longer do so', or they are 'not earning enough to support themselves', in which case 'they should normally be expected to leave the UK'.[52] The denial of benefits was felt starkly during the pandemic, particularly as the separate 'furlough' scheme to support lost employment income was at the discretion of employers and dependent on tax having been paid through the 'pay as you earn' scheme.[53] Instead of benefitting from these schemes, many domestic workers were simply dismissed without pay or notice, which could also leave them homeless where they had been live-in.[54] This underscores how, even where not directly prevented by immigration rules from bringing family members, domestic workers face an enormous risk that a change to their income or loss of their job could lead to the uprooting of their entire family, alongside being unable to rely generally on basic funds to supplement their income, such as the child support payment.

Family reunification and human rights law

Migrant families and social rights

A lack of support through social rights can amount to a practical barrier on family reunification, including in the context of internal migration. In India, a key issue is the lack of portability of benefits between states, albeit with measures currently underway to address this. The right to social security is found in the International Covenant on Economic, Social and Cultural Rights (ICESCR) Article 9, with General Comment 19 of the UN Committee on Economic, Social and Cultural Rights (UNCESCR) indicating that internal migrants 'should be able to access

[51] Home Office, 'Permitting Access to Public Funds—Version 5.0' (2025) 22.

[52] ibid 23.

[53] KD Ewing and Lord Hendy, 'Covid-19 and the Failure of Labour Law: Part 1' (2020) 49 Industrial Law Journal 497, 514–19.

[54] Devyani Nighoskar, 'Migrant Domestic Workers and COVID-19: A Call to Action' (*Futures of Work*, 5 May 2020) <https://futuresofwork.co.uk/2020/05/05/migrant-domestic-workers-and-covid-19-a-call-to-action/> accessed 29 March 2025; Caitlin Boswell, '"We Also Want to Be Safe": Undocumented Migrants Facing COVID in a Hostile Environment' (Joint Council for the Welfare of Immigrants 2022) 13–18.

social security from their place of residence, and residence registration systems should not restrict access ... for individuals who move to another district'.[55] Therefore, the measures currently being implemented to allow for better portability are of vital importance.

In the international migration context,[56] the link between social rights and the facilitation of family reunification is recognized in the Global Compact for Safe, Orderly and Regular Migration, a soft law instrument endorsed by the UN General Assembly in 2018.[57] This includes a stipulation to:

> Facilitate access to procedures for family reunification for migrants at *all skills levels* through appropriate measures that promote *the realization of the right to family life and the best interests of the child*, including by reviewing and revising applicable requirements, such as on income, language proficiency, *length of stay*, work authorization, and *access to social security and services*.[58]

In addition, General Comment 19 stipulates that non-nationals should have access to non-contributory schemes for income and family support, and that any restrictions including qualifying periods must be reasonable and proportionate, with no restrictions on access to primary and emergency medicine.[59] This calls into question barriers to access by international migrants, alongside the non-discrimination obligation in Article 2(2) ICESCR, with UNCESCR General Comment 20 confirming that Covenant rights apply to all including migrant workers regardless of legal status and documentation.[60] There is a limited exception in ICESCR Article 2(3), which states that:

> Developing countries, with due regard to human rights and their national economy, may determine to what extent they would guarantee the economic rights recognized in the present Covenant to non-nationals.

This could potentially be relevant to South Africa and Chile (and India regarding international migrants), which the IMF classes as emerging and developing

[55] UNCESCR, 'General Comment No. 19 on the Right to Social Security (Art. 9 of the Covenant), 4 February 2009, E/C.12/GC/19' [39].

[56] This section briefly addresses some key social rights matters of relevance to migrant domestic workers. For a fuller examination of social rights and international migration, see Natalie Sedacca, 'Migrants and Social Rights' in Christina Binder and others (eds), *Research Handbook on International Law and Social Rights* (2nd edn, Edward Elgar, forthcoming).

[57] Alan Desmond, 'From Complementarity to Convergence: The UN Global Compact for Migration and the UN Migrant Workers Convention' (2022) 55 World Comparative Law 83.

[58] United Nations, 'Global Compact for Safe, Orderly and Regular Migration, GA (11 January 2019) UN Doc A/RES/73/195', Objective 5(i)—emphases added.

[59] UNCESCR, 'General Comment 19' (n 55) [37].

[60] UNCESCR, 'General Comment No. 20 on Non-Discrimination in Economic, Social and Cultural Rights (Art 2, Para 2 of the Covenant), 2 July 2009, E/C.12/GC/20' [30].

economies.[61] However, it should be construed fairly narrowly, since its inclusion in ICESCR was intended to 'end the domination of certain economic groups of non-nationals during colonial times' according to the Limburg principles on implementing ICESCR.[62] It clearly is not applicable to the UK; the UNCESCR's 2025 concluding observations recommended a review of the NRTPF policy to prevent an increase in poverty and precarity among migrants and asylum seekers.[63]

At regional level, the AComHPR Principles and Guidelines require states to ensure all persons, especially those from vulnerable and disadvantaged groups (a category including both legal and illegal migrant workers as well as refugees and asylum seekers) are covered by the social security system, with non-contributory systems necessary to achieve universal coverage.[64] In the IACtHR, *Muelle Flores v Peru* recognized a right to social security, referring to an immediate obligation to ensure access to the benefits recognized by the right *without discrimination*.[65] Similar principles could potentially be used to challenge the denial of social security to migrants based on a short-term or otherwise precarious status.

In the ECtHR, access to social rights has been derived from the provisions of Protocol 1, Article 1 of the European Convention on Human Rights (ECHR) on peaceful enjoyment of possessions, and from Article 8 ECHR where relevant to family life.[66] This is subject to the Court's generally cautious approach in cases involving state support that involves financial resources.[67] In *Niedzwiecki v Germany*, which concerned the refusal of child benefit to a Polish national with a limited residence title, the ECtHR held that child benefits fell within the ambit of Article 8 and that there was a lack of sufficient justification for the differential treatment based on migration status.[68] However, in other cases it has emphasized the state's permitted discretion over migrants' access to benefits.[69] *Bah v UK* confirmed

[61] IMF, 'World Economic Outlook Database—Groups and Aggregates' (*imf.org*, 2023) <https://www.imf.org/en/Publications/WEO/weo-database/2023/April/groups-and-aggregates> accessed 2 May 2025.

[62] UN Economic and Social Council, 'The Limburg Principles on the Implementation of the International Covenant on Economic Social and Cultural Rights—Annex to E/CN.4/1987/17, 1987' [43].

[63] UNCESCR, 'Concluding Observations on the Seventh Periodic Report of the United Kingdom of Great Britain and Northern Ireland—E/C.12/GBR/CO/7' (2025) [26].

[64] AComHPR, 'Principles and Guidelines on the Implementation of Economic, Social and Cultural Rights in the African Charter on Human and Peoples' Rights, Adopted at the Forty-Seventh Ordinary Session Held in Banjul, the Gambia, from 12 to 26 May 2010' [1(e), 82(j)].

[65] *Muelle Flores v Peru* IACtHR 6 March 2019, Ser C No 375 [171–208]. On Article 26, see Chapter 3.

[66] Lieneke Slingenberg and Ingrid Leijten, 'Social Security in the Case Law of the European Court of Human Rights', *Research Handbook on European Social Security Law* (Edward Elgar 2023) 39–40.

[67] Colm O'Cinneide, 'A Modest Proposal: Destitution, State Responsibility and the European Convention on Human Rights' (2008) 5 European Human Rights Law Review 583, 585; Dimitrios Kagiaros, 'Vulnerability as a Path to a "Social Minimum"? An Analysis of ECtHR Jurisprudence' in Frans Pennings, Toomas Kotkas, and Ingrid Leijten (eds), *Specifying and Securing a Social Minimum in the Battle Against Poverty* (Hart 2019) 246.

[68] *Niedzwiecki v Germany* (2005) 42 EHRR 33 [9–11, 31–33].

[69] Colm O'Cinneide, 'Why Challenging Discrimination at Borders Is Challenging (and Often Futile)' (2021) 115 AJIL Unbound 362, 365.

that migration status could be a relevant ground of distinction for Article 14, but found the denial of social housing to a migrant mother because of her son's immigration status to be proportionate in the circumstances of the case, partly because of the 'element of choice' in bringing her son to the UK.[70] This is problematic as the Court seems to blame the applicant or at least see her decisions as 'taking place in a vacuum'.[71] Yet it was also relevant to proportionality that the applicant was never actually made homeless and other relevant duties would have applied had this become a more imminent threat.[72] Consequently, it is possible that a breach would be found in other circumstances where the violation had more severe consequences, and crucially, denials based on migration status still require proper reasoning to be deemed justified.

The right to education, found in ICESCR Article 13 and the UN Convention on the Rights of the Child (CRC)[73] Article 28, is another matter that affects the viability of migrant domestic workers having their families living with them. The empirical materials show that even where there is no explicit bar on irregular or other migrant children attending schools, there are often complications in proving eligibility. As against this, the UNCESCR has criticized parents being prevented from sending their children to school because of a lack of documentation.[74] A 2017 Joint General Comment of the Committee on the Protection of Migrant Workers and the Committee on the Rights of the Child urges states to 'expeditiously reform regulations and practices that prevent migrant children, in particular undocumented children' from registering.[75] A decision by the Committee of the Rights of the Child regarding the daughter of a Moroccan national, who was refused school enrolment for a year based on her failure to meet the correct formalities such as proving her residence, found a violation despite the state formally recognizing the right of irregular migrants to education.[76] This points to a need to reform procedures to facilitate the registration of all children, which would address one of the practical barriers to domestic workers' family reunification. Both the ECtHR[77]

[70] *Bah v United Kingdom* (2012) 54 EHRR 21 [46–52].

[71] Marie-Benedicte Dembour, 'Gaygusuz Revisited: The Limits of the European Court of Human Rights' Equality Agenda' (2012) 12 Human Rights Law Review 689, 715.

[72] *Bah v UK* (n 70) [51].

[73] United Nations, 'Convention on the Rights of the Child, (Adopted 20 November 1989, Entered into Force 2 September 1990) 1577 UNTS 3'. All case study countries have ratified the CRC.

[74] UNCESCR, 'Duties of States towards Refugees and Migrants under the International Covenant on Economic, Social and Cultural Rights—UN Doc E/C.12/2017/1—13 March 2017' [11].

[75] UNCPRMW and UNComRC, 'Joint General Comment No. 4 and No. 23 on State Obligations Regarding the Human Rights of Children in the Context of International Migration in Countries of Origin, Transit, Destination and Return—16 November 2017—CMW/C/GC/4 and CRC/C/GC/23' [59–60].

[76] UNComRC, 'K.K v Spain—Communication No. 165/2021—Un Doc CRC/C/95/D/165/2021, 28 June 2024'.

[77] *Ponomaryovi v Bulgaria* (2011) 59 EHRR 799. The court emphasised specific features of the applicant's case including becoming irregular 'somewhat inadvertently', so the finding does not necessarily suggest an acceptance that *all* irregular migrant children are entitled to education—ibid [59–63]. For critique, see Dembour, 'Gaygusuz Revisited' (n 71).

and the IACtHR[78] have likewise found violations based on restricting migrant children's access to education, as has the South African High Court.[79] Therefore, compared to the more complex position on social security access, there is a strong impetus across human rights systems towards upholding the right of migrant children to education.

Restrictions on family reunification and the right to family life

Although family reunification is not a freestanding provision in human rights instruments, it has been recognized in international and regional human rights law through other obligations, primarily on protection of the family. Relevant rights in the International Covenant on Civil and Political Rights (ICCPR) are Article 17, protecting family and private life, and Article 23, which establishes the family as the 'natural and fundamental group unit of society' that is 'entitled to protection by society and the state'. The UN Human Rights Committee has held that 'the exclusion of a person from a country where close members of his family are living can amount to an interference within the meaning of Article 17', and that differential treatment in reunification rights based on the spouse's sex also violates Article 23.[80] Furthermore, in its General Comment on Article 23, it held that 'The right to found a family implies, in principle, the possibility to procreate and live together', which in turn 'implies the adoption of appropriate measures ... to ensure the unity or reunification of families, particularly when their members are separated for political, economic or similar reasons'.[81] The inclusion of 'economic' is notable, suggesting potential relevance to labour migrants such as domestic workers rather than being limited to forced migration.

In addition, the CRC provides for the child's best interests to be a primary consideration in all actions concerning children, requires states parties to ensure children are not separated from their parents against their will except where necessary for the child's bests interests, and requires applications to enter a country for the purpose of family reunification to be dealt with in a 'positive, humane and expeditious manner'.[82] This calls into question the appropriateness of migration regimes that entirely preclude family reunification. The joint General Comment of the Committees relating to children's rights and migrant workers' rights—introduced in the last subsection—maintains that a breakup of a family unit by expelling one

[78] *The Girls Yean and Bosico v Dominican Republic*, IACtHR 8 September 2005, Ser C No 130.

[79] *Centre for Child Law v MBE* (n 39).

[80] UN Human Rights Committee, 'Shirin Aumeeruddy-Cziffra and Others v Mauritius - CCPR/C/12/D/35/1978, Decision on Merits, 9 April 1981' [9.2(b)2(i)2, 9.2(b)2(ii).

[81] UNHCHR, 'General Comment No. 19: Article 23 (The Family) Protection of the Family, the Right to Marriage and Equality of the Spouses—Adopted at the Thirty-Ninth Session of the Human Rights Committee, on 27 July 1990' [5].

[82] Articles 3, 9(1), and 10(1).

or both parents based on an immigration law violation is disproportionate, given the 'sacrifice inherent in the restriction of family life and the impact on the life and development of the child'.[83]

Turning to the regional level, the American Convention on Human Rights (ACHR) contains rights to protection of the family and of the child under Articles 17 and 19, as well as privacy and family life in Article 11. A violation of Articles 17 and 19 arose from separation during immigration proceedings in the 2013 judgment *Pacheco Tineo v Bolivia*.[84] The complex background to the case involved a Peruvian family that had been granted refugee status in Bolivia and later also in Chile, re-entered Peru to discuss a possible return, and then re-entered Bolivia without passing immigration control, following which they were deported to Peru, with the children separated from the parents in the process.[85] The IACtHR held that the right to protection of the family under Article 17 ACHR created an obligation on the state 'to promote, as extensively as possible, the development and enhancement of the family unit', such that even legal separations of children from parents can amount to a violation of this right.[86] This quite expansive obligation is significant, underscoring the seriousness of family separation. The trend towards recognition of family reunification was extended by a 2014 IACtHR Advisory Opinion on children and migration.[87] The Opinion held that measures interfering with 'the obligation to prevent family separation and to preserve family unity', must fulfil 'an essential public interest' and be strictly proportionate, with no alternative measure that would be less harmful to rights.[88] It therefore limited the state's margin of appreciation in a situation where parents were to be expelled from a country where children are legally residing or had a right to nationality, given the state's duty to factor in the family's interests.[89] The latter point is important because a high margin of appreciation tends to favour the prioritization of states' arguments based on sovereignty over the protection of migrants, particularly as migrants often lack democratic representation.[90]

Family reunification in the migratory context is also recognized in the African system, hinging on the State's duty to assist and protect the family in Article 18(1) of the African Charter on Human and People's Rights (ACHPR). Guiding Principles

[83] UNCPRMW and UNComRC (n 75) [29].

[84] *Pacheco Tineo Family v Plurinational State of Bolivia* IACtHR 25 November 2013, Ser C No 272 [229].

[85] ibid [72–107].

[86] ibid [226].

[87] *Rights and Guarantees of Children in the Context of Migration and/or in need of international protection—Advisory Opinion OC-21/14* IACtHR 19 August 2014, Ser A No 21.

[88] ibid [273–77].

[89] Belen Olmos Giupponi, 'Assessing the Evolution of the Inter-American Court of Human Rights in the Protection of Migrants' Rights: Past, Present and Future' (2017) 21 International Journal of Human Rights 1477, 1485.

[90] Jean-Baptiste Farcy, 'Equality in Immigration Law: An Impossible Quest?' (2020) 20 Human Rights Law Review 1, 18.

from the AComHPR include the right of all migrant families to protection, placing requirements on states to take 'all appropriate measures to facilitate the reunification of migrant family members with citizens or non-citizens, including in decisions about migration status' and to grant 'derivative immigration status and timely admission to family members of migrants'.[91] Notably, the Principles also refer to a General Recommendation of the Committee interpreting the Convention on the Elimination of All Forms of Discrimination against Women, which criticizes the disadvantageous terms women migrant workers can be subject to, particularly in women-dominated sectors like domestic work, and requires host states to ensure schemes are not directly or indirectly discriminatory.[92] This is relevant to migration regimes that either preclude family reunification for domestic workers or make it very difficult to access. Salient decisions of the AComHPR include *Kenneth Good v Botswana,* where the applicant's sudden deportation with no justification in the knowledge he would be separated from a minor daughter was held to violate Article 18.[93] Relatedly, the South African Constitutional Court has interpreted Article 18 ACHPR alongside Art 23 ICCPR as indicating that international human rights law 'clearly recognizes the importance of marriage and a state obligation to protect the family', in the context of migration law regarding foreign spouses of South Africans.[94] Accordingly, despite there being no explicit right to family life in the Constitution, legislation preventing the formation of a marriage relationship would violate the right to dignity in section 10 of the Constitution.[95] Applying these principles more recently in *Rayment v Minister of Home Affairs*, the South African Constitutional Court held that provisions requiring migrants on spousal visas to leave the country on the breakdown of their marriage, separating them from their children, violated the right to dignity of both the parent and child, alongside other children's rights.[96]

Taking the African and Inter-American systems alongside international obligations, therefore, indicates a growing recognition of the right to family reunification. As with other migration-related rights discussed in Chapter 7, the position in the European system is slightly different. Denial of family reunification can, in certain circumstances, breach Article 8 ECHR, but the ECtHR's findings of a violation directly on this basis are fairly rare, with the Court's approach generally showing

[91] AComHPR, 'African Guiding Principles on the Rights of Migrants, Refugees and Asylum Seekers—Adopted May 2023, Made Public October 21, 2023', Principle 31.

[92] CEDAW Committee, 'General Recommendation No. 26 (2008) on Women Migrant Workers—CEDAW/C/2009/WP.1/R' [19, 26].

[93] *Kenneth Good v Republic of Botswana—Communication No 313/05* [2010] ACHPR 106 (AComHPR) [213].

[94] *Dawood and others v Minister of Home Affairs* [2000] ZACC 8 (Constitutional Court of South Africa) [29].

[95] ibid [37].

[96] *Rayment and Others v Minister of Home Affairs and Others* [2023] ZACC 40 (Constitutional Court of South Africa) [98].

significant deference to state sovereignty.[97] Nonetheless, the exceptions to this trend merit attention, and there have also been successful challenges to family reunification policies with a disparate impact on a particular group, based on Article 14 ECHR, which prohibits discrimination in relation to the securing of other rights. A classic example of the distinct treatment of these rights (Article 8 alone, versus Article 8 with Article 14) is the 1985 case *Abdulaziz, Cabales and Balkandali ('ABC')*, which involved three migrant women in the UK who were unable to bring their husbands to join them because of immigration rules.[98] While rejecting the UK's submission that neither Article 8 nor any other ECHR right applied to immigration control, the ECtHR emphasized the state's 'right to control the entry of non-nationals into its territory' subject to treaty obligations.[99] It held that there was no violation of Article 8 as the applicants had only got married after arriving in the UK and had not shown 'obstacles to establishing family life in their own or their husbands' home countries'.[100] However, it found a violation of Article 14 based on sex discrimination since family reunification was easier for a man settled in the UK than a woman in this position, and the state's advanced justifications, including protection of the domestic labour market, were not adequate.[101]

Subsequent cases have carved out exceptions to the limited reading of Article 8, although without establishing a general right to family reunification or substantially questioning deference to state sovereignty.[102] These cases are often approached as a positive obligation, meaning the ECtHR tends not to conduct a strict proportionality analysis and instead generally applies a looser 'fair balance' test, weighing the 'general interest of the community' against individual interest, and assuming that immigration control is generally in the public interest.[103] Even so, in some cases this has led to a finding in favour of the applicant that Article 8 was violated through denial of family reunification. *Tuquabo-Tekle v The Netherlands* concerned a refusal to allow an Eritrean national aged fifteen to join her mother and stepfather in the Netherlands, where they resided on humanitarian and asylum grounds respectively.[104] Noting that similar principles applied to the state's respect for family life, whether the obligation considered was positive or negative, the ECtHR held that the state had failed to strike a fair balance.[105] Although the case turns on its own facts, it makes some points that are promising with regards

[97] Marie-Bénédicte Dembour, *When Humans Become Migrants: Study of the European Court of Human Rights with an Inter-American Counterpoint* (OUP 2015) 119–20; Helena Wray, *Article 8 ECHR, Family Reunification and the UK's Supreme Court: Family Matters?* (Hart 2023) 13, 43–45.

[98] *Abdulaziz, Cabales and Balkandali v United Kingdom* [1985] ECHR 7 [10].

[99] ibid [59–60, 67].

[100] ibid [66–69].

[101] ibid [74–83]. Submissions based on race- and birth-related discrimination were, however, rejected—ibid [84–89].

[102] Dembour, *When Humans Become Migrants* (n 97) 121–27.

[103] Wray (n 97) 56–63.

[104] *Tuquabo-Tekle and others v The Netherlands* [2005] ECHR 803 [112].

[105] ibid [42, 52].

to findings of a positive obligation to facilitate family reunification. The Court held that a parent leaving children behind when settling abroad cannot be assumed to have 'irrevocably decided' that the children should remain there permanently.[106] This is pertinent to the situation of domestic workers who often migrate ahead of their children, needing several years before seeking reunification. The *Tuquabo-Tekle* judgment also questioned the idea that the applicant exercied 'free will' in leaving her child behind, given the circumstances of her migration.[107] Again, this recognition could be important in the context of domestic work, where migration is often spurred by factors such as a lack of opportunity, low wages, and feminized poverty,[108] so domestic workers cannot necessarily be held to have made a 'free choice' to leave family members behind.

In cases that involve potential discrimination regarding another right, meaning Article 14 is engaged, the ECtHR tends to undertake stricter scrutiny and lower the margin of appreciation afforded to states.[109] Beyond the type of overt discrimination seen in the *ABC* case,[110] this can also extend to rules that have a disparate effect, as the ECtHR has increasingly recognized the concept of indirect discrimination since 2007.[111] In *Biao v Denmark*, the Grand Chamber found a rule that gave preferential treatment regarding family reunification to those who had been Danish citizens for at least twenty-eight years to violate Article 14 read with Article 8, as it disadvantaged those who obtained citizenship later in life, who were disproportionately of 'non-Danish' ethnic origin.[112] The burden was therefore on the state to put forward 'compelling or very weighty reasons unrelated to ethnic origin', which it had failed to do.[113] This creates potential avenues to challenge other family reunification schemes that are *prima facie* neutral but have a disparate effect on racialized groups,[114] as may be the case with domestic workers' migration. The same is also true regarding gendered impact, particularly as notions of 'skill' used to award more advantageous statuses carrying a right to family reunification tend to exclude women.[115]

In addition, it may be possible to claim discriminatory treatment based on exclusion of a category of migrant from family reunification rights. *Hode and Abdi v*

[106] ibid [45]. This point drew on an earlier case: *Sen v The Netherlands* (2001) 36 EHRR 81 [40].
[107] *Tuquabo-Tekle v Netherlands* (n 104) [47].
[108] Chapter 1.
[109] Wray (n 97) 58–60.
[110] O'Cinneide (n 69) 364.
[111] Mathias Möschel, 'The Strasbourg Court and Indirect Race Discrimination: Going Beyond the Education Domain' (2017) 80 Modern Law Review 121, 124.
[112] *Biao v Denmark* (2017) 64 EHRR 1 [32–35, 112–13, 138–39].
[113] ibid [114–37].
[114] Möschel (n 111) 131–32.
[115] Catherine Briddick, 'Precarious Workers and Probationary Wives: How Immigration Law Discriminates against Women' (2020) 29 Social & Legal Studies 201; Shreya Atrey, Catherine Briddick, and Michelle Foster, 'Guest Editor Introduction: Contesting and Undoing Discriminatory Borders' (2022) 22 International Journal of Discrimination and the Law 210, 211–13. See also Chapters 5 and 7.

UK was a successful challenge to excluding refugees from family reunification policies that applied to migrant workers and students, which held that if the domestic legislation 'confers a right to be joined by spouses on certain categories of immigrant', this had to be done in compliance with Article 14.[116] It underscored that protection under Article 14 is not limited to treatment based on innate characteristics, with 'other status' encompassing a wide range of distinctions including immigration status.[117] By extension, the status of 'domestic worker' is likely to amount to the type of 'other status' that is protected under Article 14.[118] This means that a scheme that specifically disadvantages domestic workers by excluding them from a benefit enjoyed in other migration routes may be viewed as a type of differential treatment that requires objective and reasonable justification in and of itself,[119] in addition to the justification required for disproportionate effects regarding gender or ethnicity.

Barriers to family reunification—Towards a contextualized proportionality analysis

In general, justifications for denying family reunification based on sovereignty and control over entry, residence and expulsion of foreigners should be carefully scrutinized, rather than being accepted uncritically. As Dembour notes, the assumption that the state's power to control migration is 'almost unfettered ... a matter of well-established international law' is both historically inaccurate given the recent nature of migration control and conceptually problematic, since rule of law principles requiring constraint of state powers should equally apply to immigration.[120] Rather than assuming that the state can deny entry to migrants without giving a reason, Schotel has argued that a proper justification for refusal must always be based on balancing the migrant's legitimate interests against properly substantiated reasons for refusal.[121]

When conducting that balancing exercise in relation to the rights of domestic workers, it is important that the proportionality analysis should be *contextualized.* This means it should give proper weight to the structural factors behind large-scale migration in the sector and the disadvantages faced by domestic workers, including

[116] *Hode and Abdi v United Kingdom* (2013) 56 EHRR 27 [43].
[117] ibid [46–47]. This was also acknowledged in the previous (unsuccessful) case *Bah v UK* (n 70).
[118] Joe Atkinson, 'Employment Status and Human Rights: An Emerging Approach' (2023) 86 Modern Law Review 1166, 1191–92.
[119] In *Hode*, the ECtHR held that 'offering incentives to certain groups of migrants' could in principle be a legitimate aim, but that it did not justify the treatment in that case—*Hode & Abdi v UK* (n 116) [51–56].
[120] Dembour, *When Humans Become Migrants* (n 97) 97, 117–18.
[121] Bas Schotel, *On the Right of Exclusion: Law, Ethics and Immigration Policy* (Routledge 2012) 17–25; Dembour, *When Humans Become Migrants* (n 97) 97, 117–18.

the harm that long-term separation from families can cause. Key drivers of the demand for domestic work include the fact that, as women increasingly enter the workforce in many industrialized countries, long working hours remain the norm despite being designed around an outdated (and never truly accurate) model of a male 'productive' worker supported by a female 'reproductive' worker.[122] States rely in part on domestic workers to allow this model to continue without providing adequate support such as publicly funded childcare or addressing work-life balance in a more systemic way. Where states benefit from services provided by domestic workers by allowing them to sustain such models, but decline to offer corresponding benefits such as the right to bring family members, this exemplifies what Gorfinkiel has described as a 'utilitarian' approach to migration, in which 'migrants are mainly regarded as workers, relegating other basic elements of their individual lives'.[123] While migrant domestic workers are permitted to 'contribute to the smooth social organization in the destination country', their own care needs and those of their families are ignored.[124]

By contrast to this overly instrumentalist and narrow view of the purpose of migration, the contextualized approach I am proposing insists that, where demand is created for migration into particular sectors such as domestic work, this comes with a responsibility towards those who enter the country as a result. It is vital 'to reject any starting assumption that care should come at the cost of rendering domestic workers—including domestic workers' own care needs—invisible'.[125] If schemes are created to fulfil a demand for migrant workers in this sector without associated conditions that allow for family reunification, the overall impact is precisely such a denial of workers' care needs. As against this, family life and work should be approached holistically to allow for an understanding of 'the migrant caring subject within a broader perspective of the social reproduction of their own and other families'.[126] Failure to take such an approach and the resulting widespread denial of family reunification directly reflects the devaluation of domestic work. The impetus to tightly control conditions on domestic workers' migration, including their potential to bring family members with them, draws on a gendered idea of their work as 'low-skilled' and not economically valuable.[127]

A further set of factors driving widespread migration for domestic work relates to conditions in workers' countries of origin, including limited job opportunities

[122] See Chapter 1.
[123] Magdalena Diáz Gorfinkiel, 'Family Rights in a Migratory Context: Whose Family Comes First?' in Maria Kontos and Glenda Tibe Bonifacio (eds), *Migrant Domestic Workers and Family Life: International Perspectives* (Palgrave Macmillan 2015) 130.
[124] ibid 133–34.
[125] Adelle Blackett, *Everyday Transgressions: Domestic Workers' Transnational Challenge to International Labor Law* (Cornell University Press 2019) 3.
[126] Eleonore Kofman, 'Rethinking Care Through Social Reproduction: Articulating Circuits of Migration' (2012) 19 Social Politics 142, 153.
[127] Mullally and Murphy (n 1) 411.

and low wages that create the need to send remittances back to family members and the impetus to escape gendered poverty and discrimination.[128] To properly take such factors into account, it is necessary to move to an understanding of differences in wealth and opportunity as 'products of a colonially structured world' as opposed to 'unfortunate or natural occurrences',[129] and to recognize the way that exclusionary policies towards migrants further entrench these systems.[130] These arguments are particularly pertinent to the UK, given Britain's status as a former colonial power,[131] but they also relate to a broader point that the political and economic context of migration should be brought to the forefront when considering justifications for limiting migrants' rights to family reunification based on migration control. While courts and legislative/policy-making bodies may not be in a position to comprehensively address these historical injustices, they should at least be aware of and sensitive to the structural disadvantages they create, rather than treating labour migration as a straightforward matter of personal choice for which the migrant and their family must personally bear the consequences.

The proportionality analysis must also give proper weight to the serious harm caused by denying family reunification. Separation of children from parents with an otherwise strong relationship is understood as 'shocking in almost any context but immigration', where it has been normalized.[132] Denial of family reunification can put severe limits on the type of family relationship a domestic worker is able to maintain[133] and tends to create 'prolonged separation and a care deficit' for children, whose care may have to be reassigned to 'members of the extended family or poorly paid local domestic workers'.[134] Given the care deficit for children that domestic workers are forced to leave behind, the large-scale movement of women without their families can be viewed as a new form of imperialism, with love and care increasingly becoming 'the new gold' as they are extracted to the Global North in lieu of the classic 'plunder of physical resources'.[135]

[128] Chapter 1.

[129] Nadine El-Enany, *Bordering Britain: Law, Race and Empire* (Manchester University Press 2020) 171.

[130] The former UN Special Rapporteur on Contemporary Forms of Racism has highlighted how European colonial migrants were able to migrate freely in the colonial era, leading to the advantages enjoyed by the global north, which today are entrenched in part by the right to exclude migrants from former colonies from sharing in them—E Tendayi Achiume, 'Migration as Decolonization' (2019) 71 Stanford Law Review 1509, 1517, 1537, 1543–44.

[131] El-Enany (n 129).

[132] Wray (n 97) 10.

[133] Maria Kontos and Glenda Tibe Bonifacio, 'Introduction: Domestic and Care Work of Migrant Women and the Right to Family Life' in Maria Kontos and Glenda Tibe Bonifacio (eds), *Migrant Domestic Workers and Family Life: International Perspectives* (Palgrave Macmillan 2015) 4–5.

[134] ILO, 'Report IV(1)—Decent Work for Domestic Workers—99th Session of the International Labour Conference' (2010) 10.

[135] Arlie Russell Hochschild, 'Love and Gold' in Barbara Ehrenreich and Arlie Russell Hochschild (eds), *Global Woman: Nannies, Maids and Sex Workers in the New Economy* (Granta Books 2003) 25–28.

My empirical findings underscore the harm caused by family separation, including the length of separation and rarity of visits mentioned in the UK and South African contexts, where the migration regimes are more restrictive.[136] Furthermore, Chapter 5 addressed how migrant workers who live apart from their own families may be more likely to view themselves as part of the employer's family, even in the context of a stronger regulatory framework in Chile that otherwise pushes against this understanding. A lack of access to family reunification has repercussions for the migrant worker's situation: the presence of children and their needs (e.g. for health and education) is an important mechanism in making migrants visible in public space.[137] The failure to allow for family reunification thus not only reflects, but also reproduces and intensifies, the devaluation of domestic work.

Conclusion

A human rights framework for the situation of domestic workers, including a focus on the right to private and family life, is valuable for facilitating the consideration of questions that are traditionally viewed as outside the remit of labour law, such as the right to bring family members to the destination,[138] which is crucial given the prevalence of migration in the sector. Across the case studies, the most direct obstacles are seen in migration regimes that specifically preclude bringing dependents to join the worker, as in the UK, and the lack of relevant legal pathways and limitation of the special exemption permit regime in South Africa, whereas Chile has greater provision for family reunification particularly since 2021 changes. By contrast, for internal migrants in India there are no formal bars on bringing family members to a destination, yet practical hindrances can exist through a lack of viable options for housing, education, and welfare support. Related issues exist in the context of international migration elsewhere, representing a further difficulty for migrant domestic workers who would otherwise have a legal route to bringing family members to join them. My empirical work reinforced how both these levels of barrier can cause long-term separation from family members, often with distressing impacts.

Against this background, the chapter has identified an increasing recognition of the right to family reunification in international and regional human rights law based on rights to protection of the family and respect for family life, including

[136] See also Chapter 6 on the impact of long working hours on family life.

[137] Gul Ozyegin and Pierette Hondagneu-Sotelo, 'Conclusion: Domestic Work, Migration and the New Gender Order in Contemporary Europe' in Helma Lutz (ed), *Migration and Domestic Work: A European Perspective on a Global Theme* (Ashgate 2008) 203.

[138] Natalie Sedacca, 'Migrant Domestic Workers and the Right to a Private and Family Life' (2019) 37 Netherlands Quarterly of Human Rights 288, 290. The analysis in this chapter builds on and extends beyond this article.

at international level and in the Inter-American and African systems. While the ECtHR has been more constrained in finding violations based directly on the right to a private and family life, there are some salient exceptions, and it has exercised stricter scrutiny of restrictive measures in cases that involve potential discrimination under Article 14. Therefore, where migration schemes deny rights based on status as a domestic worker, or have differential effects based on characteristics such as gender or race, a strict proportionality analysis should apply. I have argued that this analysis should be carried out in a contextualized way that accounts for structural factors driving migration and generalized harms of long-term separation. If these structural issues are given proper weight, schemes that either exclude domestic workers from family reunification altogether or make it practically very difficult to achieve will be difficult to justify. The aim these restrictions pursue, to the extent that this is stated, generally relates to the supposedly 'low-skilled' nature of domestic work. They are not compelling since they draw on the devaluation of domestic workers and the assumption that their family life is less important than the interests of the employers and/or the destination countries they 'serve'. They are based on extracting the services provided by the domestic worker to the host country without providing in return for their own family life, and fail to give proper weight to the structural disadvantages driving large-scale migration for domestic work or to the serious harm caused by long-term separation from family members.

9
Conclusion

Introduction

Drawing on doctrinal materials and empirical research regarding Chile, the UK, South Africa, and India, this book has examined shortcomings in labour and migration law that affect domestic workers and the relevance of human rights law to challenging these. It has analysed exclusions faced by domestic workers as resulting from two key themes. First, lack of accountability, denoting a lack of ordinary standards of scrutiny for work that takes place in the private sphere of the home and family, is exemplified by the exclusion of private homes employing domestic workers from labour inspection. Secondly, devaluation, meaning the gendered, racialized, and migration-related denigration of paid domestic labour—including its conflation with unpaid labour carried out by women in the family home—is reflected in systemic low pay, extended working hours, and unfavourable visa regimes based on the supposedly 'low-skilled' nature of the work.

Justifying the book's adoption of a human rights framework in Chapter 3, I identified shared normative values of labour law and human rights in their orientation to addressing abuses and imbalances of power, while elucidating the potential for human rights to move beyond individualistic and restraints-based approaches. I argued against drawing a sharp distinction between human rights and workers' agency, since the domestic work context necessitates a more expansive understanding of agency compared with traditional industrial workplaces. The normative value of universality at the centre of human rights law is also crucial in challenging domestic workers' exclusion from labour law protection, which arises from the designation of their work in the private sphere as distinct from 'real work', alongside the impact of harsh migration regimes. I advocated an approach to human rights law that centres positive obligations on the state to prevent and punish rights violations by private bodies, including employers, gives proper weight to social and economic as well as civil and political rights, draws and builds on feminist critique of the lack of scrutiny of the private sphere, and holds firmly to universalistic principles on the rights of migrants and other marginalized groups.

The remainder of the book contained in-depth analysis of thematic issues and their human rights implications, drawing on my empirical research across the case study countries alongside other materials. Part 2 explored shortcomings in inspection and enforcement mechanisms (Chapter 4), the devaluation of domestic work and its manifestation in systemic low pay (Chapter 5), and the challenges of

Human Rights and the Protection of Domestic Workers in Labour and Migration Law. Natalie Sedacca, Oxford University Press. © Oxford University Press 2026. DOI: 10.1093/9780198985266.003.0012

regulating and limiting working hours, particularly for live-in domestic workers (Chapter 6). Part 3 focused on issues affecting migrant domestic workers, namely the impact of restrictive migration regimes and irregular status on domestic workers' labour mobility and ability to realize their rights (Chapter 7), and barriers to family reunification (Chapter 8). The next section of this concluding chapter explores cross-cutting human rights violations across thematic areas, while the subsequent section reiterates key reforms to labour and migration law supported by my human rights-based critique. The final sections comprise reflections on the broader implications of my analysis for a human rights approach to (domestic) workers' rights.

Violations of domestic workers' human rights across thematic areas

While previous chapters contained an analysis of human rights issues arising from their specific area of focus, this section draws out cross-cutting themes across the three areas of human rights that have featured most prominently in my analysis: the right to work, the prohibition on forced labour, and the right to private and family life. References for the human rights authorities and principles referred to in these sections can be found within the relevant chapters earlier in the book; this chapter repeats references for direct citations only. In contrast with the previous chapters' engagement with counterarguments, in what follows I focus on reiterating my key conclusions on the implications of human rights for domestic workers.

The right to work

The right to work is a foundational human right relating to labour law, which can be particularly challenging to realize in the domestic work sector, but which also has the potential to offer broad protections. My analysis focused on two aspects: the negative right to work, which encompasses protection against state interference in the ability to seek employment or being coerced into labour; and the interlinked right to *decent* work, comprising just and favourable conditions of work. The negative right was a focus of Chapter 7 because it is often curtailed by restrictive visa schemes that preclude or restrict domestic workers' opportunities to change employer and sector.[1] I questioned justifications for these restrictions, which may not be borne out by evidence (as with the notion that limits on changing employer encourage reporting of abuse, seen in the UK). More generally, restrictive schemes for domestic workers are often closely related to the devaluation of domestic work

[1] It can also be undermined by practical obstacles that arise in an internal migration context, as in India.

and the notion that it is 'low-skilled', while migrants in other categories that require greater formal qualifications are viewed as more desirable and therefore afforded greater mobility and privileges.

The right to decent work has had broad relevance across Chapters 4–7. Chapter 4 argued that the right is violated by the unsafe working and living conditions that domestic workers are often exposed to, which include inadequate accommodation that may lack privacy and basic facilities such as toilet access, and a heightened risk of violence and sexual harassment. I argued that the right gives rise to a requirement for a functioning system of labour inspectorates that is adequately resourced and covers all work sectors, making the generalized exclusion of domestic work from inspection regimes in the UK and India highly problematic. In Chile and South Africa, some form of labour inspection does apply, but there are still limitations, such as the lack of a power of entry to the home, under-resourcing, and reliance on complaints rather than proactive programmes.

Chapter 4 also elucidated the importance of separating labour inspectorates from immigration enforcement. This links to the argument in Chapter 7 about the right to decent work being applicable to all rather than conditional on migration status—part of the universalistic principle that human rights apply without distinction. The denial of these rights would be concerning anyway, but is particularly so given the ways that visa regimes can fuel irregularity through complex and expensive bureaucratic requirements, a lack of options for legal migration, and the imposition of arbitrary rules that deny some workers awaiting determination of their trafficking status the right to work. The UK regime—with its 'hostile environment' for irregular migrants that allows for extensive data sharing, criminalization of work without status, and seizure of irregular migrants' wages as 'proceeds of crime'—is a major concern in this respect. In South Africa and Chile, there is a clearer recognition of irregular migrants' labour rights, although some concerns about divergence from this were highlighted, such as data sharing by South Africa's Department of Labour and new sanctions introduced in Chile's 2021 legislation.

Beyond these generalized points on applicability and enforcement, Chapters 5 and 6 addressed specific aspects of the right to decent work. Chapter 6 highlighted the component requirement for 'rest, leisure and reasonable limitation of working hours', contrary to the excessive hours often demanded of domestic workers. Chapter 5, on devaluation, examined the right to a living wage and to fair pay, identifying three interlinking aspects: fairness, equality, and provision for a decent standard of living. Most obviously, violations can arise both where domestic workers are excluded from the minimum wage applicable to other sectors, as seen until recently in the UK (for some live-in workers) and South Africa, and to date in many Indian states. In this situation, anti-discrimination provisions are relevant as a means to challenge discrepancies in wage and social security frameworks that disadvantage domestic workers. The South African Constitutional Court Case *Mahlangu*, regarding domestic workers' exclusion from benefits for injury and death at work, was especially significant for taking an intersectional approach to discrimination against domestic workers as Black women and for its strong recognition of the value of domestic work.

Yet beyond equalization with existing minimum wages, the right to just and favourable conditions of work also requires that the set wage provides a decent standard of living and is 'fair', a concept I explored based on a feminist reading of the criteria set out in General Comment 23 of the UN Committee on Economic, Social and Cultural Rights,[2] alongside observations from the empirical research. I argued for recognizing the output of domestic work in ways that go beyond direct economic productivity to encompass care and other 'essential work', but also facilitation of the employer's way of life. The understanding of fairness should also account for the complexity and range of tasks performed in household work and reflect the risks to health and safety, hardships, and impact on the worker's private and family life that arise in domestic work.

The prohibition on forced labour

The prohibition on forced labour has also been a focus throughout Chapters 4–7, and is linked to the right to decent work since it is a key corresponding justiciable right[3] of relevance to labour standards. Regional jurisprudence has recognized the protective obligations on the state arising from the prohibition, with the European Court of Human Rights (ECtHR) requiring states to put in place 'an adequate legislative and administrative framework to prohibit and prevent trafficking, forced labour, and servitude and to protect its victims'.[4] Moreover, the Inter-American Court of Human Rights (IACtHR) has identified labour-related and other relevant obligations arising from this prohibition, including to address structural discrimination, 'eliminate all legislation that legalizes or tolerates slavery and servitude', to 'conduct inspections or other measures to detect such practices', and to 'take measures to protect and assist victims'.[5] This fortifies the imperative to implement effective labour enforcement and structural changes, including through amendments to legislative frameworks, which also arise from the right to decent work.

Relatedly, the prohibition on forced labour is pertinent to the discussion on the minimum wage. This is recognized directly by the Indian Supreme Court in the *Asiad Workers* case,[6] and in the ILO's approach, in which non-payment of

[2] UNCESCR, 'General Comment No 23 on the Right to Just and Favourable Conditions of Work (Art 7 of the Covenant), 27 April 2016, E/C.12/GC/23' [10].

[3] The right to decent work is directly justiciable in the African system, but not in the other regional systems.

[4] *FM and others v Russia* App nos 71671/16 and 40190/18 (ECtHR, 10 December 2024) [293].

[5] *Workers of the Hacienda Verde Brasil Verde v Brazil* IACtHR 20 October 2016, Ser C No 337 [319, 338].

[6] *People's Union for Democratic Rights v Union of India and Others* ('*Asiad Workers* case') (1982) 3 SCC 235, 26.

minimum wages is one of the indicators of forced labour. The link is also acknowledged indirectly in domestic servitude and forced labour cases in the ECtHR, which highlighted lack of wages as a key issue,[7] albeit alongside other factors. These cases demonstrate the potential to develop a structural reading of the prohibition on forced labour, through identifying systemic violations such as widespread non-payment of the minimum wage as facilitating forced labour. In addition, the ECtHR's growing recognition of irregular status as a factor driving susceptibility to forced labour strengthens the argument for the removal of legal frameworks that deny labour rights to irregular migrants.

The right to private and family life

In contrast to the discussion of the right to work and forced labour, the book's analysis has considered the right to private and family life not only in relation to workers' entitlements, but also for its relevance on the employer side as a reason to deny or limit domestic workers' rights. In putting forward a proposal for inspection including a power of entry to the home arising from the right to decent work and the prohibition on forced labour, I acknowledged that such a power could infringe the employer's right to private and family life. However, bearing in mind that this is a qualified right, I argued that it should not be understood as requiring a complete bar to powers of entry. Instead, the interference with the right can be justified as proportionate to the legitimate aim of protecting domestic workers' rights and freedoms, provided that any inspection power is clearly delimited to ensure a focus solely on matters relevant to workers' rights. Also of relevance to this question is the parallel issue of increasing scrutiny of abuses taking place within the private sphere of the home and the family, such as domestic violence, discussed in Chapter 3. If it is sometimes appropriate for the state to intervene within an actual family unit, then, by analogy, interference in a unit that consists of a domestic worker alongside their employer(s) cannot be completely precluded by comprehensive and unscrutinized notions of privacy.

Just as notions of the employer's privacy as a reason to limit workers' rights tend to be overstated, the rights of the domestic worker to a private and family life are often neglected. Countering this trend, the book has brought the implications of this right for domestic workers to the forefront across three key areas. Chapter 6 examined the relevance of the right to the demand for proper limitation of working time, including allocated break periods outside and away from work. This is often missing in the context of demands for excessive hours and constant availability, which can leave domestic workers insufficient time to maintain

[7] *Siliadin v France* (2006) 43 EHRR 16; *CN v United Kingdom* (2013) 56 EHRR 24; *Chowdury and Others v Greece* App no 21884/15 (ECtHR, 30 March 2017).

relationships with existing friends and family members, or to develop new connections or life projects. I argued that an approach to working time based on the right to private and family life is valuable for underscoring the need for proper rest periods during which the worker can leave the employer's home, whether or not the working day consists of back-to-back tasks. This is contrary to assumptions that have been made about domestic work, including in some of the ILO discussions leading to agreement of Convention 189 (C-189). In Chapter 7, I explored how the expansive understanding of the right to private and family life, as relevant in cases regarding denial of access to employment, lays the foundation for recognizing the right to work and to free choice of employment in regional contexts where the main enforceable human rights instrument does not provide for this directly.

Chapter 8 analysed how the potential for family reunification is often denied to domestic workers as a result of specific and restrictive visa schemes, such as the UK's Overseas Domestic Worker Visa, or lack of provision, as in the limited labour migration routes and special exemption permits in South Africa. Even where a migrant's family members would formally be entitled to live with them at the destination, as for internal migrants in India, there are often practical obstacles such as the availability of housing and welfare support, which social rights, including to social security and education, are relevant to addressing. A lack of legal access and practical avenues for family reunification can lead to long-term separation and have serious implications for family relationships, with domestic workers missing out on the everyday lives of children and other relatives. The visa regimes that deny such rights often have a disproportionately negative impact on women and racialized minorities, as well as on domestic workers as a category.

In all these contexts, I discussed the need to justify infringements with the right to private and family life as a proportionate means to a legitimate aim or based on a 'fair balance' assessment. On working time, my empirical research revealed two key types of proposed justification. One related to support for families who may be working long hours in jobs outside the home, while the second entailed cultural expectations of a particular way that a service in the home is provided, requiring the worker to be constantly available. I argued that the latter point would not amount to a 'legitimate aim' for interfering with domestic workers' private and family life, since it does not entail a positive social purpose. The labour market participation argument is more complex and nuanced, as it could amount to a legitimate aim. However, I noted that measures relying on it are still unlikely to be proportionate where there is a severe impact on the domestic workers' private and family life. Straightforwardly accepting this justification obscures critical engagement with the reasons extended timetables are needed to support working families and the availability of other means that the state could use to address these, such as improving public childcare provision and addressing long working hours in other sectors.

In the matters discussed in Chapters 7 and 8, the reasons for interfering with the right to labour market access and mobility, and to family reunification, are broadly related to the question of migration control. I noted that the underlying reasons for restrictive schemes are often related to the supposedly 'low-skilled' nature of domestic work, reflecting the work's devaluation. Rather than accepting state sovereignty arguments as a given to excuse a lack of access to rights like family reunification, I argued that they should be carefully scrutinized using a 'contextualized proportionality analysis'. This would take into account key structural factors in the demand for domestic work and the benefits states gain from domestic workers' migration, as well as the substantial negative consequences of denying family reunification routes highlighted by my empirical work and other studies. This is a vital counterweight to the current position that allows labour to be extracted for the benefit of the employer and host country while constraining the worker's family life.

Reforms demanded to prevent violations

The demand for greater inclusivity and universality supported by human rights provides a basis for recognizing the exclusion of domestic workers from key entitlements as unacceptable and consequently gives rise to a series of proposals for reform. The suggestions I have identified in Chapters 4–8 and that I later reiterate are not intended as an exhaustive list of all reforms needed in domestic work, but rather, are an elaboration of the main proposals that arise from areas the book has focused on. Since these are derived from human rights obligations, they are relevant to all countries that have accepted those obligations, regardless of whether they have also ratified C-189. For those that have, they add further specificity to the stipulations of C-189 in several respects, including as regards working hours, inspection powers, and migration regimes.

With regard to challenging devaluation, equalization of the minimum wage for domestic workers with that found in other sectors is a vital first step, yet it may be insufficient where existing minimum wages do not provide an adequate standard of living to domestic workers and their families. The human rights analysis consequently supports a demand for specific uplifts beyond the minimum wage where existing levels do not meet the requirements of a living wage and fair pay, the calculation of which requires recognition of the varied outputs of domestic work, the complexity of responsibilities the role involves, and the significant hardships, risks to health and safety, and impact on personal and family life experienced by domestic workers.

The right to private and family life, alongside corresponding social and economic provisions, requires proper restrictions on working hours that leave adequate time for the domestic worker to construct their own family life, with an entitlement to leave the employer's home during time off. The concept of the 'special characteristics of domestic work' as mentioned in C-189 should not be interpreted as a justification for working hours that are unlimited or significantly higher than those in other sectors. Providing for proper restrictions requires the amendment of legal frameworks that permit excessive hours and closing enforcement gaps that give rise to inadequate monitoring and enforcement of working time. Setting new standards to take the place of such frameworks should entail consultation with domestic workers, and representative organizations where available, to determine the extent of any deviation from ordinary working patterns as required in domestic workers' interests, such as allowing those living far from their families extended periods of leave to visit them. Yet any such stipulation should be subject to boundaries and safeguards to ensure variations are not excessive and are applied only where genuinely voluntary on the part of the worker.

Ensuring that labour rights are adhered to in practice also requires an effective and properly resourced system of inspection that entails proactive visits rather than only reacting to complaints and includes a proportionate power of entry into homes. Crucially, the concept of 'due regard for privacy' should not be interpreted as barring any power of entry to the home without the employer's consent or prior court authorization. Instead, it should require that there are specific constraints on the discretion granted to inspectors and delineations to ensure that each step they take is directly related to the aim of protecting the domestic worker's rights, so that interference with privacy is proportionate. Inspections should therefore generally not take place during the night, and rather than a general power to search through correspondence and possessions, should consist of prescribed steps such as interviews with the employer and the worker, reviewing accounts of payments and records of hours worked, and inspecting the worker's living quarters (where live-in) and working environment, including access to toilets and other facilities. They must also include separate conversations with the worker and be part of a range of measures aimed at increasing both parties' awareness of rights and workers' capacity to challenge violations—such as written information and meetings about rights and relevant trade union and community organizations—and employer submission of online information about conditions of work, hours, and payment.

Furthermore, labour inspections must be strictly separated from immigration enforcement with a prohibition on the sharing of any data, since they will otherwise be a threat to rather than a benefit for migrant domestic workers whose status is irregular or 'semi-legal'. This forms part of the wider point that the right to decent work must be guaranteed to all workers regardless of immigration status, requiring repeal of measures that restrict access to rights, such as the criminalization of work without status, or bars on irregular migrants bringing claims for violations. Workers in an irregular or 'semi-legal' situation must also have accessible and viable options to regularize their status. Relatedly, even workers who have a regular status through a valid work visa are often disadvantaged by restrictive measures that tie them to the domestic work sector and make it difficult to change employer. To meet the requirements of the negative aspect of the right to work and avoid fuelling forced labour, visa regimes should be amended to ensure that migrant domestic workers have an unrestricted right to change employer and that practical barriers to exercising this right, such as short and non-extendable time limits, are removed. The right to private and family life, understood in a way that properly accounts for structural factors driving migration and the harm of long-term separation, also creates a requirement for visa schemes to have options for family reunification, including the removal of systemic practical barriers such as prohibitive fees and denial of access to key social rights.

Implications: The relationship between human rights and the rights of domestic workers

This book has argued that domestic workers' exclusion from protection in labour and migration law falls short of human rights standards, based on an approach that centres positive obligations, gives proper weight to social and economic rights, draws on feminist critique of the lack of scrutiny of the private sphere, and holds firmly to universalistic principles on the rights of migrants. Based on the material and resulting analysis, this section contains reflections about the relevance of human rights to the position of domestic workers.

Human rights standards are relevant to a range of violations and can exist in a supporting relationship to labour law

Domestic workers have routinely been excluded from the protection of labour law by virtue of factors that are related both to gender—the designation of their work as part of the 'private sphere' and therefore distinct from 'real work'—and to ethnicity and migration status, including harsh visa regimes and the lack of rights afforded to migrant workers, particularly those with irregular status. The principle of universality is foundational to human rights law and is normatively significant for countering these exclusions of domestic workers from labour law's protection. Drawing on a universalistic view of human rights, this book has challenged the view that a lower standard of protection is permissible for domestic workers as a result of their location within the private sphere of the home, or because of the need for them to provide support to those working outside the home—for example, through being constantly available. Instead, I have argued that systemic low pay, long hours, and a lack of enforcement of rights fall short of decent work requirements and the right to private and family life, as well as the protective aspects of the prohibition of slavery and forced labour. I have also used the universalistic approach to critique the restrictive nature of visa regimes as a violation of the negative aspect of the right to work, the denial of labour rights to irregular migrants as a breach of the right to decent work, and the obstacles to family reunification as violating the right to a private and family life.

It is sometimes argued that human rights have limited value for workers' rights since they are focused only on exceptional and extreme forms of abuse.[8] In contrast to this, the book has pointed to the wide-ranging role human rights standards can play in advancing the inclusion of domestic workers, including on routine violations such as low pay, excessive working hours and unsafe workplaces, and systemic issues like visa restrictions. It should also be noted that an abuse against domestic workers being 'extreme' does not necessarily mean it is exceptional or unusual, given that gaps in the regulatory framework tend to create systemic, severe violations. While not every labour law norm can be specified within human rights, the demands for greater inclusivity and universality supported by human rights standards provide the basis for recognizing widespread shortcomings of labour law and migration regimes as unacceptable, paving the way for more specific regulatory standards to be set in the labour law field.

Rather than viewing a 'labour rights as human rights' approach as de-emphasizing worker agency, I have argued for understandings of agency to be receptive to the context of domestic work. Across the case study countries, trade unions have played a crucial role in improving the rights of domestic workers, but also face constraints in organizing in a classic industrial sense because of membership coverage, the absence of representative employer organizations, the isolated nature of domestic work, and a lack of capacity for many domestic workers in the most severe conditions to engage in union activities. This necessitates a nuanced and reflective conception that recognizes methods of engagement other than traditional collective bargaining as an exercise of agency, including involvement in campaigns for better labour and migration laws, education about rights, and even individual steps such as taking the decision to leave an abusive employer—particularly where that could put the worker's status at risk.

The potential for domestic workers to become actively involved in unions and other collective organizations stands to be greater where their human rights are respected, and more difficult in a context of widespread abuses of other rights. Constraints on organization include excessive working hours leaving workers little to no time to spend outside the employer's home, a lack of information on rights and relevant organizations, and visa regimes that give workers only a very short period in a country, tie them to an employer, or put at risk of becoming irregular.

[8] This argument has been made by some in the labour law field—see eg Vera Pavlou, *Migrant Domestic Workers in Europe: Law and the Construction of Vulnerability* (Hart 2021). On human rights in relation to trafficking, see also Hila Shamir, 'A Labor Paradigm for Human Trafficking' (2012) 60 UCLA Law Review 76.

Conversely, a set of entitlements including secure and extendable visas and a prescribed level of time off that can be spent outside the employer's home, as well as the dissemination of relevant information about rights and organizations providing support, is likely to be conducive to workers' self-organization. The entitlements supported by the human rights perspective can therefore act as a foundation for greater advances to be sought, and more specific regulatory standards set, including where possible through collective bargaining.

Shifts and contestations within human rights law hold promise for improved protection of domestic workers

As against a traditional focus on state restraint, a crucial shift in human rights law since around the late 1970s has been the development of positive duties on the state with regard to abuses carried out by non-state actors, which can be referred to as 'due diligence' or the 'positive obligation'. This is important for the position of domestic workers, since the immediate cause of violations is usually a private employer. There has been some criticism of the shift to focus on positive obligations and particularly of the use of human rights to mobilize criminal law obligations.[9] Yet, while criminal law has a role to play regarding severe violations such as domestic servitude, trafficking, and forced labour where the impacted worker wishes to pursue this route, this neither is, nor should be, the sole focus of positive duties in human rights. Instead, the obligations on the state that human rights give rise to in this context include the amendment of labour law frameworks to ensure adequate protection, reform to visa regimes to protect workers' human rights and family life instead of making them susceptible to forced labour and long-term separation, and the creation of effective labour enforcement mechanisms. Alongside this, the 'integrated approach' to interpretation has increasingly filled gaps left by the greater emphasis on civil and political rights in the regional human rights systems.

Human rights jurisprudence has also developed in recent decades towards a greater willingness to find violations in relation to phenomena that were previously viewed as private matters, such as domestic violence. This view of the private sphere as open to scrutiny provides a grounding for accountability within domestic work, indicating by analogy that inspections should not be precluded simply because the workplace is in the 'private sphere'. Instead, they can be justified in order to protect the domestic worker as the less powerful party within the home, who also has the right to a private life. The pivot to establishing that the private sphere is not beyond scrutiny exemplifies the development of human rights law to become more responsive to the interests of women, demonstrating a capacity

[9] Laurens Lavrysen and Natasa Mavronicola (eds), *Coercive Human Rights: Positive Duties to Mobilise the Criminal Law under the ECHR* (Hart 2020).

for progressive change in the interests of specific sections of humanity that—while always nominally included through the principle of universality—were previously subject to blind spots and a lack of specific protection.

It is to be hoped that this capacity can also be translated to the field of migrants' rights, challenging the tendency seen in some contexts to prioritize state sovereignty, which undermines the universalistic principles of human rights. Deference to sovereignty is far from the consistent position in human rights, with a more protective approach to the rights of migrants seen in comments of the UN Committee on Economic, Social and Cultural Rights, and the jurisprudence of the Inter-American and African regional systems. Meanwhile, the ECtHR has shown some greater openness towards migrants' rights in recent years, including recognition of the vulnerability of irregular migrants and findings that certain restrictions on family reunification have an unjustified discriminatory impact. All the regional systems ultimately recognize that a state's sovereignty is not absolute but is subject to its obligations in international law, including human rights, so the question is how those human rights obligations are interpreted and whether they are given sufficient weight. When carrying out this analysis as regards migration rules that exclude domestic workers from protection, I have argued for placing substantial weight on the severity of domestic workers' conditions, the context for their large-scale migration arising from demand in destination countries and adverse social and economic conditions in countries of origin, and the serious harm caused by long-term separation from family members. On this basis, regimes that systematically deny labour rights to irregular migrants can be identified as violating the right to decent work, and the widespread denial of family reunification can be viewed as breaching the right to private and family life. Any arguments about state sovereignty must be read in this context, and are not compelling where they create systemic violations of rights.

Relevance to other regions/sectors and summary

Fourteen years on from the ILO's approval of C-189, its ratification by forty countries worldwide is significant and encouraging, but does not yet represent a drastic shift or encompass a majority of countries. Campaigns for ratification of C-189 remain essential, given the comprehensive set of standards it contains, and significant improvements seen in ratifying countries. Nonetheless, obligations on states to improve domestic workers' rights also exist independently of their ratification of C-189, stemming from the widely accepted human rights to work, private and family life, and protection from forced labour. This book has focused on countries that are subject to the jurisdiction of a regional human rights system (UK, Chile, South Africa) and/or whose domestic courts engage substantially with human rights norms (South Africa, India). Yet ratification of key international human rights treaties—such as the International Covenant on Economic, Social and Cultural Rights, International Covenant on Civil and Political Rights, Convention on the Elimination of All Forms of Discrimination against Women and Convention on the Rights of the Child—is far more widespread than these examples, meaning that rights identified as deriving from them have a broader normative relevance even in contexts where there are greater limits on enforceability. The arguments may be relevant to legal challenges, and can also be used to strengthen policy and campaigning work by and for domestic workers, lending further force to calls for change by showing how the current position is incompatible with human rights standards. In countries that have ratified C-189, the analysis remains relevant to the further development of standards, particularly in contentious areas like inspection and working time limits.

This book's analysis of the exclusion of domestic workers from protection as falling short of human rights standards may also have resonance beyond the domestic work sector—for example, in relation to groups of workers who are excluded from protections because of the mode through which their work takes place, notably workers on digital platforms and in the 'gig economy'. They are also salient in light of the increasing trend towards offering restrictive, time-limited visa schemes to migrants in lower-paid jobs, including agriculture and other forms of care, as well as domestic work, which makes it difficult to enforce rights. Ultimately, these exclusions risk a situation (which has already been closer to the reality for many countries, particularly outside the industrialized Global North) where the fulfilment of labour rights is a privilege for a select group of workers instead of a guarantee to all. This means that domestic workers, and the movement for their rights, have a crucial role to play in the broader development of labour law for the twenty-first century, through the imperative for inclusion based on principles of universality and against an exclusionary and delimited view of the application of workers' rights.

The realization of domestic workers' human rights and the challenge to their exclusion requires, as a minimum, secure visa systems with simple and accessible mechanisms for extension and change of employer, protection of the labour rights of irregular migrants, a minimum wage that is equal to that in other sectors and represents a fair and living wage, working time limits that leave adequate time for a family life, viable access to family reunification, and an effective, proactive system of inspection with a power of entry to homes that is separated from immigration enforcement. Where these conditions exist, domestic workers will have a floor of rights to build upon, creating a more favourable position to self-organize for further improvement and respect at work. Human rights law, when it centres on positive obligations, takes an 'integrated approach' to interpretation, insists on a universalistic approach to migrants' rights, and challenges the public/private sphere divide, therefore has an integral and valuable role to play in challenging the exclusion of domestic workers.

APPENDIX

List of Interviewees by Country

All descriptions of roles relate to the time of the interview. Pseudonyms (used for all domestic worker interviewees, and professional interviewees who chose to be cited this way) are denoted by a first name only in inverted commas.

UK

Interviews with domestic workers in 2018 as part of Kalayaan project

All these interviews were with Filipino nationals.
Workers with permission to work while waiting in the National Referral Mechanism ('NRM'):

- 'Leana'
- 'Josefina'
- 'Juliana'
- 'Katalina'
- 'Rachel'
- 'Sam'
- 'Lisa'
- 'Sara'
- 'Vicky'
- 'Christina'
- 'Eva'

Workers without permission to work while waiting in the NRM:

- 'Amy'
- 'Elsa'
- 'Elena'
- 'Maria'
- 'Nicky'
- 'Mian'
- 'Natasha'
- 'Joana'
- 'Stefanie'
- 'Marina'

Interviews with professionals in 2020

- Avril Sharp: Casework and policy officer at Kalayaan
- Carita Thomas: Lawyer at Anti-Trafficking and Labour Exploitation Unit

Chile

Interviews with professionals in 2019

- Jose Luis Ugarte: Academic in labour law
- 'Javiera': Academic in public law, human rights, gender
- 'Catalina': General coordinator of a migrants' rights organization
- Ruth Olate: General secretary of domestic worker union SINTRACAP ('Sindicato de Trabajadoras de Casa Particular') and federation
- 'Daniela': Academic in sociology
- Alvaro Gallego: Academic and professor of litigation clinic
- Irma Arriagada: Academic in care work and migration
- 'Francisco': Academic in migration
- 'Rocío': Academic in women's rights and human rights
- José Francisco Castro: Labour Ministry, Juridical Department
- Eduardo Caamaño Rojo: Academic in labour law
- Giorgio Jackson: Congress person
- 'Nancy': Director of university law clinic on migration
- Paulina Granados Zambrano: Works at Pensions regulator
- 'Alicia': Practising lawyer
- David Oddó Beas: Head of Juridical Department in Labour Ministry

Interviews with domestic workers in 2019

Workers introduced by the union (all Chilean nationals):

- 'Francisca'
- 'Constanza'
- 'Camila'
- 'Valentina'
- 'Romina'
- 'Josefa'

Workers introduced by the migrants' rights organization:

- 'Sofia' (Venezuelan)
- 'Maria' (Peruvian)
- 'Isabella' (Colombian)
- 'Michelle' (Bolivian)
- 'Sara' (Bolivian)

South Africa

Interviews with professionals in 2024

- Jane Barrett: Former Director of Organisation and representation at WIEGO (Women in Informal Employment: Globalizing and Organising), now retired and working on contract basis
- Amy Tekié: Co-founder of IZWI Domestic Workers' Alliance
- Abigail Osiki: Research Associate at CENTROW (Centre for Transformative Regulation of Work) and academic
- Fairuz Mullagee: Researcher and coordinator of the Social Law Project
- Thando George: Candidate Attorney at Socio-Economic Rights Institute of South Africa ('SERI')
- Yongeza Mbimbi: Candidate Attorney at SERI
- Marlese von Broembsen: Associate Professor at CENTROW and senior labour rights researcher at WIEGO
- Eunice Dhladhla: Regional leader of South African Domestic Service and Allied Workers Union ('SADSAWU') for the Gauteng province

India

Interviews with professionals in 2024

- 'Meera': Works at an international organization
- Aditi Yajnik: Coordinator for Self-Employed Women's Association ('SEWA')
- Nalini Nayak: Founder of SEWA Kerala in 1984, former national coordinator of the national platform of domestic workers, continues to provide expertise on rights of domestic workers and other sectors
- Supurna Banerjee: Assistant Professor at the Institute of Development Studies
- Samita Sen: Professor at Cambridge University
- Praveena Kodoth: Professor at the Centre for Development Studies
- 'Gita': Consultant in a Research Institute
- Anchita Ghatak: Women's rights activist and development professional, co-founder of organizations Parachiti and Maitree

Index

For the benefit of digital users, indexed terms that span two pages (e.g., 52–53) may, on occasion, appear on only one of those pages.

Tables are indicated by an italic *t* following the page number.